10.50

THE HISTORY AND CHARACTER

OF CALVINISM

The History and Character of

CALVINISM

JOHN T. McNEILL

OXFORD UNIVERSITY PRESS

LONDON   OXFORD   NEW YORK

OXFORD UNIVERSITY PRESS
Oxford   London   Glasgow
New York   Toronto   Melbourne   Wellington
Ibadan   Nairobi   Dar es Salaam   Cape Town
Kuala Lumpur   Singapore   Jakarta   Hong Kong   Tokyo
Delhi   Bombay   Calcutta   Madras   Karachi

0

Printed in the United States of America

Gratefully dedicated to the memory of my father
WILLIAM CAVENDISH McNEILL
1849–1928
an exemplar of
Calvinist faith and virtue

Preface to
the paperback edition

SINCE the first edition of this book the output of studies in the history of Calvinism has continued in ample and unceasing flow. It would have been impracticable to revise the text with adequate response to these; and the decision to leave it substantially unchanged has been rendered easier by the fact that the newer scholarship has not, I believe, invalidated any major statement or serious point of interpretation contained in it. The short Postscript appended briefly comments on some of the recent developments and viewpoints. The Book List has been substantially revised. A few sentences have been rewritten on pp. 41, 200, 213, 222, 225, 231, 234, 246, 405, 410 and 424. Otherwise the alterations are minute corrections only. I am very grateful to the Oxford University Press for making the book available to a wider reading public in the paperback edition.

J. T. McN.

Middlebury
August 1966

PREFACE

At the age of ten I was induced by my father to memorize the Westminster Assembly's Shorter Catechism. As time went by, the phrases of this classic took on meaning for me, and I came to know that what I had learned was Calvinism; but for a good many years I made no effort to extend my knowledge of that subject. When I studied theology, my interest in church history took another direction. It was not, indeed, until I had become a teacher in that field, and was under some obligation to examine the sources and literature of the Swiss Reformation, that I first began to realize the historic magnitude and religious reality of the Calvinist movement. This book has been written in an attempt to meet the needs of persons whose acquaintance with its subject matter may be as slight as mine long remained, and who may not have opportunity to read at large in the field.

Comparison of the 'literature' with the 'sources' has brought a good many surprises. Calvinism has usually been discussed in an atmosphere of controversy and has often been judged, even by academicians, with slender reference to the evidence. There would be no point in expending labor on a mere summary of other men's opinions. As far as possible, the source documents had to be searched and allowed to speak. The space available did not permit labored disputation and display of proofs; but in general, where reigning interpreters had to be challenged, specific evidence has been presented. No unverified statement has been consciously admitted. In the selection of data, the aim has been to draw attention to significant and representative facts and thoughts, without tiresome insistence upon the writer's point of view.

The work seemed naturally to divide itself into the four major sections indicated. No apology is offered for including a treatment of the German Swiss Reformation. A creative charity marked the relations between the Protestantism of Zurich and that of Geneva. The differences were not inconsiderable, but they were not allowed to become divisive. Both had the same allies and the same adversaries. They formed one communion and passed on to later generations a common heritage. There is therefore no incongruity involved in making Zwinglianism a part of the wider movement that, in the unavoidable short-hand of language, is here called Calvinism.

The longest of the four parts has taken the form of something resembling a brief monograph on John Calvin himself. This is followed by an account of the spread of Calvinism in Europe and America, and a series of chapters on its later struggles and developments in response to the revolutionary changes of modern society and thought. Here, amid an embarrassing wealth of materials, enough has been selected to give some factual body to the discussion. Although Calvinism's formative stage was passed in the sixteenth century, its subsequent history, both internal and in exterior relationships, is neither unimportant nor dull. At every period vivid figures move in the pageant of Calvinism, and it has touched the destinies of nations.

Libraries in New York, Chicago, Washington, Edinburgh, London, and Geneva have all yielded something to the volume. In the later phase of the study, the Union Theological Seminary Library, with its competent service and ample holdings, has been my chief boon. I owe a debt that is beyond measure to generations of students at the Seminary, and not less to those others who in Toronto and Chicago shared and aided my early explorations in the field. I have profited by some helpful comments offered by the readers of the manuscript, Professors Edwin Lewis and Paul T. Fuhrmann; and I am most grateful for the patience and encouragement of Mr. Wilbur D. Ruggles, Religious Book Editor of the Oxford University Press.

J. T. McN.

Dallas
March 1954

CONTENTS

PART I

HULDREICH ZWINGLI AND THE
REFORMATION IN GERMAN SWITZERLAND

When I was younger, I gave myself overmuch to
human teaching, like others of my day, and when
about seven or eight years ago I undertook to devote myself entirely to the Scriptures I was always
prevented by philosophy and theology. But even-
tually I came to the point where led by the Word
and the Spirit of God I saw the need to set aside
all such things and to learn the doctrine of God
direct from his own Word.
— Huldreich Zwingli, *Of the Clarity and Certainty of the Word of God,* 1522. Translated by
G. W. Bromiley, in *Zwingli and Bullinger,* Library of Christian Classics, Volume XXIV, London
and Philadelphia, 1953, pp. 90f.

In all that is possible for us, and to which we are
bound, as becomes pious members of the Con-
federation, we shall be glad to comply with your

requests, and to wait upon you according to our bounden duty. But in what concerns the Word of God, our souls' salvation and our consciences, we cannot give way.

— The Council of Zurich, defending acts of the Reformation that had been condemned by the Swiss Federal Diet, 1524. B. J. Kidd, *Documents of the Continental Reformation,* Oxford, 1911, p. 442.

CHAPTER I

THE BACKGROUND OF
THE SWISS REFORMATION

— I —

THE sixteenth century, like our own, was a time crowded with surprises. A German miner's son came out of a monastery with a message of God's wrath and love, to begin a widespread transformation of the Church and the religious life of Europe. A resolute emperor, defeated in a long struggle to bring to his vast domains religious unity and secure peace, sought his own peace in a monastic retreat. A patriotic Swiss humanist became a zealous church reformer, and died in battle at the hands of his compatriots. A French humanist and law scholar underwent a 'sudden conversion' and became the theologian and guide of Protestantism in its second phase of expansion. A Spanish aristocrat and soldier, convalescing from wounds, discovered the secrets of a spiritual discipline by which vigor was restored to the languishing Church of Rome. Luther, Calvin, and Loyola had each a little less than thirty years of public activity; Zwingli had only twelve. The significant labors of all these agents of religious change fell within the short span of the years 1517 to 1564. This period witnessed also the essential acts of the Reformation in England, Scotland, and the Scandinavian lands. Where else does history show a transformation so rapid, so surprising, and so permanent?

On the continent of Europe the terms 'Lutheran' and 'Reformed' refer to two clearly differentiated branches of Protestantism. In this book we shall have only such incidental reference to Lutheran churches, leaders, and teachings as is necessary to clarify the history of Reformed Protestantism. The Reformed churches took their rise from two distinct but similar expressions of the Protestant spirit. The first was led by Zwingli, who died when Luther was in mid-career, and before the Counter Reformation began. This movement was confined for the most part to German Switzerland. The second was championed by Calvin, who had never known Zwingli and who was active in French-speaking Switzerland precisely during the crucial period of Roman Catholic reform. This period consisted of the thirty years from the beginning of the pontificate of Paul III (1534) to the promulgation of the Confession of Faith of the Council of Trent (1564). The first of these dates is that of Calvin's conversion to Protestantism; the second is that of his death. The year 1534 saw also Henry VIII's break with the Papacy, and by 1564 the Elizabethan settlement of religion was complete. During these three decades Lutheranism lost most of its original energy, and in Germany and eastern Europe its prospects were dimmed by the revived activity of Roman Catholicism. Though Zwingli's teachings still had a wide influence, a period had been set to the expansion of Zwinglianism in the Swiss cantons. Without Calvin and his disciples the very survival of Continental Protestantism would have been imperiled. When Calvin died he left a series of Reformed churches, separately organized by nations and cities, but so closely associated as to form a new international Protestantism.

We must mention at the outset a historical paradox that should not escape us. On the one hand Calvin, the chief of those who gave to the Reformed their theology and morals, owed much more to Luther than to Zwingli. But on the other hand, the church that was shaped in German Switzerland under the leadership of Zwingli became attached to that which emerged in French Switzerland under the direction of Calvin. The result of this paradoxical development was that the Protestantism which had its strongholds in the Swiss cities continued to expand in Europe and to exert effective resistance against the reactivated Papacy, while the interpreters of Lutheran theology repudiated elements in the Reformed teaching and rejected projects of union with the Reformed churches. Thus the principal branches of Continental Protestantism continued in separation from each other.

— II —

During the Middle Ages a hardy race of peasant warriors arose in the Swiss valleys where Alpine streams pass to tributaries of the Rhine and the Rhone. They were poor, hard-working, simple folk, but they were possessed of a passionate love of corporate and personal liberty and unwilling to tolerate oppressive feudal control. Wordsworth's well-known sonnet on the subjugation of the Swiss by Napoleon begins:

> *Two Voices are there; one is of the Sea,*
> *One of the Mountains; each a mighty Voice;*
> *In both from age to age thou dids't rejoice;*
> *They were Thy chosen music, Liberty.*

The reference is to Britain and Switzerland as the nurseries of human liberty. The Swiss nation emerged from small beginnings in the late thirteenth century. On 1 August 1291 three German-speaking mountain communities stretching around Lake Luzern, Uri, Schwyz, and that part of Unterwalden known as Nidwalden, solemnly in a 'Perpetual Covenant,' agreed, 'for the establishment of peace,' to defend one another in case of attack and to recognize no foreign judges. Their territories lay within the Holy Roman Empire. The object of their compact was not to dissolve the bond of connection with the Empire but to exclude the rule of feudal intermediaries between them and the emperor. They were virtually asserting freedom to govern themselves according to their own desires and to develop those democratic procedures in government which they preferred to the lordship of a prince. This is apparent in their resolve to exclude all 'judges' or magistrates who were not born in their valleys, or who had purchased their offices, and by the provision for arbitration of disagreements among the cantons. The Swiss had leaders but not masters. They were not a cultivated people; their lives were hard and their manners unrefined. But they loved their freedom and with admirable courage fought to defend it.

The Confederacy expanded, meeting crisis after crisis, for more than two centuries. It was repeatedly assailed from Austria and repeatedly surprised its assailants by its brave and skillful resistance. In the fourteenth century the decisive victories of its defending armies (at Morgarten in 1315, Sempach in 1386, and Näfels in 1388) discouraged its enemies and secured the survival of the republic. Thus was provided, in the words of the Swiss historian, Wilhelm Oechsli, 'an asylum for republican ideas in the midst of monarchical and feudal Europe.' Thereafter, by a series of treaties (1389, 1399, 1412, 1474) the growing Confederacy drew from the Hapsburgs an unwilling recognition of freedom from control and exemption from taxation. The fifteenth century wove fanciful tales of William Tell and other legendary heroes of resistance to Hapsburg princelings, giving expression and encouragement to the growing tradition of Swiss liberty.

In the middle years of the fifteenth century, internal strife offered occasion for fresh Hapsburg intervention. Zurich quarreled with the canton of Schwyz over the properties of the deceased Count of Toggenburg, and the Emperor Frederick III formed an alliance with the Zurichers. Frederick drew in the services of the so-called Armagnacs, an army of freebooters, fresh from service in the Hundred Years' War, and commanded by the Dauphin of France. The invaders were halted at the gates of Basel by a small force from Schwyz and Bern, who sold their lives at such cost, 'tearing the arrows from their bodies' to fight on, that the Dauphin hastily returned from 'this amazing country' (1444). The issue between the Swiss states was settled by a Bernese arbitrator, and Frederick's alliance with Zurich was repudiated. His son, Duke Sigismund, in 1458 asserted fresh claims in Switzerland but suffered a series of defeats. Many and formidable were the attempts to crush the Confederacy, but under these blows it gained strength and unity, until at Constance, on 30 March 1474, Sigismund reluctantly signed with its leaders a new 'Perpetual Compact,' abandoning his claims. Not long afterward, Charles the Bold, enemy of Louis XI of France and ally of the emperor, after brilliant successes in other conflicts, suffered repeated defeats by Swiss infantry and finally fell in battle at their hands (1477).

Though freed from Hapsburg sway, the Swiss still retained a slender attachment to the Empire. Yet the existence and prosperous expansion of their democracy constituted a challenge to the Empire and the princedoms within it. In fact the cantons were not represented in the imperial diets and were not ruled by the emperor or the imperial council. Attempts to collect in Switzerland taxes voted in the diets only promoted the severance of the Confederacy from the Reich. The breach was completed early in the reign of Maximilian I, 1493–1517, whose wife was a daughter of Charles the Bold. Making use of the Schwabian

League, a south-German military organization, Maximilian attacked the Confederates in the spring of 1499. In the brief and sanguinary war that followed, the Swiss, though numerically outclassed, won every encounter. They soon forced Maximilian to terms, and in the treaty of Basel, 22 September 1499, he acknowledged the independence of their nation.

The original territory of three cantons had now expanded to something like the modern outlines of the Swiss republic. Luzern, Zurich, Glarus, Zug, and Bern became cantons in rapid succession during the years 1332 to 1353. By 1513 Fribourg, Solothurn, Basel, Schaffhausen, and Appenzel had been added, making the number thirteen. Other extensive territories were associated with the federation as 'allied' or 'subject' districts. The interlocking local governments of these, and their varying relations with the Confederacy, formed a pattern too complicated to be examined here. Certain frontier areas may be mentioned for their importance in the Reformation era. Lying to the southeast the allied league of the Grisons (the Gray League) was comprised of Italian-speaking communities; to the southwest lay the French-speaking Pays de Vaud, with the notable city of Lausanne, and beyond it, at the outlet of Lake Leman, the free city of Geneva. In these western areas the powerful canton of Bern was expanding its influence in rivalry with Fribourg and neighboring Savoy. Another important frontier was on Lake Constance, where lay the bailiwick of Thurgau. This was one of the 'common bailiwicks,' subject to the joint rule of a number of cantons. While the Thurgau was later (1531) to become a canton, the city of Constance itself was to be detached from Switzerland through events of the Reformation.

— III —

The inner differences and conflicts of pre-Reformation Switzerland arose in part from the tension created by the rise of cities and their admission into the Confederacy. The interests of the burgher class, which had urban education and money power, clashed with those of the rural areas. The city of Zurich, founded, it is believed, in the ninth century by a grandson of Charlemagne, Ludwig the German, became an imperial city in 1218. Some flowering of culture appeared there during the thirteenth century, and in the fourteenth (1336) Zurich adopted a constitution framed in part on the model of Strasbourg, which gave the chief authority to a guild of nobles and rich burghers. It was because of civil strife over this measure and the ensuing Austrian intervention that the Zurich leader, Rudolf Brun, led the city into the Confederacy (1351). Zurich acquired wide rural districts and showed a disposition to expand her subject areas, to the discomfort of her neighbors. In 1489 the misguided policy of the burgomaster, Hans Waldmann, goaded the peasants, who were already freemen, to revolt. In the outcome Waldmann was executed as a traitor and the peasants won only the right to bring their grievances to the council of the city, a body of two hundred members elected by the guilds, which, with the Burgomaster, continued to rule the canton.

Bern came into existence as a fortress, manned by Teutonic knights in the service of Frederick Barbarossa. About the stronghold there grew a community that became a free imperial city, filling a hairpin bend in the river Aar and expanding into the country about. Late in the thirteenth century Bern asserted her freedom by taking arms against Rudolf of Hapsburg. Thereafter Bern followed a bold policy of expansion and was often at war. She won a decisive victory over Burgundian and imperial foes in 1339, and in 1353 joined the Swiss Confederacy. But she later fought independently and continued to enlarge her territory. In 1414 the Bernese were invited by the Emperor Sigismund to snatch the Thurgau from Frederick of Austria; they promptly conquered the district, and to Sigismund's surprise continued to hold it. The city was ruled by patrician families who were descendants of its first inhabitants. An attempt by the burghers to assume power in 1469 failed because the citizens reacted in favor of their traditional rulers, and Bern remained an aristocratic community. The governing body was a council of twelve elected from the nobility and headed by an officer called the Schultheiss.

In the larger wars of the late fifteenth century, the Bernese played a brilliant part. With lands bordering on the territory of Charles the Bold, Bern was that proud adventurer's most determined foe. After Charles's death, the Bernese leader, Adrian von Bubenburg, wished to have the Confederacy annex Franche-Comté, forestalling the French plan to occupy this desirable territory. His plan was prevented by the opposition of Zurich. The restless ambition of Bern was now directed to the Pays de Vaud, where Bernese expansion took a new form in the Reformation. Meanwhile Bern received a large share of the 100,000 Rhenish guilders which Louis XI of France was induced to pay the Confederates for yielding Franche-Comté. Others paid the Swiss for fighting; Louis paid them handsomely for keeping the peace. Mules laden with gold appeared in the streets of Bern, and nobles and people were enriched by generous pensions. Easy and luxurious habits, rather than cultural advance, resulted from the repeated distribution of such tribute among a people who had formerly lived under a strict economy and had cultivated military virtues.

The Swiss in the fifteenth century were culturally retarded. Zurich and Bern had Latin schools, but there was no university in the country, and although a fair number of Swiss students went abroad for study, education was neglected for the most part and literacy was low. The admission of Basel to the status of a canton in 1501 brought into the Confederacy a center of learning and literature hardly surpassed in Europe and a university thoroughly impregnated with humanism.

Basel had been a trading center since the tenth century, and early assumed the status of an imperial principality under the rule of the bishop. In 1337, however, the guilds began to elect a chief guildmaster, and thereafter the bishop's authority in civil matters steadily diminished. The Black Death (1349) took a heavy toll of the population, and in 1356 an earthquake leveled the cathedral and other buildings and caused a destructive fire. The indomitable burghers soon erected new and better churches and homes. A generation later, having fallen under the sway of Leopold of Austria, they began to look to the Swiss Confederacy for alliance against the Austrian power.

— IV —

The new learning of the Renaissance came to Basel with the celebrated general council held there, 1431–49. Apart from its ecclesiastical importance, the council was significant because it attracted to the city a group of Italian and German humanists. One of these was Eneo Sylvio Piccolomini, later Pope Pius II, then a bright and ambitious young Italian of easy morals fresh from an adventurous mission to Scotland and England. For ten years Eneo spent most of his time at the council, and he loved

Basel. The young scholar reports the prosperity of the newly built city, the splendor of the churches, the rich furnishings of the houses, and the jeweled gowns of the ladies to be seen in the great new dance hall. Basel then possessed a cathedral school and other teaching institutions connected with churches and monasteries. A prominent member of the council, John of Ragusa, brought with him a valuable library, which he left with the Dominican house in which he lodged in the city. Its manuscript treasures were to be of use to such scholars as Reuchlin and Erasmus. The fall of Constantinople (1453) gave to Basel some expatriated Greek scholars who later became instructors in Greek. In 1459, responding to an appeal by the burgomaster on behalf of the city, Pius II authorized the founding of the university of Basel; it began to receive students the following year. Its statutes followed those of the university of Erfurt, the student body being divided by faculties and not, as at Paris, by nations. The school was almost unique in the fact that from the first it was the seat of unchallenged humanism. The celebrated Sebastian Brant (d. 1521) was a member of the school for more than a quarter of a century, from 1475 to 1501. Brant studied law and was a member of the law faculty, but his fame rests upon his satirical poem, *The Ship of Fools,* published at Basel in 1494, a facetious exposure of the decadence of the age and the futility of human pursuits. The book was provided with numerous illustrations, probably by the German artist Albrecht Dürer, who was also in Basel in 1492–4, learning the art of engraving. Brant had a low opinion of student life at Basel and at other universities. He was even more caustic in his comments on priests: they were shepherds not to be trusted with the sheep, and as skillful in their task as the miller's ass playing the lute. He was a versatile and energetic man, and was not only a law professor and a popular writer but also a judge and an editor and adviser for printers. The severance of Basel from the Empire and its attachment to Switzerland wounded Brant's German patriotism and he responded in 1501 to an appeal from his native Strasbourg voiced by his friend John Geiler, the eminent preacher of that city, and became an official there.

Basel vied with Venice as a leading center of the printing trade, and the printers served well the cause of humanist learning. A printing press was first used in the city apparently in 1468 by Berthold Ruppel, thought by some to have been a pupil of Gutenberg himself. Soon afterward John Heynlin von Stein (d. 1496), a brilliant Paris scholar, induced some eminent humanists to come to Basel to co-operate with the printers. His associate and successor, John Amerbach (d. 1513), as early as 1479 produced a Latin Bible embodying learned emendations. Through thirty-eight years, Amerbach, with the aid of such renowned scholars as John Reuchlin, Sebastian Brant, Conrad Pellican, and Beatus Rhenanus, published numerous classical and patristic texts as well as works of learned contemporaries. Reuchlin took degrees at the university of Basel in 1475 and 1477 and there he pursued the study of the Biblical languages, employing for Greek instruction a refugee scholar, Andronicus Contoblacas. John Froben (d. 1527), who was trained by Amerbach, and a score of less distinguished printers of the early sixteenth century carried on the fine tradition of the scholar-printers, who brought the art of making beautiful books to a stage of expertness never equaled in later times. When Froben died, Erasmus, his most illustrious humanist helper and author, in gracious tribute described him as a man of simple virtues 'whom you could throw dice with in the dark,' and interpreted Froben's great kindness to himself as prompted by 'the love of learning.'

Basel manufactured the paper for its printers; and Basel book firms opened distribution centers in numerous cities of western Europe. In the early sixteenth century Zurich, Bern, and other Swiss cities developed their own book-making trades, but Basel was far in the lead. In Switzerland there were no such wealthy and powerful patrons of the New Learning as appeared in the Italian cities, but the printers took their place.

While the urbanized cantons that had been added were far more populous than the rural ones, the political life of the Confederacy maintained in large degree its original character, and all the federated governments, with limitations in the case of Bern and some others, were on an elective basis. In Uri, Schwyz, Unterwalden, and Glarus the governing body was the entire male citizenry assembled in open-air meeting (the *Landesgemeinde*). These small cantons were represented in the federal diet on equal terms with the larger ones. The diet consisted of two delegates sent from each canton and one from each of the associated districts. The federal constitution was to all appearances extremely fragile. Nothing of importance affecting the inner life of the cantons could be determined in the diet. The delegates merely spoke the mind of the canton they represented, and the dissent of a single canton could halt action. Yet through many a crisis the common interest of all came sufficiently to expression to prevent permanent disruption. When in 1481 a horde of discharged mercenaries passed through many districts committing lawless acts, a notable diet met at Stans to effect a pacification. After animated debate, the warning voice of the hermit, Nicholas von der Flüe, brought an agreement. The pact of Stans obviated a fresh outbreak of civil war and provided against dangerous popular agitations. Early in the sixteenth century the young nation, still politically immature, would have to wrestle with the problems of a fundamental religious cleavage.

— V —

The Renaissance Popes frequently asserted lofty claims of power and authority in both ecclesiastical and secular affairs. Yet the Papacy was rather contributing to than arresting the moral decline of the Western Church, and was forfeiting the respect of men of character and discernment. An unprecedented stage of deterioration was reached by the end of the fifteenth century. Notes of alarm had been sounded by the faithful pastor John Geiler in Strasbourg, the Dominican Girolamo Savonarola in Florence, the Franciscan Thomas Murner in Frankfort, the Paris scholar Jacques Lefèvre, and countless other anxious observers of the trend; while Desiderius Erasmus showered upon ecclesiastical offenders the arrows of his satirical wit. The simoniacal voluptuary, Alexander VI, was followed (after Pius III's pontificate of one month) by the simoniacal militarist, Julius II (1503–13), a ruthless, able, and utterly secular-minded prelate. It was Swiss mercenaries led by a Swiss cardinal who saved Julius from the vengeance of Louis XII of France (1498–1515).

During the wars of 1509–15 the French bishops supported their king in hostility to Julius, whom they denounced in unmeasured terms. In 1511, a meeting of the French clergy demanded a new reforming council. Such an assembly was called in the names of nine French and Spanish cardinals, and actually met at Pisa (1 September 1511). Though in ineffectual strength, this Council of Pisa offered a serious challenge to the Pope, and the only way

in which Julius could checkmate the French was to call a council of his own. As a result the Fifth Lateran Council opened on
3 May 1512, the Pope's military fortunes having meanwhile
taken a turn for the better. The French-sponsored council, after
three removals, expired at Lyons, and its clerical promoters made
humiliating terms with the Pope. At the outset of the Lateran
meeting Julius was admonished by Aegidio of Viterbo, General
of the Augustinians, to give his whole attention to the reform of
morals and the advancement of spiritual life in the Church, but
the 'Pontiff Terrible' had no ear for such matters. Julius II died
20 February 1513, and the council maintained a sluggish life
under Leo X until 16 March 1517. The decision to close it then
was vigorously protested by Thomas de Vio Caietano, General
of the Dominicans, who saw that its true task was not well begun.
It had faced helplessly the moral decay of the Church and reaffirmed the declaration of Boniface VIII in 1302 that obedience
to the Pope is altogether necessary to salvation. Pope Leo, a son
of Lorenzo de Medici, spent his time and money on frivolous
entertainments and the patronage of artists, and allowed the
Church to drift. By the time of Leo's death, in December 1521,
Luther was in the Wartburg, and Zwingli was beginning to stir
the burghers of Zurich by his daring sermons.

The condition of the Church in Switzerland was similar to
that which prevailed generally in pre-Reformation Europe. Indeed, it is often stated that abuses, disorders, and secularity were
exceptionally marked in the Confederacy. The causes of the low
state of the clergy did not lie in their excessive power, for the
cantons and cities had gained a large measure of control in ecclesiastical matters. Some resistance to Italian clerical pressure
was also in evidence. Typical of this trend was the *Pfaffenbrief*,
or Priest's Charter, a measure adopted by most of the cantons as
a result of a dispute in 1370, by which foreign ecclesiastics were
prohibited from summoning Swiss citizens before any foreign tribunal, save in matrimonial and ecclesiastical cases. Nowhere else,
perhaps, had the political come so largely to dominate men's
minds at the expense of the religious. There are, of course, instances of the reverse of this. The hermit Nicholas von der Flüe
had left a career of worldly success for the exercises of devotion
—and his advice was heeded in a political crisis. But evidence
abounds that the cathedral chapters and monasteries were in-

vaded by simony and nepotism, and that the morals of the clergy were in general extremely lax.

The organization of the Swiss Church offered certain peculiarities that were unfavorable to its efficiency. The principal dioceses, having taken shape before the nation arose, extended far beyond its borders and bore little relation to the cantonal areas within them. Thus the bishop of Constance, who was subject to the archbishop of Mainz, ruled a large area of southern Germany in addition to the northeastern quarter of Switzerland, including Zurich. The bishopric of Sitten (or Sion) on the upper Rhone extended into Savoy; in 1513 it was made directly subject to the Pope. That of Chur on the upper Rhine, belonging to the archdiocese of Mainz, reached into Austria; that of Basel into Alsace. The bishops of Basel and Lausanne were under the archbishop of Besançon in France; the bishop of Geneva was a suffragan of the archbishop of Vienne; his diocese extended northwestward into France and southeastward into Savoy. The territory of Bern was shared among the dioceses of Lausanne, Sitten, and Constance; while the diocese of the bishop of Como, a suffragan of Milan, extended into the Grisons. The Swiss bishops, moreover, were feudal lords whose secular domains were confusedly dispersed. At a time when the forces favoring the Confederacy, the canton, and the city were everywhere irresistibly advancing upon the old feudal authority, the feudal claims and entanglements of the bishops were a liability rather than an asset to them.

The weakness of the episcopate was not merely the result of inconvenient units of organization. With a single exception, the Swiss bishops of the early sixteenth century were men of secular spirit and low morality. Paul Ziegler of Chur was notorious for his immoralities, and these were associated with nunneries. Hugo of Hohenlandenberg, bishop of Constance, unashamedly sold immunity for clerical concubinage, raising the fee with each child born to the priest. More celebrated was the able and ruthless warrior prelate, Matthew Schinner, who succeeded his uncle as bishop of Sitten in 1499 and was made a cardinal by Julius II (1511). He was admired and employed by that pontiff and by Leo X, and might have succeeded the latter but for his bitter hatred of the French. He secured Swiss mercenary troops for various papal campaigns in Italy, led his countrymen in the decisive victory over the French at Novara (1513), visited Henry VIII to draw him into a league with the Pope and the emperor (1516), was driven from his see by the intrigues of a rival, became prominent in the service of Pope Adrian VI, and died in Rome of the plague on 1 October 1522. The Swiss bodyguard ever since retained by the Popes was first organized by Schinner. In many respects Schinner stands in sharp contrast to Zwingli, who became a national figure about the time of the cardinal's death.

No less marked is the contrast between Schinner and the one good bishop among the Swiss prelates, Christoph von Utenheim of Basel (1502–27). Christoph was a German who before coming to Basel had been associated with John Geiler's Strasbourg group. He instituted annual diocesan synods and labored in the cause of reform through the twenty-five years of his episcopate. He was encouraged and advised not only by Geiler but also by the humanists Jacob Wimfehling, Wolfgang Capito, and Erasmus. Wimfehling joined him in 1503 and framed at that time a plan for reform, by which the bishop was partly guided. Bishop Christoph at first looked favorably upon Luther, but like Erasmus he turned against the Reformation in both its Lutheran and its Zwinglian form. His own reform efforts effected little change, and the Reformation in Basel was a fulfillment of Wimfehling's grim warning in 1503 that if the clerics would not reform themselves they would be reformed in spite of themselves by the people.

The assumption that with papal permission church offices might be trafficked in without blame is startlingly expressed in the testimony of Herman Göldli of Zurzach before the diet on 18 March 1520. Göldli denied that he had sold church benefices as horses were sold in Zurzach; that would have been simony. But he had, by permission of His Holiness, reimbursed himself for expenses in turning over a benefice and had secured from it a yearly pension, authorized by the Pope's bulls, letters, and seals.

The leaders of the Swiss Reformation were men who had undergone the intellectual emancipation of humanistic learning. The leaven of humanism spreading from Basel, Vienna, and other centers, by means of books as well as by personal association, began about 1500 to affect a fair number of the younger clergy and educated laymen in northern Europe, and to create a

mood of criticism and ridicule toward traditional ecclesiasticism
and theology. Some northern humanists, following Italian example, not only scoffed at the scholastics but also cast aspersions
upon the claims of Christianity itself, and wrote in a vein of
flippant and sophomoric paganism. Others sought by the aid of
Neoplatonist conceptions to break the hold of Aristotle and to
bring to expression an undogmatic spiritual view of Christianity.
The Florentine exponents of this Christian Platonism, Marsiglio
Ficino and Pico della Mirandola, both died before 1500, but
the influence of Pico was still potent in northern humanism.
Jacob Wimfehling and Erasmus were both indebted to him.
Wimfehling inspired many to follow the new learning, but he
also wrote a treatise to defend the scholastics against 'young
men enamored of the pagan poets.' Mutianus Rufus (d. 1526)
can be associated with both these strains. He studied with the
Florentine masters in the 1490's and later idolized Erasmus, but
he was so much captivated by ancient paganism as to propose
adding Moses and Christ to the Roman Pantheon. In his elder
years a cleric in retirement at Gotha, Mutianus wrote weighty
letters setting forth vague ethical and spiritual ideals, and made
disciples of bright young men who visited him. One of his greatest admirers was Conrad Celtis, whose students at Ingolstadt complained of his tippling and ill-temper; despite these faults, he
fascinated many young scholars there, and later at Vienna,
where Zwingli heard his lectures in 1500.

'Their unity, and the glory of their armies,' wrote Guicciardini
of the Swiss, 'have made famous the name of this so savage and
barbarous nation.' But their unity was not very secure, and it
now began actually to be threatened for the very reason of their
military glory. Swiss soldiers recruited and led by Schinner in
the service of Leo X and the Emperor Maximilian won so much
admiration for their fighting qualities that they were in greater
demand than ever as mercenaries. Schinner, in his hatred of
Francis I of France, against the wishes of the Pope induced the
Swiss to support the election of Charles V as emperor (28 June
1520). When on 8 May 1521 Charles and Leo X resolved their
differences, they agreed to employ jointly an army of Swiss mercenaries to drive the French from Italy. Three days earlier the
alert French king by liberal payments had secured from leaders
of the Confederacy freedom to recruit mercenaries in most of

the cantons. The leading voice among the few patriots who saw the menace of this monstrous traffic and boldly opposed it was that of the scholarly priest and preacher whose life and work must now engage our attention.

CHAPTER II

ZWINGLI'S EDUCATION AND EARLY PASTORATES

— I —

IN THE village of Wildhaus, far up the Toggenburg valley in eastern Switzerland, the Reformer Huldreich Zwingli was born, 1 January 1484. Sixteen years earlier the little community had passed under the control of the abbey of St. Gall, securing to itself the right to elect its *ammann,* or chief magistrate, and its village priest. Zwingli's grandfather, Heinrich, and his father, Huldreich, or Ulrich, held in turn the office of *ammann,* and at the time of the boy's birth the priest was his uncle, Bartholomew Zwingli. The maiden name of the Reformer's mother was Margarethe Bruggmann. Before her marriage to Zwingli's father she was the widow of one Meili, whose brother, John Meili, became the abbot of a monastery. While Zwingli's relatives thus included persons who had public responsibilities or clerical position, the families of both father and mother were locally respected village folk living frugally by the raising of sheep. The village lies on an exposed and windswept slope, 3300 feet above the level of the sea. The flocks were grazed on the wide, unfenced mountainside, reaching many miles northward toward Alpine peaks. The house of Zwingli's father, situated in that part of the village known as Lisighaus, was so firmly built that after nearly 500 years it still stands. The roof was weighted with stones to prevent it from blowing away. Existence for the Zwingli family was not marked by comfort or refinement. Soil and climate at Wildhaus were so unfavorable that fruits and field crops would not ripen. Until Huldreich was six, and living at Wesen with his uncle, he 'never saw harrow or plough or growing grain.' The senior Huldreich, notwithstanding his distinction in the community, probably, like his neighbors, lived the life of a shepherd, and doubtless his numerous sons went in their early boyhood to the upland pastures with their father and the sheep.

Huldreich was the third child in a family that was to consist of eight boys and three girls. He could remember long winter evenings of happy family associations, and a grandmother who told him the folk tales that sometimes appeared later as illustrations of his sermons. Although the boys had to sleep two, or even three, in a bed, and to share the other inconveniences of a large family with small resources, they were well fed and healthy. Two of Huldreich's younger brothers found their way into ecclesiastical life, and two of the sisters became nuns. The others remained in the peasant status of their birth. In 1522 Zwingli, who was then beginning his reforming work in Zurich, wrote to his brothers at Wildhaus:

> Be assured that I will keep myself informed of you as long as I live, and that I am happy in the thought that, like your ancestors, you live by the work of your hands, maintaining the nobility that you hold from Adam.

The words may recall to some readers the song of the peasant revolt led by John Ball in England in 1381:

> *When Adam delved and Eva span*
> *Who was then a gentleman?*

Adam was the peasant's favorite ancestor, since he antedated the founders of all families of nobility. Tennyson could remind the Vere de Veres that

> *The gardener Adam and his wife*
> *Smile at the claims of long descent.*

Zwingli always liked to call himself a peasant, and although there was no boorishness about his manners, his successor, Bullinger, remarked that 'he spoke as they speak in the country.' He was familiar with the tasks and the language of Alpine shepherds. When he translated the Twenty-third Psalm he rendered the sentence that in English reads, 'He maketh me to lie down in green pastures,' in the words: 'In schöner Weyd *alpt* er mich.' His utterances incidentally reveal a close observation of the ways of wild creatures and record his awe of 'the great mountain masses that make firm the earth as bones do flesh, and proclaim the might and majesty of God.'

From childhood he felt an ardent local patriotism, which was stirred by tales of the regional history, and he grew up with a boundless admiration for the Swiss national heroes and intense zeal for the honor and welfare of the Confederacy. He had probably very little practical experience of his father's occupation. At about the age of six, he was taken from his home to be cared for by his uncle, Bartholomew, who had now become a rural dean and lived at Wesen on a near-by lake. This uncle undertook the principal care for the boy's education. Huldreich remained here until he was ten, displaying exceptional talent as a schoolboy. Bartholomew, observing this with admiration, determined to see that the boy should receive the best education possible. In 1494 he was placed in the school of St. Theodore conducted by Gregor Bünzli in Klein-Basel. The master was kind, but severe in discipline. The pupils had to converse, if at all, in Latin. Zwingli made rapid progress in Latin, music, and dialectic. After two years Bünzli felt that the pupil was outgrowing the school and recommended a more advanced institution in Bern. Here a competent humanist, Heinrich Woelfli (Lupulus), taught the Latin classics and awakened the minds of his students by accounts of his own travels in the Holy Land and by stories drawn from Swiss history.

Zwingli's school experience was making him a humanist and at the same time intensifying his patriotism. But his greatest delight was in music, for which he had a remarkable talent. He rapidly learned to play numerous instruments with skill, and he sang so well that the Dominicans of Bern, with a view to the improvement of their choir services, sought to recruit him to their number. We do not know how near he was to becoming a friar. It may have been the influence of his family that prevented this. Much as he loved music, he decided that he would not take this step in order to pursue it as his life's work. It was this Dominican house that a few years later was disgraced by the proof that its leaders staged 'apparitions' in the cell of a terrified novice, Johann Jetzer, who was driven frantic by their treatment. This was a part of their controversy with the Franciscans over the Immaculate Conception of the Virgin Mary. The apparitions affirmed the damnation of Duns Scotus and other Franciscan advocates of that doctrine. Even Woelfli, Zwingli's former teacher, was for a time credulous of the deceit. These Dominicans were condemned by a commission of ecclesiastical judges (which included Cardinal Schinner) in 1509. Zwingli was by that time far from the circle of their influence. One wonders whether, if he had joined their company twelve years earlier, he would have sprung forth a Reformer from the Dominicans as Luther did from the Augustinians. Everything we know of him points to the assurance that he would not have been party to a fraud.

Zwingli never lost his devotion to music. He is said once to have subdued a disorderly class of boys by a tune played on the lute. It is noteworthy that both Luther and he were highly gifted, and greatly interested, in music. More versatile than the Saxon in musical talent, Zwingli yet probably regarded music less seriously than did Luther who considered it a divine gift for the comfort of souls.

— II —

Fulfilling the wishes of his father and his uncle, Zwingli next moved to the university of Vienna. We are poorly informed of the circumstances of his first period there; but it was evidently brief and unfortunate. The records show that he matriculated in 1498 and that in 1499 he was sent away (*exclusus*). It is conjectured that this action had something to do with his outspoken Swiss patriotism. This was the year of the Swabian war, when feeling ran high and his nation was fighting for survival. To be for the first time away from one's own country and amid sympathizers with her enemies, who are menacing her very life, is for a boy of fifteen an experience that is not conducive to patience and silence. But Vienna had attractions that drew him back (1500) after his countrymen had won the war. Conrad Celtis, the celebrated humanist, was there, and the university was rich in classical learning. Zwingli's studies probably included some scholastic philosophy and a considerable range of classical literature. Also, in Vienna he was closely associated with two gifted young Swiss scholars, Joachim von Watt (Vadianus) of St. Gall, later a notable minor Reformer, and Heinrich Loriti (Glareanus) of Glarus, afterward a distinguished schoolmaster, first in Basel and then in Paris. Johann Heigerlin (Faber), who was to confront Zwingli later as an opponent, and John Eck, who would be the great antagonist of Luther, were also in the circle of his university friends.

In 1502 he returned to Switzerland, visited his birthplace and family, and entered the university of Basel. He added to his labors as a student those of a teacher in St. Martin's school, while in due course he took the degrees of bachelor (1504) and master (1506) of arts. He passed courses in philosophy and theology, and pursued his favorite humanistic studies with zest and freedom. Apparently he felt nothing of the serious self-questioning that led Luther, a master of arts, to the monastery door (1505). It was natural that Zwingli should be inclined to the profession of his uncle and of other educated relatives. No special inner call to the priesthood seems to have been thought of. Nor did he devote himself to the special study of scholastic or patristic theology. The writings of the Florentine Neoplatonists, especially of Pico della Mirandola, began to interest him deeply. But it was more important for him that he came in 1505 under the instruction of the ablest and most impressive teacher then at the university, Thomas Wyttenbach of Biel, lately brought to Basel from Tübingen. This serious-minded humanist and Biblical scholar, who was also a caustic critic of scholastic trifling and of prevalent abuses, made an enduring impression upon the young men in his classes. Zwingli owed more to his brief contact with Wyttenbach than to any other personal influence. This was not only a matter of intellectual stimulation; Wyttenbach was keenly interested in the practical work of pastors, to which calling he would soon (1507) devote himself. Zwingli's companion and friend at Basel, Leo Judä, wrote gratefully in later years of Wyttenbach's guidance of himself and Zwingli, referring to the ease with which he passed in his lectures from literature to the earnest study of Holy Scripture, and noting his condemnation of the papal doctrine of indulgences. Zwingli's own testimony is similar.

— III —

The death of the priest of Glarus, and the good offices of Zwingli's always helpful uncle, Bartholomew, led to his being invited to be the pastor of that community. The post thus opened to Zwingli was one of some prominence, for Glarus was the principal town of the canton of that name, lying to the southeast of Zurich. He readily accepted and, being still unordained to the priesthood, went to Constance for ordination by Bishop Hugo. After this, he preached his first sermon at Rappersweil, read his first mass in the church of his native village, and, in December 1506, undertook his duties at Glarus. His correspondence of the time with scholar friends indicates no discontinuance of his humanist interests. But it is apparent, too, that he was attentive to pastoral tasks and was a conscientious priest working in the spirit of Wyttenbach's conception of the office.

> Notwithstanding my youth [he wrote in 1523] the ecclesiastical functions aroused in me more fear than joy, for I knew, and I remain convinced, that I must give account for the sheep that should perish through my negligence.

The ground floor of his house was the headquarters of his parish work; the upper floor was his study, equipped with the learned books in which he delighted; on both floors he continued to practice music. We may suppose that Zwingli felt no incompatibility between his pagan classical studies and his Christian duties. They were in fact intimately related and complementary. The link between them was the Greek language. Wyttenbach had emphasized the value of Greek as a key to the interpretation of the New Testament, and Zwingli seems to have measured his own conscientiousness as a priest by the degree of his devotion to Greek. From 1513 he was eagerly at work on it, intent on preparing himself to use it in gaining an understanding of the Scripture. Later Bombasius, secretary to Cardinal Schinner, became his instructor in Greek; but the competence he gained in it was due to his own persistence. Erasmus now became the young priest's greatest inspiration. He read the works of the eminent humanist and was led by them to an intensive study of the Latin Church Fathers, especially Jerome and Augustine; but the Greek Fathers also were now accessible to him in their own language. It is often assumed that the Reformed theologians were indifferent to the Church Fathers. Their works bear ample evidence to the contrary. This is emphatically true of Oecolampadius, Bullinger, and Peter Martyr Vermigli, and not less so of Zwingli. He probably knew the patristic literature not less intimately than either Luther or Calvin—both of whom knew it well.

In 1516 Erasmus' Greek New Testament came from Froben's press in Basel. This was a great event in the history of publishing, and for men of the Reformation an event of the first importance. At Basel Zwingli had been admitted to Froben's learned circle, and he had kept himself familiar with the progress of learning there. Soon after his removal from Glarus to Einsiedeln, with an almost worshipful admiration he visited Erasmus in Basel, and came away with the commendation of that prince of humanists. With his own hand Zwingli copied the Pauline Epistles in Greek, and later filled the wide margins of his manuscript with learned notes in Latin. Zwingli would outgrow his glowing enthusiasm for Erasmus as he more and more subordinated literature to religion and exalted the New Testament that Erasmus had so much helped him to comprehend. He was a man of the people, and he could not share the aristocratic detachment of Erasmus. He would bring directly to the people every conviction that he formed, and labor for the spiritual welfare of his compatriots. Herein lay the difference between a sixteenth-century humanist and a Reformer, and in Zwingli the humanist would yield to the Reformer.

— IV —

During the Glarus period, Zwingli twice visited Italy, not as many scholars did, for study in the Italian centers of humanism, but as chaplain to mercenary troops from his canton in the service of Pope Julius II against the French. Politically, he came under the influence of Cardinal Matthew Schinner, and he shared that warlike ecclesiastic's hostility to France. In 1510 he wrote *The Fable of the Ox*, a poetic allegory warning his countrymen (here represented as a fat ox) against taking bribes to serve the leopard of France, the lion of the Empire, and the fox of Venice. A later fable, *The Labyrinth* (1516?), exposes mercenary service by reviving the classical tale of the Minotaur. The child-devouring monster within the maze here consumes the sons of the Swiss people. Probably by the time the latter work was written Zwingli had become a stout opponent of all Swiss mercenary service to foreign states. The years that intervened between these allegories saw his service with the troops. He went to Italy in 1512, was probably present at the battle of Novara in 1513, and certainly saw the tragic defeat of his countrymen at

Marignano in 1515. His own letters tell with vivid detail the
brilliant actions of his companions in battle, including the incident in which the athletic Swiss stripped off their clothing, keeping only their halberds, swam the Adda, and put to flight the
German *landsknechts* on the French side—thus opening the way
to the capture of Pavia, where soon the shout arose: 'Julius, the
Swiss have conquered!' Zwingli had studied the history of war
and doubtless felt something of its glory and romance. But the
butchery of Marignano may have rid his mind of any illusions
he had entertained regarding the military life.

He found on his return to Glarus that French gold was flowing there, and that the people were prepared to appease the
victorious French king and to agree to furnish troops for his
service. Zwingli opposed this move, and his position was so unpopular that he was obliged to resign his charge. He was considerately permitted to retain his title to the parish and to appoint a vicar to serve it. Thereafter he uncompromisingly opposed the recruiting of mercenaries in Switzerland. To take this
stand was to challenge an entrenched system: most wars of the
time were waged with mercenary forces obtained wherever they
were available and loyal primarily to their paymasters, and no
hired soldiers were so sought after as the Swiss. Some years later
(1522) Zwingli wrote a tract (*Divine Warning to the Confederates*) which shows that he had reflected deeply not only on the
moral damage to the nation of the mercenary traffic, 'that school
of blasphemy, that source of a bad conscience,' but also on the
horrors and evils of war itself. He was not so near as Erasmus to
absolute pacifism; some wars, he thought, might still be just and
necessary; but he had no excuses for the wanton militarist. He
desired that his nation be (as she has been in the present century)
armed and prepared against aggression but devoted to peaceable
and friendly policies. In defense of his position he cites the similar warnings of the much admired saint and hermit, Nicholas
von der Flüe (d. 1487); but he notes sadly that in this respect
the saint's advice had not been taken.

Leaving Glarus, Zwingli accepted a call to Einsiedeln in the
canton of Schwyz, where he was to preach in a monastery church.
The monastery dated from the ninth century, but its renown
was associated with an impressive legend of the later consecration of the church by Christ with the songs of angels. The church

was dedicated to the Virgin Mary, and in Zwingli's time a black statue of the Virgin within the building was frequented by many pilgrims, especially at the annual feast celebrating the angelic consecration. The administrator of the monastery, Theobold von Geroldseck, a follower of the New Learning, welcomed Zwingli and encouraged his work, even when his bold preaching was criticized by others. That Zwingli had then no fixed objection to pilgrimages is apparent from the fact that he joined a pilgrimage to Aachen in 1517. But he did object to the indulgences that formed the chief attraction for pilgrims. He seems to have been greatly impressed by a poem of Erasmus, which he read in 1515, on the common ungrateful neglect of the abounding love of Jesus, by which alone men are saved.

— V —

The time of Zwingli's return from Italy, his transfer to Einsiedeln, and his visit to Erasmus marked a renewal of his zealous attention to Greek, and to the New Testament. He reported his new resolution to Vadianus, declaring that it was formed not out of vanity but that he might be equipped to understand the Scriptures. In 1522 he referred to the decision taken 'six or seven years ago' to devote his whole strength to Scripture study. 'I began,' he said, 'to implore God for His light, and the Scripture became much clearer to me.' He learned extensive portions of it by heart. His understanding of it was not in accord with the claim inscribed on the entrance to the monastery: 'Here may be obtained a plenary remission of sins.' Despite the fact that his income depended on the gifts of pilgrims to Einsiedeln, he boldly preached against the belief that pilgrimages are a means of obtaining pardon. Some pilgrims on their way to the shrine turned homeward when they met others who had been there and who told them of Zwingli's preaching that 'Christ alone saves and that He saves everywhere.' If there were fewer pilgrims now, visitors began to be attracted to the place by the fame of Zwingli's sermons. Some of these strangers were from Zurich, where the young preacher now came to be spoken of favorably.

For the obscurantist aspects of medieval religion Zwingli had a high disdain. But he had been a keen political supporter of the papal cause, and he was still in favor with the Roman Curia. For his services in Italy he had received from Leo X a papal pen-

sion of fifty florins a year, which helped to provide him with
books. Papal legates were occasionally in Einsiedeln, and in 1518
Zwingli received fresh recognition from the Pope through one
of these, Cardinal Antonio Pucei. He received the title of acolyte-
chaplain to the Pope, and was given to expect further honors.
It is probable that this action was taken because some expressions of dissatisfaction with Rome had escaped his lips, and the
Papacy, having trouble enough in Germany, wished to avoid
alienating an influential Swiss cleric. Cardinal Schinner, driven
from his own see of Sitten, at times sojourned at Einsiedeln.
Zwingli afterward stated that about 1517 he told the cardinal
frankly that the Papacy had a bad foundation and urged prompt
reform if the edifice was not to crash. He also gave Pucei to
understand that he would rather surrender his papal pension
than suppress the truth; but he continued to receive it until 1520.

In 1518 there came to Einsiedeln the Franciscan indulgence
seller, Bernardino Samson, who had been busy in Uri and parts
of Schwyz. Zwingli heard reports of his ill behavior and of his
unguarded claims for the merits of indulgences. With the full
support of Hugo, bishop of Constance, conveyed in a letter from
his vicar, John Faber, Zwingli denounced Samson's traffic in
vehement terms. Rather than purchase indulgence certificates,
Zwingli urged the people to trust in the saving merits of Christ
alone. It has been supposed that his motives in assailing indulgences were as much national and economic as religious. He had
not thought so deeply about the issue as Luther had, or been so
much concerned over the peril to souls that the practice involved.
Yet he showed in his preaching that he had taken a step in the
direction of the Reformation. A few years later, when opponents
were calling him a Lutheran, he said that in 1516, before Luther
was heard of in Switzerland, he himself had 'begun to preach
the Gospel,' and that he had earlier learned 'the fraud of indulgences' from Wyttenbach in Basel. Nevertheless, the real beginning of the Swiss Reformation was still in the future.

In one respect Zwingli was ill qualified to lead a movement
of reform. His private life had not been free from moral lapses.
As a priest he had broken his vow of celibacy. He wrote a statement of his faulty record to a canon of the Great Minster in
Zurich in 1518. He had three years earlier resolved to live a chaste
life and had maintained his resolution thereafter during the

half year before leaving Glarus and his first year at Einsiedeln.
Then he had been overcome by the blandishments of a woman.
He wrote that he was now aware of his weakness, but that he
was not entangled in the chains of Venus. It should perhaps be
noted that in the year of this letter Zwingli's bishop complained
of much worse behavior on the part of large numbers of his
clergy. The bishop's lax policy of fining offenders was not calculated to improve matters.

— VI —

The question of Zwingli's personal morality, to which this
letter was an answer, had been raised in connection with the
proposal to bring the now celebrated preacher to the city of
Zurich. The 'people's priest' at the Great Minster had resigned
his office to enter a monastery, and the canons were inquiring
about Zwingli's fitness for the post. It so happened that during
his visit to Erasmus at Basel, Zwingli had met, and very favorably
impressed, a modest young Swiss of Luzern named Oswald Geiss-
haüsler, who answered to the name of Myconius, bestowed on
him by Erasmus. A scholar and a friend of humanists, Myconius
was now master of the principal school in Zurich, which was attached to the Great Minster. He was instrumental in inducing
the canons, with whom election to the vacant office rested, to consider Zwingli, and he helped to convince Zwingli that he should
become a candidate for the position. In course of the decision
Zwingli visited Zurich, and his manner and appearance made an
excellent impression. Neither Myconius nor the influential canon
Utinger, to whom the letter was addressed, felt the offenses he
confessed to be such as to disqualify him; nor, as it proved, did
the body of canons, although, as Zwingli urged, there was no con-
cealment of the facts. Such behavior was then so common as
scarcely to be scandalous; and Zwingli's principal rival for the
position was reputed to be the father of six boys. So it came about
that Zwingli was elected by a vote of seventeen to seven. He was
warmly congratulated by many admirers, and the choice was
hailed with celebration by Swiss students in Paris.

Men sensed in his promotion to a notable center of influence
in Switzerland that some beneficial change impended for the
Swiss Confederacy and the Swiss Church. Preaching would be
his primary function, and he would have many eager hearers.

He himself fully realized the key position he would hold in Zurich. 'If the grace of Christ,' he said to one of the canons of the Great Minster, 'can be preached in so notable a place, the other Swiss cantons will hardly fail to follow the example.' He came to Zurich in December 1518 and took up his new duties on his thirty-fifth birthday, 1 January 1519. The shepherd's son out of the Toggenburg was now in the prime of manhood, moderately tall and notably handsome, a personality at once vigorous and gracious; equipped with solid learning and accustomed to diligent study; an expert mighty in the Scriptures and gifted with unusual oratorical powers. What would he make of his opportunity?

CHAPTER III

ZWINGLI AND THE
REFORMATION IN ZURICH

— I —

IT WAS not without apprehension that the canons of the Great Minster invited Zwingli to be people's priest. When he was initiated into the office, the provost took care to impress upon him responsibility for the maintenance of the payment of tithes and other revenues of the church. Zwingli in reply referred to quite other matters. He startled his colleagues by declaring his intention to preach on the life of Christ, beginning with a course of sermons interpreting the Gospel of Matthew. Moreover, he would preach Christ *ex fontibus scripturae sacrae* — from Scripture sources — without employing man-made commentaries.

Here was something new and strange. The preaching familiar in Zurich, as elsewhere, did not range over books of the Bible but referred to the readings for the day, and ordinarily followed a beaten path of interpretation. What danger lurked in this revolutionary method? The canons were worried. Some of the men who had voted for Zwingli now tried to dissuade him from his novel plan. He denied that it was an innovation: Chrysostom and Augustine had discoursed at length on whole books of Scripture. On 1 January he announced the plan to the people, and on the following day, Sunday, began the series on Matthew.

From beginning to end, Zwingli's preaching in Zurich was electrifying. It was marked by ample scholarship and the fruits of daily study, and at the same time by simplicity, conviction, and fervor. One hearer said that he felt as if lifted up by the hair and suspended in space. People who had ceased to be churchgoers became constant attendants. Those of the poorer classes were made to feel the preacher's sympathy for them and his understanding of the conditions of their lives, and their marked response was a little disturbing to the more comfortable burghers. In frank language Zwingli examined the motives and exposed the behavior of the citizens and the political and moral faults of their leaders, while he continually summoned them to repentance and a scriptural faith in the Redeemer. Zurich was now for years to experience the excitement, tension, and conflict that so often accompany a profound change in religion. The change involved a revival of religion and of conscience, the repudiation of hierarchical authority, and the affirmation of the authority of Scripture, with revolutionary consequences for doctrine, worship, and discipline. A few of the vivid happenings of this process of transformation demand our attention.

Samson the indulgence seller, having been driven from Einsiedeln before Zwingli's removal to Zurich, and having made a profitable round of Zug, Luzern, Unterwalden, and Bern, came to Bremgarten near Zurich. There he was vigorously resisted by the dean, Heinrich Bullinger (father of the Reformer of that name), who brought the issue before the Zurich magistrates. Zwingli denounced the friar and his mission, proclaiming that Christ alone can remit sins and that sellers of pardon are emissaries of Satan. Samson, none the less, came to Zurich to press his claims, but the Greater Council bade him depart. In a wagon drawn by three horses and laden with Swiss money, Samson took his way over the Alps. Whatever may have been thought of this in Rome, Hugo of Hohenlandenberg, bishop of Constance, approved Zwingli's stand against this dealer in pardons, as he had done before.

Feeling the strain of his new responsibilities, Zwingli sought to recuperate at the baths of Pfäffers, but news of a violent outbreak of the plague in Zurich brought him promptly back to his flock. Ministering daily to the victims, he himself was stricken, and his recovery was virtually despaired of. Prayers were offered for him, and we learn of anxious inquiries from his brothers and from distant friends. His religious feelings in expectation of death and when beginning to recover, he later vividly described in simple verses. These have been regarded as evidence of a significant religious change; but they will be found to reflect thoughts that he had previously expressed, framed in a personal piety to which he was no stranger. But it was now significant for him that he had faced death with his Christ-centered faith, and that his faith had not failed him. The death by plague of numerous friends and parishioners, and a year later of his beloved young brother, Andrew, who had visited him in Zurich, saddened him and increased his seriousness. He now returned to the pulpit physically weak, but was soon more effective than before, stressing the doctrines of sin and redemption and the sufficiency of Christ's love and sacrifice. His sermons touched on the lives of his hearers and the events of the hour, and he lashed out against whatever he thought to be selfish and irresponsible political and moral conduct.

He was already testing all religious observances by a strict rule of Scripture. This led him to discount ascetic orders, the invocation of saints, and the doctrine of purgatory. He was attacked from monastic pulpits and replied hotly in his own sermons. Some of the canons of the Minster were alarmed when he affirmed that the payment of tithes rested on no scriptural basis. Numerous opponents hoped to make Zurich so uncomfortable for him that he would leave it. In a letter from a well-wisher, who did not venture until later to disclose his name, Zwingli was warned of a plot to poison him.

Supporters of the mercenary service were his most aggressive opponents. On this matter, Zwingli was now adamant. When in 1521 Francis I succeeded in obtaining hired troops from the other cantons, Zwingli's protests induced Zurich to reject the king's offers. This decision was confirmed on consultation of the local communities throughout the canton; but it was resented by the rest of Switzerland. There was fear that the issue would result in the secession of Zurich from the Confederacy. Pope Leo X now hoped to offset the French move by inducing the Zurichers to permit the recruiting of mercenaries for the papal forces, and Zwingli's former associate, Cardinal Schinner, was sent to negotiate the agreement. Zwingli had resigned his papal pension a year earlier, and he now resisted the Pope's proposal as vigorously as he had the French offer: he even assailed the cardinal as a trafficker in the blood of youth. Schinner succeeded in obtaining a small force, on terms of restricted service. These stipulations were soon violated, and the Zurich councils called the contingent home again the same year. In January 1522, responding to Zwingli's persistent demand, the magistrates resolved to permit no more recruiting for foreign wars. Religiously, on the indulgence question, and now politically, on the mercenary issue, Zwingli had taken a stand in direct hostility to the papal policy; yet Rome made no move to silence him. Luther had been treated less patiently.

— II —

During this controversy Zwingli had pilloried those who regarded eating meat during a fast as a great sin while thinking it no offense to sell human flesh to foreigners to be slaughtered. The Zurich printer, Christopher Froschauer, was a warm supporter of Zwingli and took pleasure in printing and circulating his sermons and treatises. At the Frankfort book fair, Froschauer had learned something of Luther's opinions. He fully adopted Zwingli's view that the Church fasts were unscriptural and hence not obligatory; and he resolved to act upon it. At a dinner during Lent, 1522, Froschauer and others ate sausage meat. Zwingli, who was present, approved, but did not partake of the forbidden food. The act was done in no sacrilegious spirit; but some others in the community were dramatizing their emancipation, and shocking their neighbors, by holding meat dinners on Fridays. The council, long accustomed to regulating the citizens' conduct, to allay disquiet commanded that there be no further violation of the Lenten rules, but recognized therewith that the New Testament does not authorize the fast. Zwingli preached, and some weeks later published, a sermon *On the Choice and Free Use of Foods,* leaving the Christian free to fast or not to fast according to his conscience, provided he does not scandalize his neighbor.

The bishop of Constance, appealed to by opponents of Zwingli, felt the situation to be grave enough for episcopal action. His coadjutor, Melchior Wattli, came with two other clerics to investigate and correct the Zurichers. First they assembled the clergy, but Zwingli addressed the meeting with convincing effect. They took their plea before the Little Council, of which Zwingli was not a member. It was more favorable to the bishop than the priests had been; but some of its members got the matter referred to the Great Council, which included in its number the fifty who composed the Little Council. This move frustrated the efforts of the commissioners, who had hoped to avoid a debate. After some delay, Zwingli was admitted to the Great Council.

In reply to the appeal of the commissioners not to leave the Church in which alone is found salvation, he pictured the Church of true believers in every nation, and argued that the observance of fasts is a matter of indifference which ought not to be compulsory or held to determine membership in the Church of Christ. No decisive action resulted. The council thanked the bishop for his fatherly admonition, weakly renewed its regulation against violating the fast 'without special cause,' and commanded all to avoid harsh judgments and keep the peace.

In Constance, if not in Rome, Zwingli was now regarded as a schismatic. His old friend, John Faber, turned from him and became an ardent opponent of the Reformation. Bishop Hugo wrote to warn the canons of the Great Minster not to be seduced from the Church. Zwingli had now been appointed to a canonry, and being present when the bishop's accusing letter was read, he undertook to reply to it. In August 1522 his defense appeared, *Archeteles* (Beginning-End), so entitled, he explained, in the hope that this first reply would be the last required. It is written with the vigor of conviction and is highly argumentative and strewn with rhetorical questions. What harm, he asks, will come if the whole rubbish heap of ceremonials be cleared away? God declares that they are vain. Who denies that Christ is one, and that there is one Church founded upon the rock? But some hold that the 'rock' is the Fisherman, others that it is the Creator of all things. 'The downfall of your ceremonies is at hand.'

This audacious reply brought forth a warning letter from Erasmus, with whom Zwingli's relations were to be no longer friendly. About this time the impoverished, diseased, and unhappy refugee, Ulrich von Hutten, whose brilliant role in Germany had ended with the failure of the Knight's War, was repulsed by Erasmus in Basel and threw himself on the charity of Zwingli. The Reformer's hospitality and personal kindness to the discredited and friendless radical during the last months of his life (1523) were in marked contrast with the self-protecting attitude of the humanist.

In July 1522, Zurich was visited by François Lambert, a gaunt Franciscan from Avignon, almost converted to the Reformation, yet a seeker, traveling about to inquire what truth might be found from the new teachers. He was well recommended by Berthold Haller, who was then instituting the Reformation in

Bern — discussed in the next chapter. Zwingli welcomed Lambert and permitted him to preach, but challenged his position on prayer to the Virgin. A friendly public disputation ensued, after which Lambert confessed himself convinced that he must pray to God only. He then mounted his donkey and set out for Basel and Wittenberg. We shall encounter this roving inquirer again.

Zwingli had been invited to nominate his successor in Einsiedeln and had chosen his former student companion, the little Alsatian, Leo Judä (1482–1542). In July 1522 a group of eleven evangelical priests met in Judä's house, among them Zwingli and three others from Zurich. Their purpose was to draft an appeal to the bishop of Constance for permission for clerical marriages. The document they prepared assumes as common knowledge the widespread violation by priests of their vows of celibacy. Quoting Scripture proofs, they hold clerical marriage right and proper and in the interests of true chastity, and ask that its unwise prohibition be removed. The petitioners refer to the 'tyranny' of Rome and to their own Swiss nationality, and seem to suppose the reform possible by territorial or episcopal action. Bishop Hugo could not but recoil from this view; nor would he, a German, share their Swiss national sentiment. Further, after efforts to check concubinage among his priests, he was now enjoying a large income from fines imposed upon those who had concubines and children. Most of the petitioners were following the common practice.

As for Zwingli, in this year, after a secret ceremony, he took into his house Anna Reinhard, who for nine years had been a widow and was a person of good reputation. Zwingli had earlier taught and befriended her gifted son, Gerold Meyer. His friend, Myconius, spoke of Anna as Zwingli's 'wife,' but two years elapsed before the Reformer publicly avowed the union (April 1524). Little is known of the personality of Anna, but Zwingli thanked God for His blessing on their marriage. Of the four children of the marriage the eldest, Regula, became the wife of Rudolf Gwalter, who edited Zwingli's works. William (1526–41) died of the plague while studying in Strasbourg; Ulrich (1528–71), minister and professor, married a daughter of Zwingli's successor, Heinrich Bullinger. The youngest, Anna, died in infancy.

— III —

The events of 1522 strengthened Zwingli's position in the city and canton. The Great Council and the burgomaster, Marcus Roust (like Zwingli a veteran of Marignano), were prepared to act on his principle that the Bible should be the norm of doctrine and worship. In a synod that autumn, the rural clergy showed a remarkable readiness to adopt this principle. Zwingli's whole movement would not have amounted to much if it had not readily won the support of the great majority of the priests. It must be remembered, too, that all concerned were accustomed to the determination of church affairs by action of the political powers. In Switzerland the bishops had little real authority. The clergy were subject to the rules and laws of the communities that supported them. No canton was more independent of the hierarchy than Zurich. It had recently refused military aid to the Pope, and now it had failed to satisfy the bishop of Constance.

Nevertheless fear of serious trouble for the Reformers lay in the attitude of most of the other cantons, with whose leaders Zurich's rejection of mercenary service had made her unpopular. Zwingli was looked upon with anxiety or detestation by many Swiss. The federal diet meeting at Baden in July 1522 had instituted procedures against the evangelical pastor of Fislisbach near by. Popular violence, too, was a possibility on the part of exasperated Zurichers who felt antagonistic toward the Reformer. Leo Judä, who late in 1522 had come from Einsiedeln to St. Peter's Church, Zurich, was set upon and injured after confuting an Augustinian in the street. Zwingli knew not what to expect for himself. His brothers wrote to him in consternation, supposing that like John Huss he would be burned at Constance — and the family dishonored by an heretical member. He replied that he had weighed the consequences of his action and had no fear; his sole aim was to proclaim the treasures of Christ. His grief would be inconsolable if his brothers by nature were not his brothers in faith. Zwingli was undaunted, but Zurich was in a state of nerves. The situation called for decision. The bishop had failed, and Rome was silent.

At Zwingli's request, the Great Council, without waiting for what the Pope or the hierarchy might do, called a public disputation on the questions at issue, in order to bring them to a per-

manent settlement within the canton. It was stipulated in the
invitation to the meeting that the arguments were to be based
on Scripture, and that the language used was to be German. The
bishop of Constance was courteously invited to attend in person
or send deputies. From the point of view of canon law the whole
plan was, of course, quite irregular; but the bishop was in no
position to interdict it. He decided to send his vicar, John Faber, *old frie...*
and three others to the meeting. Thus came about the First Disputation of Zurich, held in the town hall under the presidency
of the burgomaster on 29 January 1523. About 600 persons attended, half of whom were clergy, gathered from the whole canton. Zwingli had drawn up and published for the occasion his
Sixty-seven Conclusions, the first formal summary of his doctrines. He here asserts the authority of Christ, as the only High
Priest and Mediator, and the brotherhood and communion of
Christians in Him, who constitute the Church Catholic. He affirms that Christians are free with respect to works that are not
enjoined in Scripture. The authority of the Pope, transubstantiation, saint worship, purgatory, fasts, and pilgrimages are all
repudiated. Zwingli deplores the scandal that priests should not
be permitted lawful marriage but are allowed, on payment of
money, to take concubines or mistresses.

These Conclusions received little attention in the Disputation
itself. The meeting lasted through only a forenoon and a short
afternoon session. The bishop's deputies took the position that
the matters in discussion belonged to a church council, not to a
town meeting, and would not dispute. Faber stated (too opti-
mistically) that a general council would be held at Nuremberg
within a year, and he maintained that only the learning of Paris
and Louvain would be adequate to deal with the controversy.
'Why not Erfurt or Wittenberg?' asked Zwingli; and he affirmed
that a Christian assembly competent to treat the points at issue
was present in the hall. He had at hand copies of the Bible in
the original languages, and here were scholars fully capable
of interpreting them. He had letters from Nuremberg that
showed no expectation of a council there. After a silence Zwingli
implored his critics to present their arguments, but no response
followed, save a taunt for his opponents in a raucous voice from
the rear.

A loaded question posed by a priest concerning the pastor of

Fislisbach, prosecuted by the federal diet and now imprisoned at Constance, led the vicar to explain that he himself had by Scripture convinced the prisoner of his errors. Zwingli, springing to the attack, pressed him to produce the convincing passages; but in vain — Faber's instructions did not permit him to dispute. Zwingli took full advantage of Faber's unwillingness to join battle, and those present were impressed by the evident strength of the evangelical position. Faber's only chance lay in the possibility of eliciting a strong local resistance to Zwingli; but although the latter had many tavern critics, and some learned ones, in the city, no Zuricher rose to challenge him.

After a noon recess, the assembly met to hear the verdict of the magistrates. The burgomaster declared on behalf of both councils that, since no one had refuted Zwingli's articles, he should continue to proclaim the Gospel, and that all the priests of the canton should also follow the Scripture in their preaching. Apparently Faber had not read Zwingli's Conclusions until after the morning session. He now offered criticisms of some of them, and a brief and animated exchange followed. But the business in hand was really ended with the magistrates' decision, and the burgomaster dismissed the meeting. This outcome was decisive for the canton of Zurich. It was not only a commitment of the whole community to the preaching of evangelical doctrines; it was also by implication a withdrawal from the jurisdiction of the bishop of Constance, and of the Pope.

From the first Zwingli had been treated by Rome with singular patience and caution. A severer course had been unsuccessfully followed with Luther; but the policy of forbearance toward Zwingli was not more successful. Adrian VI (1521–3), the last non-Italian Pope, was a Dutchman trained in the northern learning and in the Spanish Inquisition. He had sought, with strong inducements, help from Erasmus against Luther. He hoped to halt Zwingli's course and prevent his irrevocable repudiation of the Papacy. Zwingli was now approached by an officer of the Swiss papal guard, none other than the son of Burgomaster Roust, and by a papal legate, with a letter from Adrian. The Reformer was addressed as the Pope's well-beloved son, was greeted with an apostolic benediction, and was led to expect liberal promotions and honors if he would change his message and show his obedience. A papal agent, authorized to negotiate with him, jocularly stated that Zwingli could have anything but the papal throne. These approaches were completely ignored by Zwingli, and did not for a moment halt him in his pursuit of reform. Faber's adverse remarks on his *Sixty-seven Conclusions* gave him more concern, and set him to labor on a defense of them. His *Exposition and Basis of the Conclusions,* a closely argued treatise of 300 pages, appeared the following June.

— IV —

Radical elements now arose to challenge and distress the victorious Reformer. At various points his own doctrines had given encouragement to these. His negative Scripture test — what is not authorized in Scripture being rejected — meant the exclusion of images from worship; and the affirmation that Scripture is the sole norm of doctrine left the possibility of an endless variety of interpretations of Scripture. What had been authorized by the authorities of Zurich was in effect Zwingli's own interpretation. But others, on the same assumption of the source of authority, might differ from him on the inferences to be drawn. Now that his views had become official policy, some began to associate them with the denial of that very liberty of the Gospel which he had originally extolled.

A pamphlet appeared from the pen of an Anabaptist, advocating the prompt destruction of images used in worship; and minor acts of iconoclasm took place in two Zurich churches. Nicholas Hottinger, a shoemaker with some education, aided by companions, in Stadelhofen beside Zurich overturned a large wooden crucifix that had been a landmark and an object of reverence. These iconoclasts were arrested; but agitation was heated, and the Council determined to hold another disputation in order to frame a policy on images. Invitations went out to all the cantons, to the university and the bishop of Basel, the bishops of Constance and Chur, and the abbot of St. Gall. Most of the replies were unfavorable to such public discussion of important issues. Bishops Hugo of Constance and Christopher of Basel wished the matter to be held for the meeting of a council. The assembly, 900 in number, predominantly Zurich citizens and clergy, met on 26 October 1523. The sessions were continued for three days. Zwingli won an easy victory over all advocates of images, and it was decided to abolish them. The doctrine of the

Mass was next discussed, under the presidency of Zwingli's friend Vadianus, who had come as a representative of the town of St. Gall. Zwingli's view that the Mass is not a sacrifice but the remembrance of a sacrifice prevailed. Here, as at the previous disputation, every opportunity was given for contrary argument. One courteous speaker, Conrad Schmied, commander of the Knights of St. John from Küssnacht, merely observed that in worship 'pictures are the staves of the weak' — to which Zwingli made a courteous reply. Representatives of the friar orders, who in their sermons had defended the old ceremonies, kept silence now, or acquiesced in the decisions. Such warmth of unanimity prevailed at the close that Zwingli wept with emotion.

The question of authority in reform measures had not been fully sifted by Zwingli and his supporters. They had affirmed the sole authority of Scripture; but in order that Scripture should produce the reform of abuses, it must be interpreted. One source of the effectiveness of Zwingli's arguments lay in the fact that nobody really questioned the authority of Scripture. His training, too, had made him alert and eloquent and ready to interpret the Word, as his opponents were not. But in order that the Reformation should succeed, Zwingli never doubted that in addition to preaching community action was required. In the disputations, the Great Council of Zurich, which controlled the canton, made decisions for the community. Both Zurich councils were strongly under Zwingli's masterful influence. But he himself did not wish to admit their authority in these matters. During the First Disputation he had replied to the demand for action by a church council with the statement that the whole assembly, with its 'bishops' (that is, the pastors), had the powers of such a council. In the October Disputation he affirmed again the right of the then present assembly to decide, as representing the church of the canton. In this, he believed he was returning to the principles of the primitive Church before general councils were held. The action of the Zurich magistrates was welcomed because it accorded with Scripture and with the mind of the Christian Assembly. The magistrates, on their part, however, simply considered themselves authorized to reform the Church within their territories. These positions were theoretically divergent, but practically they coincided, making it possible for the question of ultimate responsibility to remain an open one.

The radicals, on the other hand, were prepared, on their own reading of Scripture, to challenge the decisions reached. There were iconoclasts who were unwilling to take the slow pace that Zwingli recommended, and the councils of Zurich intended, in the elimination of images and the reform of ritual. Some impatient souls were offended that Masses were not at once abandoned. But the most serious objections came from a group of Anabaptists that now began to agitate for still more basic changes. They discarded infant baptism, rejected all state ordinances affecting the Church, opposed the collection of tithes, and denied that the Church was properly composed of all members of the community. The brilliant but ill-disciplined young humanist, Conrad Grebel, brother-in-law of Vadianus, and Felix Manz, the son of a clergyman, who was also well educated and had studied Hebrew, became the most notable spokesmen of the group. In 1523 they proposed to Zwingli and the council that a true church of the regenerate should be assembled, entirely self-governing and with the means of excommunicating unfaithful members — a church 'without sin.' Zwingli asked whether they themselves would qualify for membership, and held that in this world all churches must have tares amid the wheat.

This was the beginning of a protracted controversy. The Anabaptists wanted to employ Zwingli's own method, a public disputation. They were joined by a former monk from Chur, Brother Jacob, known from his blue cloak as Blaurock. This zealous sectary had interrupted the service in the neighboring parish of Zollikon, pounding with his walking stick and shouting, 'I am a door, I am a good shepherd.' There was a strong fanatical strain in the movement, though this was not prominent in Zurich. Thomas Münzer, the violent mystic of the Peasant Revolt in Germany, visited Waldshut on the Austrian side of the Rhine in 1524 and got in touch with some of the Swiss Anabaptists. Grebel later wrote to him, praising his writings and charging that Zwingli taught 'a sinful, pleasant Christ.'

Zwingli was caught at a disadvantage. He had some affinity with the Anabaptists, much as he was offended by their separatism. He had suggested that infant baptism is not clearly indicated in the New Testament; he had denied the scriptural basis of tithes, and he had affirmed the paramount authority of Scripture. But the idea of a church of approved saints made sinless by regeneration seemed to him utterly unrealistic as well as un-scriptural. These Anabaptists were to Zwingli what the Witten-berg radicals were to Luther: Carlstadt, indeed, was one of their inspirers. But Zwingli was himself more of a radical than Luther. He showed some sympathy with the rebelling peasants and was regarded in Germany as their partisan. He was instrumental in having some of the demands of the Zurich peasants met by the councils (1525). As long as possible, he treated the Anabaptists with patience.

On 17 January 1525, a conference was held with the Anabap-tists before the magistrates. Its outcome was a measure com-pelling all parents to have their children baptized by the eighth day of life and forbidding separatist religious meetings. This was compulsion; and it only intensified the claims, and the resolu-tion, of the sectaries. They now began the practice of rebaptism: Grebel baptized Blaurock, who baptized numerous others, pour-ing the water over the head. The chief leaders were imprisoned, protesting that they were not subject to secular jurisdiction. There was another futile conference in March. On 6 November a full-scale disputation took place, so well attended that it had to be held in the Great Minster. A surprising number of Ana-baptists came from distant parts of Switzerland and beyond. The heated exchange lasted for three days. Again the magis-trates gave their judgment, as could have been anticipated, in Zwingli's favor, excoriating his opponents for their shameless wrangling, conspiracy against God, and contempt for authority. Totally unconvinced, Grebel, Manz, and Blaurock were again imprisoned, but soon released. Balthazar Hübmeier, a distin-guished Anabaptist, forced by the Austrians out of Waldshut, came to Zurich, professed a change of mind, but reverted pub-licly to his former views. The numbers of the party grew and the magistrates were at their wits' end.

The possibility of tolerating a separatist minority seems not to have been considered. Nor would the Anabaptists have been satisfied with that solution. They thought of their own groups as alone constituting the true Church, and condemned govern-ment churches in principle. They alarmed the state authorities by their opposition to military service and to participation in political life. Early in 1526, the Council turned to severe meas-ures. Those in prison were more harshly treated than before.

On 7 March the death penalty by drowning was ordered for those who practiced rebaptism, though professedly it was for their subversive political attitude. If the magistrates hoped that the threat of death would deter the Anabaptists, they were greatly mistaken. Still they hesitated to enforce the regulation. It was not until nine months later that the penalty was inflicted. Manz and Blaurock were condemned to death; but the latter, not being a Zuricher, was scourged and expelled. Manz was drowned on 5 January 1527; his aged mother, tearless and proud of her martyr son, witnessed his brave death from the shore. The movement shrank to its core of faithful adherents, but was still active in other parts of Switzerland. In St. Gall and Appenzel it exhibited instances of extreme fanaticism. One overwrought devotee, Thomas Schugger, decapitated his brother with a sword.

Zwingli had found it necessary in this controversy to revise somewhat his earlier views. His defense of infant baptism involved an argument from the early Church Fathers, since the evidence of the New Testament, on his admission, left the matter undetermined. He did not reverse his opinion that tithes have no scriptural basis, but he pleaded for their maintenance on grounds of practical necessity. In both these instances we see a modification of what we have called his negative scriptural principle. He had come to feel also that complete freedom of religion held the danger of anarchy and had approved stern measures which earlier he would have thought tyrannous. He was, no doubt, honestly convinced that the Anabaptists were politically subversive, and he had always been a patriot jealous for the safety of the Confederacy. The enthusiasts constituted a menace to the public institutions that he approved, and to the Church in the early stage of the new life of the Reformation. Like the magistrates, he hesitated to begin persecution, but in the end he sadly approved, and probably helped to frame, the severe measures taken. It is idle to conjecture what would have happened if he had held to a course of tolerance. The sixteenth century was not ready for modern liberalism, and Zwingli, with his heart set upon reform by public action, was not the man to move toward the separation of Church and state. Even today our systems of toleration are challenged anew, and we shall not maintain them without effort. Nor is there any evidence that at this period the resolute martyrs of Anabaptism would themselves, if successful, have proved more tolerant than their unwilling persecutors.

The other principal sufferers from the policy of reform were the monks, friars, and nuns. They had been much criticized, and the government had been petitioned from parts of the canton to have their properties taken over for poor relief. In 1523 the chapter of the Great Minster was itself drastically reformed. Foreseeing their own suppression, the nuns of the Frauminster in Zurich, the canons of Embrach, the Cistercians of Cappel, and the Augustinians of Winterthur made terms for the dissolution of their communities and for their own maintenance. But the Dominicans, Franciscans, and Augustinians in Zurich, whose pulpits had rung with denunciations of Zwingli, refused to take such a course. Suddenly, on 3 December 1524, the councils of Zurich took action to bring the three orders together, permitting any who so desired to depart with pensions. The magistrates and police escorted the Dominicans and Augustinians to the Franciscan house, directed them how to live together, made provision for their food supply, and left them to overcome as best they could their old mutual antipathies in their common adversity. The vacated properties were confiscated and disposed of in the interests of the city hospital and schools. Zwingli began to build up the school of the Great Minster, which was called the Carolinum, and to invite scholars of standing to it. Notable among these was the eminent Conrad Pellican, who settled in Zurich on 1 March 1526, having already served in the beginning of the Reformation in Basel.

— V —

Meanwhile a transformation of worship and discipline was in process. The decisions of 1523 affected chiefly the pulpit message. In Zurich, as everywhere, the Reformation proceeded by means of a preaching closely drawn from the Bible. Such preaching sometimes, without the preacher's intention, incited hearers to hasty action against features of the cultus. In instances of iconoclasm, such as the Hottinger case referred to above, Zwingli held the offense to consist in the fact that what was done had not yet been authorized by the government. Hottinger was banished from Zurich; soon afterward he was beheaded by action of the federal diet. In accordance with the decision of October 1523 a commission, formed of eight members from the two councils and six of the clergy, was established to plan steps of reform. Zwingli wrote *A Short Christian Introduction,* intended as an instrument of the commission and an interim directory for the clergy of the canton. It dealt briefly with the Law and the Gospel, images, and the Mass. The commission instituted a preaching campaign to explain the temporary policy throughout the canton, and planned the orderly removal of images from the churches. This was done, despite the protest of the bishop, in the spring and summer of 1524. Along with the pictures and images went the treasures of shrines. Processions were discontinued, and the revered bones of saints were decently buried. One of Zwingli's applications of Scripture to worship was the rejection of organs in churches; they were removed or silenced. The omission of singing followed in December 1527. It is remarkable that the man responsible for this innovation was personally so fond of music that he had been charged with frivolity for his attention to it. Zwingli interpreted the Bible as excluding instrumental music and the traditional chants in public worship. Undoubtedly the well-known artificialities that had invaded the choir music of the time had something to do with this extreme and indefensible measure.

During his second period in Italy, Zwingli had found time to make some inquiries regarding the variation in the liturgy of the Mass between Rome and Milan, and later he had introduced simplifications of the rite at Zurich. He had now for several years spoken of the Mass as idolatrous, and taught a doctrine of the Eucharist that laid emphasis upon the memorial aspect of the sacrament as opposed to the Roman view of transubstantiation and a re-enacted sacrifice. The positive aspects of Zwingli's Eucharistic doctrine have been overlooked for the most part, since, among his contemporaries, what distinguished his opinions was his repudiation of the doctrine of the corporeal presence in both its medieval and its Lutheran forms. The definitive suppression of the Mass in Zurich was delayed until April 1525. A simple and impressive form for the administration of the sacrament, written by Zwingli, was then introduced; this will call for reference in another chapter.

Zwingli claimed to have 'preached the Gospel' before Luther was known in Switzerland, and he resented the designation

'Lutheran.' Yet he showed at first only good will toward Luther, and encouraged Froschauer to promote the circulation of his books. He probably owed only a minor debt to Luther as a writer, and the success of Luther's movement was no more than a general encouragement to his own. Differences in the experience, training, and temperament of the leaders, and still more, perhaps, differences of social environment, caused the Reformation movements in Germany and Switzerland to diverge greatly. The doctrine of the Eucharist was the topic chiefly debated. But the difference here was entangled with political preferences and policies, and attended by misunderstandings natural in that era wherever Germans of the Empire met Germans of the Confederacy.

By 1524 the Eucharistic issue was fairly defined. Luther had affirmed a doctrine of the corporeal presence: in 'This is my body,' I Cor. 11:24, 'is' meant nothing but 'is.' Desiring to stress the priesthood of all Christians, he excluded the priestly miracle of transubstantiation, and adduced instead, to explain the presence, his doctrine of the ubiquity of Christ's resurrected body. To give the body this more than bodily nature, he revived and adapted the patristic concept of the interchange of characteristics (*communicatio idiomatum*) between the body and the spirit. Zwingli escaped these subtleties and reached a very different result by a figurative interpretation of 'is' ('This signifies my body') and by corresponding interpretations of other passages. The Eucharist became an expression, and an experience, of faith, the appropriation of the spiritual presence of Christ through commemoration of His redemptive sacrifice. Christ, Zwingli said in 1530, 'is present to the contemplation of faith.'

The visit of Hinne Rode, a Netherlands scholar, to Wittenberg, Strasbourg, Basel, and Zurich (1522–3) helped to clarify the points of view of the Reformers on this topic, especially of Bucer and Zwingli. Rode bore with him a treatise in letter form, written by Cornelius Hendrix Hoen, a follower of the pre-Reformer, Wessel Gansfort. Zwingli conferred with Rode and soon after published Hoen's letter with approval. It contained an explanation of the Corinthians passage to which Zwingli gave currency: 'This signifies my body.' The discovery of this congenial treatment of the sacrament corroborated impressions he had gained from Pico and Erasmus. He may also have made use of the treatise *On the Body and Blood of Our Lord* by Ratramnus, a ninth-century monk of Corbie, who used the expression 'Hoc figurat corpus meum' — 'This figures forth my body.' Luther was displeased and shocked by the denial of the corporeal presence and failed to see in Zwingli's doctrine any element of true faith. Zwingli in turn countered the doctrine of ubiquity with the argument that according to Scripture the body of Christ is spatially absent, being in heaven. In 1527 he set forth his view in opposition to that of Luther in a treatise entitled *Friendly Exegesis, or Exposition of the Eucharist*. Luther replied in his *Great Confession concerning the Holy Eucharist* (1528), one of the angriest of the tracts of the great Reformer. Zwingli in turn, while professing to avoid harsh invective, answered in kind. He and Oecolampadius made it clear, however, that on many other points of doctrine they and their Swiss associates were on common ground with the Wittenbergers. All this was background for the Marburg Colloquy, 1529.

A notable feature of church life in Zurich was the 'Prophecy,' or public meeting for Scripture exposition and discussion. Similar exercises were later employed by Calvin, in the Church of Scotland, and in the 'Prophesyings' suppressed in Elizabethan England (See below, pp. 318 f.).

— VI —

Zwingli had gained ascendancy in Zurich, but his intrepid policy was bearing fruit in Zurich's increasing isolation. The diet meeting at Luzern in January 1525, hearing complaints from the bishops of Basel and Constance, warned Zurich, quite in vain, against further innovations, and at the same time adopted an elaborate project of reform in forty-seven articles. This plan was very different from the Zwinglian one. But the preamble to the long document states that because the chief shepherd (the Pope) is 'silent and asleep,' the Swiss must take care of themselves. The diet condemns alike 'the Lutheran or Zwinglian sect' and 'Roman indulgences' granted for money. While the Scriptures are to be freely circulated, the seven sacraments are to be retained and the books of Reformers to be suppressed. Highly informing as this document is concerning the state of mind of the Swiss, it bore no fruit of reform. In Luzern, Zwingli was burned in effigy, and this canton, along with Uri, Schwyz, Unterwalden, and Zug, formed at Beckenried (April 1524) a separate alliance to combat the Reformation. Zwingli now began to seek security for Zurich by alliances with south German cities and with France, at the same time promoting the spread of the Reformation in other Swiss cantons where it had made a beginning.

Postponing the story of this extension of the Reformed Church, we note the development of Zwingli's religio-political plans. In December 1527 Zurich and Constance, whose citizens favored the Swiss against the emperor, formed an agreement called the Christian Civic League. Six months later, Bern joined this pact. The result of the Disputation of Bern (May 1528) greatly encouraged the other cantons and districts to rally to the side of Zurich. By January 1530, St. Gall, Biel, Mühlhausen, Basel, Schaffhausen, and Strasbourg had taken the same step. Zwingli hoped for yet wider alliances. The opposing group of cantons took alarm, responded to the advances of the ancient enemy, Austria, and in February 1529 formed with Austria an agreement called the Christian Union. An extension of this alliance to include Bavaria, Savoy, and other principalities was actively promoted. It seemed that Switzerland would be torn apart and would become, with a great region of Europe, the theater of a major war.

Zurich was pursuing an aggressive policy of intervention on behalf of adherents of the Reformation in St. Gall and was sending evangelists into the free bailiwicks. One such Gospel preacher, Jacob Kaiser, was seized by officers of Schwyz and burned at the stake, 29 May 1529. On 8 June, Zurich declared war on the five opposing cantons. When the forces confronted each other at Cappel near Zurich, the soldiers began to fraternize and the commanders to negotiate. Agreement was reached 26 June. The terms were favorable to the policies of Zurich in allowing freedom of preaching in the common bailiwicks and in the payment of compensation to the family of Kaiser. The five cantons also repudiated the Austrian alliance, which had profited them nothing in the crisis. But Zwingli saw loopholes in the treaty and anticipated a renewal of trouble. He wrote a hymn which is an outcry of deep distress with overtones of faith. This may be translated:

> O Lord, unless Thou take the rein,
>   The chariot sinks and doomed are we,
> While foes make mockery of our pain,
>   In swaggering pride that fears not Thee.

Show forth Thy glory in our land:
  Confound the vaunting troops of hell:
Renew our souls, that we may stand
  Thy faithful flock who love Thee well.

O help us, till the strife be o'er;
  O let all bitterness depart;
The old-time faithfulness restore,
  And praise shall rise from every heart.

The Zwinglian doctrine of the Lord's Supper had penetrated the south German cities; but there the mediating view of Martin Bucer, the Strasbourg Reformer, gained ascendancy. Philip, the Margrave of Hesse, a prominent Lutheran prince, shared Zwingli's political outlook and tolerated his theology. Philip was engaged in complicated diplomacy, designed to utilize the French hostility to the Hapsburgs and to unite the forces of the Lutheran League of Torgau with those of Zwingli's Christian Civic League, so as to form a common front against possible attacks. The diet held at Speier in the spring of 1529 had increased the tension in Germany. Some of the southern cities had joined with the Lutheran princes in the celebrated Protest of Speier, which gave currency to the word 'Protestant' in its now historic sense. Philip labored to bring about a conference between the chieftains of the Reformation, Luther and Zwingli, in the hope of consolidating the Protestant movements. Zwingli's anxieties made him eager to co-operate in this. Luther and Melanchthon, distrustful of Zwingli, were with difficulty prevailed upon to meet him.

Philip persisted until he arranged the conference at Marburg. Zwingli rode away from Zurich in secrecy, without the consent of the council, and without telling his wife what his destination was. In three weeks he reached Marburg, accompanied by his ablest theological supporter, John Oecolampadius, the Reformer of Basel. At daylight on 1 October the discussions began; apparently they were concluded on the night of Sunday, the third. The participants came with different intentions. Luther and Melanchthon, still hoping for the Lutheranizing of the Empire, anxious to avoid political entanglements with the Swiss that might offend Charles V, and at the same time holding a low opinion of Zwingli's theology, simply did not wish or expect an agreement. Zwingli and Oecolampadius earnestly hoped for a theological *rapprochement* that could be used as the basis of a political and military alliance.

These facts explain in part the intractable manner of Luther and the intensity and even tearful emotion of Zwingli that appear in reports of the conference. The seventeenth-century Lutheran historian, Baron von Seckendorf, recognized that Luther here showed himself hostile and arrogant, insisting simply on submission to his opinion. At first Luther was closeted with Oecolampadius, Melanchthon with Zwingli. Later, Philip presiding, these four were together at a table while a score of other German theologians sat about them. Luther began this session by pulling back the velvet tablecloth and writing on the table, 'Hoc est corpus meum' — 'This is my body' — and repeatedly, when the argument took a turn unfavorable to him, he returned to the phrase as an anchor for his thoughts.

The points raised were not new. The Reformed theologians tried to get Luther to admit that the resurrected body of Christ is 'in a place,' namely in heaven, and hence not in the sacramental elements. They cited many passages in support of a figurative interpretation of 'is' in the quoted text — an argument that Luther dismissed as 'mathematical.' In support of it, Zwingli, well versed in the Church Fathers, quoted Fulgentius and Augustine. Luther claimed that all the other Fathers were on his side and later produced some supporting texts from Chrysostom and Ambrose. During the discussion taunts were exchanged, and it was only the landgrave's firmness and diplomacy that prevented the talks' breaking off in anger and futility. Neither party conceded a particle of theological conviction, but each gained a new respect for the other. In the end, at Philip's request, Luther framed fifteen articles to propose to the Swiss, believing that they would not be accepted. He was surprised that no objection was taken against any of those dealing with points other than the Eucharist. The fifteenth article was so framed as to be an agreement to reject the Roman Catholic position on the sacrament and its celebration, and to hold in mutual charity the divergent views that had been expressed by the two parties.

And although at the present time we are not in agreement as to whether the real body and blood of Christ are corporeally present in the bread and wine, yet each party shall extend Christian charity toward the other, as far as conscience permits, and both shall implore Almighty God that He confirm in us by His Spirit the true understanding of His Word.

Luther's insistence on the clause, 'as far as conscience permits' (a strange limitation on 'Christian charity'), and his refusal at the close to clasp hands with Zwingli as a brother indicate the suspicion that still dogged their relationships. But the fifteen Articles of Marburg in reality constituted a positive outcome of what might have proved a disruptive quarrel. On the other hand, the conference left the possibility of full agreement remote indeed, and failed to produce what Philip had hoped for, the basis of an armed alliance.

— VII —

It was for Zurich and her Reformer that the resulting situation was most perilous. While the emperor disappointed Luther by his effort at the diet of Augsburg to procure the suppression of the Reformation, he was not in a position to proceed at once by war, and in the Schmalkald League the Lutheran cause gained a measure of security. But Zurich was virtually isolated. From Zwingli's point of view, the previous peace of Cappel was appeasement of a resolute foe. At Augsburg the south German cities had presented their own statement of belief to the diet: it was dismissed without consideration. Bucer, its author, sought to interest the Swiss in it, or in some other possible mediating statement, to which he hoped the Lutherans might assent. But Zwingli grew weary of his shifting phraseology and finally repulsed him, with the advice: 'Spare your paper.' At the time of the Augsburg diet Zwingli also sent to the emperor (July 1530) a short confession of faith (*Fidei ratio*). Frank and uncompromising, it could hardly have been expected to win favor in the eyes of Charles V, but Zwingli may have hoped by it to add to the number of his friends in Protestant circles.

He was now entangled in diplomatic schemes to secure Zurich and Protestant Switzerland against attack. There were busy but fruitless negotiations with Venice and with France. The propaganda of hate against the Zurichers, incited partly by Zwingli's utterances, swept the Forest cantons. Zwingli, having gained political ascendancy in Zurich, looked for no terms of peace short of the complete freedom of preaching in the opposing cantons. He seemed now able to do nothing effective to prevent a war, which he dreaded and for which Zurich was not prepared. Bern, which had also adopted the Reformation, wished to maintain peace and proposed an embargo on shipments to the five cantons of grain, salt, wine, and iron, commodities they needed and could not otherwise obtain. They still refused to yield the point of tolerating itinerant evangelists. Bern remained unwilling to fight, and there was great misgiving in Zurich. Zwingli offered to resign his office; he labored to arouse the citizens to arms; and then, fully realizing the tragic situation in which he and his fellows stood, he courageously awaited the blow.

The five cantons, having been assured of aid from the Pope, set their armies in motion on 6 October 1531. The Zurich troops who responded to the summons of the magistrates were few and unprepared, and there was no adequate plan of battle. Zwingli had bidden farewell to Heinrich Bullinger, who would succeed him, saying: 'Be faithful to Our Lord Jesus Christ!' Myconius, who had been his closest friend, with profoundest grief saw the Reformer, as chaplain of the soldiers, ride out with them, into the tempestuous night. Late the next evening, 11 October, the battle was joined at Cappel. After hours of desperate fighting against odds of three to one, the surviving Zurichers took flight. Zwingli's old friend Geroldseck, his step-son Gerold Meyer, and many magistrates and ministers of Zurich were among the fallen. Zwingli himself was struck while bending to comfort a wounded man. He was found in the darkness helplessly wounded and, having been identified, was vindictively slain. The last words heard from his lips were words of Socrates that he had often re-called in days of peril: 'They may kill the body, but not the soul.' A former canon of the Zurich Frauminster, now with the enemy, bent over his corpse and exclaimed, 'Whatever you believed, you were a good Confederate.' His body was quartered and burned to ashes.

CHAPTER IV

PROGRESS UNDER OECOLAMPADIUS
AND BULLINGER

— I —

IN THE last chapter attention was centered on the career of
Zwingli and his work as it affected the canton of Zurich. His life
was lived under high pressure, and it was cut off before he or
others could measure his achievement or judge whether it would
endure. Meanwhile, under the the leadership of men who were
in touch with him, the Reformation had been advancing in other
parts of Switzerland. These were men who had been drawn into
the sphere of Zwingli's influence; but they were not his converts
or disciples. Some of them, indeed, had been affirming or preaching scriptural versus hierarchical authority and stoutly assailing
medieval abuses before Luther or Zwingli became famous. They
had adopted these positions, like Zwingli himself, under the influence of Christian humanists, particularly of Erasmus. But the
ecclesiastically indeterminate humanist reform ideal fell short of
satisfying them and was left behind as they pursued their study
of the Bible. The bolder programs of Luther and Zwingli called
forth their general approval. Since in experience and training
they had much in common with Zwingli, they found many of
their own thoughts reflected in his teachings. Most of them were
fascinated by his brilliance and boldness. Although Caspar Hedio
played little part in the Swiss Reformation, his adherence to
Zwingli is typical of that of many of the awakened and scholarly
clerics. At Whitsuntide, 1518, Hedio, already a Basel doctor of
divinity, visited Einsiedeln and heard Zwingli preach on the
story of the paralytic in Luke 5. He was completely captivated.
He described the preacher's masterly presentation of the forgiveness of sins as 'beautiful, thorough, solemn, comprehensive,
penetrating, evangelical.' He felt as if he had been listening to

one of the early Church Fathers. It is not evident that Hedio's mind was changed: rather he was immensely gratified, and confirmed in judgments already formed. It was thus with most of those who became Zwingli's colleagues in reform.

Oswald Myconius was a self-effacing man with great capacity for appreciation of others. The object of his admiration changed from Erasmus to Zwingli and he moved with Zwingli from humanism to reform. Wolfgang Koepfel (Capito), another Erasmian, and Johann Hussgen (Oecolampadius), whose humanist teachers were Reuchlin and Wimfehling, were Biblical humanists who, so to speak, voted for the Reformation. Thomas Wyttenbach, who as early as 1505 magnified the evangelical points of Erasmus' teaching — the authority of Scripture, faith, and the reconciling work of Christ — later showed a disposition to active reform like that of his own pupils, Zwingli and Judä. As pastor of Biel, 1507–26, with an interval at Bern, 1519–20, he promoted the Reformation. Conrad Kürschner (Pellicanus) learned much from Pico when in Italy, and thereafter naturally associated himself with the workers for reform in Switzerland. Vadianus moved similarly from the new learning to the new gospel.

None of these men, it appears, passed through anything like the throes of Luther's inner struggle, or felt a 'sudden conversion' after stubborn resistance such as Calvin was to experience. They did not, like Luther, publicly quarrel with Erasmus or other humanists. They graduated from Christian humanism to Zwinglian Protestantism, extending rather than basically revising their theology, and translating thought into action. The Bible, studiously consulted, often in the light of the Church Fathers, in whom they delighted, rather than the frame of any theological system, shaped their message. The relatively slight inner anxiety of Oecolampadius, stressed by E. Stähelin, scarcely constitutes an exception to this. The one among them all who underwent a specific conversion was Zwingli's successor, Heinrich Bullinger, and apparently no Swiss or other Reformer's influence had much to do with this experience.

Capito (1478–1541) and Oecolampadius (1482–1531) were the beginners of the Reformation in Basel. The son of a blacksmith of Hagenau, Capito was trained in Pforzheim, Ingolstadt, and Freiburg and was qualified in medicine, law, and theology. His scriptural condemnation of traditional practices began about

1512, when he became pastor of Bruchsal near Tübingen. In that year Pellican and he discussed approvingly together the spiritual concept of the Lord's Supper. About the same time Capito met and formed an enduring friendship with Oecolampadius, with whom he was to be briefly associated at Heidelberg and at Basel. He taught and preached at Basel for four years, 1515–19, introduced slight changes in the worship at the cathedral, and prepared his hearers for more fundamental reforms. Capito was appointed chaplain to Albert of Mainz; but since his theological position was unsatisfactory to that opponent of Luther, he broke this connection in 1522. His reputation as a Reformer rests on his work in Strasbourg, 1523–41, where he co-operated with Bucer and maintained good relations with the Swiss leaders. A more radical innovator (later an Anabaptist), Wilhelm Röubli, having zealously attacked the Mass and purgatory, was banished from Basel in 1522, the year in which Oecolampadius began his permanent residence there.

This gifted man was born at Weinsburg in Würtemberg of a well-to-do family named Hussgen. This family name (which is variously spelled) is a diminutive of the word for 'house,' but the learned form he adopted, 'Oecolampadius,' means 'house lamp.' To satisfy his father's wish that he should study law, he attended the university of Bologna, but he turned to theology and the languages and continued his work in German universities. At Heidelberg he was stimulated by Reuchlin, whom he ultimately rivaled as a master of Hebrew; at Tübingen he felt strongly the influence of Wyttenbach and made the acquaintance of Melanchthon and Capito. Despite a notably retiring disposition, he early obtained a reputation as a preacher. In 1515, Bishop Christoph von Utenheim, at the suggestion of Capito, appointed Oecolampadius to be penitentiary priest of the diocese and chief preacher at the cathedral of Basel. The presence there of Erasmus, then preparing for publication his New Testament in Greek, was one of the attractions of the post for Oecolampadius. He proved a helpful assistant in the final stage of this work, and was closely attached to Erasmus, although he never became completely a disciple of the Dutch humanist. The office of penitentiary, which gave him supervision over cases of penance, led to his close study of patristic texts on this subject, some of which he translated; and he went on to read extensively in the

Church Fathers. He was of an earnest reforming temper: he denounced in pulpit and in print the customary *risus pascalis,* or unseemly ludicrous tales introduced into the Easter services.

He was soon called away to Augsburg; and, somewhat unsettled by the Luther controversy, he sought opportunity for study by entering the Brigittine monastery of Altomünster, near that city (April 1520). But he had already become a reader of Luther's treatises and was moving toward the adoption of his views of penance. The monastic brethren charged him with heresy, but allowed him to avoid arrest and ride away with an armed band of protectors (January 1522). For a brief period he was in the company of Franz von Sickingen, leader of the Knights, whose revolt was about to begin. In November 1522, he arrived in Basel, accompanied by Ulrich von Hutten, who, as we have seen, was obliged to depart for Zurich because of Erasmus' hostility. Oecolampadius was at this period in friendly correspondence with Luther. It was to him that Luther wrote his celebrated comment on Erasmus, that he would die like Moses in the land of Moab (1523). It was in part through Luther's influence that Oecolampadius had moved away from Erasmus and 'Moab' into the Promised Land of the Reformation, yet he was not to be drawn into the circle of Luther's disciples.

Back in Basel, he was made preacher in the Church of St. Martin's, and lecturer in theology at the university. He now began to cultivate the friendship of Zwingli and to press for reform. His alliance with Erasmus was severed, and some of his university colleagues were unfavorable to his teaching. He enjoyed the confidence of Conrad Pellican, who taught Hebrew, and suffered with him the suspicion of the conservatives. When the latter became hostile, the city council, which by charter controlled the university, dismissed the objectors and promoted Oecolampadius and Pellican to full professorships. In 1523 the feudal authority of the bishop, which before the Reformation had been progressively reduced, was finally extinguished, and the aging Christoph von Utenheim removed the episcopal residence from the city. The preaching of scriptural doctrines was free, and changes in the services were cautiously introduced, including the use of the German language in singing and in the service of Baptism. In 1524 a priest of the canton of Basel, who had married, posted in the university and elsewhere five theses against the prohibition of clerical marriage; nobody came forward to dispute with him. The Basel Franciscans, on their refusal to substitute sermons for Masses, were deprived of their incomes by action of the magistrates. The printing houses of Basel were issuing much Reformation literature. 'They print everything favorable to Luther,' said Erasmus in 1523, 'nothing in favor of the Pope.'

— II —

At this period a beginning was also made in Bern. Here a talented poet, Nicholas Manuel (d. 1530), aroused public interest in reform, especially by his satirical plays. In 1523, at the carnival, two of these were enacted, in which the Pope and the hierarchy were vigorously attacked. In one, Manuel contrasted Christ crowned with thorns and riding on an ass, followed by the humble and afflicted, with the Pope splendidly mounted and armed, surrounded by military weapons, trumpets, and drums, and attended by soldiers and camp followers.

The leader of the reform in Bern was Berthold Haller (1492–1536), a native of Aldingen in Würtemberg, who had been at Pforzheim a fellow student of Melanchthon, and had taught in the academy of Rothweil on the Neckar; he had also assisted Wyttenbach at Biel before coming to Bern (1518). In 1520 he succeeded Wyttenbach as priest of St. Vincent's, Bern. In 1521 he visited Zwingli and formed with him an enduring alliance. He was soon in the center of controversy, a situation most uncongenial to him. He lacked the valiant spirit of Zwingli, and when he became discouraged by opposition it was Zwingli's exhortations that held him to his task. He summoned new resolution and remained active in Bern, a firm contender for the Reformation and guide to the Reformed Church, until his death in 1536. Haller was aided by the support of a distinguished Bernese family, the De Wattevilles, of whom Jakob was the presiding magistrate, while his son Nicholas was provost of the church of Bern and had been thought of as the probable successor to the bishop of Lausanne. Nicholas de Watteville, however, advised the bishop not to visit Bern with the intention of suppressing Haller's work, and later threw in his lot completely with the Reformation. Other valuable helpers of Haller were Sebastian Meyer, a Franciscan who from 1518 had decried abuses in the

Church and preached from the Epistles of St. Paul; and Franz Kolb, who was forced out of Bern for some years but returned in 1527 to preach reform with great energy.

The movement in Bern was delayed by the opposition of the aristocratic Little Council of the city, which attempted to expel Haller and Meyer (1523) and repeatedly prohibited innovations in worship and the reading of the books of Reformers. The Great Council, on the other hand, favored the new preachers and refused to permit their expulsion. The events of the German Peasant Revolt, 1524–5, increased the fear of change and produced fresh cautionary measures. But the continued preaching of the ministers and the writings of Manuel gradually persuaded both the people and their magistrates.

In St. Gall the learned and widely traveled Vadianus, first a Christian humanist, then a Protestant Reformer, and always a friend of Zwingli, labored unremittingly in the cause. He was not only a distinguished man of letters but also a practicing physician, so that Zwingli spoke of him as 'physician of body and soul' to his countrymen. As burgomaster of St. Gall (1526–51) he held a position of dignity in the Confederacy. The resistance of the abbot of the venerable abbey of St. Gall was the chief obstacle to adoption of the Reformation in the canton. Vadianus was aided by reforming preachers from Zurich, but none of his associates was so influential as John Kessler (d. 1572), a St. Gall workman's son. Having studied at Basel and Wittenberg, Kessler settled in his native town, supporting himself as a saddler and a teacher of Latin, and taking opportunities to discourse on the Bible in private houses and guild meetings. He wrote an important diary in which he records the events of the time. He was one of the two Swiss students who had the luck to meet, in an inn at Jena in 1522, an armed knight with a Hebrew Bible later identified as Martin Luther returning to Wittenberg from the Wartburg.

By 1524, preachers of the Reformation, encouraged by Vadianus and Zwingli, awakened a response in Appenzel, the last of the thirteen cantons to join the Confederacy. The cantonal assembly of citizens (*Landesgemeinde*) in that year left the abolition of medieval worship to the vote of the local communes and forbade compulsion in matters of faith. Johann Schurtanner, a correspondent and friend of Zwingli, was one of Appenzel's chief preachers of the new doctrines. In the Toggenburg valley similar efforts were made, and from 1524 it was there required that preaching be based on the Scriptures. A brother of Zwingli's mother was a supporter of the reform in Wildhaus. In Glarus, Valentin Tschudi, one of Zwingli's students in the Theodore school at Basel, whom Zwingli had nominated as priest and inducted into the charge in 1522, led a gradual movement toward the Reformation, avoiding conflict and intolerance. In Sebastian Hofmeister (1476–1533), a Franciscan of Constance, Schaffhausen had a preacher of Zwinglian doctrines from 1520. In the Grisons, Johann Dorfmann, called Comander (d. 1557), pastor of St. Martin's in Chur, went about preaching the new message, attended by a voluntary bodyguard until support grew strong. Having been charged with heresy by the suffragan bishop of Chur and an abbot, he convincingly defended at the Disputation of Ilanz, 7–8 January 1526, a set of theses of the Zwinglian type. The diet, meeting five months later, declared for scriptural preaching and enacted a liberal statute of reform without persecution. The bishop's powers were reduced, and monasteries were forbidden to receive new members.

In these instances of a rapid process of adoption of the Reformation in the cantons, we see an extraordinary readiness of the citizens to welcome the new concepts of religion. This would be unaccountable had not the hierarchical church already lost the affections of the people. The common clergy were not very unpopular: in most cases they moved with their flocks into the Reformed Church. But the bishops had been political more than religious figures, and had resisted the rising burgher democracies, which were too strong for them. Generally the procedure for reform was by vote of the effective political power, the citizens, or their elected magistrates. But no such vote would have been taken if it had not been preceded by the intrepid preaching of zealous Reformers. It was these men of conviction who brought the burghers to the point of decision.

— III —

The tension and conflict attending the Reformation affected the entire Confederacy. Zwingli and the other leaders hoped to extend the movement throughout the nation; their opponents desired to see it crushed. The issues involved inevitably came to the attention of the federal diet. As early as September 1523 a diet, meeting at Baden, condemned religious innovations. Zurich and Schaffhausen were not represented in the diet of Luzern, 1525, which produced the elaborate proposal of reform to counter that of the Reformers (p. 47 above). Basel, Appenzel, St. Gall, and the Grisons proved unwilling to accept its suppressive clauses, and Bern reached the same position. It was also too severe against clerical abuses to satisfy the defenders of the medieval Church.

There now arose on the papal side a proposal for a disputation to wrest victory from the Zwinglians and lead to their downfall in the Confederacy. John Eck of Ingolstadt had crossed swords with Luther at Leipzig in 1519 and believed that he had won the encounter. He sought a similar engagement with Zwingli. In 1524 he proposed to the Swiss federal diet that a disputation be held under its auspices. The situation about this time became tense through the execution of Hottinger and the even more atrocious treatment accorded to the deputy bailiffs of Stammheim and Nussbaumheim. The charges against these men were connected with the destruction of the Carthusian monastery of Ittingen, the act of an aroused mob in revenge for the arrest and prosecution of an evangelical pastor. Actually these officers had tried to prevent the action of the populace. They were surrendered to the federal diet by Zurich on condition that they would be tried solely for their action at Ittingen, but since this offered no basis for their condemnation, they were savagely tortured and beheaded by the authority of the diet, at Baden, August 1524, for their implication in the removal of images from churches in their respective communes. Two sons of Hans Wirth, the deputy bailiff of Stammheim, were evangelical pastors: one of these was freed; the other suffered, like his father, with great steadfastness. This cruel and dishonorable action by their opponents exasperated the evangelical party and fortified their resolution throughout the country.

In these circumstances the prospect of a free public debate before the diet was unfavorable. Eck's formal proposal, dated a few days before the execution of the bailiffs, was readily accepted by the five cantons that in the previous April had leagued themselves against the Reformation in the union of Beckenried (pp. 47 f.). Zwingli would gladly have battled Eck in Zurich, and a safe-conduct was offered the German champion of the Papacy to come to Zurich; but this was no part of Eck's plan. Nor would he accept an invitation to Bern, St. Gall, Basel, Constance, or Schaffhausen. The disputation was set for Baden, the scene of the recent act of judicial murder; and the Zurich magistrates would not allow Zwingli to endanger his life there. A safe-conduct was, indeed, offered him, but he was urgently warned by a Bernese councilor not to trust it. With this advice, he was himself in full agreement: 'I will not bathe (baden),' he said. Myconius, in his memoir of Zwingli, deeply regrets this decision, and its wisdom has been discussed by historians to the present generation — not without references to Luther at Leipzig and at Worms. The reader of history who knows the fascination of dramatic clashes of personality may have other reasons than those of Myconius for regretting Zwingli's absence from the Baden disputation. If the two giants had contended in an atmosphere of free discussion the debate would have been a momentous one. Both were experienced in disputations and equipped with knowledge and eloquence. It might have been one of the greatest debates of all time; but the decision was predetermined and would hardly have differed.

Zwingli's absence from Baden did not prevent the disputation from proving significant, however. The banner of the evangelicals was carried by the meek but resourceful Oecolampadius, who would gladly have played a part second to Zwingli's. Actually he profited by notes secretly sent him by Zwingli, who was kept informed by messengers of the discussions from day to day. At some points in the debate he had the not very effective assistance of Haller, who was somewhat intimidated by the disfavor of certain magistrates of Bern. As for Eck, he carried lightly the full burden of his side, enjoying the controversy and assured of an easy victory. He was accompanied by Faber; and numerous clerical emissaries from Constance, Basel, and Chur were in attendance.

Nicholas Manuel described in sarcastic verse Eck's loud, ostentatious oratory. But Oecolampadius, combining modesty with the alertness of a highly trained mind, was able to gain some advantages in the argument. There were some hearers favorable to Eck's cause who blushed for his overbearing manner, and wished that the lank, sallow man from Basel had been on their side. The discussion was prolonged over sixteen days, 21 May to 8 June 1526. Eck brought to it a set of seven theses, the last two of which, on original sin and Baptism, were not handled in the arguments. The other five affirmed respectively: the corporeal presence; the Mass an oblation for the living and the dead; the invocation of Mary and the saints; the retention of images in churches; and purgatory. The authority of the Pope, it will be observed, was not among the theses. No one except the secretaries appointed was permitted to make a record of the speeches. At the close of the disputation the victory of Eck in defending his theses was affirmed by a vote of 87 to 12, whereupon Faber and the Alsatian Carmelite Thomas Murner, then of Luzern, delivered abusive judgments on Zwingli.

The victory of the German champion was to prove strangely fruitless of the result intended. There was prepared for publication in the name of the participating cantons a document that contained the theses of Eck accepted by the conference, with editorial material by Faber and Murner strongly adverse to Zwingli and Zurich. But Bern, Basel, and Schaffhausen withheld their signatures of this. Bern particularly resented pressures now brought to bear by the five cantons. Murner's publication of his *Almanac of Heretics,* in which Zurich was menaced and some respected Bernese families were lampooned, did not help the author's cause. Instead, Bern felt herself inclined more to Zurich than to her opponents. Some measures were, indeed, taken in response to the Baden decision, but they were unpopular. Berthold Haller declined to obey the magistrates' command to resume the use of the Mass, and went unpunished. The people were coming more and more under Haller's influence, and into sympathy with Zurich. The advance of the Reformation was recorded in the Bern elections of Easter week, 1527, which constituted a political unheaval. The members of the Little Council were henceforth to be nominated by the Great Council, which represented the citizens, and both councils were now favorable to the Reformation. Representatives of Bern, Basel, Appenzel, and St. Gall met in Zurich and promised not to desert the Zurichers. The allied districts of Biel and Mühlhausen, southwest and northwest of Basel, respectively, were also associated in this agreement.

— IV —

Bern now projected a new disputation on a national scale, at which it was hoped that Zwingli would at length meet Eck. This plan involved in effect a repudiation of the Baden decision, and the five cantons would have nothing to do with it. Eck sent a contemptuous refusal, as did also the other leading Roman Catholics who were invited — Thomas Murner, already mentioned, and Johann Cochlaeus, then chaplain of Duke George of Saxony, one of the most scholarly of Luther's opponents. Only second-line advocates of the Roman cause condescended to attend. The bishops of Basel, Constance, and Sitten declined the invitation, and the bishop of Lausanne sent only French-speaking delegates, who could not participate in the main debate since this was held in German, and soon went home. The emperor, in an effort to prevent the meeting, wrote from Speyer holding out the prospect of a church council, but without effect.

The Bern Disputation, 7 to 26 January 1528, proved a rally of the evangelical forces. The Swiss leaders welcomed Bucer and Capito from Strasbourg, Ambrose Blaarer, who had made a powerful impression in Constance, others of distinction from the south German cities, and Guillaume Farel, who had opened a campaign in the Pays de Vaud. Haller rejoiced to see in Bern his colleagues from Zurich and Basel. Oecolampadius punned happily: 'I bathed at Baden; Zwingli shall lead his bear-dance at Bern.' Zwingli came to Bern with numerous Zurich preachers and scholars, and with other Swiss and German participants who had gathered in Zurich to the number of one hundred. Since they had to pass through unfriendly territory, they were escorted by an armed guard of three hundred men commanded by the burgomaster.

The sessions were held in the Franciscan church and opened on 7 January, Vadianus presiding. For the discussion, a statement in ten short theses had been prepared by Haller and Kolb, and circulated in Zwingli's Latin and Farel's French translation. The Ten Theses of Bern constitute a highly condensed sum of Zwinglian teaching in its negative aspects, and will call for reference in our next chapter. During the period Zwingli, besides taking leadership in the debate, twice preached powerfully to city congregations.

Though Oecolampadius and Bucer spoke frequently, and many others occasionally, it was Zwingli's voice that ruled the disputation, which was more one-sided than that of Baden had been. Conrad Traeger, an Augustinian of Freiburg, was the principal defender of the old order. A disappointed priest of Solothurn who was present, and who was an admirer of Erasmus, sadly describing the debate, remarked that the Roman cause was defeated for lack of learned advocates: when Scripture proofs were called for, Traeger fled the argument. Of Zwingli he noted: 'That beast is more learned than I thought.'

For five days the assembly argued over the first of the theses, which reads: 'That the holy Church of God, of which Christ is the only Head, is born of the Word of God, abides in it, and hears not the voice of strangers.' This is an expansion of the first of the theses presented by Comander at Ilanz two years earlier. The phrase that is added, 'of which Christ is the only Head,' invited controversy over the papal claims. The weaker party made a spirited defense of the papal authority and was confuted chiefly by Bucer's exegesis of the Gospel commission to St. Peter. The fourth thesis, on the presence in the Eucharist, also consumed five days. More briefly disputed were the others, which dealt in the Zwinglian manner with laws based on tradition, the sufficiency of Christ's sacrifice, the Mass as a sacrifice, intercession of saints, purgatory, images, enforced celibacy, and clerical unchastity. Zwingli and his aides easily outmatched the opposition on these familiar points. Convinced by Zwingli's treatment of the Mass, Nicholas de Watteville took his final step of identification with the Reformation, giving up his thirteen benefices and his prospects as an ecclesiastic; he later married a former nun and aided the Reformed Church as a layman.

The Disputation of Bern more than compensated the Zwinglians for the Disputation of Baden. The reforming party was vindicated in the country; in Bern it was triumphant. The magistrates promptly took a bold course of reform. On 7 February they ordered a series of changes that swept away the old system. The bishops of Constance, Basel, Lausanne, and Sitten, whose dioceses extended into Bernese territory, were notified that, having long shorn rather than fed the sheep, they were henceforth deprived of their jurisdiction in the canton. The Mass was discontinued and Zwinglian practices in the sacraments were adopted. The use of images was abolished, and rules of clerical celibacy and seasons of fasting were likewise set aside. Clerics holding benefices retained their incomes, but at their deaths the funds were to be appropriated for public services. Monks and nuns were given the option of remaining in their convents or leaving them; in the latter case they were to receive small pensions. Pastors were commanded to preach on not less than four days of each week except during the busy seasons of sowing, harvest, and vintage. A commission was sent about the canton to bring these decisions into effect. A colony of brothels in the city was destroyed and the occupants were exiled. A college was established for the training of ministers. The revolution in Bern was complete and irrevocable. Its significance was even greater than the elated Zwinglians realized at the time: it established a headquarters for the labors of Farel, who in turn prepared the way for Calvin.

Oecolampadius returned from the Bern Disputation to his post in Basel with fresh resolution, and preached vigorously against images and the Mass. The Baslers were divided, the majority favoring the preacher, while the magistrates were indisposed to innovations. A spontaneous revolt ensued (9 February 1529) in which mob pressure induced the council to authorize changes similar to those adopted in Zurich. Without waiting for such approval, the people excitedly tore down statues and images in the churches, burned crucifixes, and defaced or obliterated wall pictures. The Mass was abolished and a new liturgy of the Eucharist replaced it, accompanied by a directory of church discipline, issued on 1 April 1529. The demand for reform had broken the bounds set by a conservative magistracy. It is remarkable that the cultured university city of Basel witnessed more violent internal strife during the crisis of the Reformation than occurred in any other major Swiss center. For a time the magistrates took the step of separating the contenders by keeping 2500 Protestants in the Franciscan church and 900 Roman Catholics in that of the Dominicans. In the atmosphere of strife Glareanus, Erasmus, and a number of the professors in the university departed in disgust to Freiburg in the Breisgau.

As for Oecolampadius, his spirit was not that of a radical or a preacher of violence. In most respects he was more cautious, or more patient, than Zwingli. His plan of discipline will receive attention in our next chapter. After the first excitement of 1529, he succeeded in directing the popular urge for reform along constructive lines. Though less aggressive than Zwingli, he was hardly less active. He formed many contacts and friendships in Switzerland and Germany, and he wrote a number of treatises, translations of the Fathers, and Scripture commentaries. He exchanged weighty letters with many persons in various lands. Late in his short life he married a widow. His three children were given the Greek New Testament names of Eusebius, Irene, and Alethea, i.e. Pious, Peace and Truth. After his association with Zwingli in the Marburg Colloquy he engaged in important discussions with representatives of the Waldensians. With Bucer and Blaarer, he toured southern Germany, furthering the Reformation in Ulm and other cities. In February 1531, on his initiative Basel, Zurich, Bern, and St. Gall formed a plan to hold representative synods whenever matters of doctrine were to be decided. He was never robust, and under the strain of the civil strife in Switzerland his health failed. The news of Cappel and of Zwingli's death is thought to have hastened his own. He declined an invitation to become Zwingli's successor, and soon fell into a fatal illness. His death took place seven weeks after Zwingli's, 24 November 1531. Three days before this the civil war was brought to a close with a treaty that was in many respects unfavorable to the Protestant cantons.

— V —

Neither of the two outstanding leaders of the Reformation in German Switzerland reached the age of fifty, and both died in the same autumn, leaving the cause they had labored for at what seemed an insecure stage. Had they lived on in active co-operation another ten years, they might have been instrumental in its further expansion in Switzerland and beyond. Ferdinand of Hapsburg exulted in Zwingli's death, as ending a threat to his house and to Roman Catholicism. Luther spoke of the dead Reformer with a bitterness highly discreditable to himself. Five years later, in a kindlier temper, he wrote to Zwingli's successor that he had been deeply grieved by the deaths of Zwingli and Oecolampadius. Zwingli has been called a martyr; he was not the kind of martyr whose death gives a new impulse to his cause.

The political role which Zurich under his leadership had unsuccessfully played was discontinued. By the terms of the treaty of Cappel, Zurich's foreign connections were dissolved. Thenceforth the stream of Zwinglian influence in southern Germany was cut off. Its activity in the promotion of the Reformation in eastern Switzerland was also ended. Most of the canton of St. Gall was reclaimed to Roman Catholicism. Solothurn, which had favored Zurich and reform, was induced to return to the old church order. But Zurich itself, Bern, Basel, and Schaffhausen, the town of St. Gall, areas of the Grisons and of Glarus, and some communes of the common bailiwicks remained firmly Zwinglian.

It is not to be denied that the crippling of Zurich in the Peace of Cappel was a grave setback to Swiss Protestantism. The greater part of eastern Switzerland was sealed off from the agents of Zwinglian evangelism. Protestant expansion in Switzerland was not, however, brought to an end. The base of the mission was no longer Zurich but Bern; its direction no longer eastward but westward; the communities it won no longer German-speaking but French-speaking. We shall treat in due course the audacious thrust of the Reformation, under the aegis of Bern, westward into the Pays de Vaud. While Bern sponsored this historically momentous effort, Zurich remained, until the ascendancy of Geneva, the paramount center of Swiss Protestant theology. This fact is largely a consequence of the personal qualities and labors of one man, the eminent successor to Zwingli, the talented, wise, firm, and compassionate Heinrich Bullinger (1504–75), *antistes,* or presiding minister, of the Zurich church.

We have noted that one Heinrich Bullinger was the dean of Bremgarten who in 1519 repulsed the indulgence-seller, Bernardino Samson. At that time the dean's fifth son and namesake was about fourteen years old, and was a schoolboy in a Latin School at Emmerich on the Dutch frontier of Germany in Cleves (1516–19). It has been stated by numerous scholars that he was there under the influence of the Brethren of the Common Life, but Professor Blanke of Zurich in his *Young Bullinger* (1942) finds no evidence of this, and Bullinger's own account does not mention the Brethren. His eldest brother, Johann, had been there some years before him. Under the severe discipline and exacting instruction of the school, young Heinrich learned Latin, reading the letters of Cicero, Pliny, and St. Jerome and the works of a Carmelite poet, Baptista of Mantua. He went next to the university of Cologne (1519–22), a stronghold of the old theology and then recently the butt of the celebrated satire, *Letters of Obscure Men,* a humanist attack. Here Bullinger proved himself an independent student. He studied Gratian and Peter Lombard, but, observing that these guides of the scholastics followed the Church Fathers, he turned to the study of Chrysostom, Augustine, Jerome, Ambrose, and Origen. The Fathers, he found, themselves rested on earlier authority, and this authority was the Bible: he must go to the New Testament. He also discovered the writings of Luther and felt that they were more in accord with the Fathers, and with the Scriptures, than were the scholastics. The doctrine of justification by faith laid hold upon his mind. He had entertained a desire to join the Carthusians; but the monastic life no longer appealed to him. Early in 1522 his conversion to a position similar to Luther's was completed, and it was confirmed by the reading of Melanchthon's *Loci communes.* His was a conversion through reading, not through anybody's personal persuasion. He was then in his eighteenth year and about to leave the university.

Bullinger took his master's degree at Cologne, in April 1522, and returned to his father's house. In the following year he was appointed to teach in the school of the Cistercian house at Cappel. During the six years in which he was thus employed, he succeeded, with the full co-operation of the abbot, in bringing the members of this monastic community to evangelical beliefs and led them to acquiesce in the dissolution of the institution (1527). In 1525 he aided Zwingli in the contention with the Anabaptists. In August 1528 Bullinger wrote a long, self-revealing letter proposing marriage to Anna Adlischweiler, a former nun. She became his wife and the mother of six sons and five daughters. By her devotion in the tasks of a pastor's wife, especially in bearing the burden of her husband's hospitality and charity to the poor and sick and to needy refugees for religion who frequented Zurich, Anna Adlischweiler deserves a place in Christian history. In 1565 Bullinger was stricken by her death, of the plague, along with that of three of their daughters — one of whom, Anna, was the wife of Zwingli's son, Ulrich.

In 1529, Bullinger went to Bremgarten to succeed his father,

who had also embraced the Reformation. While at Cappel, the
son had become well known in Zwingli's circle and had shared
the confidences of Zwingli himself. After Cappel, the distressed
Zurichers, unable to secure the services of Oecolampadius and
unsatisfied with the gifts of Leo Judä, turned hopefully to the
able young pastor of Bremgarten. By the treaty of peace, Bremgarten was lost to the Reformation. On 20 November, Bullinger,
his father, and his brother Johann, leaving all their possessions,
fled for their lives to Zurich; Anna and the children joined him
there. He was appointed to be people's priest at the Great Minster and, on 9 December 1531, entered Zwingli's pulpit. His first
sermon was as a *sursum corda* to the saddened congregation.
'Many people thought,' said Myconius, 'that Zwingli was not
dead, or that, like the phoenix, he had been restored to life.'

Bullinger possessed the qualifications needed for this post of
critical responsibility. His preaching was able and inspiriting.
His published sermons carried the Reformed teaching far beyond
Zurich, and in translation far beyond Switzerland. His associate,
Pellican, in a chronicle written at the height of Bullinger's career,
called him 'a divine enriched by unmeasured gifts of God.' His
private life was exemplary, filled with acts of thoughtful and
sacrificial kindness; and this was extended to some whose opinions were widely different from his own. During visitations of
the plague he endeared himself to the people by his self-forgetful
ministry to the sick and dying. While he was able for the most
part to avoid controversy, his constant and consistent testimony
made him a bulwark of the Reformed Church in the tumult of
thought of that age. His forty-four years in Zurich (1531–75)
include all the thirty years of Calvin's activity as a Protestant
(1534–64). The period saw the rapid growth of the Reformed
churches of Europe. If Calvin was the theologian of the Reformed beyond Switzerland, Bullinger was the personal friend
and adviser of many of the leaders in this movement. And his
skill in framing statements of belief was unsurpassed even by
Calvin.

It is characteristic of Bullinger that he extended the hospitality
of his home to Zwingli's widow and children, who had been left
without means. He felt a deep loyalty to the memory of Zwingli;
but at some points he diverged from the position of his predecessor. Before the civil war, he had striven hard to prevent the rise

of warlike passions. He declined to promise silence on political subjects in Zurich, but he, unlike Zwingli, did not hatch political schemes, and he had little to do with public affairs. He endeavored to give the Church a function distinct from that of the state, and claimed for it the right to admonish magistrates. He modified Zwingli's view of the Eucharist, and gave ampler and more systematic expression to other theological ideas hastily set down by Zwingli. He promoted the work of education. Pellican and Judä continued as professors in the Carolinum, and the daring exegete, Theodor Buchmann (Bibliander, d. 1564), joined the faculty in 1531. A native of Bischofszell in northeastern Switzerland, Bibliander had been trained under Ceporinus, Pellican, Oecolampadius, and Capito, and was a linguistic genius. Pellican says that he was 'very highly skilled in the sacred languages, very expert and eloquent, in all doctrinal matters.' In 1540, he startled his contemporaries by publishing a translation of the Qur'ân. He was among the first Protestant advocates of foreign missions. His position on the doctrine of predestination was adopted from Erasmus but was unsatisfactory to Calvinists such as his colleague, Peter Martyr (Pietro Martire Vermigli, d. 1562). This eminent Italian scholar had been a refugee in England and had fled from Queen Mary to Strasbourg and Zurich, where he became Pellican's successor on the latter's death in 1556. The Carolinum was disturbed by controversy between the Italian and the Swiss: this was resolved by Bibliander's dismissal, on salary, in 1560, but both men remained Bullinger's personal friends.

Fortunately for the Reformed Church, the intercourse between Calvin and Bullinger was entirely amicable, and they were able to agree on essential matters. The correspondence between them was frequent and intimate. With Bucer, however, the relations were not close, and Bullinger was cool to the Strasbourger's attempt to unite the Zwinglians with the Lutherans on the basis of the Wittenberg Concord of 1536. This agreement on the Eucharist, highly important for Lutheranism, since it drew together the South Germans with the Wittenbergers, was promulgated just after the First Swiss Confession, which had been framed by Bullinger himself. Bullinger entered into a friendly correspondence with Luther, who showed some good will toward the Swiss for two years and then assailed their doctrines violently (1544).

Calvin now tried to allay the righteous indignation of Bullinger over this attack. Bullinger's able reply (1545) was not answered by Luther, who had not long to live when it appeared. When the emperor, Charles V, seeking to enforce his *Interim* of 1548 — a misconceived attempt at religious settlement — drove numerous Lutherans to flight, some of them took refuge in Zurich, where they were accorded hospitable shelter.

A book might be written about Bullinger's hospitality to distressed religious refugees. It was the English exiles who owed most to him. A few of them, such as John Hooper, later bishop of Gloucester, came to him during the reign of Henry VIII; but far more numerous were those who fled to Zurich from Queen Mary's persecutions (1553–8). Some of Elizabeth's most prominent bishops — such as John Jewel, bishop of Salisbury, author of the *Apology of the Church of England,* Archbishop Edmund Grindal, and John Parkhurst, bishop of Norwich — owed and acknowledged a deep personal debt to Bullinger and the Zurich community; others were his correspondents and readers. Jewel in particular estimated very highly Bullinger's influence in the renewal of the Reformation under Elizabeth.

Bullinger was a prolific author: he is credited with 150 titles, including unpublished manuscripts. A number of his more popular works were translated into English, Dutch, or other languages. In the *Decades* (completed in 1557), a work that consists of five series each containing ten long and thoughtful sermons, he presents a simplified summary of Reformed theology and ethics. A complete English translation of this work appeared in 1577. In December 1586, the Canterbury Convocation, presided over by Archbishop John Whitgift, endeavoring to improve the pulpit message of Anglican ministers, commanded those of them who were not yet masters of arts to provide themselves with copies of the *Decades.* They were also required to keep notebooks and to record each week the essential contents of one of the sermons and present their notes quarterly for examination by competent ministers, who were to report to the archdeacon and the bishop. To meet the need for copies a new edition of the work was issued (1587). If we except the New Testament Paraphrase of Erasmus, Bullinger's *Decades* was the only work by a foreign Reformer that was given such official status in Anglicanism.

Bullinger was the author of a number of books of a historical nature, including a general history of Switzerland of which the section on the Reformation was published in three volumes, 1838–40. It is far more broadly conceived than the short sketch of Zwingli's life furnished by Myconius (1532), yet it represents Zwingli as the prime leader of the whole movement in Switzerland. Closing with the year 1534, Bullinger includes modest references to his own participation in the movement, and writes of his father with admiration. The work is an extended and, for the sixteenth century, a well-balanced account of events, and is a primary source for the modern historian. His *Diarium* also has much interest, but is rather scant in content. Among his other works that had a wide circulation were *The Anabaptists, Origin, Growth and Sects,* (1560), written in German, and his Latin treatise, *On the Authority and Certitude of Holy Scripture and the Institution and Function of Bishops.* He was also the author of a short handbook for the sick, written in 1538, during one of the numerous visitations of plague that took place in his lifetime. It is a little treasury of comfort and exhortation, one of the earliest Protestant books designed to guide the thoughts of the sick and dying.

The best-known monument to Bullinger's genius, however, is the Second Helvetic Confession, which will be considered later. Through his preaching, his numerous books, his wide correspondence, his doctrinal statements, and his rich personal associations and ministry extending over many years, Heinrich Bullinger had an indispensable and distinguished part in the maintenance and early growth of the Reformed churches. His writings were eagerly read in Poland, Hungary, and Bohemia; he was in correspondence with persons eminent in Church and state in many countries of Europe, and exchanged arguments with Lutherans, Anabaptists, Anti-Trinitarians. He died on 17 September 1575, sincerely mourned and honored. His son-in-law, Josias Simler, wrote a well-informed account of his life, to which is appended a long series of tributes to his memory, in Latin and Greek verse, by his learned colleagues.

CHAPTER V

DOCTRINE, DISCIPLINE, WORSHIP

— I —

ONE who follows attentively the progress of the Reformation in the German-speaking cantons of Switzerland cannot but observe its insistently Biblical character. The leaders adopted without question the view that the Scriptures furnish authoritative and final direction for the Church with respect to doctrine, discipline, and worship. The principal stages in the movement were marked by disputations in which this position was taken as basic. It was the first premise of the Reformation argument.

Zwingli professed to rest every statement of his Sixty-seven Conclusions of 1523 upon the evidence of Scripture, and declared in the preface to this document:

> If I do not correctly understand the Scripture, I undertake to allow myself to be better instructed, yet only from the aforementioned Scripture.

This position was taken in hostility to the claims of tradition, in which the Reformers saw the source of the abuses and deterioration prevailing in the Church.

The first of the Conclusions declares it a blasphemous error to hold that the Gospel is nothing without the approval of the Church. The Eighteen Theses of Comander at Ilanz (1526) begin with the proposition that 'The holy Christian Church was born of the Word of God: it abides therein and hearkens not to another voice.' This statement was, as we saw, in substance repeated in the Ten Theses of Bern (1528). Throughout this notable document is exhibited the negative Scripture theology of Zwinglianism. The Church does not establish laws beyond the Word of God (*extra Dei verbo*). To recognize any satisfaction for sins

other than Christ's satisfaction for the sins of the whole world
is to deny Christ. It cannot be proved from Scripture that the
body and blood of Christ are corporeally present in the Eucharistic elements. The Mass is contrary to Scripture, and blasphemy
(ii-v), et cetera.

The modern Protestant is not satisfied with this negative application of the doctrine of scriptural authority. He has trouble
with the notion, too, that the Church has been born of the Word
(*Ecclesia nata est ex Dei verbo*). Is this historically true? If the
'Word' is taken to mean the canonical Scriptures, it may be replied that the Church came into being before the New Testament was written, and that it was only in a very limited sense
'born of' the Old Testament. Yet this ready answer does not embrace all the facts. It is also true that the Church was being
brought into existence, as ecumenical fellowship and locally visible institution, by the written Epistles and Gospels as these appeared. Moreover, the 'Word' was never thought of by the Reformers without a mental reference to the interpretation supplied by the Holy Spirit to the mind of the devout reader or
hearer. 'God reveals himself,' wrote Zwingli in 1522, 'through
His Spirit, and nothing is learned of Him without the Spirit.'
The balance between written Word and Spirit-prompted interpretation is not always to be found in Zwingli and his associates. But there lies in this view a truth that is also historically
validated. Through the centuries the Church has seen a repeatedly renewed growth through the activity of the Word of
Scripture spiritually grasped in the thoughts of men. The Reformers were following a golden thread of truth in affirming
that the Scripture is the matrix and directive of the Church. In
scholastic theology, tradition had assumed equality with Scripture; and the authority of the Bible had largely ceased to bear
directly upon ecclesiastical practice. Zwingli confronted all this
on Scripture ground with flat and confident denial.

The Ten Theses of Bern and similar utterances represent,
however, only one aspect of the Swiss Reformed theology. The
Reformed took the Bible also positively as the guide to daily
living and personal faith. Zwingli had complete assurance that,
in a simple sense, the Word is our teacher. In his sermon 'On the
Clarity and Certainty of God's Word' (September 1522) he affirms
that 'there is one true and very simple sense of the divine Word,'

in which it may and should be understood. The Bible presents for Zwingli a unified body of teaching, comprehensible to all who hearken to the voice of the Spirit, and supplies not only true doctrine but also the basis of brotherly agreement and unity. He was willing to believe that if the Bible were given free course the faithful would, under its unitive impulse, abandon their contentions and dwell together as brethren. Even the Anabaptist commotion did not entirely disabuse him of this rather naïve supposition. But he stressed the distinction between the 'outer Word,' consisting of spelled-out letters, and the 'inner Word of God,' which is the outer illuminated by the Spirit (*Commentary on True and False Religion*, 1525). In his two confessional statements of 1530 and 1531, addressed respectively to Charles V and to Francis I, he states his reliance upon 'the oracles of God,' and his recognition of the Church when it 'judges according to the Scripture at the bidding of the Spirit.' To King Francis he writes:

> We teach not an iota that we have not learned from the divine Oracles; and we assert nothing for which we cannot cite as guarantors the first teachers of the Church, prophets, apostles, bishops, evangelists, Bible-expositors.

The recognition here of early Church writers as interpreters of Scripture is notable; but the primary and ultimate authority of the Word remains unqualified.

It is the Bible in its original languages to which appeal is to be made in all doctrinal decisions. The Latin Vulgate has no status for the Swiss theology. Copies of the Hebrew and Greek texts were, symbolically and for reference, placed on the table at the disputations. While on principle a knowledge of the Bible was important for all Christian people, not many of them could be expected to read it in the original tongues. As in Luther's movement, there was among the Swiss Reformers a zeal to provide a scholarly translation of both Testaments into the spoken language. The labor of preparing it was lightened by the use of Luther's New Testament and Pentateuch in German. It displeased Luther that his Saxon German was altered to make it intelligible to the Swiss. The prophetic literature and the poetical and wisdom books were carefully rendered into Swiss German by Leo Judä with the assistance of Caspar Grossmann (Megander), Michael Adam (a Christian Jew), and others. Zwingli himself had a hand in this task. The complete 'Zurich Bible' was published in 1529, and handsome editions by Froschauer followed in 1530 and 1536. The scholarship of the Zurich version was excellent; the style has not been so highly esteemed. The widespread use of the Bible in the mother tongue was of inestimable value in confirming the faith of laymen and their adherence to the Reformation.

— II —

The Reformed theologians diverged from the Christian humanists, who were their teachers, in the emphasis they placed upon the majesty and holiness of God, the sinfulness of man, and the gulf between God in His holiness and man in his sinful state. Zwingli and Oecolampadius are in this respect not far from Calvin. The natural law itself is for Zwingli the working of God's spirit in man's heart. Man's nature has been 'shattered' in the Fall. For this reason he requires political government. Even the Christian, says Zwingli, remains a wretch in God's sight (*Gottschelm*) and needs the compulsion of the state. Without divine aid, man can no more perceive the being of God than can a beetle the being of man. True, Zwingli must make his favorite ancient philosophers exceptions to the general rule of man's total incapacity to understand God. But the dim knowledge of God their works exhibit was theirs only because God especially vouchsafed it to them. Zwingli repudiates the service of philosophy in this realm; yet he tries to describe God in philosophical terms. 'That alone is God which is perfect, that is, absolute, and to which nothing is lacking, but everything is present that belongs to the highest good.' All things in us and in the whole created world are ordered by God's providence, and each man's eternal state is predestined. God's justice is not ours: what is unjust for us may not be so for Him, since He is above the law which we obey. Man must acquiesce in the divine will, as clay in the potter's hand. Man's works earn no reward from God: if his actions are good they are not his own but arise from God's activity within him. We should not ascribe to the hammer what is done by the smith wielding it: and God does not reward His own work (*Treatise on Providence*).

The austerity of this doctrine of God is modified by the insistence that God is our Father, to whom we have recourse in need, kindlier than an earthly father. The grace and mercy of the Father are revealed in the Son. Herein lies the essential message of the New Testament:

> The sum of the Gospel is that Christ, the Son of the living God, made known to us the will of the Heavenly Father and by His innocence redeemed us from eternal death and reconciled us to God.

No merit of our good works, or of the saints, has any reality, but the merit of Christ's sacrifice avails for us. He fulfills the law for us and sets us free from its condemnation. He is given to be the leader and commander of the whole human race and is the Head of all believers, who are His body. All who have life in Him are members of the Catholic Church, the Communion of Saints. All Christians are brothers of Christ, and of each other (Sixty-seven Conclusions).

Zwingli thinks of the Church primarily as the spiritual, invisible body of all the faithful, 'the spotless bride of Jesus Christ governed and refreshed by the Spirit of God.' But in his *Commentary on True and False Religion,* which embodies his slightly earlier *Reply to Emser,* he shows the application of the term 'Church' to the assembled people who profess to be Christians, including those who are 'not very faithful.' Over against this defective body of those who live within 'the company of Christians' there is 'a glorious and noble Church, the spouse of Christ, without any spot or wrinkle' (Eph. 5:27). This, unlike Plato's Republic, is not imaginary; it has real existence, its members being the true believers in Christ as the crucified Son of God. It refuses to be locally confined, but spreading throughout the world receives members everywhere: the vaster it is, the more beautiful also it is.

Zwingli contrasts this holy, universal Church with the Church of the pontiffs: the former rests upon the Word of God as understood in the light of the Spirit and therefore cannot err. The identity and number of its members are concealed from men's eyes. His teaching on the Church is formally summarized in his *Account of the Faith* (1530), prepared for Charles V, wherein he explains the uses of the word 'Church' in Scripture. It is applied to: (1) the body of the elect known to God alone; (2) the universal perceptible Church of nominal Christians; and (3) parts of the latter, to each particular congregation. It is not claimed that the members of the holy Church of the elect are themselves perfectly holy and sinless. Its holiness rests upon the redemptive work of Christ; when we firmly believe in this work, however, we are marvelously transformed. It is this Church that is 'the Catholic Church, the Communion of Saints,' that we confess in the Creed.

Zwingli sometimes asserts that the particular congregation as a member of the whole Church exercises discipline, rejecting offenders and receiving penitents, and judging of pastors and doctrine. In this view, he did not intend to authorize, however, an autonomous church jurisdiction in discipline. Church discipline is interwoven with the life of the Christian state and prescribed by civil law. In his *Exposition of the Faith* (1531), addressed to Francis I, Zwingli's thought revolves around the concepts of the visible Church of the whole nominally Christian people and the invisible Church of the elect. The argument here involves a recognition in strong terms of the authority of the state in maintaining the integrity of the visible Church. Zwingli had always assumed that the Church properly comprises all the people. He had recoiled from the notion of the Church of separated Christians, advocated by the Anabaptists. He was now asking the state to provide security for the Church, as a visible society having the same membership as the political community.

It is true that some of his utterances seem capable of a different construction. Certain statements in his Conclusions of 1523 seem to favor a church discipline independent of the state power:

> No private person may pronounce excommunication; but the church in which the person to be excommunicated lives, together with its pastor (xxxi). Nobody can or ought to be excommunicated but one who has publicly offended by his misdeeds (xxxii).

Yet he did not then or later project a separation of the church authority from the state authority in discipline, and the outcome of his work in Zurich was to draw the two together, the compulsive element being supplied by the state. When in his *Commentary on True and False Religion* he connects the ban with the local church, as distinct from the universal Church, he does not have in mind any autonomous 'church,' as distinct from secular government, but the authority of the local community which is both Church and state. Oecolampadius, as we shall see, held a different position.

In 1525 Zwingli, co-operating with the magistrates, wrote *Advice on Excluding Adulterers and Usurers from the Lord's Supper*. In this he assumes that the government is to undertake enforcement of the regulations: no autonomous action by the churches is involved. Despite some inconsistencies, the tendency of his thought was to yield to the state the effective power in discipline. He gave decreasing attention to the scriptural concept of 'binding and loosing,' and was concerned rather with guarding against scandal and deterioration of morals. The most original legislation that he fathered affecting the lives of the people is found in the marriage ordinances of 1525 and 1526, which have nothing to say of church authority as such. A board of six judges was appointed to deal with sex offenses and pleas concerning marriages and their disolution. In applications for divorce not only adultery but such factors as insanity, leprosy, desertion, and indecent behavior were to be considered.

A wide field was left, however, for the pastoral care of souls. In March 1524, Zwingli published, in revised form, a sermon he had delivered to the clergy attending the First Zurich Disputation. A hearer who was to become a notable leader of reform in Appenzel, Jakob Schurtanner, had induced him to print it. Its title, *The Pastor*, was suggested by the *Pastor* of Hermas, but Zwingli knew this ancient classic only from Jerome, and his own book bears no resemblance to it. It is an impressive and devout, if somewhat controversial, exhortation. Zwingli first describes with scriptural phrases the true shepherd of souls, then assails the false pretenders in clerical office. He urges faithful preaching of repentance, and not less the direct guidance of individuals and loving devotion to their upbuilding. He does not hesitate to stress the extreme difficulties encountered in the pastoral office, but calls for a sacrificial commitment to its tasks. 'The shepherd must deny himself, suppress self-love, and every day make ready to bear a new cross.' He is to contend courageously in the strength of God for the Word of God; but he must win the enemies of God by love, the pastor's most necessary virtue. He must pray God to be set on fire with His love.

— III —

Between 1527 and 1531 Zwingli and Oecolampadius were in occasional correspondence on points concerning discipline and excommunication. The Basel Reformer sought to secure for the Church a distinct power of discipline, but Zwingli was disinclined to this and their letters show a divergence of view which is also reflected in the practices that arose in the two cantons. It was not to Zwingli that Oecolampadius owed his doctrine of the Church, although, apart from the important issue of its autonomy in matters of discipline, the two Reformers were in substantial agreement.

In 1525, when replying to a Louvain professor's defense of the confessional, Oecolampadius wrote:

> I know and love with all my heart the Church which our heavenly Father has chosen before the ages to be the spotless bride of his Son, our Lord Jesus Christ.

This church he calls 'The Catholic Church' which 'God the Father foreknew and elected, the Son by his blood cleansed, redeemed, and adorned, and the Holy Spirit indwells and guides.' It is not visible, since it is not assembled and because faith itself is invisible. Its members are known only to God and to the consciousness of each. God builds this Church by the proclamation of His Word, and in this proclamation lies the power of the Keys of the Kingdom of Heaven. Those who possess the Holy Spirit have this power, which is not exercised arbitrarily and depends not on man but on God's bestowal of the 'efficacious Word.' The 'rock' on which the Church is built is 'confession of and faith in Christ,' and often the simplest persons are instruments of the Holy Spirit and exercise the power of the Keys. This resembles the language of Luther in his various references to confession, absolution, and the priesthood of believers. But Oecolampadius attempted to render effective lay participation in discipline, and to assert an ecclesiastical authority operating independently of the state. From the time of his experiences as penitentiary priest of Basel (1518) he had felt keenly the need of a discipline that would include excommunication and public penance. In this he was of the same opinion as the Strasbourg Reformers, Capito and Bucer. In 1524 Bucer had written: 'Where there is no discipline and excommunication there is no Christian community.' In 1526 Oecolampadius put forth a plan of church procedure (*Agende*) toward offenders in which excommunication was provided for; but apparently resistance and the lack of a supporting organization rendered this null.

In Basel, as we saw, the most notable steps toward reform were taken after the iconoclastic disturbances of early February 1529. On 12 February, in a solemn meeting of the combined councils of Basel, it was declared that the government is the instrument and handmaid of God and is obligated to serve God's honor and the civic peace. The magistrates swore acceptance of these principles and subsequently induced the guild members to make oath accordingly, promising to support the government in establishing the Word of God, Christian morals, civic peace, and unity, and pledging thereto their lives, honor, and goods. They were instructed to elect to the councils men obedient to God's Word, considering neither private friendship nor enmity but only the honor of God and the common good.

On 1 April, the Tuesday of Easter week, the government adopted a new Order of Worship and directory of conduct prepared by Oecolampadius. It was designed to subject public worship and the Christian life alike to the test of Scripture, and to eliminate the abuses of the old order. It provided for the pure, clear, and joyous preaching of the Evangel, and for necessary brotherly censures and penalties. Shameless and hardened offenders were to be excommunicated. In the services for Baptism and the Lord's Supper the *Agende* of 1526 was substantially copied. The sacraments were treated as symbolic of the inner working of the grace of God in Christ. The Lord's Supper was described as established by Christ to bring to mind with thanksgiving, and to declare, his holy passion and to cultivate Christian love and unity. It was to be everywhere celebrated at Easter, Pentecost, and Christmas, and each Sunday in one of the churches of the city. The sick were to be visited, and comforted from the Word of God by the ministers and deacons. A schedule of preaching services was laid down. Three hours each Sunday afternoon were to be set apart for theological lectures in the cathedral. Images were to be removed from the churches and not replaced, and holy days reduced to Christmas, Easter, Ascension Day, and Pentecost. Professors were to be appointed for Old and New Testament

theology, and the whole university and the schools of the city
reoriented to the new order of the Church.

— IV —

While Oecolampadius strove to establish this disciplinary authority in Basel, Zwingli was encouraging the development of
agencies of Church and state co-operation in discipline. He obtained (26 March 1530) a sweeping ordinance to set standards
of morality, with penalties not only for grave moral lapses but
also for indulgence at taverns, dancing, luxurious clothing, profanity, and non-attendance at church. This 'morals mandate'
(*Sittenmandat*) was revised after Zwingli's death (1532). Roger
Lei, in a thorough examination of the Zurich discipline, points
out that the ordinance grew out of the work of the synods, which
Zwingli had introduced. In origin as in content it exhibits the
close interaction between Church and state always characteristic
of the Zurich Reformation. A committee had been appointed in
1527 to plan a synodical organization, and the first synod of the
canton of Zurich was held in April 1528. It consisted of the
pastor and two lay deputies from each parish. In these meetings
the pastors themselves were subjected to censure by one another
and by laymen and were often closely examined on relatively
trivial charges. The system spread to other Reformed areas and
was to have importance as a means of maintaining standards for
the ministry. In Zurich it was in no sense a rival of the political
authority. Representatives of the government were present in the
synods and took a leading part in the proceedings.

Oecolampadius also instituted semi-annual synods for the pastors of the canton of Basel: the first was held in May 1529. These
meetings passed regulations that constituted them an organ of
the Church as, in some degree, an autonomous institution, and
hence they were viewed with apprehension by some of the burghers. Synods of May and November 1530 asserted the view of
Oecolampadius regarding the distinction in jurisdiction of
Church and state. Oecolampadius was anxiously determined to
provide within the framework of the Church for the treatment
of offenders. To hand them over to the government, he wrote to
Zwingli (17 September 1530), was to betray them. 'A government
that takes away the authority of the Church is worse than Antichrist [the Papacy],' he adds. Zwingli wrote to Vadianus that he

was more favorably impressed by this than were his colleagues; but his actions do not show any response to the Basler's zeal for a truly ecclesiastical jurisdiction.

From the May synod of 1530, Oecolampadius, with the approval of the pastors, went to the magistrates and delivered a notable 'Oration on the Restoration of Excommunication.' Christ, he argued, had given his disciples power to bind and loose, to expel from the churches and receive again, and to hold stubborn offenders as publicans and sinners, i.e. to excommunicate. Oecolampadius perceives here the fact, not admitted by Zwingli, that Church and state were not truly composed of the same members, and that their censures have different objectives. The state counts as citizens heathens, Jews, and excommunicated persons. It punishes those who have repented of their crimes and to whom the Church extends mercy. It recognizes violators of marriage and other evil doers, when their legal punishment has been endured, without evidence of repentance, while the Church cannot admit such to communion. Oecolampadius meets the charge of 'tyranny' by saying that the censures of the Church are more remedial than punitive, and by a mature plan for associating lay officers with the pastors in discipline. He proposes a board of twelve censors consisting of the four pastors, four magistrates, and four representatives of the lay people. This democratic plan would, he held, avoid all tyranny and uphold the dignity of the Church.

When a member is guilty of manifest sin, the college of twelve censors is to send a carefully selected monitor to warn him as a brother. If this fails, two or three are to be sent to admonish him, and if he is still unmoved, he is rebuked by all twelve in the name of the whole Church. If he is so obstinate as to despise this third warning, he must be excommunicated in the name of the Lord. If he then seeks the removal of the ban, he is to be released from it when he has taken upon himself a suitable penance. Here Oecolampadius affirms the governing principles of 'charity, zeal for God's glory, and edification of our neighbor.' He claims that this discipline will drive out idolatry, superstition, and false teaching, restore Christian freedom, and make the Church 'a people distinguished by sincerity of faith and holiness of life in all the earth, unto the glory of God.'

In all this, we see Oecolampadius the true forerunner of Calvin. Ernst Stähelin points out that he created a new office, that of lay presbyters, and a new jurisdiction, the Presbytery, composed of these and the pastors.

This grand scheme of church discipline was actually adopted, and its author so informed Zwingli on 23 June. But its success depended upon the full support of the magistrates of Basel and upon the approval of the other members of the Christian Civic League, especially Zurich and Bern. Oecolampadius was soon aware that he could not count on either of these factors. Berthold Haller was very sure that the system he sponsored in Bern was superior. In this, a consistory of eight members, representing the Church but acting in the name not of the Church but of the Council, exercised discipline. At a meeting of the League in Aarau, 27 September 1530, Bern objected to the Basel plan. A synod in Zurich a month later took up the matter, but avoided any commitment to the principle of an autonomous church discipline. A conference at Basel, 16 November, considerately agreed to place no hindrance on any city's adoption of the ban by church action. In the following December, there was a new attempt in Basel to make the earlier decision effective, though with some important modifications. The obstinate offender who remained for a month unrepentant under excommunication was to be punished by the government. Thus in the end, reliance on the state was only in degree less in evidence in Basel than in Zurich. This was perhaps the maximum of church autonomy possible in a German-Swiss canton in the sixteenth century. The Reformation leaders assumed the unity of the territorial church and its recognition and support by the state. In general they were willing to concede much to the state in order to maintain a relationship in which ideally the Church is the divinely instituted organ of the spiritual life of the community and both Church and community are committed to 'the Word of God.'

— V —

An extreme simplification of worship resulted from the application of the rule of Scripture to the cult. The number of sacraments was reduced to two, and the rites of these were completely stripped of medieval ceremonial and interpretation. Invocation and adoration of the Virgin and saints, pilgrimages, indulgences, images, instrumental music, and much of the traditional material

of public prayer were swept away. The Reformed worship stressed
the text of Scripture and utilized the language of the people.
Psalm singing in German was introduced apparently by Oecolampadius, who wrote of its effect enthusiastically to Zwingli,
12 August 1526.

From the early 1520's both Oecolampadius and Zwingli opposed the view that the Mass is a sacrifice, but the former retained
longer than the latter an emphasis upon the corporeal presence
of Christ 'under [sub] the bread and wine.' A letter of Oecolampadius sent to Hedio 21 January 1523 shows the influence of
his previous evening's interview with Hinne Rode of Utrecht —
who, as we saw (above, p. 46) brought the statement of Cornelius
Hoen on the Eucharist that was to prove pleasing and suggestive
to Zwingli. Whether they discussed Hoen's letter at this time or
not, Oecolampadius thenceforth spoke the language of the spiritual rather than the corporeal presence. He was in touch with
Farel and François Lambert at the time, and the sources of his
change of view are uncertain. In sermons and tracts he made
clear his position, which closely approximated Zwingli's and
sharply diverged from Luther's. If Bucer occupied ground between Luther and Zwingli, Oecolampadius may be said to have
stood between Zwingli and Bucer. In the *Genuine Exposition of
the Eucharist* (1529), he freely cited the Greek and Latin Fathers
to disprove the corporeal presence, arguing learnedly over their
use of terms such as 'mystery' and 'sacrament.' Probably the
Lord's Supper was felt by him more deeply than by Zwingli to
be a religious experience of great value for faith and fellowship;
it creates a fraternity in repentance and amendment of life. As
he defended his views against Johann Brenz and other Lutherans, he found himself with Zwingli in denying what these critics
affirmed, and at the Marburg Colloquy he was Zwingli's able ally.

The German-speaking Swiss Reformed Churches retained the
use of the font in Baptism and unleavened bread in the Lord's
Supper, which the Church of Geneva was to abandon. But in
the bareness of its liturgy it was more extreme. W. D. Maxwell, in *An Outline of Christian Worship*, calls the Zwinglian
rite of the Lord's Supper 'the least adequate of all the Reformation liturgies.' In 1523 Zwingli renounced the canon of the
Mass and proposed to substitute for it a radically simplified
service. Yet the Mass was continued for two years more. In April

1525, Zwingli and the other pastors of the city of Zurich, with Myconius and Megander, appeared before the Great Council to appeal for the abolition of the Mass. A high official, Joachim am Grütt, opposed this, but was unsuccessful in meeting Zwingli's scriptural argument. The service that replaced the Mass (13 April) was contained in Zwingli's *Action or Use of the Lord's Supper*, published at this time. A month later a brief form of Baptism was introduced, featured by a prayer that the light of faith may be kindled in the child's heart, that he be given newness of life, and that he follow Christ daily through life. The passage in Mark 10 about Christ blessing the children was read.

In the rite for the Lord's Supper the sacrament is called a memorial and a thanksgiving. The young people were to communicate on Maundy Thursday, the middle-aged on Good Friday, and the old people on Easter Day. Communicants were to be seated in the nave and served by the ministers from a table placed there, the unleavened bread and wine being presented in wooden vessels, 'that no pomp come back again.' Bullinger reports that the faithful received the Eucharist 'with great wonder and still greater joy.'

By 1531, as is evident from the Appendix to Zwingli's *Exposition of the Faith*, Bern, Basel, and the other Protestant parts of Switzerland were using substantially the Zurich communion service. A number of traditional elements remain in this simple rite, such as the *Gloria in excelsis* and the Apostles' Creed. The Scriptures invariably used consist of I Cor. 11:20–29 and John 6:47–63. Readings from John 13 may be added. The communicants partake from a sitting position and kneel during the prayers. The Supper is called 'a spiritual and sacramental eating [*manducatio*] of the body of Christ.' But the whole emphasis is upon the commemoration of Christ's sacrifice, and gratitude for redemption and spiritual unity.

As Cyril Richardson has indicated, Zwingli's numerous writings on the subject stress the presence of Christ as divine and hence omnipresent, rather than His presence in the elements of the sacrament. The sacrament does not itself convey grace; yet it is prized as a special means of appropriating grace. Its value was felt to be largely in the experience of group association in the commemoration of Christ's passion and sufficient sacrifice, and in the accompanying stimulation and nurture of faith. Zwingli will go only so far as to say to Charles V:

*Credo quod . . . verum corpus Christi adsit fidei contemp-
latione* — Christ's true body is present by the contemplation
of faith; that is, those who give thanks to the Lord for the
benefit accorded us in His Son are aware that they have par-
taken in His true flesh, that in His flesh He has truly suffered, truly cleansed away our sins by His blood, and thus
everything wrought by Christ becomes, as it were, present
by the contemplation of faith.

This language is not satisfactory to advocates of the corporeal
presence. But it is the language not so much of rationalism as
of mysticism. A great solemnity attended the simplified Eucharistic service in Zurich, and in the faith of the worshipers Christ
the Redeemer was truly present.

— VI —

Sacramental doctrine was developed by Bullinger from the
groundwork laid by Zwingli, but with some modification through
the influence of Calvin and the careful reading of the Church
Fathers. In his *Fifth Decade,* he enlarges upon Augustine's treatment of sacraments as signs of holy things, or visible signs of invisible grace, and makes use of passages from Augustine, Chrysostom, Irenaeus, and other Fathers, numerous scholastic writers,
countless Scripture passages, and frequent learned references to
ancient customs. With a good deal of repetition Bullinger im-
presses upon us a few salient points of interpretation. The sacraments are instituted by God, under the forms of natural and
common things — water, bread, and wine. By these earthly and
visible signs sacraments 'represent the deep mysteries of the Gospel.' They are symbols that 'admonish us of brotherly love.'
Christ's body is in heaven, but the believer perceives it with the
eyes of the soul. Mystically and sacramentally the bread and wine
are the body and blood of Christ. Corporeally we receive the
signs, spiritually we comprehend the things signified. Participation in the Eucharist is for Bullinger at once a very personal matter and a profound group experience. It involves belief that
Christ suffered for the individual worshiper himself. It also involves 'reconciliation and friendship,' a realization of *synaxis,* or
communion. A plain simplicity in the vessels used in the service
is supported by many citations from the Fathers. A sitting position is preferred, since 'the Lord sat at table with his disciples,'
and because it is quieter than when the people rise and move.

The frequency of taking communion is left to the decision of each man's conscience, with a counsel from Augustine of peace among those who differ on this. Doctrinally there is no conscious divergence from Zwingli (who is freely quoted) in this exposition. There is, however, a more positive, perhaps we may say a more religious, temper in its presentation.

Bullinger's treatment of Baptism contains a reasoned defense of the Baptism of infants as members of the household of God. He struggles with the problem of Baptism as the sacrament of regeneration in the case of children who have no conscious faith, and argues mainly that God imputes faith to them. Holding that in God's mercy those who die in infancy are saved, he opposes as needless and superstitious the baptism by midwives of infants about to die. On the other hand he condemns the Pelagian view that infants, being innocent, are not to be baptized. The position here is common to the Reformed theologians and will be discussed further in a later chapter.

It was Bullinger's task to provide the Reformed Church with its first extended confession of faith. We saw that Zwingli, in addition to writing his Sixty-seven Conclusions and numerous theological treatises, set forth two short confessional statements addressed respectively to Charles V and to Francis I in 1530 and 1531. In 1534, Myconius, who succeeded Oecolampadius as antistes of the church of Basel, produced a short and bare outline of doctrine, usually known as the First Basel Confession. Its authority was confined to Basel and Mühlhausen. The First Helvetic, or Second Basel, Confession followed in 1536. It was principally the work of Bullinger. Adopted by a conference of theologians at Basel, it became authoritative for German-Swiss Protestantism. An important agreement between Bullinger and Calvin, the Consensus of Zurich (1549), drew the French and German-Swiss Churches into fuller agreement than before on the doctrine of the Eucharist. Bullinger's position was not surrendered in this document. He had, however, felt in some degree the influence of Calvin, a fact to which the Second Helvetic Confession bears witness. It was prepared in 1562 not as a formulation of the theology of the Church but as a statement of the author's own position amid the new theological discussions of the time. In 1566, however, after Peter Martyr Vermigli and Theodore Beza had been consulted and some alterations made in response to their opinions, it was adopted by all the Swiss Reformed Churches, except those of three cantons; and these accepted it soon afterward.

This important Confession, as adopted, bears the marks of the growing ecumenical consciousness of Swiss Protestantism and the enlargement of its theological horizon during the era of Calvin and Bullinger. It is addressed 'to Christ's faithful people everywhere, throughout Germany and the nations beyond.' It was promptly approved by the Reformed Churches of Scotland, Poland, and Hungary, and has always been held in high esteem in all branches of the Reformed Church. Its length and comprehensiveness, and its wide approval, constitute this Confession an authoritative compendium of Reformed theology. It is too extended for analysis here. It presents in fresh terms the assertion of Biblical authority and the condemnation of images. The saints are to be honored, and loved as brethren, but not invoked in prayer. Providence and predestination are affirmed in phrases that attempt to guard man's will and responsibility. We are not to regard particular persons as reprobate. It is interesting that this Confession accepts (Chapter XI) the *communicatio idiomatum,* or interchange of properties, in the relation of the divine and human in Christ, which Luther brought from the Fathers to support his view of the Eucharist. Here, however, the sacrament is explained in terms far from Lutheran (Chapter XXI). The body is in heaven, whither our hearts are raised in the service of communion. To confess sins privately to God, and in the public services, is sufficient, but to seek from a minister counsel and comfort in time of trial is commended. Faith is God's free gift and is the source of good works, which are motivated by gratitude and a desire to glorify God. Simplicity in worship is supported on the ground that the accumulation of rites in the Church takes away Christian liberty and substitutes ceremonies for faith.

With this brief notice of a notable statement of faith we turn from the German-Swiss thought and leaders to the more momentous work of John Calvin. What has been said should help us to realize how far the foundations of Reformed Church doctrine and polity had been laid by his German-Swiss predecessors.

PART II

CALVIN AND THE REFORMATION IN GENEVA

——————

GESTA DEI PER JOHANNEM CALVINUM piae recorda-
tionis hominem dicere aggredior. — Alexander
Morus, *Calvinus* (address before the Geneva
Academy), 1648, p. 2.

CHAPTER VI

YOUNG CALVIN

— I —

IN THE year 1551, the canons of the cathedral of Noyon in Picardy celebrated in solemn procession the death of that city's most eminent son, John Calvin the Reformer. An illness of Calvin, unverified rumor, and wishful thinking had induced this celebration, which was premature by thirteen years. A year later, when Noyon suffered a disastrous fire, Calvin expressed his sorrow for the ruined city, but remarked: 'I survive my birthplace that last year gave solemn thanks for my supposed death.' When he died in Geneva in 1564, an eyewitness wrote that his corpse was 'followed by almost the whole city, not without many tears.' In these incidents lies a kind of allegory of Calvin's fate in history. He has been execrated and defamed, admired and extolled. His influence has sometimes been jubilantly reported to have expired; but it has survived the authors of the reports. He remains so famous that, as is wont to happen with the great, persons ignorant of his life and work pronounce judgment upon him with the utmost finality. But he will not be thus easily dismissed. It is remarkable that in this age of stress and perplexity, when most people are absorbed in problems that seem far removed from his interests, Calvin's writings have been read with renewed attention and have vitally affected trends and movements in every sector of theological and Christian social thought.

The Reformer was born at Noyon, 10 July 1509, the son of a notary, Gérard Cauvin, and his wife, Jeanne Lefranc. Gérard's ancestors had been boatmen on the river Oise, and he had early left the family home at Pont l'Evêque to advance himself in the cathedral town. Some time before 1500 he married Jeanne. She was the daughter of Jean Lefranc, a successful innkeeper of Cambrai who, having acquired the means of comfortable retirement, had become a citizen of Noyon. The scant references we have to Calvin's mother indicate that she had a reputation for both beauty and piety. That her piety was of the medieval type may be inferred from the fact that she took John at an early age to visit shrines in the neighborhood: on one such occasion he kissed a fragment of the head of St. Ann. Calvin was the fourth son in the family. The fifth, Antoine, was to play a humble role at his brother's side in Geneva. Two of the other three died very young. One older brother, Charles, had a stormy career as a cleric of Noyon and died excommunicate in 1537. The mother's life was cut off when John was about three, and we know little of her influence upon her household. Gérard remarried, but nothing is known of Calvin's stepmother except that she became the mother of two daughters, one of whom, Marie, accompanied or soon followed her half-brother to Geneva in 1536, and there married Charles Costan, an undistinguished citizen.

Gérard Cauvin had acquired a practical knowledge of legal matters and held numerous responsible minor offices as a notary in the service of clergy and magistrates. He acted as attorney for the cathedral chapter and was secretary to Charles de Hangest, bishop of Noyon, 1501–25. This historic bishopric, dating from the sixth century, was an ecclesiastical center of exceptional dignity among the sees of France, and the life of the city gravitated around the cathedral. The episcopal office had been held for generations by members of the de Hangest family. Other prominent representatives of this aristocratic connection were Louis, the seigneur de Montmor, and Adrien, the seigneur de Genlis. Gérard Cauvin enjoyed good relations with these locally important people, and his sons were schoolfellows of their sons. Adrien's son, Claude, who became the abbot of a Noyon monastery, was a close friend of John Calvin in his boyhood and young manhood. The language used by Calvin in dedicating to him his first book, 'brought up in your house,' has led to the suggestion that he was adopted into the family, but it points rather to a familiar attachment and association in early studies. With the de Hangest boys he received instruction from private tutors; and he attended with them the Collège des Capettes, a boys' school of Noyon. He later expressed warm gratitude for the happy privilege of being tutored, though himself *unus de plebe homuncio* (a mere plebeian), with sons of the aristocracy for whom personally he had a lasting regard.

We have no reason to doubt the statements of early authorities, especially of Théodore de Bèze (Beza), Calvin's colleague and successor, that point to the brilliance and precocity of young Calvin. It was natural that his father should plan for him a university education, and the university of Paris, which was both pre-eminent and near, was the obvious choice. Moreover, Gérard used his influence with the ecclesiastics to provide church benefices for his son's maintenance during the years of study. When not yet twelve years old he was appointed to a chaplaincy in the cathedral, in which office he received a modest emolument without performing any duties. Such arrangements were frequently made on behalf of juniors, in defiance of canon law. In this case, the irregularity furnished scholarship money to an eager student. Calvin later held in turn two other benefices on similar terms. Meanwhile, in August 1523, Joannes Calvinus, aged fourteen, was registered at the Collège de la Marche in the university of Paris. 'Cauvin' had been Latinized as 'Calvinus': de-Latinized again, the name appears as 'Calvin.'

— II —

Calvin was now in the greatest of universities and at the heart of the greatest of nations. The narrow realm of Noyon was left behind, save for contacts with students from there and occasional communications with his father. Through the university echoed the political, intellectual, and religious excitements of the time. In contrast to Germany, France was a united nation; in contrast to democratic Switzerland, France was a monarchy in which all political initiative came from the king. A long series of Capetian and Valois kings had added little by little to the royal prerogative. Protests on behalf of any element of popular or responsible government had been silenced. The *Parlement* was a legal fraternity rather than a legislative body; it could, if it dared, delay, but it could not prevent, the enforcement of the king's edicts.

Even the Church had yielded to the monarchy. It is true that the Pragmatic Sanction of Bourges, 1438, an agreement between France and the Papacy, recognized the authority of church councils. But although this agreement had been unilaterally reaffirmed (1499) by King Louis XII during his protracted quarrel with Pope Julius II, and although it represented the traditional view of French churchmen, it was abandoned by Francis I (1515-47) in the Concordat of Bologna, 1516. In that year Francis reaped the fruit of his victory at Marignano. He made at Noyon a treaty with the ministers of the young emperor, Charles V, and he induced Pope Leo X to yield to him in this concordat control over the elections of bishops and abbots in his kingdom. With commendable boldness the *Parlement* and the theologians of Paris protested in vain against this measure, the latter especially on the ground of the surrender of the principle of conciliarism. But in the end Francis had his way, and his triumph here reinforced the absolutism of his rule. There was no meeting of the Estates General of France during his reign. The king made full use of his vast authority. The clergy he appointed became to a large degree his grateful instruments, and he did not hesitate to distribute lucrative benefices to his useful lay political servants.

This was not a situation favorable to the spiritual health of the Church. Secularity prevailed among clergy and monks, accompanied by moral laxity and neglect of discipline. Clerical education was low. The theological faculty at Paris (the Sorbonne) had lost its former vigor and was more intent upon the suppression of novel views than upon the pursuit of truth. Novel views were indeed appearing. Most of those who espoused them were pupils or adherents of Jacques Lefèvre of Etaples in Picardy (Faber Stapulensis). Lefèvre had spent some years in the schools of Italy and felt strongly the influence of Pico della Mirandola. In Greek he was a pupil of the eminent refugee scholar, John Argyropoulos, and he acquired some facility in reading the Greek Fathers. Lefèvre did not excel in the languages, but he was awake to their importance for a knowledge of the Bible; and he did much to interest others in them and to blaze a trail for Christian humanism in France. In 1512 his Latin translation of St. Paul's Epistles appeared, with a commentary that marked him as a heretic, in the eyes of theologians of medieval outlook, on the questions of transubstantiation, justification, and the merit of good works. This book and his earlier work on the Psalms (1509) greatly stimulated Luther. Lefèvre was later to present a translation of the Four Gospels into French and to extend this to the entire New Testament (1523). Under patristic influence he interested himself in historical points of New Testament study. He diverged from traditional assumptions and in 1517 shocked the Sorbonne by differentiating Mary Magdalene from both the 'woman who was a sinner' (Luke 7:37) and Mary of Bethany.

At the abbey of St. Germain-des-Près, where Lefèvre resided, the abbot, Guillaume Briçonnet, fell under his influence, and after Briçonnet became bishop of Meaux (1516), the leaven of the new teaching began to work in that diocese. Lefèvre shrank from controversy and had no intention of causing a schism; but the ideas he expressed were rightly judged to be revolutionary, and he entertained hopes of far-reaching reform. 'God will renovate the world,' he said to Farel in 1512, 'and you will live to see it.' He was denounced by Noël Bédier (Beda), leader of the Sorbonne and anxious guardian of orthodoxy, and was in danger of suffering the fate of heretics when Briçonnet invited him (1520) — with his pupils, Guillaume Farel and Gérard Roussel, and others of his circle, including the able Herbrew scholar, François Vatable — to share the work of reform in the diocese of Meaux. What followed there will call for attention in a later chapter.

Meanwhile the Latin treatises of Luther began to circulate in France. Their condemnation by the Sorbonne, 15 April 1521, did not effect their suppression. At least three of them were published in translation, the author's and the translator's names being withheld. The printer, Simon du Bois, issued an edition of Lefèvre's New Testament and also, some years later, the celebrated *Mirror of a Sinful Soul* by Marguerite d'Angoulême, the talented sister of the king, which also fell under the censure of the Sorbonne (1532). This combination of disapproved books suggests the alignment of elements of opposition to the Sorbonne. Briçonnet had been Marguerite's spiritual director, and she was herself an admirer and patron of Roussel and was warmly committed to the cause of reform as represented by these disciples of Lefèvre.

The man who did most to interpret Luther to the French, and who was probably the translator of some of his work, was the nobleman Louis de Berquin. Like Lefèvre and Calvin, de Berquin was from Picardy. He was condemned by the Sorbonne in 1523 but on that occasion was saved from death by the king's intervention, in response to Marguerite's plea. His release took place in the month in which fourteen-year-old Calvin entered the university. Even so young a freshman could hardly escape knowledge of the affair; not only was it widely discussed but the students celebrated by presenting a clever satirical play, *La Farce des théologastres,* in which de Berquin is the hero, Erasmus, Lefèvre, and Luther are favorably mentioned, and the Sorbonne doctors are derided. Calvin may have learned, too, that on the day of de Berquin's release, 8 August, Jean Vallière, an Augustinian, was burned at the stake in Paris for Lutheran opinions.

— III —

Calvin had an uncle in Paris, Richard Cauvin, by occupation a smith, in whose house he at first found a home. He enrolled in the Collège de la Marche, where at once his eager, brilliant mind attracted the interest of a very distinguished teacher of Latin, Mathurin Cordier, a priest of Rouen who had taken up teaching and was a regent of the Collège. Long years afterward, Cordier was to respond to Calvin's invitation to Geneva, and there to spend fruitfully his declining years. It is remarkable that a teen-age boy made a life-long friend and admirer of a scholar thirty-two years his senior. The period of Cordier's instruction of Calvin was brief; but it was sufficient to impart to his pupil the spirit of humanism at its best. It was perhaps due largely to Cordier that Calvin discovered the delights of good learning and acquired that unfailing sense of style and diction that marks all his writings.

For reasons not known but possibly connected with his intention to enter the priesthood, Calvin soon transferred his enrollment to the more celebrated Collège de Montaigu. This had long been an austere institution. Its former president, John Standonck, a member of the Brethren of the Common Life, had given it a character of gravity and asceticism; his successor, Noël Beda, vigilante of orthodoxy, had aimed to make it a fortress of resistance to innovations. He had been succeeded by Pierre Tempête, known to his students because of his exceptional severity as *horrida tempestas,* and satirized by Erasmus and Rabelais. Calvin does not seem to have collided with this stern pedagogue: Tempête's rod of discipline would naturally have fallen upon those less studious than Calvin. Erasmus had complained of Montaigu's stale eggs and not less stale theology; it is possible that Calvin's later bad digestion began in the refectory of Montaigu. But even with the best of meals, a youth who labored at his desk as he did would have risked ill health. We are informed that he ate little and slept little, but devoured books.

The Collège de Montaigu proved, indeed, a suitable nursery for Calvin's mind. It is usual to suggest that he was at this stage an unsocial being, austere and harshly critical and condemnatory of his fellow students. The statement is attributed to his opponent, François Baudouin, that as an undergraduate Calvin was commonly called 'the accusative case.' Actually Baudouin wrote nothing to this effect. The statement apparently originated with another hostile writer, Lavasseur, more than a century later (1633). It has been gleefully repeated as history many times, even since the facts were exposed by Emile Doumergue. It is an example of how misstatements gain credence. Actually what it probably rests upon is a remark by Baudouin that Calvin's cousin, Olivétan, was nicknamed 'the ablative case' because of his eagerness to 'throw off' his academic gown after lecture. Beza, however, in his *Life of Calvin* states that as a student Calvin was a censor of the vices of his fellows, and we may well believe this. Perhaps what Gregory the Great said of St. Benedict might truly be said of Calvin also: 'From his younger years he carried always the mind of an old man.' He gave an impression not only of studiousness but of maturity.

But there is no evidence that young Calvin was uncompanionable: much, indeed, to the contrary. He maintained good relations with his former schoolfellows of the de Hangest families, with three of whom, and their tutor, he had come to Paris. He was closely associated with his scholarly cousin, Pierre Robert Olivier (Olivétan), three years his senior, whom he had known also in Noyon. He became a welcome guest in the homes of two of the greatest men of the university, Guillaume Cop, a medical scholar and the king's physician, and Guillaume Budé, the most learned Hellenist of France and the most effective liberal opponent of Beda. Calvin formed close ties with the sons of both these distinguished men, and later both families were represented among French religious refugees to Geneva. Through his influence a number of the de Hangest family also later became Protestants; but not his best companion among them, Claude. All the facts belie the picture of young Calvin as morose. It would be difficult, indeed, to discover a teen-age student of his time who attracted so many choice friends. The fact that his

friends were not of the rank and file, and that they were all older
then he, has no doubt some significance. We may suppose that
as a student he felt no attraction toward intellectual mediocrity.

In the Collège de Montaigu he was fortunate, too, as he had
been earlier, in his teachers. Beza refers favorably to a Spaniard
with whom Calvin continued his lessons in Latin. This was most
likely Antonio Coronel. It is highly likely that he came under
the instruction of the celebrated Scot, John Major, or Mair, who
returned to Paris in 1525 after a period of teaching in his native
country. He was a very learned scholastic philosopher of the
Ockhamist persuasion. Among his works were a valuable *History
of Greater Britain* (1521) and a commentary on the Gospels
(1529), in which he assailed the writings of Wyclif, Huss, and
Luther. It may be reasonably inferred that Calvin heard from
his lips some of the material of the latter book before its publication; Major's lectures may indeed have given him his first substantial knowledge of Luther. François Wendel, who makes this
suggestion, believes also that, in view of his later familiarity with
the Church Fathers, Calvin probably began then his acquaintance with them.

It is certain that at his college emphasis was laid on the favorite medieval school discipline of dialectic, which involved a
practical training in vocal argumentation. The instructor in this
subject was none other than the redoubtable syndic of the Sorbonne and ex-president of Montaigu, Noël Beda. We may imagine young Calvin under his stern tutelage, a slender lad of seventeen or eighteen with flashing eyes and ringing voice, contending
in flowing Latin sentences, and nimbly disrupting an opponent's
syllogisms, on the nature of universals or the inspiration of the
prophets or the doctrine of attrition, or on some subtlety of the
schoolmen such as he himself reports: whether a hog is led to
market by the rope attached to him or by the man who holds the
rope. When we find Calvin's *Institutes* and tracts strewn with
such expressions as:

I pass over far greater absurdities;

I shall not treat them with the severity which they deserve;

The argument is too puerile to need any answer;

But it affords me no pleasure to contend with them in such
fooleries,

we realize the lasting effect of this training upon his mental habits. Its effects went deeper, we may be sure, than to supply him with a ready set of disparaging connective phrases. It sharpened and invigorated the thinking process in his brain and brought to activity his latent endowments. It was a type of educational experience well calculated to produce the mental preparedness and promptness of which he would later show constant evidence. 'Reading maketh a full man,' wrote Lord Bacon, 'conference a ready man, and writing an exact man.' Calvin under his Montaigu instructors acquired two of these disciplines: he would later practice the third.

— IV —

The rising scholar was only eighteen and a half years old when, early in 1528, he received the master of arts degree. We reserve the discussion of his religious conversion to the next chapter. Here we must notice, however, a change in his vocational expectations. We know nothing of Calvin's father that would suggest a continuous close relation with his children. Probably young Calvin's feelings toward him had never been quickened by parental warmth. He was dutiful toward his father rather than attached to him. Gérard Cauvin was now in strained relations with the canons of Noyon cathedral, by whom he was employed. Apparently he was offended by their demand to see his accounts of certain properties left to the chapter. He stubbornly refused to present his books. The quarrel was prolonged. Possibly Gérard relied upon the support of the new bishop, Jean de Hangest, a brother of Calvin's friend Claude. The bishop was also in open controversy with the canons, who criticized him for his modern ways and for daring to wear a beard. But the bishop did not deliver Gérard from his troubles, and the willful notary's resistance ultimately brought upon him excommunication.

Meanwhile, in 1528, he was reconsidering his son's future. Perhaps he feared that the benefices which supported John in Paris would be withdrawn. He himself had been a lawyer of sorts, and he appreciated the opportunities of wealth for well-trained experts in the law. It may be that Gérard had become obsessed by concern for the worldly prosperity of his family. His son at least attributed his new plan for him to the desire to make him rich. Calvin was virtually commanded by his father to turn from the clerical to the legal profession, and to enter upon the study of law at Orléans, where the law faculty of greatest repute in France was then to be found. Luther at twenty-two had declined to accede to his father's similar wish, and had entered a monastery. Calvin, in his nineteenth year, obeyed without demur, though not eagerly, and migrated to Orléans. He does not seem to have approved his father's decision, but he gives us to understand that he accepted it as within the sphere of God's providence. He soon found the new study interesting. During the year and a half of his continuous attendance at Orléans, he was a pupil of the foremost teacher of jurisprudence in France, Pierre de l'Etoile. For this stalwart and devout conservative, who after his wife's death had taken priestly orders, Calvin had great respect.

At Orléans Calvin lived in the home of Nicholas Duchemin, a disciple of Etoile, and became a warm friend of this thirty-year-old law scholar. Another of his friends was François Daniel, a law student who lived with his brothers and sisters in Orléans, among whom Calvin was a welcome visitor. There is an unconfirmed possibility that in Daniel's company Calvin became acquainted with François Rabelais, who like Calvin was yet to achieve great fame. The eminent jester had his own views of religion, and was sympathetic with the moderate reform policy of Lefèvre. François Conan, afterward distinguished as a legist, was also of the group. Calvin's association with his Orléans friends was maintained for about five years, and in the case of Daniel it was prolonged by correspondence later. It is not implied that Calvin was now wholly immersed in law studies. His attachment to these companions was more a result of their being personally congenial than because of their legal interests. This may have been true even of Etoile, who was something of a Biblical humanist as well as a jurist. Probably it was also at Orléans that Calvin first enjoyed the instruction of Melchior Wolmar of Rothweil in Würtemburg, a German under Lutheran influence, who had written a book on Homer and under whose guidance Calvin entered upon the study of Greek. This study now invaded his time schedule, but he applied to himself an iron discipline, and so labored that he was regarded as a rising legal scholar.

There arose a new star on Calvin's horizon. Andrea Alciati of Milan was invited by Marguerite d'Angoulême, who had become Duchess of Berry, to occupy the chair of Roman law at Bourges in that duchy. Marguerite also induced Wolmar to join the Bourges faculty. There was something of a migration from Orléans to Bourges, and Calvin joined the movement. He was eager to learn from the Italian celebrity; he was happy also to continue his association with Wolmar. Before the end of 1529 Alciati, Wolmar, Nicholas Duchemin, and Calvin were all at Bourges.

Calvin's real passion as a student was not for the law but for the languages, literatures, and cultures of antiquity. Alciati, too, was a humanist; but after experience with the pious and conservative Etoile, the Italian's irreverent radicalism and unbounded self-esteem repelled the sensitive youth. Calvin and Duchemin alike soon regarded him as pompous, vain, and coarse, even though they admired his talents. They resented his contempt for the French jurists, and when he made Pierre de l'Etoile the special object of his sarcasm and attacked him in print under a pseudonym, their loyalty toward their old master flamed. In 1529 Duchemin wrote a defense of Etoile (*Antapologia*); it was published in 1531, with a preface by Calvin, in which Etoile is lauded as the man who 'for his penetration, competence, and expertness in law is the unrivaled prince of our age.'

This preface, Calvin's first published writing, is dated 6 March 1531, when he was correcting the proof of the book in Paris. Few dates are available for this period; but we know that he was in Noyon on 14 May to attend his dying father, at whose death he was present on the 26th. Calvin reported the event with strange indifference. He may have continued to resent his father's determination, on no creditable motive, to make a lawyer of him. In 1530, on the advice of Calvin's senior friend, Budé, Francis I had taken the important step of establishing the College of Royal Lecturers in complete independence of the university, with professors in Greek and Hebrew. These chairs were filled respectively by Pierre Danès and François Vatable — Erasmus having declined the king's invitation. Calvin spent most of the summer and autumn of 1531 in Paris attending their lectures.

— V —

His father's death left Calvin free to make his own choice of a career. He was not inclined to enter the profession of the law, yet, not to leave a task unfinished, he proceeded to the doctorate in law at Orléans. This was completed sometime before 14 January 1532. He was in that year appointed to the office of 'annual deputy of the proctor for the nation of Picardy,' i.e. the Picard students who formed a 'nation' in the university of Orléans. In May and June 1533, he was engaged in legal duties involved in this office. There, so far as record goes, his connection with the law ends, save for his contribution to the reform of the laws of Geneva in 1543.

At Paris in 1531 his energy was not confined to studies under the Royal Lecturers. He was hard at work in the preparation of a noteworthy book. His *Commentary on Lucius Anneas Seneca's Two Books on Clemency* appeared in Paris, 4 April 1532. It is the principal monument to young Calvin's humanistic attainments. The treatise had been written by Seneca in an effort to impart some element of humaneness to the rule of the emperor Nero. It is impossible to suppose that Calvin in commenting on it was oblivious of its bearing upon the policy and character of Francis I, who with all his brilliancy was frivolous and capable of ruthlessness. At the time a few professors of evangelical beliefs had suffered death, a considerable number had been imprisoned, and even their sympathizers were insecure. Some historians have read the *Commentary* as a plea for the toleration of Protestants; but if any such intention was present, it was so concealed as not to be discoverable except by inference from Calvin's later position.

The book is to be thought of as an ambitious humanist contribution to political ethics. To Seneca and Calvin alike clemency is a virtue of princes. Seneca describes it as the lenient attitude of a superior toward an inferior in determining penalties. The task Calvin sets himself resembles that which had been undertaken in the many treatises of the 'Mirror of Princes' type, of which Erasmus' *Christian Prince* was the culmination. Calvin's political philosophy has points of resemblance to that of Erasmus and may have been influenced also by Budé's *Education of the Prince* (c. 1516). This work had not yet been published, but the manuscript may easily have been accessible to Calvin as a friend of the Budé family. Calvin ascribes to kings a high authority by divine right; yet he freely assails their vices, pride, and inhumanity. He condemns arbitrariness, denounces tyranny, and stresses the importance of the voluntary submission of the king to law. A tyrant is for Calvin one who rules against the will of his subjects. There are evident here elements that became permanent in his political doctrine (see below, p. 224).

The work is of interest as Calvin's first 'commentary.' The others would be on Scripture books but would follow a method closely similar. The method was not new. It was basically what had long been practiced in the interpretation of Scripture and other documents — such as the Sentences of Peter Lombard — and by humanists and jurists in commenting on historic texts. Erasmus' *Paraphrase of the New Testament* and Budé's *Annotations on the Pandects of Justinian* may have served Calvin as models. Calvin sets down a short passage from the treatise and subjects it to critical examination. He writes informally, studying the words employed, often referring to their use in other contexts, supplying historical details, explaining philosophical concepts, and indicating his own judgment of the author's views. Seneca's ideas are often freely commended, sometimes rejected. Calvin admires the Stoic moralist but makes it very clear that he is not himself a Stoic. He repudiates in Seneca what is contrary to 'our religion.' Seneca condemns the emotion of *misericordia*, compassion or mercy, which for him is no part of clemency but 'a vice of the mind.' Calvin as a Christian holds that *misericordia* is a virtue, and that no man is good who does not possess it. Yet it is remarkable that he goes for authority here not to the Bible but to Cicero and Aristotle. He is evidently writing for a humanist public. There is nothing very original or profound in these corrections of the Stoic ethics, commendable as they are from a Christian standpoint. The glory of the book lies rather in its exhibit of what in a man of twenty-two years was prodigious learning in classical and patristic literature, both Latin and Greek, and of remarkably mature understanding of ancient authors. It is written in clear and polished Latin.

— VI —

Calvin not unreasonably expected a good reception for his book. Seneca was a favorite 'good heathen' to Christian humanists, and in the general state of things clemency was a theme that might well have stirred interest. Yet the learned world made no response. The *Commentary* never reached the readers Calvin had in mind: it went unsold and unread. The fact that he had ventured to differ at some points from Erasmus may have harmed its chances; but it seems rather to have been simply overlooked. To Calvin (as to other authors) indifference was more bitter than disapproval. Nor was it comforting for him to remember that he had expended his own money for its publication. Some have thought that this discouraging experience was a factor in turning him from the Christian humanist to the evangelical ranks; but he himself explains the change otherwise.

It must be recognized that, judged by the Seneca *Commentary,* Calvin in 1532 was not concerning himself with the religious issues of the time. In religion, the months in which he wrote his work were exciting enough. The Augsburg diet of 1530 had been followed by the Schmalkald League of Protestant states, the Swiss civil war, and the deaths of Zwingli and Oecolampadius. Francis I had inaugurated his policy of support of Protestants abroad against the Pope and the emperor, together with persecution of Protestants in his own domains. Calvin does not comment on these things. With a more than Erasmian detachment from passing events, he delights in the literature of pagan antiquity and seeks by considerations drawn from it to promote the triumph of benevolence and moderation in government, for the betterment of man's mundane life. He has only three casual citations of Scripture passages, and these are applied politically. The Calvin known to history is a man with another outlook and other primary interests.

CHAPTER VII

CALVIN'S CONVERSION

— I —

IF HE had been as self-revealing as Bunyan or Wesley, Calvin would have made this chapter easier to write. By a few helpful notes he could have prevented a wasteful flow of ink from the pens of modern scholars seeking to explain his 'sudden conversion.' The sources for this event are scant and inharmonious, while the subject is of salient importance. Calvin would have been insignificant if he had not been a convert.

We have to consider here both the date and the nature of that transformation in Calvin's interests, loyalties, and activities which made him an evangelical Reformer. The question of the date has proved the more puzzling. I take his words, *subita conversione*, in their most obvious sense, 'by a sudden conversion.' Now it is perfectly clear that he was aware of, and inclined toward, the evangelical position for some time before he openly espoused Protestantism. Some have placed his sudden conversion at the beginning, others at the end, of this time of indetermination. A few have ingeniously read *subita* as equivalent not of (French) *subite* but of *subie* (as the past participle of *subeo*), and made the phrase mean 'by a conversion undergone.' But in view of the context, which indicates a sharp and pronounced change, this interpretation seems forced.

The words quoted are from the Preface to Calvin's *Commentary on the Psalms,* written in 1557, one of the few passages in which he offers his readers anything of an autobiographical nature. Here he says that God, who made the shepherd David a king, has advanced Calvin himself from lowly beginnings to the honorable office of a minister of the Gospel. His father had intended him for theology, but, changing his plan, had set him to study law, hoping that a legal training would open the way for him to grow rich. He had forced himself to obey his father; but God by His secret providence turned him from that course.

> Since I was more stubbornly addicted to the superstitions of the Papacy than to be easily drawn out of that so deep mire, by a sudden conversion, He subdued my heart (too hardened for my age) to docility [*animum meum, qui pro aetate nimis obduruerat, subita conversione ad docilitatem subegit*]. Thus, having acquired some taste of true piety, I burned with such great zeal to go forward that although I did not desist from other studies I yet pursued them more indifferently, nor had a year gone by when all who were desirous of this purer doctrine thronged to me, novice and beginner that I was, in order to learn it.

In the same passage Calvin tells us that being of a retiring nature (*natura subrusticus*) he had vainly sought to escape these inquirers, but every retreat had become for him a public school. God had always countered his desire for ease and brought him unwillingly to public notice. The continued effort to escape to retirement led him to seek 'an obscure corner' in Germany.

The only date that we can at once connect with this statement is that of his passage to 'Germany.' He went to Metz and thence to Strasbourg and Basel in January and February 1535. Observing that the effort to avoid attention began within a year of his sudden conversion, and was attended by repeated changes of residence, we should naturally look for the date a year or more before the departure to Basel, that is, in 1533 or early in 1534. But we must consider other evidence.

The impression we obtain from Beza's *Life* that Calvin in his Paris days 'began to withdraw himself from papal superstition' and was converted through the influence of Olivétan before the latter's flight from Orléans early in 1528 is entirely without corroboration. Calvin was then not yet nineteen and could hardly have lived through the protracted stubborn adherence to Rome which he reports. Nor does this date accord with the nature of his writings in 1531 and 1532, to which we have called attention. There is no reason to doubt that Olivétan, who through the late 'twenties was a pronounced Protestant, sowed seeds that later bore fruit in Calvin's mind. But the sudden conversion was by Calvin's own testimony followed immediately by a burning zeal for the Scriptures and a lessened attention to 'other studies.'

Nothing of this sort is discoverable either in his defense of Etoile, which belongs in the field of law, or in the Seneca *Commentary*, which exhibits the author's absorption in the classics. Since Etoile was known to have advocated the persecution of heretics — a point not raised in Calvin's Preface to the *Antapologia* — and since the *Commentary* tends distinctly toward toleration, we may perhaps argue that in 1531-2 Calvin was unconsciously progressing toward a new position. A letter written by Calvin, after his conversion, to Bucer was formerly dated by editors September 1532. It is now recognized to be of a later year, probably 1534.

It should be remembered that Beza's short *Life of Calvin* was hastily composed and, although fairly reliable for the period of the two men's association in Geneva, is not a work of sifted research for the earlier period. It has been supposed that Beza as a boy of nine may have known Calvin at Bourges, but this is not mentioned by Beza. It would in any case be unwise to give much weight to a boy's impressions recalled thirty-five years later.

— II —

We may not doubt that throughout his years at the universities Calvin was exposed to the influence of what was often inaccurately called 'Lutheranism,' through many contacts and considerable reading. There were occasional burnings for heresy, the most renowned of the victims being Louis de Berquin, who died on 17 April 1529, about the time of Calvin's arrival in Bourges. De Berquin's death did not end the circulation in France of Luther's books and opinions. While writing the Seneca *Commentary* Calvin lived in the house of a cloth merchant, Etienne de la Forge, a devout Waldensian from Piedmont. This man was an ardent reader of Luther and a fearless propagandist of Protestantism. He made a practice of distributing to the poor packages accompanied by tracts and passages of Scripture, and he kept open house for religious refugees from the Netherlands. Calvin must have observed these evidences of incautious zeal, for which de la Forge would later pay the penalty of death by fire. Who can say what influence Calvin's host ultimately had upon his religious attitudes? He himself was apparently unaware at the time that it was significant for him.

Ascribing to God alone his escape from the 'mire,' Calvin in the Preface to the *Commentary on the Psalms* mentions none of those who by their oral or written persuasions may have been human instruments in this deliverance. It is likely that he had read a number of Luther's tracts. In a statement of 1556 he implies that prior to the Marburg Colloquy he read and accepted a typical characterization by Luther of the Zwinglian doctrine of the Eucharist. By the date of this conference, 1529, much Luther material was abroad in France. Calvin was then in association with the Lutheran Wolmar, to whom he was greatly drawn. If at this time his spirit was stirred to the depths by contact with Wolmar, de la Forge, and their associates, it is strange indeed that his writings of the period reveal nothing of such an experience. Can we suppose that he wrote these in a tremendous effort to escape a personal response to the Reformation argument — that by an effort of the will he thrust such matters into a subconscious realm of the mind? It seems hard to believe that the author of the Seneca *Commentary* was struggling with the religious issue. If some manifestations of the Reformation had interested him, any personal response to its challenge could easily have been postponed. After his father's death in May 1531, he probably assumed that he would continue in clerical offices and live out his days as a scholarly and modern-minded priest of Noyon. In 1533, however, he would enter the arena of controversy, and in 1534 the ranks of Protestantism.

— III —

Calvin's personal association with Nicholas Cop, which began early in his Paris days, was renewed in the early 'thirties. In 1533 Cop was rector of the university of Paris. When the Sorbonne condemned Marguerite d'Angoulême's *Mirror of a Sinful Soul*, Cop aroused the university in her defense, and Calvin reported this with admiration to his friend François Daniel. On 1 November of that year Cop delivered a rectorial address that startled the old believers into a vigorous reaction. The long accepted view, first published by Beza in 1575, that Calvin was Cop's ghost writer for this discourse has been abandoned by most authorities. Yet a strong probability lingers that he was in some way associated with it. Cop employed materials from Erasmus to blast the Sorbonne and, in unacknowledged quotation, passages from a sermon of Luther (1522) contrasting the Gospel and the law and emphasizing free grace. But the address (which is cast in sermon form) is not merely a tissue of extracts; it is a passionate attack upon the censors and persecutors, and an espousal of the cause of those who represent the new point of view in religion. The argument is Biblical and evangelical, and anti-Sorbonnist. There is nothing distinctly anti-papal in the discourse, and it contains at the end of the exordium a formal salutation to the Blessed Virgin. Cop boldly urges that the peace of the Church be based on the Word, not on the sword. He lauds those persecuted for God and justice as more admirable in their courage than Regulus or Socrates. He calls for an end of the dissimulation that is practiced through fear of those who kill the body but cannot harm the soul.

There is preserved in Geneva a copy in Calvin's hand of a part of this daring manifesto, but it is almost certainly not the original draft, nor is the complete copy that rests in Strasbourg the original. Calvin's having transcribed Cop's text need occasion no surprise, in view of the close friendship between them, and from the fact that Calvin shared the unhappy consequences. It is quite possible that he saw it before it was delivered, and, indeed, that Cop had invited his suggestions for it. But it is antecedently unlikely that an accomplished scholar such as Cop would have asked another to write for him a public discourse of first importance, and hardly probable that Calvin would have accepted such a commission. The address is rather exclamatory in style and lacks the persuasive orderliness characteristic of Calvin. Cop takes as his text: 'Blessed are the poor in Spirit.' It has been shown that Calvin's treatment of this beatitude offers a quite different interpretation. The assumption of Calvin's authorship breaks down.

We may assume, however, that it substantially represents Calvin's views in the autumn of 1533. If so, had he, as many believe, already experienced the 'conversion'? Since, as we have seen, he refers prominently to his obstinate attachment to the Papacy prior to that event, we naturally look for a repudiation of the Papacy as a mark of its effect. The Papacy is, however, not in question either in this document or in any of Calvin's extant letters of 1533. If the rectorial address is read as a sequel to Cop's very recent spirited defense of Marguerite's book, it appears not as a Protestant document but as the voice of the party of Marguérite and of Lefèvre's followers. At the moment this party was both menaced by the Sorbonne and encouraged by some measure of immunity then apparent in the king's policy. Could the balance be turned against the Sorbonne in favor of Marguerite and her protégés? Cop had temporarily won a victory for Marguerite in the university: he was her champion here with reference to the broad religious policy of France. He avails himself of some Luther material, but the outlook is not that of Luther, or of the later Calvin. If Calvin approved the utterance he was, we may say, ripe for conversion rather than fresh from it. The date of the *subita conversio* must be put later.

All that we know of Calvin in 1533 bears testimony that he had not changed his religious allegiance. In June, with Nicholas Cop, he visited a nunnery and interviewed the abbess in order to arrange for the admission to it of a sister of his friend François Daniel. On 23 August he was in Noyon attending (though not a member) a session of the chapter, in which it was decided to hold a solemn procession to allay the plague. In October he presented to Daniel a book by Gérard Roussel, Lefèvre's eloquent disciple, who had been imprisoned for a short time after Cop's address and who was also of the number of Calvin's friends and correspondents. Neither Roussel nor Daniel ever moved from the position of Lefèvre to Protestantism.

Cop's sermon associates its author and his friend with the advocates of a new spirituality within the old Church rather than with those who bade farewell to Rome. Whatever hopes were entertained by Cop and Calvin on All Saints Day, 1533, were soon to be disappointed. Proceedings for heresy were instituted by the Sorbonne and the *Parlement* against both men. The charge against Calvin was not the authorship of the address but 'familiarity with the rector.' The king was induced to authorize prompt extirpation of the 'Lutherans' (10 December). Late in November, Cop fled to Basel. Calvin, according to one chronicler, escaped from the Collège Fortet in Paris, where he had been lodging, by a window, improvising a rope from twisted bed curtains, and then — excellent walker that he was — he went afoot in the costume of a vine dresser to Noyon. The police who came to arrest him seized his books and papers. Marguerite may have interceded for him: he was soon in the Paris area again. Then

he set out for a friendly retreat in Saintonge, where he spent the
first half of the year 1534.

— IV —

Louis du Tillet, a member of a prominent family, was a cultured young cleric of Lefèvre's persuasion, who had somewhere
formed a friendship with Calvin. He was a canon of the Cathedral
of Angoulême in Saintonge and had inherited from his father
an extensive library. Calvin found a happy home with du Tillet
at Claix near the city of Angoulême and, if the hostile historian
Florimond de Raemond (d. 1602) is not entirely misinformed,
became a prominent figure in a group of liberal clerics who associated with his host. De Raemond is responsible for the view
that Calvin wrote the *Institutes of the Christian Religion* in
Angoulême; by a gross error he supposed that Calvin was there
for three years. We know from his own letters that he studied
with du Tillet, and that the two young men stimulated each
other. He is reported, too, to have composed sermons for pastors
in the neighborhood. Probably it was for him a time of intellectual growth and of deep heart-searching. The *Institutes* may
have profited from the reading done in du Tillet's library; but
we have no real evidence that he was then writing the book.

At this time Marguerite, who had in 1527 become the Queen
of Navarre, was protecting Roussel and the aged Lefèvre at
Nérac. On 6 April 1534, possibly the hundredth year of his life,
Lefèvre welcomed from the press the final edition of his French
Bible. About the same time he received for an interview an eager
and perhaps perplexed young man who had journeyed to his retreat. Despite his father's excommunication Calvin had retained
his benefices and was in good standing with the chapter of Noyon.
In about two months he would be twenty-five and would be expected to proceed to ordination. He was under necessity of de-
ciding whether to go through with this. He had known Lefèvre
by reputation from boyhood and had been a companion of some
of his pupils. The patriarch and the young scholar, both natives
of Picardy, had never met. Lefèvre had been ordained in his
youth: he might have something to say to Calvin about that
problem. No doubt Calvin wanted to talk with the inspirer of
the group to which he had in a general way belonged. Lefèvre's

movement had won many competent advocates, yet was not succeeding. Cop's address had been a plea for its liberation, but what had followed was a grave setback for his party. Lefèvre himself had suffered defeat, first at Paris and later at Meaux. Calvin must have been reaching the conclusion that the course the aged scholar had pursued, of seeking reform within the hierarchical system, was not fruitful or justifiable. The timing of the visit to Lefèvre seems, despite the youth's apparently favorable circumstances at Angoulême, to coincide with the culmination of a period of inner tension and the confrontation by Calvin of a painful but unavoidable decision.

A knowledge of what was said in this interview would be priceless; but that is denied us. If only because of Lefèvre's eminence and advanced age, Calvin's silence about it is exasperating. Beza tells us only that a gracious reception was given the visitor, and alleges a prophecy of Lefèvre that Calvin would be 'an instrument in the establishing of the Kingdom of God in France.' Guillaume Farel reported at the time of Lefèvre's death, two years later, that the dying scholar in anguish accused himself of failure 'to confess the truth of God.' These statements cannot be verified. Yet it is not inconceivable that his talk with Calvin tended to encourage a bolder course than he himself had taken.

Whether or not Lefèvre sought to evoke on Calvin's part a resolute course of behavior, the situation cannot have failed to impress upon Calvin the futility of cautious methods. It must have come upon his mind with irresistible conviction that, with their inspirer very aged and in forced retirement, those reforming spirits who scrupulously remained within the Roman communion and subject to its hierarchy would assuredly never gain the reforms they sought. Not only a few Sorbonne reactionaries but the whole weight of the established Church of France and of Rome opposed them. Obedience to the ecclesiastical authorities was itself the frustration of reform. Behind the harsh reaction of the Sorbonne he saw the whole medieval papal, hierarchical, and sacramental system sunk through long deterioration into a state of corruption and superstition, inert in the chains of tradition, negligent of the Word of God. Here lay the ultimate hindrance to reform, the stronghold of the persecutors of those who sought it. Cost what it might, Rome itself must be repudiated: others had paid the price. He had known this in an impersonal way for some time; but he had resisted the suggestion, having been 'stubbornly addicted' to the Papacy and to the system in which from boyhood he had expected to participate through his later years. Now it was all clear, and it was personal. There could be no postponement, no rationalized evasion. The hand of God was laid upon him.

With thoughts such as these, John Calvin proceeded from Nérac across France to Noyon, and there on 4 May surrendered his clerical benefices. More clearly than any utterance, this action proclaims that his conversion had taken place. It may have preceded the visit to Lefèvre, but it is not impossible that it was on that occasion that his personal attachment to Rome quite ended. The appeal of Lutheran literature with its uncompromising denunciations of Popes, contact with Etienne de la Forge and other saintly Protestants, the valiant suffering of martyrs to a Biblical faith, the obscurantism and idolatry of saint cults, processions, relics, indulgences, and ceremonial, conference with friends, and intense study of the Bible and the Fathers, all were factors that exercised a cumulative pressure within his soul and finally broke the barrier of resistance. This barrier, which had protected his ecclesiastical plans, now appeared a sacrilegious defense against the will of God. Calvin was already accustomed to see the providence of God in the crises of his life. Now men and books and other instruments of that divine direction were forgotten. 'God subdued my heart to docility.'

— V —

In our review of the events by which to date the conversion of Calvin, we have called attention to some of his own phrases that suggest the nature of the experience. His word 'sudden' is obviously not intended to suggest that it was unrelated to the past. Rather it was precisely that outcome of past experiences against which he had tried to fortify himself. He had clung loyally to the old system; he had been 'not easily drawn out of that deep mire,' and had no doubt resisted much persuasion. He could not explain in terms of human motivation how it happened that he resisted no longer: at once he found himself docile, tractable, obedient, alert to do the will of God, and completely freed from every hindering sense of obligation to do what he now clearly apprehended to be under divine disapproval.

The French text of the key passage to which we have referred has *coeur* where the Latin is *animum*. It was a matter of the heart and spirit: 'God subdued my stubborn heart.' There is a strange impression in many quarters that Calvin was a man without emotions. It is a judgment easily made of those who do not talk much about their emotions. The whole story of his youth, his studies, his many friendships, and his correspondence shows that he was in fact of an unusually ardent nature. His conversion was not merely enlightenment; it was that unreserved, wholehearted commitment to the living God that is symbolized in the seal which he later used — a flaming heart on the palm of an extended open hand. God had rescued him from the depths; Calvin remained a man astonished by the mercy of God — *la miséricorde de Dieu* — mercy wholly undeserved and beyond man's earning.

In his *Reply to Cardinal Sadoleto* (1539) Calvin meets the charge of heresy and schism laid against converts from Romanism. The cardinal had enforced his argument by picturing the sorry plight of such persons called to account 'before the awful tribunal of the Supreme Judge.' Calvin takes up the challenge and presents two hypothetical converts, a minister and a layman, who, addressing God, explain the reasons for their course. One cannot read these speeches without feeling that they are brilliantly and rather adroitly designed by Calvin as an *apologia pro vita sua*. Yet it is not clear to what degree they represent a personal record. The minister affirms his conviction that the light of saving truth is kindled by the Word of God only, and that the introduction of human inventions into the Church was sacrilegious presumption. He has observed that leaders in the Church cared little for the Scripture, but deluded the wretched people with their strange dogmas and stupidities. The people, indeed, greatly revered God's Word, but from afar, and without examining it, and thus piety deteriorated through error and superstition and useless trifles fabricated as a means of winning the favor of God. But

> Thou didst shine upon me with the brightness of Thy spirit, that I might detest these things, and recognize how impious and injurious they were; Thou didst bear the torch of thy Word before me that I might loathe them as they deserve; Thou didst arouse my soul.

We may conjecture that Calvin here writes with a
own conversion and with a lively sense of the c
that, with a realization of the abuses in the Chu.
been laid upon him.

The layman's defense is of no less interest for its ap,
bearing on the nature of Calvin's conversion. It emphasizes:
the failure to find peace of conscience through the medieval system of satisfactions, and the soul's 'terror' in this plight; (2) the
impact of a new and 'very different doctrine' of the sufficiency of
Christ's work of satisfaction; (3) an aversion felt toward the new
teachers on the ground of reverence for the Church and the
avoidance of schism; (4) persuasion that their effort to correct
the faults of the Church — of which, he notes, 'they spoke nobly'
— was far different from schism; and (5) that the Papacy was not
constituted by the Word of God but was a tyranny resting on
empty claims. It will be found that these considerations, presented here as reasons for leaving the Roman obedience, are all
frequently treated in Calvin's writings, though elsewhere generally with no autobiographical suggestion.

No other Reformer, not even Luther, stressed more urgently
the objections to compulsory auricular confession where there
is no thought of 'internal renovation of the mind.' Calvin holds
that through the complicated and indefensible explanations
given of attrition and contrition 'the wretched conscience is
wonderfully tormented,' and the penitent is invariably driven
either to despair or to pretense (*Institutes* III, IV, 1–2). So feel-
ingly does he treat these matters that he seems to be recalling an
experience of his own of the distress of an unhappy and misguided penitent, at the time unaware of the abundant grace of
Christ. We may say the same of his treatment of the other points
here. He habitually insists that an assurance of salvation is found
only in 'the mercy of God shown to us in Jesus Christ; for in Him
alone is accomplished that which appertains to our salvation'
(*Commentary on the Psalms*, 6:2). In many passages he affirms
his horror of schism. While he justifies separation from Rome
and rejects the papal claims of authority, he nonetheless extols
the glories of the true Church of God, visible and invisible, from
which to depart is defiance of God.

It would seem that in the *Reply to Sadoleto* we have, particularly in the layman's speech, a more or less conscious tabulation

f some of the principal problems that were exercising Calvin's mind before his conversion and the solutions of them found in that experience. Here, as is not the case in the *Commentary on the Psalms*, men as well as God play a part — the 'new teachers,' he calls them. The conversion was thus the culmination of a process of thought and discussion. But again in the minister's speech, it is the divine intervention that is definitive: 'Thou, O Lord, didst shine upon me with the brightness of Thy Spirit.' The paradox here need not surprise us. Psychologists and biographers are familiar with the phenomenon of long-unresolved perplexity, unrewarded toil, and agony of spirit followed by sudden illumination and direction, with a resolution of the distressing problems, for which there is no rational explanation apart from that of divine deliverance.

Suddenly, in the prime of life, Calvin found himself a new man, a man whom God had claimed. Humbled and surprised, he prepared himself for new tasks.

CHAPTER VIII

THE INSTITUTES OF THE
CHRISTIAN RELIGION

— I —

CALVIN's *Institutes of the Christian Religion* is one of the few books that have profoundly affected the course of history. It was in March 1536 that the first edition of the work came from Thomas Platter's press in Basel. Almost two years had then elapsed since Calvin's resignation of his benefices in Noyon. That event had been followed in the same month by the prosecution of his brother Charles for heresy, and his own arrest (26 May 1534) for connection with 'an uproar made in the church.' Possibly this disorder was occasioned by the affair of Charles and was not incited by John. At any rate after two short periods of imprisonment John was permitted to leave Noyon.

His life through the rest of the year 1534 corresponds to the statements quoted in the last chapter from the Preface to the *Commentary on the Psalms:* he moved from place to place, as those who were 'desirous of purer doctrine' sought his guidance. We find him first in Paris, associated with his former host, Etienne de la Forge. Calvin had undertaken not to speak publicly, but he was privately in contact with men emerging into Protestantism. Of these, a paralyzed shoemaker, an upholsterer, a military officer, a mason, and an advocate are known by name; there were also nobles, professors, and students. A socially miscellaneous group, surely, were these first Calvinists. Others whom he met were far from being his disciples — persons of 'Libertine,' Anabaptist, or Anti-Trinitarian opinions. It was apparently at this time that Michael Servetus failed to meet him for a promised conference — an incident that helped to fix in Calvin's mind an unfavorable judgment of that Spanish radical who was later to go to the stake in Geneva. Later in the year Calvin went in turn to Poitiers, Angoulême, and Orléans. He again became the center of a large group of inquirers, some of whom would afterward be evangelical ministers or laymen of some local celebrity. At Poitiers he was intimate with a few legal and theological scholars. Florimond de Raemond affirms also that while there Calvin, without being ordained, administered the Eucharist in a simple rite. It is certain that he wrote his *Pyschopannychia* in 1534, and that the preface of this book was written at Orléans. It was designed to refute the views of some Anabaptists regarding 'the sleep of the soul' between death and judgment. But he was apparently dissuaded by Capito from publishing this strangely peripheral contribution to theology until 1542, by which time he had written on weightier topics. In 1534, too, were written the two prefaces to his cousin Olivétan's translation of the Bible, which was to appear at Neuchâtel in June 1535. Calvin's Preface to the New Testament in this Waldensian Bible contains a passionate avowal of Biblical faith, his first distinct public utterance of this kind.

Calvin was now in a state of detachment from ecclesiastical and academic responsibility, and unwilling to form permanent ties with the variant groups he consorted with. When on 18 October 1534 placards against the Mass were found affixed to many doors in Paris and elsewhere in France, the situation of Protestants suddenly became grave. Before many weeks — about the beginning of 1535 — Calvin was beyond French jurisdiction. With his friend du Tillet he journeyed to Metz, Strasbourg, and Basel. Calvin, as we saw, ascribes his departure from France to the desire to find an obscure spot where, undisturbed by inquirers, he might pursue his studies. But he undoubtedly felt also the peril of persecution. In the months that followed many of those inclined, or adhering, to Protestantism were imprisoned, tortured, and burned. One who suffered was his brave friend, Etienne de la Forge (15 February). The French king, in order to divert foreign sympathy from his victims, declared in a manifesto of 1 February that those punished were only Anabaptists and seditious men. To Calvin they were 'faithful and saintly persons,' and 'holy martyrs'; and that the king should add calumny to cruelty was not to be borne in silence. Calvin then resolved to publish the *Institutes*. It was, he says, his two-fold object

first, to vindicate from undeserved insult my brethren whose
death was precious in the sight of the Lord and secondly,
since the same sufferings threatened many pitiable men, that
some sorrow and care for them should move foreign peoples.

We do not know when the book was begun. By August 1535,
when he wrote the masterly dedicatory letter to King Francis,
the manuscript was substantially ready for printing. Six months
later the modest volume of 520 small octavo pages appeared,
under the title, *Christianae Religionis Institutio*. Nobody in
Basel, he tells us, had known that he was the author. Living
under the assumed name of 'Martianus Lucanius' (the latter an
anagram for Calvinus), he probably succeeded in concealing his
identity from all but a few friends. Jean Oporin, the publisher,
and Thomas Platter, the printer of the book, Simon Grynaeus,
Wolfgang Capito, and not improbably Pierre Viret, Heinrich
Bullinger, and Guillaume Farel, all of whom were then in Basel,
are to be counted among his associates and confidants. The con-
cealment of his name was a device not for safety from persecution
in Protestant Basel but for protection against the distractions
of publicity, that he might concentrate on his book. To read and
write without interruption and without nerve-wracking responsibilities was for Calvin this life's best boon. Not for long, however, was he to enjoy this busy retreat. The *Institutio* was on the
bookstalls, and its title page bore unambiguously the words,
'John Calvin of Noyon, Author' (*Joane Calvino Noviodunensi
autore*). He did not linger in Basel to autograph copies. He was
already on his way to Ferrara, now answering to the name of
Charles d'Espeville, which he had earlier employed in Saintonge.

— II —

The work was to be expanded greatly in later editions, but
even in its first form it was a fairly comprehensive and well-pro-
portioned summary of Christian doctrine. The introduction takes
the form of an admonitory letter to King Francis and is written
with burning eloquence. It is likely that Calvin had serious
hopes of persuading the king. A few months earlier Francis had
invited Bucer and Melanchthon to Paris to formulate a plan for
reforming the French Church, and had sent an emissary to treat
with the Zwinglians and Lutherans. John Sturm of Strasbourg,
then in Paris, had written to Bucer in commendation of this plan,

but also remarking that he now understood what was meant by the passage, 'the heart of the king is in the hands of God' — such was the unpredictability and fickleness of Francis. Calvin knew that there had been in 1534 a possibility that the royal policy might take a turn favorable to the Reformation: might that possibility again arise? He writes with formal courtesy to His Majesty, while indignantly and vehemently denouncing the 'cruel persecutors' who pour into his ears their lying clamors and inflame the people with hatred against the evangelicals. The latter are being condemned unheard, on fabricated charges.

> It is for this reason that I ask you, most invincible King, to take full cognizance of this cause . . . And do not think that I am here concerned with my own personal defense, in order to gain a safe re-entry to my native land. For it I feel a due natural affection, but as matters now stand, I do not much regret being excluded from it. But I plead the common cause of all the faithful, and even of Christ himself.

Certain 'moderate men,' he scornfully states, shrug off the issue by talking of the 'error' and 'imprudence' of those who merely voice the sure truth of God. No one ventures to oppose the persecutors' fury.

> Thus all are ashamed of the Gospel. It is, then, for you, most gracious King, not to close your ears or your heart from so just a defense, especially when it is a matter of such importance as to involve the secure maintenance of God's glory on earth . . . a matter worthy of your attention, of your cognizance, of your royal throne! For this consideration makes a true king: that he recognize himself as a minister of God in the government of his kingdom.

Calvin affirms that the evangelical teaching ('our doctrine') cannot be overthrown since it is that of the Word of God; and he supports his claim by reference to 'the analogy of faith' in Romans 12:6, the rule for all interpretation of the Scripture. Acknowledging ourselves morally naked, blind, and weak, we ascribe all righteousness to God; assured that He is a benign Father we expect all benefits from Him, Whose great love toward us was revealed in Christ. For this trust and hope in God and Christ, believers are being imprisoned, scourged, tortured, or exiled. Calvin becomes vituperative in his indignation against the comfortable advocates of persecution whose kitchen is their religion.

One by one the current charges against Protestantism are now reviewed and refuted. The first is that of novelty: but God's Word cannot be accused of novelty, new though it be to the accusers. It has, indeed, been concealed, but through human impiety. Nor is it, as they allege, dubious and uncertain: so assured are the devout that they fear not death or judgment. It is unreasonable to demand miracles in proof of this faith. If it were new, this might be asked, but 'we forge no new Gospel.' Besides, Satan employs miracles, and they are the stock-in-trade of magicians. There is a weighty section on the authority of the Church Fathers and the tenor of their teachings in relation to contemporary strife. It is only the errors of the Fathers, Calvin asserts, that are cherished by his opponents. If they must allegorize Proverbs 22:28, 'Not to remove the ancient landmarks, which our fathers have set,' why not apply the verse to the Apostles who preceded the Fathers? He quotes from the patristic literature numerous passages that lend themselves to arguments against the ceremonies of the medieval Church, the doctrine of transubstantiation, fasts, celibacy, and the sophistical subtleties by which the Scripture is obscured.

Calvin repudiates the allegation that the Protestant position involves the necessity of affirming the true Church to have been long extinct. The Church has not ceased to be, and will continue to the end of time: but it has not always been visible, and it does not consist of an external organization. To the charges of schism and sedition Calvin hotly rejoins that the devil, disturbed by the new preaching of the Gospel, has raised up pestilent sects, and points out that the Apostles themselves had to contend with the same evil. Here he has reference to the Anabaptists ('Catabaptists,' he calls them), undoubtedly bringing to mind the violent scenes at Münster which had ended just two months before the date of his epistle. But God is the author of peace, and those who obey the Gospel have always lived simple and peaceable lives, practicing all the virtues and presenting an example to their detractors. Envy itself has had to bear witness to their civic integrity. There are laws and penalties for those who would cloak their carnal liberty with the liberty of the Gospel: let not the Gospel be blasphemed through their wickedness. 'Though your heart is now alienated from us and even inflamed against us,' Calvin adds, 'we yet trust that we shall be able to win it, if you will but once, with a quiet and attentive mind, read this confession of ours, which we offer as our defense before Your Majesty.'

Calvin was apparently aware that his book was adapted to serve a double purpose. It was a 'confession' in the sense of being an apology to win immunity from persecution for those who held his opinions; and it was a book of instruction for religious inquirers. At the outset of the epistle he states that he had begun the book to meet the needs of 'multitudes hungering and thirsting after Christ' who had little knowledge of Him. While preparing a simple work of this type, he had been startled by the rising fury of persecution and he had decided to direct the book to the persecutors and to the king. It has still, he implies, its original simple structure, but it is a confession exhibited in justification of its adherents. He refers to it both as 'my confession' and as a 'summary' of the doctrines held by the persecuted. His 'this our confession' at the end of the epistle, and other passages in it, show that he regards himself as speaking for a group united in belief, numerous and resolute, a group that has had no spokesman hitherto and has been grossly defamed and condemned to merciless destruction. The catechetical and apologetic aims of the work were in fact never to be disentangled. If Calvin spoke *for* the French Protestants, he also spoke *to* them. He instructed them while he defended them, and brought them to unity by his instruction. In later editions of the *Institutes* we see Calvin thinking more of the instruction than of the defense. This is the reason for most of the amplification and reordering of materials which we observe in his several revisions of the treatise. Through a quarter of a century, like an inventor perfecting a machine by repeated alterations, he kept reworking it, until at last he pronounced it satisfying to his own mind.

— III —

The *Institutio* of 1536 contained only six chapters. Four of these dealt with the Law, the Creed, the Lord's Prayer, and the sacraments of Baptism and the Lord's Supper. Calvin may have taken this sequence of topics from Luther's catechisms; but he could have found them in numerous medieval books for the instruction of the laity — with the sacraments numbering seven instead of two. Chapters v and vi add controversial arguments to the catechism material. The former is on the five rites miscalled 'sacraments,' because not so regarded in Scripture and the Fathers, i.e. penance, ordination, confirmation, extreme unction, and marriage. The final chapter, on 'Christian Liberty,' treats of the relation of Church and state and amid much thoughtful interpretation of the duties of the Christian life in effect resumes in a systematic way the argument of the epistle to the king.

From the standpoint of public demand Calvin's *Seneca* was, as we saw, a disappointment. The *Institutio,* on the other hand, was a pronounced success. Within a year the publisher informed him that the stock was exhausted and that a revised edition was called for. It has been supposed that a French version either preceded or soon followed the first Latin edition of 1536; but this view rests on slender evidence and no copy of such a text exists. If a French translation did exist, it most probably remained unpublished. Calvin's literary labors were interrupted by his work in Geneva and it was not until after his removal to Strasbourg in 1538 that he had time to complete the revision for the second greatly enlarged edition. Its appearance was delayed by the dilatoriness of a Basel printer, from whom the impatient author recovered it to have it printed in Strasbourg, August 1539, by Wendelin Rihel, printer to the Strasbourg Reformers. The words of the title were interchanged to read *Institutio Christianae Religionis,* and Calvin added here words that may be rendered, 'now at length truly corresponding to its title.' In a part of this edition intended for circulation in France, the author's name was given as 'Alcuinus,' again an anagram for his true name.

Some of the original topics were expanded under new chapter titles, and so much new matter entered the book that its bulk was nearly three times what it had been. The number of chapters was increased from six to seventeen. Of the eleven new chapter titles, two precede the first chapter of 1536 and three follow what had been the final one, while others are elsewhere interspersed with the original six. Some matter has been shifted from the old to new chapters, but in general the additional titles represent new material. Of special weight among these are the chapters on the knowledge of God, on the similarity and differences of the Old and the New Testaments, on predestination and providence, and on the Christian life. Some of the added matter seems to bear the mark of Bucer's influence: the exposition of 'the Christian life,' for example, apparently reflects Bucer's notable book on *The True Cure of Souls*, which had appeared a year earlier, when Calvin was laboring on the revision and had come into happy relations with Bucer at Strasbourg.

In a brief epistle to the reader Calvin indicates that the aim of the revision has been to produce a textbook that would be serviceable in 'the preparation of candidates in theology for the reading of the Divine Word.' He expects to make references to it in Scripture commentaries that he may write, and thereby avoid long digressions. Thus Calvin's book, at first mainly an apologetic treatise exhibiting in a favorable light the faith of his fellow-religionists, was transformed by skillful expansion into a compendium of scriptural doctrine for student use. It was accordingly published in a format adapted for the desk rather than the pocket. Each of the 436 pages measures about 13 x 8 inches and has wide margins inviting the reader's notes.

— IV —

The French version, which came from Jean Giraud's press in Geneva two years later (1541), is Calvin's own translation of the 1539 Strasbourg Latin edition. It is also a landmark in the history of French prose. This is commonly affirmed on two grounds. The first is the fact that no similarly elaborate and serious work of thought had ever appeared in that language. The other reason is its literary distinction. By an almost unanimous verdict of the scholars, the 1541 *Institution de la religion chrestienne* is a French classic, and through it Calvin, with no rival except Rabelais, stands in the van of the fathers and creators of the French literary tradition. It is an impressive fact that this scholar who had been thinking in Latin and writing it with great facility and force shows an instinct for discovering the resources of the mother tongue in the treatment of the highest themes. The style is marked by clarity and dignity, and by sonorous oratorical sentences wrought under the influence of Latin rhetoric. Pannier, in a characterization of Calvin's style, remarks:

The rhythm is now slow, now hastened, it is the work of a man who loves singing, the style of a man cultivated and well-bred, a charming talker and an eloquent orator.

The reader's attention is encouraged by the apt use of vivid images, familiar proverbs, and expressions drawn from common speech. Legal terms in the Latin are sometimes rendered by non-technical approximations — as when *manumissio* becomes *délivrance*. Calvin once more added to his title a new description:

> Institution of the Christian Religion, in which is comprehended a summary of piety and what it is needful to know of the doctrine of salvation. Composed in Latin by John Calvin and by him translated into French, with a Preface addressed to the Most Christian King of France, by which the present book is presented as a confession of Faith.

The 'confession of faith' was, however, the scholarly compendium of 1539 in a new dress. Only in the format is there a resemblance to the 1536 edition. There are 822 small pages in small type. The text was worthy of a better garment. Enough copies got into France to cause anxiety in ecclesiastical and government circles. In February 1544, it was burned at Notre Dame, and later it was formally suppressed.

The Latin edition of 1543, in twenty-one chapters, shows considerable expansion and some free changes of the order of treatment. One of the principal insertions is a chapter (IV) on Monastic Vows. This edition was reprinted in 1545 and with minor revisions in 1550, 1553, and 1554. With the 1550 edition Calvin introduced a subdivision into numbered paragraphs. There were French translations in 1545 and 1551, with numerous printings. The final revision of the Latin *Institutes* appeared from the press of Robert Etienne in Geneva in 1559. In his Preface to this definitive edition Calvin notes that the unexpectedly favorable reception accorded to the book has stimulated his repeated efforts to improve it. Yet he was not satisfied with it until it was brought to its present form, which he hopes will be approved by his readers. He has looked upon it as a service to the Church of God, and has toiled over it while ill, so that if he should not recover it might be left complete as a grateful return to those who encouraged his labors. As in 1539, he states that the object of his revision is 'to prepare students of theology for the reading of the Divine Word.'

— V —

The *Institutio* was now full-grown and nearly five times its original extent. It is divided into four books, and these in a general way follow the topics of the Apostles' Creed: the Father, the Son, the Holy Spirit, and the Holy Catholic Church. Calvin thus treats of God as Creator, as Redeemer, and as Inspirer of men, and describes the Church as the divine society through which and in which God chiefly works with man. The noble symmetry of the structure is suitable to the grandeur of the theme. Each book is divided into chapters with titles; these number eighty in all, and they are conveniently subdivided by numerals. In the interests of order and coherence the arrangement of topics has again been freely altered, and a large amount of new matter is so introduced as to expand and corroborate the lessons of the earlier recension.

We shall later review some of the main elements in Calvin's thought. Almost the whole of his theology is epitomized in the *Institutes,* and the various parts of his system are there displayed in their relative proportions. His other writings gravitate from and cluster about this work. It strikes the discerning reader as a work of literary as well as of theological genius. Calvin is here, as Emile Doumergue has written, *'l'homme de la parole* — the man of the word — of the word of God, of the word of man.' He would have the reader understand that God has been from the beginning communicating Himself by His created works, and by His Word spoken to patriarchs, prophets, and apostles, and that it is in the Holy Scriptures that 'God preserves His truth in perpetual remembrance.' In Calvin's book, the word of man is elevated and vivified by the Word of God, and is employed to communicate its message anew, with deep conviction and arresting eloquence. It is not Calvin's logic but the vigor of his rhetoric and his rarely matched powers of communication, under the sway of religious conviction and emotion, that constitute him, through the *Institutes,* one of the makers of the modern mind.

CHAPTER IX

CALVIN JOINS FAREL
IN GENEVA

— I —

ON THE eve of the publication of his book, John Calvin, alias Martianus Lucanius, disappeared from Basel, to reappear as Charles d'Espeville in Ferrara. We have no record of the journey; it may have led across Switzerland and through the Graubünden or by a more easterly route through the Tyrol. Apparently he went with a double purpose. Like other educated men, he wanted to see something of Italy. And he wished to confer with the gifted French princess Renée (1510–75), daughter of Louis XII, whom ill fortune had made duchess of Ferrara. In her youth Renée had come into the circle of her cousin Marguerite and of Lefèvre, and her sympathy with reforming spirits was well known. Calvin may have hoped that through her favor Ferrara would become the center of an expanding Protestant movement in Italy, and even the base for a mission to France. For a short time she was permitted to make the court of Ferrara a place of refuge for Frenchmen of untraditional and evangelical views. The duke, her husband, Ercole II d'Este, a son of Lucrezia Borgia and thus a grandson of Pope Alexander VI, was, not surprisingly, of another persuasion. His mother, a generation earlier, had peopled the court with Renaissance scholars and artists; would the Reformation here, as frequently elsewhere, follow the Renaissance? Ercole found his wife's friends uncongenial; and her hospitality to religious suspects compromised his position in relation to his natural allies. Under pressure from the Pope and the emperor, he would soon scatter the nest of evangelical refugees. Calvin did not await this conclusion; but during his sojourn (April and May 1536) some of the company were called before the Inquisition.

We know something of Calvin's contacts at Ferrara. He undoubtedly met there the gifted poet, Clement Marot (1496–1544), whose Psalms in French would later be employed in the worship of Geneva. It is not evident that Marot, thirteen years Calvin's senior, took any interest in him at the time. Calvin, always a guide of souls, at Ferrara counseled a French girl, Françoise Bousiron, and formed a friendship with her fiancé, a German medical scholar, Johann Sinapius. Their international love affair, disapproved by the parents of Françoise, was, for the sixteenth century, strangely romantic. Three years later, Sinapius, having married Françoise, wrote to thank Calvin for the advice he had given her, and to recall his own very happy association with him then. It is historically more significant that Calvin found Renée herself responsive to his opinions, and that he made a permanent impression upon her mind. Although he was not to meet her again, he was to be, through occasional correspondence, her trusted spiritual adviser until his death. A year younger than her guest, a woman of no outward attractiveness but of noble spirit, Renée was to live through troublous years in Ferrara and later to maintain at Montargis in France a refuge for her persecuted countrymen.

The city of Ferrara itself was undisturbed by the Reformation, and perhaps its unquestioned acceptance of the Roman ceremonies increased Calvin's vexation against these. He was distressed, too, by the news from France, and by the failure of old friends to take a firm stand on issues he felt to be crucial. Nicholas Duchemin wrote to ask his advice on attendance at unreformed worship services, and in a long letter Calvin warned his friend against 'the sacrilege and filth of Babylon.' On learning that Gérard Roussel, whom he had regarded as an evangelical voice in the French pulpit, had accepted a bishopric, he sent him a vehement and reproachful letter, which begins sharply: 'John Calvin to an old friend, now a prelate.' Assuming that Roussel has deserted the evangelical cause for worldly rewards, he exclaims: 'O Rome, Rome, how thou dost corrupt noble minds!' He writes in a mood of extreme and embittered hostility. Calvin was later to regard more favorably his one-time friend turned prelate, but not basically to modify his antagonism to Rome. These long letters were published in 1537.

The way back from Ferrara, the birthplace of Savonarola,

was evidently through Aosta, the birthplace of St. Anselm. Legend has enlarged upon Calvin's Italian visit to make him a prisoner of the Inquisition, escaping at Bologna, and a bold preacher rejected by the populace at Aosta, where, in fact, a misdated record of 'Calvin's flight' on a stone slab remains to puzzle historians. We may conclude that he paused there on his way and took the St. Bernard Pass over the Alps. The French king had then recently offered a temporary amnesty to religious exiles. Availing himself of this, Calvin visited Paris and, with his brother Antoine and his half-sister Marie, formed a settlement (2 June) of the Noyon property they had inherited. He then set out from Paris for Strasbourg, hoping there to resume the life of a scholarly interpreter and inspirer, from a quiet nook, of the movement in which he preferred to let others take the posts of danger and of power.

— II —

'But God,' writes Calvin, 'thrust me into the game.' It happened through an unexpected contretemps. There was a detour sign on the road from Paris to Strasbourg. Francis I and Charles V were in the opening stage of their third major war. Armies sprawled across the roads forbade passage. Calvin bent his way southward by Geneva, whither his friend du Tillet had preceded him. He went to an inn, planning to spend one restful night and be gone. But du Tillet talked to the reporters. There was a knock on the door of Calvin's chamber, and an importunate caller entered, who felt himself commissioned to remake the scholar into a leader. This was, of course, Guillaume Farel (1489–1565), the venturesome, big-voiced, red-bearded little evangelist and controversialist who had been changing the religious scene in the French-speaking districts west of Fribourg and Bern.

Farel, born in Gap in the Dauphiné of a well-to-do family, was Lefèvre's most aggressive pupil, a second-rate scholar and a hot gospeler. As early as 1523 he had fled from France. Some years later Roussel and others urged him to return, but he had found his function elsewhere. At Basel he was befriended by Oecolampadius, who counseled against fanaticism: but the influence of Erasmus caused his expulsion. Bern rather than Basel was to be his sponsor and base of operation. He spent a period in Montbéliard, where he wrote three small books: an exposition of the Lord's Prayer (1524), a liturgical handbook (1525), and a summary of the Faith (1525). These booklets mark him as a pioneer in Protestant worship and doctrine and have recently begun to attract fresh attention from historians. At the suggestion of Berthold Haller, the Reformer of Bern, Farel went in 1526 to the Pays de Vaud and settled at Aigle as schoolteacher and evangelist. Later he brought Neuchâtel into the Reformed camp. During a sojourn at Orbe, he made a Protestant of the Paris-trained scholar, Pierre Viret (1511–71), later the Reformer of Lausanne and a close associate of Farel and Calvin. A highly provocative preacher, Farel had much experience with angry mobs and bore a charmed life amid physical dangers. He responded to the approaches of the Waldensians of Piedmont when they inquired of Oecolampadius and others concerning the Reformation, and attended their notable synod at Chanforan in 1532. This synod forged a lasting bond between the medieval scriptural heretics and the Reformed Church, and projected the new French Bible that was to be prepared by Olivétan and published with prefaces by Calvin (see above, p. 120). From Chanforan, Farel, with Antoine Saunier and possibly Olivétan, turned to Geneva, which he entered 4 October 1532.

Geneva was the scene of both a religious and a political revolution. From the beginning of the 'twenties, Luther's writings had been attracting the interest of some of the citizens. In 1522, as we have seen, François Lambert, in the midst of his conversion from Franciscanism to Lutheranism, paused there and voiced his novel doctrines. The city's political agitations in the years that followed rendered the situation less uninviting to Protestant preachers. On 1 October 1531, Farel himself had reported to Zwingli that Christ was being imparted to the Genevese. On 2 June 1532, a sale of indulgences having been authorized in Geneva, placards assailing Pope Clement VII were spread about the city. Farel knew that, however roughly he might be received, he could count on some willing hearers. He and his helper were soon hustled out. But a month later another of his aides, Antoine Fromment, a modest and courageous young man, opened a school in Geneva. A Paris Dominican, Guy Furbity, appointed advent preacher by the Council, bitterly denounced Lutherans and 'Germans,' thereby arousing the wrath of the Bernese magistrates, who felt themselves alluded to in this language. Fromment made bold to challenge him, offering to give his body to be burned if Furbity had not spoken 'falsehood and the words of Antichrist.' Fromment had to take shelter in friendly homes; but Furbity soon found himself in prison. On 1 January 1533, Fromment began to preach to numerous hearers. He was set upon and obliged to leave Geneva; but he left converts, and he soon returned. In March came Pierre Viret, who was impressed by the eagerness of many 'to hear the Word.' On 20 December 1533 Farel re-entered Geneva. Less than two years thereafter the city had cast in its lot with the Reformation.

The political story of Geneva is one of the most fascinating of the late medieval city histories. For a century and a half the burghers had been taking to themselves political autonomy at the expense of the bishop, while the counts — after 1416, dukes — of Savoy tried to gain control of both bishops and townsmen. The liberties of Geneva dated back to the 'Franchises' of 1387, by which the judgment of cases between laymen was taken from the bishop's court and given to a board of four syndics elected by the citizens. In 1519 the final stage began in the struggle of the citizens to free themselves from feudal and episcopal rule. The patriots took from the Swiss Confederates (*Eidgenossen*) their party name, 'Eidguenots,' the source, as some believe, of the word, 'Huguenots,' the later designation of French Protestants. After a failure in 1519, they rose again in 1525, and in 1526 formed alliances with their neighbors, Bern and Fribourg. The treaty with Fribourg was to be torn up by that city in 1534, as the struggle went on. In 1528 the *vice-dominus* (*vidomne*), who represented the interests of Savoy, was expelled. The bishop of Geneva, Pierre de la Baume (1522–38), was in bad repute and in the crisis long showed only vacillation. He fled in 1527, and in 1530 called on the duke of Savoy to crush the burghers. Having returned in 1533, he soon took flight again (14 July). The syndics declared the episcopal office vacant (October 1534) while the bishop (from Gex) excommunicated the liberators. With Savoyard aid, the bishop attempted to subdue the city but was long held off by the stout resistance of the citizens, now encouraged by the new preachers. Bern then intervened, though with no worthy aim, in behalf of the beleaguered city (January 1536), and soon scattered the attackers. Bern proposed to take over the authority of the exiled bishop and *vidomne*; but the magistrates replied that Geneva, having suffered for her liberty, would not accept the yoke of a foreign power (February 1536). Bern would meddle in Genevan affairs thereafter, but would never secure mastery of the spirited Rhone city.

When Farel's permanent work began, 20 December 1533, Geneva had no functioning bishop. Although the bishop's vicar sought to keep the episcopal revenues flowing, church authority was being assumed by the magistrates. The vicar forbade the reading of Holy Scripture (January 1534). Bern, taking occasion by this, and resenting Furbity's insults, demanded that a disputation be held in which the evangelicals could be heard against him, and that a church be put at the disposal of the preachers. A Bernese embassy inexorably required that Geneva bring Furbity to debate. Consequently a formal disputation took place in Geneva, 27 January — 3 February 1534, in which Furbity was worsted. Later he was induced to confess that his argument was based on Aquinas, not on the Scripture. He was held prisoner for two years, when he was exchanged for Antoine Saunier, who had been arrested in France. Meanwhile the cause of the preachers was manifestly gaining adherents. The commodious house of Jean Beaudichon was a center of worship, and on 1 March 1534 Farel got the use of a Franciscan chapel. Later that year the services of Farel and Viret on the ramparts where the citizens were meeting the assaults of the bishop's forces won for them the confidence of the people. An unsuccessful attempt to poison them also brought a reaction highly favorable to their message. A second disputation, lasting nearly four weeks, was held in May and June 1535. Wide circulation was given in advance to the five theses on which the preachers offered to debate, and many invitations were sent to foreign theologians; but it was only near the close that two friars appeared to oppose the Reformers, who meanwhile had expounded their theology. The opposition was weak and ineffective. The populace, which earlier had been aroused against the ministers, now tumultuously demonstrated in their behalf. Farel obtained the pulpit of the Madeleine and of St. Gervais, and on 8 August 1535 he was carried by the crowd to St. Pierre, and that venerable cathedral heard its first Protestant sermon. Iconoclastic disorders followed and the councils, moved by a fervent oration from Farel, ordered that the Mass be suspended (10 August).

The old church order seemed to crumble away. I
duced services according to his liturgy of Montbéliarc
course was followed in the dependent villages. The
ship and the new preaching proved acceptable. But th
demands of the preachers with respect to behavior w
eagerly received. A set of severe regulations was adopted (28
February 1536) governing dress, drink, games, and church attendance. Geneva had been accustomed to sumptuary laws and
government directives but it had not always obeyed these. Its
people were given to pleasure and (says a French critic of the
Reformers) 'had a fondness for cabaret life.' In accepting the
Reformation they can hardly have realized what a transformation of conduct would be entailed by their choice.

— III —

Geneva was now governed by a series of councils. The four
syndics, with their four latest predecessors, the city treasurer,
and sixteen others, formed the Little Council, which held responsibility in routine matters. A Council of Sixty had long stood
behind it, and in 1527 a Council of Two Hundred was instituted,
which was still, in 1536, accumulating power. The General Council, or Commune, was the assembly of all citizens; it was summoned only where grave decisions affecting all were to be made.
The syndics and the treasurer were elected by the whole citizenry; the Two Hundred annually elected sixteen members of
the Little Council and were themselves elected by the latter.
The decision of Reformation made by the Little Council and
the Two Hundred required, as Farel was convinced, ratification
by the General Council. It was assembled on Sunday, 21 May
1536, in the cathedral. With uplifted hands the citizens pledged
themselves to live by the Word of God and to abandon idolatry.
They also agreed to maintain a school to which all would be
obliged to send their children, and where the children of the
poor would be taught gratis. Saunier, fresh from imprisonment
in France, was put in charge of the school and given two as-
sistants. 'Thus,' says Eugène Choisy, 'was born the free and compulsory public school.' (Charlemagne and his great bishop, Theo-
dulf of Orléans, had had the same idea, but not much had come
of it in the intervening centuries.)

It was two months later that Calvin came to Geneva. His deathbed statement that confusion then reigned in the Genevan Church is an exaggeration. Farel and his associates were intent on reconstruction and had taken some significant steps in the ordering of discipline, worship, and education. The enforcement of the new regulations was fraught with trouble. For refusing to listen to the preaching, Jean Balard, a former syndic, was ordered to leave the city. The situation was tense and unsettled; it called for talents of a higher order than Farel possessed. Farel apparently assessed truly his own limitations. When du Tillet let it be known that Calvin had come for the night, Farel eagerly sought him out, resolved to enlist him in the Geneva work. The interview was both dramatic and historically momentous. Farel was twenty years Calvin's senior, and a man of flaming zeal. Calvin longed for the library and the study; to Farel this would be desertion of the cause of the Lord. 'If you refuse,' he thundered, 'to devote yourself with us to the work . . . God will condemn you.' Calvin later testified that he had been terrified and shaken by Farel's dreadful adjuration, and had felt as if God from on high had laid His hand upon him. And Farel, when Calvin lay dying, wrote of their unexpected meeting as an act of divine providence.

Such was Calvin's call to Geneva. He picked up some possessions at Basel and was soon back in Geneva, prostrated with a cold. About 1 September his voice was heard by a few listeners in St. Pierre, when he began a course of lectures on St. Paul's Epistles. He was designated by the academic title, 'Professor of Sacred Letters.' It was not until the following February that payment for his services was voted by the Little Council. When Farel proposed this, 5 September 1536, the secretary, not catching the young stranger's name, could only call him in the record 'Ille Gallus' — that Frenchman.

Probably early in 1537, Calvin was admitted to the company of the pastors, by what act or ceremony we do not know. The widely held opinion that he was never ordained to the ministry seems to rest upon the absence of evidence bearing on the point amid the scant records of his early weeks in Geneva. It is sometimes, I believe unjustifiably, supported by citation of his denial in a late tract against Gabriel Saconay (1561) of the statement that he had entered the priesthood and celebrated Mass at Noyon.

There, Calvin, referring to his Noyon period, calls himself 'a simple laic, as they would say,' and adds that he always abhorred the flavor of oil (*Opera* IX, 448). This language has no connection with a possible ordination at Geneva. Nor, on the other hand, should the statement of Francis Junius, who at the time of Calvin's death had been for some years in Geneva, that 'those who preceded Calvin ordained him' (*Francisci Junii Opera*, 1608, II, 1189) be taken as determinative. Both Calvin and Beza refer to his authorization by the 'presbytery' without using the word 'ordination.' Bucer, in November 1536, calls Calvin his fellow minister. Sadoleto, in his attack on Calvin's ministry (1539), does not imply the absence of ordination. Calvin replying to him states, 'I accepted the charge having the authority of a lawful vocation.' There is no evidence that 'those who preceded him' in Geneva were themselves ordained, although it is not unlikely that one of them, Elie Corauld, had been a priest. Corauld was a French ex-Augustinian, now old and blind, who had joined Farel in Geneva. Calvin himself strongly urged ordination, with the imposition of hands, at a synod held in Zurich in 1538, and in various writings he stresses the importance of the rite. It is unwise to dismiss the possibility that he was solemnly set apart to the ministry in some Protestant circle.

— IV —

Lausanne, now under political pressure from Bern, was the scene of Viret's labors. In the Swiss manner, a disputation, to which all the clergy of the Pays de Vaud were summoned, was held there at the beginning of October 1536. Nearly 200 priests and monks came; but competent interpreters of the Roman position, some of whom had been personally invited by the Bernese, failed to appear. Calvin joined Viret and Farel in maintaining five theses, which were circulated in advance. On the third, which affirmed the spiritual as against the corporeal presence in the Eucharist, Calvin took up the challenge of an opponent who claimed the support of the Fathers for his position. By a nimble and surprising flourish of remembered passages from Tertullian, Chrysostom, Augustine, and other Fathers, he put to rout the opposition. But it was Viret who carried the chief burden of the argument. After the disputation, reforms were introduced in accordance with the system of Bern, and these were presently extended throughout the whole territory. A minority of priests who resisted were ultimately banished (1539).

Hitherto the magistracy and citizens of Geneva had adopted Protestantism only in terms of the decision of May 1536 — to live according to God's law and God's Word and to abandon idolatry. On 16 January 1537, the Little Council received from the ministers and adopted a document entitled: 'Articles concerning the Organization of the Church and of Worship at Geneva.' This set of articles was designed as a constitution for the Church, securing to it existence and status apart from the temporary measures taken by the government. Articles now lost, written by Farel and approved the previous 10 November, may have contributed to the January constitution; but it is likely that Calvin was its principal author. It begins:

> Most honored lords: it is certain that a church cannot be called well ordered and regulated unless in it the Holy Supper of Our Lord is often celebrated, and attended— and this with such good discipline that none dare to present himself at it save holily and with singular reverence. And for this reason the discipline of excommunication, by which those who are unwilling to govern themselves lovingly, and in obedience to the Holy Word of God, may be corrected, is necessary in order to maintain the Church in its integrity.

Thus in Calvinism the proper, reverent, and frequent administration of the Lord's Supper, and its protection from profanation, are the central motives of the church discipline. This is emphasized later in the document:

> But the principal order that is required, and of which it is appropriate to take the greatest care, is that the Holy Supper, ordained and instituted to join together the members of Our Lord Jesus Christ with their Head, and among themselves in one body and one spirit, be not stained and contaminated . . . For this reason our Lord, has placed in His Church the discipline of excommunication.

The 'reason' for the Calvinist discipline is not, as is often supposed, to be discovered in premises of ethical or scriptural legalism, but in the sense of 'the Holy' and in reverence for the sacra-

ment as the meeting of Christ and his people, and
as one body in Christ. This is the position of Ca
stitutes, and it is here wrought into his rationale
actually prescribed. Here is the focus of the Ch
norm of membership in the Church is fitness
without profanation, to the mystery of the sacrament, in w...
'we are made partakers of the body and blood of Jesus Christ, His
death, His life, and all His benefits,' and are 'joined in true peace
and fraternal unity.'

Calvin desires that the communion be 'frequently' celebrated
— 'at least every Sunday' — but demands it only once a month
by sequence in the three churches, St. Pierre, Rive, and St. Gervais. To enforce the discipline it is requested that there be appointed 'certain persons of good life and repute among all the
faithful,' steadfast and incorruptible men, who in all quarters
of the city will keep an eye on the life and conduct of everyone.
They are to report notable offenses to one of the ministers and
join with him in fraternal admonition of the offenders. If one
remains unrepentant, he will be notified that his faults must be
reported to the church. If there is still no salutary confession,
the minister is to declare the matter openly, and new efforts are
to be made to overcome the sinner's obduracy. As a last resort,
he is to be excluded from the company of Christians and left
in the power of the devil (cf. I Cor. 5:5) until he gives evidence
of repentance. In this period, in the hope that the Lord will
touch his heart, he is still enjoined to attend the preaching.

If faults of conduct are thus to be detected and corrected, Calvin sees even greater reason to deny toleration within the Church
to 'those wholly contrary to us in religion.' Those who prefer
the Pope's kingdom to Christ's are to be discovered by means of
a confession of faith; and the magistrates are invited to set the
example by making their own confession, whereby it may be
understood that this faith is that by which all the faithful are
united into one church. They should then appoint from their
company some who, with the ministers, will test doctrinally each
of the people.

'We desire,' Calvin adds, 'that the Psalms be sung in the
church,' according to ancient usage and the testimony of St. Paul.
Psalm singing has power 'to arouse us to lift up our hearts to
God'; but there is need of training for this, and he proposes a

oir of children who are to be taught 'modest and churchly singing,' that listening to their clear voices the people may 'little by little' join in praise. A catechism is also to be prepared for the instruction of children; and regulations regarding marriage are to be laid down.

— V —

Such was the project of the ministers early in 1537. The Little Council and the Two Hundred authorized it but showed little enthusiasm for its implementation. Town governments of that age habitually adopted numerous rules for the behavior of the citizens and often failed to enforce them. Geneva had a body of such regulations before the Reformation. It had long been a penal offense, for example, to play at cards, bowls, or dice during church services. In February 1536 a fresh list of prohibitions and restrictions had been adopted. The novel element in 1537 was the association of the restraint of private extravagance and immorality with fitness for admission to the communion. Calvin's intention was that the church authority should determine the communicant's fitness, and that the government should support any ecclesiastical decision to excommunicate. He had probably been influenced by the Basel plan of 1530 (above, p. 82). But the magistrates tended to view their function in another light. For them standards of behavior were the affair of the state and, sharing the common view that the old ecclesiastical discipline had been oppressive, they were unwilling to have the ministers vested with the power of excommunication.

For fourteen months the issue was undecided, while Calvin and Farel strove to establish a system of instruction. As an instrument for this Calvin published early in 1537 his *Instruction in Faith,* a brilliant summation of the main teachings of the *Institutes,* intended for lay readers. This weighty little book was long unknown but came to light in Paris in 1877. Paul T. Fuhrmann's English edition (1949) contains, with copious notes, only about sixty pages of text. The work remains a masterpiece of condensation and simplicity and is unsurpassed as a key to Calvin's teaching. With this went a still more briefly framed Confession of Faith, which had been presented to the magistrates in November 1536 and to which all the inhabitants of Geneva were to be solemnly pledged. It begins with the words: 'First,

we protest that for the rule of our faith and religion we are resolved to follow the Scripture alone.' In twenty-one short paragraphs it succinctly expresses what the Scripture is held to teach
concerning God, law, salvation, grace, prayer, sacraments, the
Church, excommunication, the ministry, government, and other
points of doctrine.

Calvin's conception of the Church involved insistence upon
the personal affirmation of a body of teachings by everyone who
belonged to the community. The medieval Church made baptism
in infancy the basis of membership, and only opinions and conduct that betrayed disregard of the Church's teaching called in
question the individual's status as a member. Calvin applied a
creedal test and wished to invoke the penalty of loss of citizen
ship for failure to meet the test.

Controversy on other grounds than the discipline dogged the
ministers. A visit was paid to Geneva by two Dutch Anabaptists,
whom Calvin met in a two-day debate before the Council of
Two Hundred in March 1537. The Council declared against the
visitors and ordered them out of the city. Calvin's Trinitarian
orthodoxy was challenged by Pierre Caroli, a brilliant Paris
scholar, but highly unstable, who after two periods as a Protestant died in the Roman communion. At this time he had become
pastor of the church in Lausanne, where he attacked Farel and
Viret and reverted to some teachings that the Reformers had
abandoned, such as the doctrine of purgatory. Calvin visited
Lausanne to aid Viret, to whom he was already warmly attached,
and showed Caroli the Geneva *Instruction in Faith*. Caroli responded that such a new creed was uncalled for. The matter
came before a Bernese deputation then in Lausanne; Caroli accused the three ministers of heresy and demanded that Calvin's
Instruction be set aside and that all agree to the Apostles', the
Nicene, and the Athanasian Creed. Calvin objected strongly to
the reaffirmation of the last-named, with its list of condemned
heresies that might become a basis of unfair charges. The outcome was a synod held in Lausanne, 15 May 1537, in which Calvin assailed Caroli in intemperate language but with convincing
evidence that the charge of Arianism was baseless. Caroli was
deprived of his charge in Lausanne. At a later synod in Bern (31
May) he was accused of gross immorality and was forbidden to
preach, while Farel and Calvin were completely exonerated.

While Calvin rejected the requirement of the Athanasian Creed on grounds of liberty of conscience, he saw no inconsistency in requiring the acceptance of his own confession. This he regarded as transparently and undeniably scriptural. Almost naïvely he thought its rejection a violation of the resolution of the people to live in accordance with Scripture. On pressure from him and Farel, the Little Council, in March, April, and May 1537, made repeated efforts to obtain the assent of all citizens. At the end of July there was a gathering in St. Pierre at which groups of people, summoned by the police, gave their adherence; but a good many remained in opposition, and even when the councils gave them the alternative of banishment, their resistance continued.

Bern showed her political hand in Geneva's unrest and began to demand that the rites in Geneva and Lausanne be made uniform with hers. The French-speaking churches had abandoned, under the puritan leadership of Farel, the use of baptismal fonts in the churches and of unleavened bread in the Lord's Supper, and the observance of Christmas, Easter, Ascension Day, and Pentecost; Bern retained these usages and desired their resumption by her neighbors.

On 4 January 1538, the Two Hundred forbade the ministers to exclude anyone from communion. The annual election a month later produced a group of syndics who were opponents of Calvin's policy and a Little Council weighted on the same side. Certain of the former syndics were cast out of the Council, allegedly for unpatriotic negotiation with France, but really for their adherence to the preachers; and the latter were enjoined to avoid politics and preach the Gospel. Without consulting the ministers, the Two Hundred adopted the Bernese ceremonies. Bern had summoned a synod to Lausanne to obtain assent to the ceremonies, and there, at the end of March, Calvin and Farel heard in silence the predetermined action of the synod. Thereupon they appealed to the Bernese to delay enforcement until a general Swiss synod, to meet in Zurich 28 April, should deal with the matter. The request was denied.

— VI —

It was no doubt expected in Geneva that the ministers would yield. But they stood firm, and Corauld, their blind associate, preached with such vehemence against their opponents that he was forbidden to preach again until he should be cleared by the magistrates. He disobeyed, and intensified his attack, but was imprisoned. The magistrates, although greatly embarrassed by their commitments to Bern, offered to delay the introduction of the ceremonies if the other ministers would consent to Corauld's dismissal. They declined both this and the adoption of the disputed ceremonies. They, too, were forbidden to preach, but, since they had not been arrested, they mounted the pulpits on Easter Sunday, Calvin in St. Pierre and Farel in St. Gervais. They refused, however, to administer the communion: to do so in the prevailing controversy would be, said Calvin, 'to profane the Holy Mystery.'

The magistrates, regarding themselves as competent to determine the affairs of the Church, could not tolerate such defiance. The councils immediately took action, and on 23 April a majority of the General Council commanded Calvin, Farel, and Corauld to depart from the city within three days. The secretary of the Little Council records that when the decree was announced to Calvin his reply was, 'Well and good. If we had served men we would have been ill-requited, but we serve a Good Master who will reward us.' Beza's version of the last phrase is, 'I have served Him Who never withholds from His servants what He has promised.'

Calvin afterward felt that he had been unworthily glad to be out of the tumult of Geneva. During preceding days and nights he had been frequently insulted. Obscene songs had been sung, and gun shots fired, under his windows. He and Farel repaired to Bern, where they reported the affair in such a way that the Bernese now sought to allay the trouble their policy had helped to arouse. The Reformers hastened to Zurich, where a synod of the churches of the Protestant cantons was to meet (28 April). At this synod they presented their case and offered conciliatory conditions of agreement coupled with proposals for the establishment of discipline in Geneva. It was not the Bernese rites that they opposed but the imposition of these by act of the magistracy. The synod favored these terms of agreement, and the Bernese deputies were asked to enlist the Council of Bern in seeking their adoption. As a consequence, an embassy was sent from Bern to Geneva. Bullinger, at the same time, wrote from Zurich in the interests of peace. The Geneva councils, however, were induced to reaffirm their decision. Calvin and Farel were turned back as they approached the city.

Calvin was again a traveler. He was soon in the house of his learned friend Simon Grynaeus in Basel, while Farel was lodged with the printer John Oporin. The blind Corauld first joined Viret at Lausanne but soon after, at Orbe, succumbed to his misfortunes and died (4 October). It was believed that he had been poisoned. Calvin was deeply grieved, and so perturbed that he could not sleep. Meanwhile he imagined that Basel would again be an agreeable retreat for his scholarly endeavor. Somewhat humbled by the way his call to Geneva had turned out, he wanted no more of ecclesiastical responsibility and contention. He had no means of livelihood, but he sold his books and rejected proposals of support from du Tillet that would have led him back to the papal Church. He was warmly attached to Farel, and at first they planned to remain together. But when Farel hearkened to a call to the scene of his former labors at Neuchâtel, Calvin declined to follow him thither. Bucer and Capito in Strasbourg urgently invited him to that city. Early in July Calvin was in Strasbourg, where the pastorate of the French-refugee church was offered him. He shrank from the task and hastened back to Basel; and he flatly refused a renewed invitation from the Strasbourg Reformers. Bucer now adopted Farel's startling and once successful method of winning a decision from Calvin. He menaced him with the Divine wrath. 'God will know how to find the rebellious servant, as he found Jonah.' On this stern admonition, Calvin abruptly reversed his decision. At the beginning of September he slipped out of Basel and went down the Rhine to Strasbourg, once again leaving his scholarly utopia for the exacting duties of a pastoral charge.

CHAPTER X

CALVIN'S STRASBOURG PERIOD

— I —

DURING Calvin's three years at Strasbourg, that city was a flourishing center of the Reformation. Evangelical worship had been introduced as early as 1524, when Diebold Schwarz, a young cleric, introduced a German translation of the Mass, with alterations reflecting Lutheran beliefs. Later Bucer and Capito had succeeded in establishing good order in the Strasbourg church, with a full program of preaching, sacraments, catechising, and mutual edification in group life. Their complicated plan for a board of lay workers (*Kirchenpfleger*), three from each of the seven parishes, to co-operate with the ministers in visitation, discipline, and church government was in operation within the limits prescribed by the magistrates, who reserved to themselves the power of excommunication. Jacob Sturm (1489–1553), who for many years headed the government of the city, an able statesman spoken of as 'father of his country' (Alsace) and widely respected in Europe, had supported the cause of the Reformation and had been the principal founder of primary schools, Latin schools, and a school for the children of refugees. The Paris-trained humanist John Sturm (1507–89) (not a relative of Jacob) had just been installed as rector of the Strasbourg *gymnasium*, which he was to make the most renowned and successful of Renaissance schools. He, too, was wholly committed to the Reformation, though he remained one of the most liberal-minded of Protestants, long continuing friendly relations with Roman Catholics and hoping for Christian reunion.

Calvin's Strasbourg period was much more than an interruption of his activities in Geneva. Both church and school had much to teach him, and he was in a mood to learn. From the first he was welcomed, befriended, and advised by Bucer, who was eighteen years his senior and for whose judgment and opinions he had high respect. With John Sturm, whom Calvin had known as a recognized scholar in Paris, he was soon on terms of intimate friendship. They were separated in age by only two years and were from the same general region of France. Sturm's birthplace was Sleide near Aix-la-Chapelle, and John Sleidan the historian, who chose to be known by the name of the village, was his friend and schoolfellow. Sleidan visited Strasbourg more than once while Calvin was there, became his correspondent, and numerous notices in Sleidan's *History of the Reformation* testify to his appreciation of Calvin's work. Sturm's objective in teaching is summarized as the inculcation of a *sapiens et eloquens pietas,* or, as he otherwise expressed it, 'to form men who are pious, learned, and capable of expressing themselves well.' The curriculum was heavily weighted with classical literature, Cicero overshadowing all other authors. Sturm promptly appointed Calvin 'lecturer in Holy Scripture.' Later the *gymnasium* would expand into an academy with a wide curriculum. Calvin's teaching, and that of Bucer, served toward the preparation of candidates for the ministry. Calvin participated happily in Sturm's school; it would later prove a useful model for his academy in Geneva.

In January 1539 Calvin informed Farel that Capito had induced him to give public lectures, so that he would either lecture or preach daily. He was also appointed pastor of the French-refugee congregation. It had been the policy of Jacob Sturm and of the ministers to welcome persecuted evangelicals to Strasbourg, and most of those who came were French-speaking. Florimund de Raemond called Strasbourg 'the receptacle of France's exiles.' The gracious wife of Matthew Zell, one of Bucer's colleagues, had announced the hospitable policy:

> Whoever recognizes in Jesus the true Son of God, the only Saviour, may boldly present himself at our house; we will receive him under our roof, and at our table. One day we also will have a part with them in the Kingdom of God. Lutherans, Zwinglians, Schwenkfeldians, Anabaptists — the wise and the foolish according to St. Paul's phrase — all have free access to our home.

Zell and Capito harbored many distressed fugitives for religion, and Bucer's house near the church of St. Thomas, was, for the same reason, called 'the inn of righteousness.'

The French colony in Strasbourg had listened to the preaching of Farel in 1525, when a number of families had arrived and men so distinguished as Lefèvre and Roussel were in their midst. But the refugees came and went; no organized congregation had been formed, and they were without any preacher when Calvin undertook to be their minister. He preached his first sermon to them on 8 September 1538. The following July he became a citizen of Strasbourg and a member of the guild of tailors.

— II —

Bucer had described the French community as 'a little company,' and Calvin sometimes called his Strasbourg flock 'ecclesiola Gallicana' — the little French church. It seems to have numbered some hundreds: an estimate for a few years later is a little under 500. The congregation first met in the church of St. Nicholas near the southern wall of the city. Two months later it was removed to the chapel of the Penitents (Franciscans) on the left bank of the river Ill; whence it migrated again in 1541 to the church of the Dominicans in the center of Strasbourg, next to the old convent that housed John Sturm's school. As a preacher, Calvin was well received. After a favorable beginning he wrote to Farel:

> The brethren intend, whenever there is evidence of a little church, to permit the administration of the Supper.

'Walloons and others speaking French,' we are told, were present when in November the sacrament was celebrated in the chapel of the Penitents. It must have been a memorable experience for the exiles, and not least for Calvin himself. The atmosphere of fraternal peace and holy gladness was in marked contrast with the troubled scene in Geneva a few months before.

The 'little French church' was remarkable for the hearty congregational singing practiced in its worship. In 1545 a Walloon student in Strasbourg wrote to a friend in Antwerp that he had been unable to refrain from weeping for joy during the first days of his sojourn there when all, men and women, joined together in the psalmody.

> You would not believe the joy that is experienced in singing the praises of the Lord in the mother tongue, as is done here. Each one has in his hand a book of music.

The 'book of music' had been compiled by Calvin and published at Strasbourg in 1539. It was entitled *Aulcuns psaulmes et cantiques mys en chant* (Some Psalms and Canticles with Notes), and contained seventeen Psalms in French meter, one in prose, and the Apostles' Creed, all set to music. Psalms 25, 36, 46, 91, and 138 of this collection were Calvin's own texts; the other Psalms were by Clément Marot, a court poet of France and satirist of abuses, strongly inclined toward Protestantism, who had been with Calvin at the court of Ferrara in 1536 (above, p. 130). A number of Marot's French Psalms were sung at the French court, and were circulated in manuscript, for years before their publication by him in 1542. Indeed, a pirated edition, with alterations of the text, appeared at Antwerp in 1541. Apparently from a manuscript copy of this altered version (the work of Pierre Alexandre, a Carmelite monk), as yet unpublished, Calvin obtained the twelve of Marot's Psalms that were included in the book. Calvin's five Psalms of 1539 were inferior in style to those of Marot, yet not without merit. He also presented the Ten Commandments, with introductory and concluding stanzas, in a poem of twelve quatrains to be sung in the church. His best poem, 'Je Te salue, mon certain Redempteur,' an utterance of warm and personal faith, appeared first in the 1545 Geneva edition of the Psalter. During the conference at Worms in 1540 he found time to write a controversial Latin poem entitled 'Epinicium,' attacking the Papacy. Later Calvin abandoned the writing of verses, having a low opinion of his success in this art. He substituted Marot's versions for his own in the editions of the Psalter.

Calvin's theory of church praise is best understood from the preface to his Psalter of 1542 and its later enlargement. Basically he identifies singing in public worship with prayer: public prayers, he says, are of two kinds, spoken and sung. St. Paul authorizes both.

> And in truth we know by experience that singing has great force and vigor to move and inflame the hearts of men to invoke and praise God with a more vehement and ardent zeal.

Calvin's 'experience' of this had been gained for the most part at Strasbourg, but, as we have seen (p. 139), he had expressed himself similarly in 1537.

It is interesting that years earlier the French refugees at Strasbourg had been a singing group. Gérard Roussel, in retreat there in 1525, when Farel was preacher to them, wrote to Bishop Briçonnet: 'The singing of the women mingling with the voices of the men produces a marvelous effect most pleasing to hear.' Even at that time versions of the Psalms in French were beginning to gain circulation. If the psalm-singing practice had been interrupted, it was now resumed under Calvin. We saw that he had planned to introduce the exercise in the Geneva church. Now he had his great opportunity, and he made the most of it.

Back in Geneva in 1543 he wrote a thoughtful addition to the preface of 1542 to which we have referred, and this he incorporated in the 1545 edition of the book. Here he has in mind the extension of psalm singing to 'houses' and 'fields.' He wants the human voice to become 'an organ of praise to God.' Music, he says, is the first gift of God, or one of the first, for man's recreation and pleasure, and we ought carefully to avoid permitting it to serve dissoluteness and lasciviousness. He cites Plato and St. Paul, and claims music, in words and melody, for morality and worship. It has power to enter the heart like wine poured into a vessel, with good or evil effect. When we have sought thoroughly, we shall find no songs more suitable than the Psalms of David. Since they are inspired Scripture, when we sing them, 'God puts the words in our mouth, as if He Himself sang within us to extol His glory.' Chrysostom bids women and little children, as well as men, to accustom themselves to psalm singing, as a sort of meditation to associate them with the company of angels. The linnet, nightingale, or parrot may sing well, but it is peculiar to man to sing with intelligence, heart, and affection. The book provides the opportunity to commit to memory these 'divine and heavenly hymns of David' in order never to cease from singing them to the exclusion of songs that are frivolous, dull, or vile. The music was to serve the text, not vice versa, to match and convey the 'weight and majesty' of the words.

— III —

As preacher, pastor, and lecturer, Calvin labored hard. He was able to keep in touch with the members of his relatively small congregation, to give thoughtful attention to its discipline and worship, and to shape these in accordance with his principles and the demands of the actual conditions. The Strasbourg authorities gave him a free hand. A plan of discipline was introduced in the spring of 1539, apparently by action of a congregational meeting. He encouraged his people when in trouble to come to him for 'counsel and consolation,' and sought in private interviews the amendment of lives. At Easter, 1540, he required a personal examination before admission to communion. He required students to lay aside the swords they liked to wear to the classroom. An immoral student was excluded from communion until he repented. The *Kirchenpfleger* system of Strasbourg extended to the French congregation: John Sleidan served for a time in that office at Calvin's side.

Calvin's form of public worship in Strasbourg was of historical significance. We know it from his book of liturgy, *The Form of Prayers and Manner of Ministering the Sacrament according to the use of the Ancient Church*. This manual was printed in 1540, but the Strasbourg edition of 1542 is the earliest extant. In that year, too, a slightly different edition appeared in Geneva, and a third Strasbourg edition in 1545 contains an explanation of the various steps in the service of the Eucharist and, as is usual with Calvin, advocates frequent communion. In Strasbourg he tried to obtain consent for a weekly communion, but the magistrates permitted it only monthly.

Calvin's design was to restore essential features of the worship of 'the ancient Church.' His main source for *The Form of Prayers* was Bucer's liturgy, which was a free modification of that of Diebold Schwarz. The outline of the Roman Mass is still readily discernible in Calvin's Eucharist. Indeed, at the beginning he recovered the words of Psalm 124:7 ('Our help is in the name of the Lord') retained by Schwarz from the Penitential Preparation of the Mass but not in Bucer's revision. The *sursum corda* took the form, 'Let us lift up our spirits and hearts on high.' The prayer of confession is followed by a declaration by the minister of absolution from sin for all who truly repent. This is followed by the singing of the First Table of the Decalogue (Commandments 1–4), each Commandment being followed by the *Kyrie Eleison*. After a short prayer the Commandments of the Second Table (5–10) are sung. This treatment of the Commandments illustrates Calvin's emphasis upon the moral law and no less upon the value of singing in worship. The sermon, the collection

of alms, and a long paraphrase of the Lord's Prayer
communion rite.

The Consecration Prayer is mainly Calvin's own cor
It begins, 'Heavenly Father, full of all goodness and
craves the faith that perceives Christ as 'in truth the ho
of heaven for our vivification' and grace to magnify the Name
of God 'by works and words.' After the Words of Institution
Calvin introduces an exhortation in which an exalted view of
the grace of the sacrament is coupled with warnings against the
participation of unfit persons in the holy mystery. The latter
feature became known as 'the fencing of the tables.' At this point
Calvin had been anticipated by Farel in his liturgy of 1525 (above,
p. 132), entitled *La Maniere et fasson quon teint es lieux que
Dieu de sa grace a visites*. The 1533 edition of this liturgy explicitly warns away those who have not true faith, as well as
idolaters, perjurers, frivolous persons, those disobedient to parents and rulers, those who injure and hate their neighbors, the
drunken and dissolute, and all who live wickedly and against
the holy Commandments of God. Calvin's language is similar
but more formal:

> In the Name and by the authority of Our Lord Jesus Christ,
> I excommunicate all idolaters, blasphemers, contemners of
> God, heretics and all who form separate sects to break the
> unity of the Church, perjurers, all those who are disobedient
> to their fathers and mothers, and to their superiors, all sedi-
> tious, unruly, violent, injurious persons, adulterers, rakes,
> thieves, ravishers, the covetous, the drunken, the gluttonous,
> and all who live a scandalous and dissolute life: declaring to
> them that they must withdraw from this holy Table, from
> fear of polluting and contaminating the sacred food that
> Our Saviour Jesus Christ gives to none but the faithful of his
> own household.

not what Christ did

Calvin includes in this exhortation a summary expression of
his doctrine of the Eucharist. Christ, he states, wishes us to participate truly in His body and blood that we may so completely
possess Him that He lives in us and we in Him:

> And though we see only bread and wine, nevertheless let us
> not doubt that He accomplishes in our souls spiritually all
> that He shows us outwardly by these visible signs, that is to

say, that He is the heavenly bread to refresh us and nourish us unto eternal life.

He is not to be sought, says Calvin, in the earthly and corruptible elements that we see and touch. Our souls must be raised to heaven and must enter the Kingdom of God where He dwells. We should regard the bread and wine as signs and testimonies, and seek the truth spiritually where the Word of God promises that we shall find it.

The minister then notifies the people to come reverently to the holy table. He himself first receives the bread and wine, then gives the bread to the deacon and to all the communicants, saying, 'Take, eat, the body of Jesus which is delivered unto death for you.' The deacon presents the wine saying: 'This is the cup of the New Testament of the blood of Jesus, which is poured out for you.' During the distribution of the elements the congregation sings Psalm 138. A noble prayer of thanksgiving and aspiration follows, including a petition for growth in the faith that is effectual in all good works. The service closes with the *Nunc dimittis* and the benediction of Numbers 6:24–6.

The Marriage Service in Farel's *Maniere et fasson* was incorporated in Calvin's *Form of Prayers*. It was short and simple. Included in the husband's vow are the words: 'as is agreeable to the evangelical precepts,' and in the wife's: 'as is prescribed and commanded in the sacred Word of God.' The direction for the office of visitation of the sick leaves all details to the discretion of the minister.

— IV —

At Strasbourg Calvin wrote a number of notable books besides those mentioned above. His *Commentary on Romans* was published in 1539. It was a product of his lectures on the Epistles of St. Paul, begun in Geneva and continued in Strasbourg. This earliest of Calvin's Bible commentaries is one of his best. It is dedicated to his Basel friend, Simon Grynaeus, with whom he had once discussed the principles of scripture interpretation, and who had agreed with him on the importance of 'clearness combined with brevity.' He briefly characterizes the commentaries of Melanchthon, Bullinger, and, with special approval, Bucer, whose work is, however, too extended and too profound for 'humble and not very attentive' readers. In May 1540 Calvin wrote with similar discrimination of Capito, Zwingli, Luther, and Oecolampadius as expositors of Isaiah.

Calvin's *Commentary on Romans* has been in circulation ever since its appearance. He shared Luther's admiration for this Epistle but gave more weight than Luther to historical and philosophical points; but unlike Melanchthon he did not concentrate on difficult passages to the neglect of simpler ones of equal value. The commentator on Seneca was now to be the eminent commentator on the entire New Testament except Revelation (a book which, he acknowledged, he could not fathom) and on all but eleven books of the Old. Most of his commentaries on the New Testament had appeared by 1550; that on Isaiah, the first of the Old Testament series, was published in 1551. Throughout these extensive works, he adheres to his conception of the commentator's task and employs his extraordinary resources of knowledge with surpassing clarity and insight.

In 1540, the year of his first *Form of Prayers,* Calvin published in French his *Little Treatise on the Holy Supper of Our Lord,* a simple and lucid exposition in the form of sixty brief chapters with titles. It is excellently designed as a layman's handbook on the controverted doctrine of the Eucharist, and in its form and style bears a resemblance to his *Instruction in Faith* of 1537 (above p. 140). It will be best to postpone discussion of Calvin's handling of the theme. It may be remarked, however, that a mystical element is present in his exposition of it, and that he stresses the sinfulness of irreverent participation along with the importance of frequent communion. In the closing sections of the *Little Treatise,* he seeks to bring mutual understanding and agreement between the Zwinglian and Lutheran disputants. In 1545 the book was published in Latin and was thus made available to Luther. Melanchthon's son-in-law, Christoph Pezel, reports that Luther picked it up in a book shop and praised it highly, saying: 'I might have entrusted the whole affair of this controversy to him [Calvin] from the beginning. If my opponents had done the like, we should soon have been reconciled.'

Another writing of this time is Calvin's *Reply to Sadoleto,* celebrated as one of the ablest of controversial tracts. Jacopo Sadoleto (1477–1547) of Modena, bishop of Carpentras in the Dauphiné and one of the cardinals appointed by Paul III in

1536, was one of the most admirable of the leaders of the reforming party among the hierarchy. In his encounter with Calvin we see the first notable challenge of the Counter-Reformation seeking the recovery of Protestant territory. Calvin and Farel having been expelled from Geneva, there seemed an opportunity to secure the return of the bishop, Pierre de la Baume, and the restoration of the city to the papal obedience. With this end in view, Sadoleto wrote to the Geneva magistrates a persuasive Latin letter, urging the necessity of unity with Rome and imputing base motives to the Reformers. Unmoved by this argument, the magistrates, having consulted with the ministers of Bern, invited Calvin to answer the cardinal's letter. Since in the previous year they had driven the Reformer out in anger, this course of action was doubtless not expected by Sadoleto. Calvin's reply, dated 1 September 1539, was written in six days. It shows due respect for Sadoleto's learning and worth, but with devastating eloquence dissolves his argument, and hurls back his accusations.

We have already mentioned (pp. 116 ff.) certain passages in the reply that shed light on Calvin's conversion. A marked feature of the piece is the way in which the Protestant conception of the true Catholic Church sharply confronts the medieval view represented by his opponent. Calvin passionately repudiates the charge of schism from the true Church. The Protestant layman testifies that the evangelical teachers 'spoke nobly [*praeclare*] of the Church,' and the minister called to judgment declares that his conscience does not accuse him of having lapsed from the Church:

> Unless indeed one ought to be held a deserter who, seeing the soldiers disordered and dispersed and departed far from their ranks, raises aloft the ensign of a commander and summons them back to their posts.

Such was the Reformer's view of the Reformation — a rallying of the disorderly ranks of the faithful. He protests his devotion to the unity of the true Church, which is based upon the Word of God, not the claims of men, and thus ends his manifesto:

> May God bring to pass, O Sadoleto, that you and all of your persuasion may perceive that there is no other bond of unity than this, that Jesus Christ, who has reconciled us to God the Father, should gather us again from this disorder and unite

us into the communion of His Body, that through His one Word and Spirit we may grow together in one heart and one soul.

A few weeks after this letter was written Pierre Caroli appeared in Strasbourg. Charging Calvin with deriding the creeds and with Anti-Trinitarian heresy, he sought to turn Bucer and Capito away from him. At Zell's house Calvin let himself go in a fit of anger, of which he wrote (8 October) to Farel: 'I have sinned gravely [*graviter peccavi*].' The incident is of little importance save as evidence of a personality defect in Calvin, an ungovernable temper under provocation, which he himself called the 'wild beast.' Caroli's charge was so absurd that Calvin would have done better to smile than to fume.

— V —

Strasbourg was in contact with the whole sixteenth-century reform movement and was now concerned with the efforts of the emperor to pacify the religious parties through negotiations connected with the imperial diets. Calvin's letters of March 1539 show him at a convention in Frankfort, where he had 'a long conversation' with Melanchthon. He reports that Melanchthon shares his views on the Lord's Supper, but he is disquieted by Melanchthon's willingness to make concessions to the emperor. He attended the succeeding conferences of Hagenau and Worms, 1540, and Regensburg, 1541. He sometimes found himself at variance with his Protestant associates, who seemed to him to be insufficiently on guard against damaging concessions to the Roman negotiators. At Regensburg, where Gasparo Contarini and other Roman Catholic theologians conceded the substance of Luther's doctrine of Justification, the hope of reunion of Lutherans with the Papacy was seriously entertained by some on both sides; but Luther was not there, and Paul III was not committed to the views expressed by his own emissaries. Calvin saw the futility and artificiality of the long-drawn-out discussions and was impatient with Bucer and Melanchthon for their resort to 'ambiguous formulae' in order to secure the appearance of agreement. Calvin's letters are among the important source documents for these conferences; they do not indicate, however, that he took a prominent part in them. Evidently he participated without enthusiasm. At the end of a letter describing the Hagenau discussions, he observes that the opposing theologians 'do nothing but amuse themselves,' and remarks wryly that his own sole object, and that of Capito, in attending the conference is 'recreation' (28 July 1540). The same letter, however, affirms on the Protestant side 'inflexible resolution to advance the Kingdom of Christ.' His primary aim in the relations of the churches was to overcome the alienation of Lutherans and Zwinglians, which, he saw, would prove a tragic hindrance to the advance of Protestantism.

In Strasbourg Calvin occupied a conveniently located apartment, where he had a housekeeper and kept a *pension* for a few students, thus adding something to the meager one florin a week that was a belated allowance from the government treasury. The students had been attracted by Calvin's fame, and in his house formed a group for instruction and prayer. In May 1539 we have the first evidence that he had begun to think of marriage. He confided to Farel that the beauty he desired in a wife was that she be modest, obliging, not fastidious, thrifty, patient, and likely to care for his health. His friends proposed in turn two possible choices. He thought the first unsuitable because she was an aristocrat and did not know French. When he was expecting to marry the other he had information about her that caused him to break off the relationship. Then he made his own choice, from among his parishioners.

Early in August 1540 he was married by Farel to Idelette de Bure, the widow of an artisan from Liége, Jean Stordeur, who had been among Calvin's Strasbourg converts from Anabaptism and had fallen a victim of the plague. Idelette was the mother of a teen-age boy, a student to whom Calvin showed kindness, and of a younger girl (Judith), who resided in the Calvin home until her marriage in Geneva. Calvin's marriage would have been one of unsullied happiness had not both parties suffered much from ill health. Idelette became an invalid, and Calvin was increasingly distressed by numerous ailments. On 7 and 10 April 1549 he wrote to Viret and Farel respectively reporting his wife's then recent death. These letters reveal his profound grief, his deep attachment to her, and his high admiration for her qualities. Late in the following year, referring to her as a most exemplary woman, he stated his intention to 'lead a solitary life.' He had shared with her disappointments and griefs. A son born in 1542 died in infancy: 'a severe wound,' wrote Calvin then, 'but our Father knows what is best for his children.' When enemies scoffed at him for having no offspring he answered that God had given him countless spiritual sons.

— VI —

Less than a year after Calvin's departure from Geneva, the magistrates began to discuss his recall. Hostile parties contended over the city's policy toward Bern. The Artichauds were so nicknamed by a play on the word articulants, because their platform was a set of articles of agreement with Bern. The opposing Guillermins, so called from Guillaume (Farel), regarded the expulsion of the Reformers as a blunder and worked for Calvin's return. New severe regulations were introduced but could not be enforced. The four ministers then laboring in Geneva were unable to give competent leadership to the church in so critical a time. The two of these who had been commissioned to Geneva by Bern, Antoine Marcourt and Jean Morand, resigned and left the city in September 1540. The suppression of a riot staged by the Artichauds had left the Guillermins in the ascendant the previous July. On 21 September 1540, the Little Council voted that Calvin should be recalled. Two deputations, and numerous communications, from the Geneva councils were employed to persuade him. Emissaries, finding in Strasbourg that he was in Worms, rode on thither in haste. A letter of 22 October, sent on behalf of the councils and signed by the syndics, was sealed with the motto, 'Post tenebras spero lucem' — 'after the darkness I hope for the light.' This is the basis of Geneva's Reformation motto, 'Post tenebras lux.' The remaining ministers supported the plea in extravagant language.

Calvin expressed privately his genuine dread of Geneva, and long declined the call. Yet he had formerly felt sure that he had been divinely appointed to labor there, and a sense of obligation to the city and its church haunted him. His correspondence gives proof that the decision to return cost him a struggle. The Strasbourgers, too, did what they could to retain him. Finally, persuaded by letters from Switzerland, Bucer consented to his going for a time only. Farel was plying him with appeals, in his urgent, prophetic vein. Calvin received imploring petitions from Swiss

Protestant communities, and from individuals who thought his leadership in Geneva vital to the hopes of Protestantism. His own letters increasingly implied ultimate acceptance. But he insisted on fulfilling his appointment from Strasbourg as a deputy to the Regensburg conference. In June 1541, however, he left the conference under escort of a herald sent by Geneva. Returning to Strasbourg, he prepared to depart. Bucer and the Strasbourg magistrates still insisted that after a sojourn in Geneva he should return to them. They urged him to keep his Strasbourg citizenship and his salary. He declined the latter but complied with the former proposal.

On 1 September he set off to resume his labors and conflicts in the city of which he had written to Viret six months before: 'There is no place under heaven that I am more afraid of.' Having renewed friendships in Basel, intervened helpfully in a church quarrel in Neuchâtel, and paid his respects to the leaders in Bern, he was welcomed with public acclaim in Geneva on 13 September 1541.

CHAPTER XI

REORGANIZATION, STRUGGLE,
AND VICTORY

— I —

WHEN Calvin left Strasbourg he was literally in tears, and he approached Geneva with apprehension amounting to dread. Neither the laudatory phrases in which he was implored to return nor the gracious reception accorded him on his arrival aroused in him any rosy expectations. Only the fraternal support of Viret, who remained with him until the following July, made the first months tolerable. Three other ministers served with him, but he doubted their fitness and loyalty. In 1540, when Farel had been urging him to return, Calvin had written to him the tremendous avowal (24 October):

> When I consider that I am not in my own power, I offer my heart a slain victim for a sacrifice to the Lord . . . I yield my soul chained and bound unto obedience to God [*cor meum velut mactatum Domino in sacrificium offero . . . animum meum vinctum et constrictum subigo in obedientiam Dei*].

Now that he had come back, the difficulties seemed almost too great to be endured. It is not eagerness but an almost sullen resolution that breathes in his first report to Farel three days after his return: 'As you wished, I am settled here: may God direct it for good.' It was Farel whom he associated with the stirring of that inner compulsion that drew him again to the scene of his former defeat. On 15 October, so busy as to be almost distraught, he wrote to Bucer reassuring him that he would unfailingly follow a course of moderation and brotherly kindness. In the following March he confided to Oswald Myconius that the first month had almost worn him out — again affirming that he was scrupulously gentle toward his former opponents. The situation was tense, and very trying to his temperament.

We may well ask, Why? Outwardly all was peaceable. On his arrival, 13 September, Calvin promptly proposed to the Little Council such a reconstitution of the Church of Geneva as would bring it into accord with the Word of God and the ancient Church. At his request the Council appointed a commission of six to frame the project with him. The other ministers co-operated, but rather by assent than actively. The Council also voted Calvin, in view of the necessity he would be under of entertaining guests, the substantial annual salary of 500 florins, together with twelve measures of wheat and two *bossets* (perhaps 250 gallons) of wine. They purchased for his use a house in what is now the Rue de Calvin, and (regardless of elections or of Strasbourg) stated plainly that they would 'keep Calvin always.' They provided for the passage to Geneva, with the family furniture, of Mme Calvin and her daughter, who had prudently remained in Strasbourg.

Calvin was touched by all this compliance and generosity. Yet he knew well that his reception did not imply a basic commitment by magistrates or people to the principles to which he must continually testify, to his concept of a church rightly constituted and truly reformed and of a Christian community properly disciplined and instructed. Actually it was to take him fourteen stormy years to win Geneva (1541–55).

The years at Strasbourg had clarified Calvin's pattern of reform. He knew what he would now attempt in Geneva. His plan soon took written form. In a letter Calvin refers to the work of preparing, with the commission of the Council, 'articles concerning the whole ecclesiastical polity.' A document was promptly drafted, submitted to the magistrates, altered in detail by the Little Council, and further modified by the Two Hundred. Then, without being shown in its changed form to the ministers, it was adopted by the General Council, on Sunday, 20 November. It is known as *Ordonnances ecclésiastiques,* the *Ecclesiastical Ordinances of the Church of Geneva.*

— II —

This historic document may justly rank as one of the most important of ecclesiastical constitutions, since in it the principles of later Reformed Church polities found classical expression. There is no indication that the framers had any thought that their work would prove momentous far beyond Geneva. Like the Rule of St. Benedict, it claims no sway beyond the environment of its origin and no sanction but its own worth and its accord with Scripture and early usage. In both these great legislative documents, however, are laid down general principles of organization and discipline that were bound to command growing attention.

It is abruptly affirmed that Christ instituted in the Church four classes of office-bearers: pastors, teachers, elders, and deacons. The functions of these ministries are defined. Pastors are to preach the Word, instruct, and admonish, to administer the sacraments, and, with the elders, to make 'fraternal corrections.' Candidates for the pastoral office must give proof of their vocation to it, first by passing a test in doctrine and being approved in conduct, and second through the stages of presentation by the ministers, acceptance by the Little Council, and consent of the people. The imposition of hands, though held to be apostolic, is for the time omitted because of then current superstition regarding its use. In view of Calvin's claim at Zurich in 1538 'that the imposition of hands ought to be in the power of the ministers,' without interference by the magistrates as in Geneva, it is probable that the real reason for its omission had to do with the unresolved issue of authority. Even the initiative here assured to the ministers in accepting ordinands would be challenged later by the Council. It was required that new ministers swear obedience to the magistrates and the laws of Geneva. The oath taken by four newly appointed pastors, 16 July 1542, guards, however, liberty to obey God in work and teaching.

Many alterations made by the councils in the original draft were manifestly intended to strengthen government control of church affairs. Nor should we overlook the probability that the draft reported out of the commission was itself the compromise outcome of debate. The accepted document offered numerous departures from Calvin's ideal, yet it retains many of the essentials of his concept of the Church.

The provision for a weekly discussion meeting of the ministers in Geneva and the dependent villages instituted a notable feature of church life. Intended to promote doctrinal unity, these meetings had also possibilities of contention. In such case the elders are to be called in, and if they fail to allay the strife the magistrates are to pronounce judgment. By such regulations the supremacy of the magistrates over the ecclesiastics is safeguarded. Other notable features here involved are the discussion method itself and the authority accorded to elders.

The ministers were also required to attend quarterly meetings for such administration and mutual discipline as they could exercise independently. The principle of 'fraternal admonition' was to be employed when a brother offended. This quarterly assembly, called the Venerable Company, although not a political organ and very limited in authority, held a notable place in the moral structure of the reformed city.

By the annexation of three former small parishes to the parish of St. Pierre, the Church of Geneva now had three parishes only, St. Pierre, St. Gervais, and the Madeleine. On Sundays, there was a service at St. Pierre at daybreak, one in each church at nine, and one in each of the first two at three o'clock. The 'little children' of each parish were to be brought at noon for instruction. Preaching services were held also in each church at successive hours on Monday, Wednesday, and Friday mornings. Only a popular interest in the unfamiliar doctrines of the Reformation, and in the Bible, made possible the maintenance of so heavy a schedule of services in a city of 12,000 people.

The order of doctors, or teachers, was distinguished by Calvin from that of pastors (cf. Eph. 4:11). The teachers were charged to guard the purity of doctrine and to secure a succession of well-equipped ministers. Lectures in theology constituted the most advanced labor of the teachers. Since knowledge of languages and sciences is a requisite for these studies, it is declared that a college must be established to instruct the young and prepare them both for the ministry and for civil government. Girls are to have a school, as formerly, apart from the boys.

— III —

The order of elders (*anciens*) takes a remarkable place in this constitution. Here we have Calvin's mature provision for a class of lay associates in discipline and the guidance of souls. Similar proposals had been made by Oecolampadius and Bucer, and by Farel and Calvin himself in the Articles of 1537. In the latter, the description is merely: 'persons of good life and good repute, dependable and not easily corrupted.' But, as is evident from the 1539 edition of the *Institutes,* Calvin had come to regard the elders as a divinely authorized order of ruling (as distinct from preaching) presbyters (*Institutes* IV, *xi*, 1, 6). Some have supposed that at this point he had felt the influence of the Strasbourg Anabaptists. It has been argued by Jaques Courvoisier that this new emphasis corresponds to, and is derived from, Bucer's *Kirchenpfleger,* lay curators of the church, in Strasbourg (above, p. 145). Bucer, however, did not assert the autonomy of the Church as over against the state. Calvin wished to secure this, and doubtless had it in mind in according to the lay officers a scriptural authority.

Yet nowhere do we see more clearly than in this ordinance the extent of the concessions wrung from Calvin by the politicians. The twelve elders were chosen from, and by, the magistracy. They were nominated by the Little Council: two were members of that council, four of the Council of Sixty, and six of the Two Hundred, which council finally ratified the choice. Their work and fitness came under annual review by the Little Council, which could dismiss them. The word 'elders' was repeatedly explained in the revised document not as an apostolic ministry but as 'commissioners and deputies of the Council to the Consistory.' The ministers were merely consulted in the nominations.

Though politically appointed, the elders were entrusted with tasks that were, in Calvin's eyes at least, ecclesiastical. They were to be chosen from the various districts of the city, and selected for their good character and spiritual wisdom. They were to watch over the lives of all, to admonish lovingly the disorderly, and, where necessary, report to their brethren in the Consistory, who would take measures for the 'fraternal correction' of the offenders. 'Fraternal correction,' * or 'admonition,' is a favorite expression of Calvin. Based upon such passages as Heb. 3:13, and occurring often in the Church Fathers, it became an emphasis in the pastoral theology of the Reformers.

The twelve elders were joined with the ministers — who at first numbered only six — to form the Consistory. This was

* It is unfortunate that a widely used and usually accurate college textbook (J. H. Robinson's *Readings in European History,* II, 133) has 'paternal' for 'fraternal' in the translation of this passage.

the principal organ of church discipline, and in it, ordinarily, not Calvin or another minister but one of the syndics presided. Calvin states in the *Institutes* (IV, xii, 4–5) that in discipline, in accordance with II Cor. 2:7, severity ought always to be tempered with mildness. He values discipline for the protection of the Church's purity and as a means of inducing repentance. Corrections, he says, are medicine to restore sinners to the Saviour. Yet the Consistory of Geneva has been regarded as the engine of a tyrannical discipline. We have seen that narrow regulations were long familiar in Geneva: it was surprising only to insist upon their enforcement. In the confusions of the years 1538–41, with Calvin absent, the authorities had adopted a severe course. They had forced compliance with the new beliefs and practices on pain of exile and had visited the homes in order to destroy images. The councils were inclined to be oppressive through anxiety. The severity of the regime after 1541 is also much more connected with the councils than with the Consistory. The Ordinances required the latter to turn over to the magistrates for punishment stubborn and criminal offenders. The cases that were finally judged in the Consistory were minor, and most of them trivial. The position of the Consistory was long ambiguous, since it had no power of corporal punishment and claimed none, and for many years was unable to act independently in excommunication. Nevertheless, from its first meeting, 6 December 1541, it introduced a new systematic supervision of the morals and habits of the people.

The fourth order recognized in the Ordinances of 1541 is that of the deacons. They are said to be of two kinds, those who manage the funds of the church and those who minister to the sick and needy. Both of these were to be elected in the same manner as the elders. Provision was made for a charity hospital (in addition to the recently established one for travelers, and the pest-house); a physician and a surgeon were appointed to attend patients in the hospital and in the homes of the poor.

The Ordinances contain also brief statements on Baptism, the Lord's Supper, marriage, burial of the dead, and visitation of the sick and of prisoners. For greater publicity Baptism was to be administered at preaching services, and near the pulpit. Calvin's plan that the Lord's Supper be celebrated in one of the three parishes each month and in all thrice a year was altered to provide for a communion in all churches four times a year, at Christmas, Easter, Pentecost, and on the first Sunday in September. The use of a communion table in a space near the pulpit is prescribed. Marriages on any day are approved, with the exception of communion Sunday, 'for the honor of the sacrament.' Matrimonial disputes are to go to the magistrates, who may at their discretion ask advice from the ministers. At funerals, 'superstitions contrary to the Word of God' are to be excluded. When any one falls sick a minister must be notified within three days: relatives and attendants are to be enjoined not to delay this, lest religious consolations come too late. The magistrates are to permit a minister to visit, for exhortation and consolation, prisoners under sentence of death.

— IV —

It is needful to add some details on the discipline in Geneva. As was natural, the magistrates frequently arrested offending citizens without action by the elders. Weekly, on Thursday mornings, offenders noted by the watchful elders were haled by a police officer before the Consistory. They were often privately counseled and admonished in advance by Calvin or another minister. The records of the Consistory and of the councils exhibit extraordinary minuteness and variety in the offenses reported for correction. Non-attendance at church and contemptuous deportment during services are very common. Other cases show a hankering after medieval religious practices. Many are the ordinary misdemeanors of an ill-disciplined town, such as drunkenness, gambling, profanity, family alienations, wife beating, and adultery. The Consistory's penalties ranged from admonition to humiliating acts of penance resembling in some degree those employed in the second and third centuries, which, indeed, they were designed to imitate. In many instances the experience seems to have effected a real 'correction' of conduct and attitude. In others the discipline was hotly resented, and the issues raised convulsed the city. The conscientious censors apparently overlooked nothing and exempted no one. Many of those penalized were loyal partisans of Calvin: they included his brother's wife. Minute misdeeds and casual flippant utterances were treated with gravity by the Consistory. The wife of Ami Perrin, commander of the militia; the treasurer of the city,

Pierre Tissot, his vindictive mother, and his wife; and the free-living old patriot, François Bonivard, 'the Prisoner of Chillon,' could testify that no class of offender escaped the 'fraternal correction' of the austere tribunal.

The more important cases were dealt with in the Little Council before or after they were handled in the Consistory. Co-operation between these two authorities was, on the whole, well maintained. The elders, being appointees of the Little Council, had an eye to its approval. Yet being closely in touch with Calvin, they evidently fell under the influence of his thought and zeal. Despite many rebuffs, Calvin also gained the increasing respect of the magistrates, who in time took courage to assail the corrupting forces in the community. There was no thought of a separation in membership of church and citizenry. The Christian community envisaged by all parties was composed of the same people as the civil community. Calvin was well aware that environment forms character and habits, and he pressed for the extermination of the community sources of moral delinquency. The censorship over amusements went to excess. Games of chance were permitted only under severe restrictions; dancing was regarded as a diabolical incitement to lust and was prohibited. Léon Wencelius has pointed out that Calvin had only praise for the dancing to express joy in God recorded in the Old Testament. But as it had been practiced in Geneva dancing featured kisses and embraces and was undoubtedly lascivious in a high degree. In fact, it had been forbidden by the syndics before Calvin was born, but the regulation had gone unenforced.

Moral conditions were, indeed, such as to invite drastic reform. Medieval Geneva, by common consent of historians, abounded in centers of dissolute pleasure. Even contemporary opponents of the Reformation freely accuse the pre-Reformation clergy and friars of appalling misbehavior; and while this was resented by the people, it was also imitated by them. Genevese gaiety was often associated with intemperance, obscenity, and licentiousness. Calvin and the authorities resorted to repressive measures to eliminate the numerous taverns and houses of prostitution. An attempt was made in 1546 to replace the taverns by centers of innocent entertainment, called *abbayes*. The keepers of these were to be watchful against excessive drinking, protracted games of cards, obscene or irreverent songs. They were to keep a French Bible displayed, encourage religious discourse and conversation, serve no food to those who did not say grace, and close at 9 p.m. But the *abbayes* were boycotted, and in three months the taverns reopened. The censorship of drunkenness and vice and the establishment of closing hours for the public houses tended, however, to chasten the nighttime behavior of the Genevese. Prostitution, it would seem, was rather effectively suppressed.

The drama, which had never been other than trivial in Geneva, survived only as an occasional school exercise. Calvin was fond of thinking of the created universe, or of the Church, as 'the theater of God's glory.' He thought less highly of the theater in which the actors are human. It was with his approval, though without his interference, that a play about Hercules was forbidden in 1546. Immediately afterward, a play written by the pastor Abel Poupin, dramatizing incidents from the Book of Acts, was produced, with elaborate stage setting and costumes paid for in part by the city. It was presented about ten times, with the approval of the Venerable Company, when one of their number, Michael Cop (a brother of Calvin's old Paris associate, Nicholas Cop), in a sermon violently condemned it as 'shameless.' There ensued an angry quarrel, in which Cop's freedom to preach became the issue. To secure this freedom, and quiet the contention, the ministers, led by Calvin, asked for the suspension of the play until a more favorable time (12 July 1546). Thus, almost inadvertently, Calvin lent himself to the supression of the drama. The favorable time never came. Thereafter the only plays in Calvin's Geneva were those acted by schoolboys. One, at least, was a comedy of Terence; one was in remembrance of five Protestant students burned at Lyons, and *The Pope Nearing His Death* was the title of another.

The drama was not the commanding art that it later became. Shakespeare was an infant when Calvin died. The dramatist may have read in the English edition of Calvin's Sermons on Job the equivalent of his line, 'All the world's a stage.' Calvin perhaps appreciated the use of drama in education, but he made no contribution to its development as a community activity or a companion of the Church. Nor did the Reformer have any substitute for the indecent dances that he and his colleagues condemned. Calvin's view of the dance in effect closely parallels that often expressed by medieval moralists, who regarded its contemporary practice as sin, mortal or venial according to circumstances. Thus Etienne de Bourbon, Dominican preacher (d. 1223), condemns dancing in churchyards as 'kindling the fire of lechery' and Thomas of Chantimpré (c.1260) would 'partly but not wholly' excuse wedding dances, not others. Without repudiating the drama or the dance as such, Calvinism so condemned their contemporary expressions as almost to extinguish them, and did nothing to revive them in more desirable forms.

— V —

Calvin's progress in Geneva was a campaign marked by battles fought and victories won against numerous opponents. To some of these we must give brief attention. In 1542, Sebastian Castellio (1515–63), a humanist turned Protestant through witnessing persecutions, came to Geneva as rector of the school. Finding his salary inadequate for his large family, he sought admission to the pastorate, and the Little Council approved the request. Constitutionally, admission to the ministry rested, however, with the ministers. Calvin led them in rejecting the candidate, while proposing that his salary be raised. The difficulty lay in points of doctrine and in the fact that Castellio in translating the Scriptures used language Calvin felt to be intentionally debased and shocking. Moreover, Castellio held the Song of Solomon, which Calvin like most others was prepared to interpret as an allegory of Christ and the Church, to be an obscene composition in which the royal author 'described his wanton amours.' The Biblical basis of Calvin's system was endangered by such an attitude to a canonical book.

Castellio tried to find work elsewhere: indeed, Calvin asked Viret to help to get him a post in Lausanne. But a sojourn there was fruitless. In April 1544 he was back in Geneva, renewing his appeal. At a weekly meeting of the ministers, some scores of laymen also being present, Castellio somewhat ineptly denounced Calvin and his colleagues not only as utterly unlike St. Paul but as gluttonous, drunken, and wanton playboys. Two weeks later, after full inquiry, the Little Council decided that 'Monsieur Bastien' should leave the city. In July he departed for Basel, bearing with him a letter from Calvin and the other ministers, in which they warmly approved his former work and explained the theological reasons for their refusal to admit him to their ranks. Jean Oporin gave him part-time employment in proof-reading; but he lived in poverty until he became a teacher of Greek in the university of Basel (1553?). By his important book, *Whether Heretics Ought To Be Persecuted* (1554), he became the most distinguished sixteenth-century exponent of religious toleration (see below, p. 176).

The word 'Libertine' was used by Calvin to designate a religious sect, widespread in France and the Netherlands, which in emphasis on the 'Spirit' rejected the law. Later the term came to be applied in Geneva to a party of opposition to the discipline, which included persons who flouted the moral law and others more politically motivated in resistance to Calvin. The wife of Pierre Ameaux, a manufacturer of playing cards, advocated and practiced 'free love.' To Ameaux's anger, Calvin hesitated to sanction a divorce from her; but this took place, and she was imprisoned. At a dinner Ameaux became eloquent against Calvin and his supporters, impugning his teachings. Imprisoned by the Council, Ameaux was called upon to ask pardon of Calvin; but to Calvin a condemnation of his doctrine was an attack upon Holy Scripture and called for no casual penalty. Finally the Little Council forced Ameaux to traverse the city coatless and hatless, at three places pleading on his knees for mercy, and to promise future conformity and obedience (5 April 1546). Sympathy for him was silenced by the erection of a gallows near his home and by the dismissal of two preachers who had been compromised by association with him.

François Favre and his family represented a class of well-to-do citizens whose easy morals were incompatible with the new regime and who fancied that their social station would secure to them immunity from penalty. In February 1546 Favre was accused of immorality and excluded from communion. Soon afterward, his son Gaspard had to answer a similar charge. When set free he took revenge by playing a noisy game outside a church where Calvin was preaching. Franchequine, daughter of François, was the wife of a distinguished citizen, Ami Perrin. On 21 March 1546 Perrin, his wife, and a gay company danced at a wedding. They were promptly imprisoned by the Council, then released, and sent to the Consistory for a reprimand. Franchequine screamed defiance and abuse, particularly against Calvin, who sarcastically inquired whether the Favres were above the law and must have a new city built for them. He looked upon their false denial of the charges against them (which they later admitted) as 'contempt of God.' A further clash with the authorities resulted in the flight of the father and the daughter from Geneva. Another Favre, Jean, when being married by Abel Poupin, responded to the essential question by shaking his head in derision: he was imprisoned. Calvin sought the repentance of François Favre and his daughter; they returned and were finally reconciled to him, and to the Church.

Perrin was sent to France to pay Geneva's respects to the new king, Henry II (1547). Calvin, whose return to Geneva had been strongly advocated by Perrin, now wrote him seeking an understanding. But after Perrin had returned, a French friend of Calvin, Laurent Maigret, exposed the fact that Perrin had engaged in unauthorized discussions with French diplomatists. Countercharges were raised against Maigret, who was imprisoned. The 1547 February elections had registered a reaction against Calvin. He now felt his position in Geneva highly insecure. He was frequently insulted in the streets. While he expected a repetition of the experience of 1538, he made no compromises. Perrin now attacked on a new sector, that of the restriction on clothing. He was commander of the militia. Might the *arquebusiers,* he asked, wear slashed breeches at the May target festival, in the manner of Bern? It was a trifle, Calvin said, but the gay patches would prelude unrestrained luxury. The Council's answer was no. Perrin nursed his grievances.

— VI —

Calvin thought Perrin 'a comic Caesar,' but tragedy was to follow. Jacques Gruet was another of the political Libertines who resented the discipline. He held extremely negative views on religion. He was arrested when an anonymous threatening note, written in a curious Savoyard patois, was found affixed to the pulpit of St. Pierre. Calvin was much more hostile to Gruet than he had been to Perrin; and the prevailing sentiment toward Gruet's opinions was one of horror. He was tortured in the manner of that age, and his papers were searched. Some of the evidence on his views came to light only later, but enough was shown to convict him of blasphemy, scoffing at divine and human law, advocating licentiousness, and treasonable correspondence, besides threatening the ministers. He was beheaded on 26 July 1547, Calvin consenting to his death. Calvin was moved by a dread of the perversion of Genevan youth (letter of 24 July); but a certain vindictiveness appears also in his references to the case.

The tide seemed to be rising against Calvin. On 13 December 1547 he quelled a tumult raised by the Libertines. Rushing into an armed crowd that had gathered to intimidate the Two Hundred, he cried out: 'If you must shed blood let mine be the first.' He finally secured a hearing and delivered an address, which subdued the excited populace. But the next day he wrote, 'I despair of holding this church any longer,' and two weeks later, 'I wish God would grant me my discharge.' The ensuing Christmas communion was preceded by a reconciliation with the Perrinists, effected by Calvin and ten appointed 'peacemakers'; but mutual distrust continued, and Perrin soon resumed his public hostility to Calvin.

In May and July 1548, Calvin reproached the Little Council, now for the most part unfavorable to him, for permitting disorders. A new opponent, Philibert Berthelier, son of a noted patriot, with his uncle, Pierre Vandel, organized an active opposition party, whose members, in contempt of the law, wore a party badge — a white cross. When Calvin protested, the Council turned its censure upon Calvin for condemning this infringement of the rules. He virtually challenged the magistrates to dismiss him for taking his stand against this dangerous faction. They evidently did not feel, then or later, that the dismissal of Calvin, which they were free to order, would be safe or wise. After February 1549 Perrin's supporters were in full power, but their aim was to subdue Calvin rather than to dismiss him. He bore constant annoyances and insults, certainly with no stoical composure but with an invincible spirit that sometimes won tribute even from opponents — all the while maintaining an intellectual activity far beyond the possibilities of most scholars more comfortably situated. The conviction of divine approval mightily sustained him; but he never enjoyed his conflicts. There was something in Luther and in Knox that made them capable of delight in combat. Calvin winced with sensitivity and apprehension, even while to opponents he appeared hard as steel. Not without reason, he called himself timid. He suffered under hostility and shrank from his fellowmen in their moods of violence. But to Nehemiah's question, 'Should such a man as I flee?' he continued to give the answer of a dedicated spirit.

— VII —

The struggle took new forms, with new opponents. In October 1551 a refugee from France, Jerome Bolsec, ex-Carmelite and physician, denounced Calvin's doctrine of predestination as false and absurd. Calvin charged him before the Council with errors and misstatements. The trial that followed was a test for Calvin and his influence, and involved a theological discussion before the magistrates. Basil, Zurich, and Bern were consulted: they failed to condemn Bolsec without qualification. But the Council finally voted to banish him. After other Protestant associations, Bolsec returned to the Roman obedience. In 1577 he published a life of Calvin abounding in defamatory falsehoods.

Predestination was the point of attack also of Zeraphin Trolliet, a Genevan ex-monk who had been excluded from the ministry and now practiced law. When he took issue with Calvin the Council again heard this topic debated. It prudently rendered one verdict to the effect that Calvin was a true teacher and a good man, and another that Trolliet was a good man and a good citizen (15 November 1552). This did not end the matter, but a reconciliation came later, and when Trolliet lay dying he asked for and received the consolations of Calvin.

In Geneva as elsewhere, witchcraft was a capital offense, and the mode of death was burning. Many thousands of alleged witches suffered this inhuman penalty in sixteenth- and seventeenth-century Europe. During the plague, charges of witchcraft were certain to be made. For two years, 1543–5, Geneva was afflicted with the plague, and witch trials and burnings were numerous. In one year there were more than twenty victims. Calvin held traditional beliefs about witchcraft, was involved in the prosecutions, and did nothing to assuage this irrational cruelty. He believed, too, that depraved persons were spreading the plague by smearing infected matter on door latches. A minister, Pierre Blanchet, volunteering to serve the plague-stricken, soon died of the disease. Calvin and Castellio both offered themselves, but the magistrates forbade Calvin to undertake the work, and Castellio, for reasons unknown, did not enter upon it. Unjust aspersions have been cast upon Calvin in this connection. He had earlier in visits to the sick exposed himself to the pest in repeated instances during his ministry in Strasbourg.

— VIII —

In the statistics of judicial burnings in Geneva some historians have confused witchcraft with heresy; and they have even charged Calvin with the burning of both types of offenders. But this is to befuddle the whole matter. Only one man was burned for heresy; in this case Calvin tried to have the penalty changed to decapitation; and Calvin had no power to burn or otherwise execute anybody. Witchcraft had, indeed, been treated as heresy in a celebrated papal bull of 1484, but it was hardly so considered in Geneva; and certainly the number of deaths for witchcraft should not in twentieth-century books be reported as deaths for heresy.

The singular case of Servetus has become the most celebrated of executions by fire for heretical teaching. Michael Servetus (1511–53), of Villanova in Aragon, was educated in theology, law, and medicine. At Toulouse he read the Bible and took it as authoritative, but employing his speculative gifts, drew from it the basis of a drastic revision of traditional beliefs. He traveled widely, forming the acquaintance of Melanchthon, Oecolampadius, Bucer, and other theologians, who sought in vain to modify his startling opinions. His work *On the Errors of the Trinity* (1531) affrighted the theologians. A marked man, he followed Calvin's example by disguising his name, calling himself Villeneuve from the family estate of Villanova. At Paris he became a brilliant medical scholar and wrote on various scientific subjects. For years he practiced medicine at Vienne. Through a third party he engaged Calvin in an epistolary controversy, in course of which Calvin detected that Villeneuve was that Servetus who had once failed to honor an appointment with him in Paris, and who had challenged the doctrine of the Trinity. A copy of the *Institutes* sent for his instruction was returned with copious and contemptuous marginal notes. In long letters he proposed to deliver Calvin from his delusions.

As a thinker Servetus was learned, original, challenging, and resourceful, but disorderly. He crowned his theological revolt by his *Christianismi Restitutio* (1553), directed for the most part against Calvin's *Institutio*. Thirty letters to Calvin are inserted in it, and a section on the Trinity is addressed to Melanchthon. Servetus regarded the doctrine of infant baptism as diabolical, and he denied original sin. But it was his assault upon the doctrine of the Trinity that attracted most attention. The traditional Trinity is likened by him to a three-headed Cerberus; the Godhead is indivisible; the mystery of the One in Three is rejected. Jesus was not Eternal Son, but was human and became divine. Because of the Trinitarian error, Jews and Mohammedans deride Christian stupidity and are repelled from Christianity. Servetus casts himself in the role of another Michael — the archangel leading the angelic host against the minions of Antichrist.

Calvin soon obtained a copy of the *Restitutio*. To his mind it was 'a rhapsody patched together from the impious ravings of all the ages.' As early as February 1546, referring to a letter of Servetus, Calvin had written that should the heretic come to Geneva he would use what authority he might have to prevent his getting away alive. The enmity of Calvin now reached Servetus in Vienne. Guillaume de Trie of Lyons lived in Geneva and was in Calvin's confidence. He informed a Roman Catholic correspondent in Lyons that Villeneuve the physician was Servetus the heretic, and the author of the *Restitutio*. Pages from the book and manuscript materials supplied by Calvin were sent in evidence, though, as De Trie stated, these were drawn from Calvin 'with the greatest difficulty' and after an earnest plea. No real reason has been shown to doubt this statement. Had he wished, Calvin might have exposed Servetus to the Inquisition years earlier. But he must have known that the documents would be of the greatest interest to any Inquisitors who might see them. So, indeed, it proved. At Vienne, Servetus was tried and, after much prevarication about his identity and other matters, was in danger of his life when he escaped an inattentive jailor. He was sentenced in absence to be burned alive, and was burned in effigy, with much of the stock of his new book.

He hoped to reach Naples, but a fatal fascination drew him to Geneva, like a moth to the candle flame. He was a guest at the 'Golden Rose' on Sunday, 13 August 1553, having arranged to take a boat on the way to Zurich; he attended church, was recognized, accused by Calvin, arrested, and imprisoned. Calvin later fully acknowledged his part in the detention of Servetus and in the preparation of charges of heresy against him, adding, however: 'I never moved to have him punished with death.' This is possibly true in a literal sense. Yet he certainly hoped that Servetus would be 'punished' and had vowed seven years earlier to bring him to death if he could.

— IX —

It should not be forgotten that not only Calvin's authority but also his security of tenure had fallen low. The elections had consistently gone to his opponents. He appears to have believed that Servetus came to complete his overthrow. He was aware that a member of the firm that printed the *Restitutio* had been connected with the Geneva Libertines. The day after the trial began, Philip Berthelier took up the cause of Servetus. Shortly afterward, Berthelier's excommunication was revoked by the Council. Servetus was encouraged to expect that he would win the verdict. Calvin so vigorously protested the Council's action on Berthelier that the latter heeded advice to absent himself from communion as before. As E. Morse Wilbur points out, the Libertines had no interest in Servetus or his doctrines save as a means of embarrassing Calvin. The part played by Calvin was that of an expert for the prosecution. He provided evidence from Servetus' works, learnedly refuted his arguments, and at times privately reasoned with him in the hope of obtaining a repentance or recantation. Servetus often used highly exasperating and abusive language. The prison conditions were indecently uncomfortable; humane treatment was promised and ordered, but not provided. This was not conducive to gentle responses by the accused. At times, however, he felt hopeful of vanquishing Calvin. He asked for a *poena talionis* to be awarded against Calvin, by which he would become possessor of Calvin's goods and house.

The Council did not wish to act until it had obtained the judgment of the ministers and magistrates of Zurich, Bern, Basel, and Schaffhausen. To these centers copies of the documents of the trial were sent. Bullinger had already expressed a judgment that Servetus ought to be put to death, and the Zurich leader gave the tone to the replies from the other churches. The Bernese replied that in Bern the penalty would be death by fire. All expressed horror at the heresies revealed, and advocated punishment. The Council was now decided, and Perrin's plea for acquittal or delay was brushed aside. In the end the verdict was unanimous. Servetus was found guilty of spreading heresy and was sentenced to death by burning. Calvin continued to argue with him, and Farel came and plied him with persuasions at the end, not without kindness but with little understanding. They failed to realize that a man so far from orthodoxy could be, nevertheless, fundamentally pious and earnest in the quest for truth. In the morning of 27 October 1553, on the hill of Champel, the sentence was carried out. Servetus died with the prayer on his lips, 'Jesus, Son of the Eternal God, have mercy on me.' The prayer was also a testimony of his conviction: he would not pray, 'Eternal Son of God.'

Embittered anti-Calvin writers deny the well-attested fact that Calvin had sought to have the Council decree death by the sword rather than the flames. Farel had indeed reproached him (8 September) for his undue leniency in taking this position, though Farel appears to have shared it later. When the sentence was rendered Calvin noted that his effort had been in vain. Calvin wanted Servetus killed, but by a more merciful death than the flames. Yet when challenged by some who deplored the whole business, he followed the event with a book (*Defense of the Orthodox Faith*, 1554), in which, like the most obdurate inquisitor, he declares that in cases of heresy the glory of God must be maintained regardless of all feelings of humanity.

Calvin, and Geneva, were congratulated and applauded for the execution of the arch-heretic; but Calvin's defense of it was so harsh as to leave some of his sympathizers dissatified. The time was opportune for the appearance of Castellio's *De Hereticis, an sint persequendi,* a plea for toleration directed for the most part against Calvin (1554). 'To burn a heretic,' said Castellio with powerful effect, 'is not to defend a doctrine, but to kill a man.' The views of Castellio on this topic have now long prevailed among the followers of Calvin. In 1903, a group of loyal 'sons of Calvin,' acting on a proposal of the historian Emile Doumergue, erected on the scene of Servetus' martyrdom an 'expiatory monument.' The example is to be commended to other branches of the Church of Christ. If it were followed, Europe would bristle with expiatory monuments; but after all it is permitted to ask whether monuments can expiate. The deed was done. When all is understood, admirers of Calvin must still look upon it with shame.

But Calvin obtained a new lease on life in Geneva. His foes had not been able to take advantage of the Servetus issue. Many of them, indeed, had no patience with the foreign heretic, and they voted for his death. Perrin and Berthelier were discredited. The next election showed a gain in support for Calvin. But the old issue of authority in excommunication was raised anew by a resumption of the Berthelier discipline case. The three councils finally voted, ambiguously, to abide by the Ordinances. The ministers were allowed to interpret this as authorizing the Consistory to excommunicate. Nothing could have been more gratifying to Calvin. Yet he was still exposed to public insults, and in Bern and Basel he was vilified and despised. He was in fact in a personal quarrel with the Bernese authorities. But in February 1555 his fortune rose. His friends were again strongly vindicated in the elections.

The admission of foreign refugees to citizenship had been stoutly resisted by the old families. The refugees were Calvin's admirers and friends. Now action was taken to admit a large number of new citizens. Some distinguished names were included, and the number represented real voting strength. Perrin's adherents staged adverse demonstrations. Following a tavern supper there took place a rather trivial but ominous breach of the peace (16 May 1555). The Council, prompted by Calvin, viewed the riot as evidence of a plot. A protracted trial followed, in which torture was employed to obtain testimony. Perrin and Berthelier fled to Bern: Geneva sentenced them to death as traitors. Their wives were banished and a number of their sympathizers executed. On 6 September 1555, the escaped Perrinists were forbidden to return on pain of death, and Geneva was at last Calvin's to command.

CHAPTER XII

GENEVA UNDER CALVIN'S SWAY

— I —

WHEN the Perrinist commotion had ended, Beza, describing the peace and concord that ensued, remarked: 'It is said that the devil departed with the fugitives.' Geneva would henceforth be often menaced from without but rarely torn by strife within. John Knox, the Scottish Reformer, arrived in time to witness the overthrow of the Libertines. He resided there most of the time for three years thereafter, and in 1558 became a citizen. In December 1556 he wrote to an English friend, Mrs. Anna Locke, in glowing praise of Calvin's city:

— where, I neither fear nor am ashamed to say, is the most perfect school of Christ that ever was in the earth since the days of the Apostles. In other places, I confess Christ to be truly preached; but manners and religion to be so sincerely reformed, I have not yet seen in any other place.

In the following year Farel, after a visit, declared that he 'would rather be the last in Geneva than the first elsewhere.' About the same time, John Bale, bishop of Ossory, expelled under Mary's government and then resident in Basel and a visitor to Geneva, wrote:

Geneva seemeth to me to be the wonderful miracle of the whole world: so many from all countries come thither, as it were into a sanctuary, not to gather riches but to live in poverty . . . Is it not wonderful that Spaniards, Italians, Scots, Englishmen, Frenchmen, Germans, disagreeing in manners, speech and apparel, sheep and wolves, bulls and bears, being coupled with the only yoke of Christ, should live so lovingly and friendly, and that monks, laymen and nuns, disagreeing both in life and sect, should dwell together, like a spiritual and Christian congregation.

Such tributes are numerous; but they come chiefly from men who were refugees for a faith like Calvin's. Geneva supplied the answer to their longing for a holy discipline, which they found lacking elsewhere and which those who preferred a morally lax environment were glad to escape.

The refugees to Geneva and the refugees from Geneva offer an instructive contrast. The remnant of the defeated party made their headquarters in Bern and moved about in the French-speaking areas controlled by Bern and adjacent to Geneva. Bolsec was in their midst; and Perrin had the favor of the Bernese government, which had long regarded Calvin as an obstacle to its influence over Geneva. The Geneva ministers complained that André Zébédée and another pastor under Bernese supervision had denounced Calvin's doctrine of predestination, and that in their circle Bolsec was calling him 'heretic' and 'antichrist.' In March and April 1555 Calvin was with a deputation sent from Geneva to Bern to seek satisfaction in this matter and the renewal of the old alliance with Bern. The Bernese were induced to banish Bolsec; but Calvin's eloquent plea failed to win vindication of his own doctrine or the silencing of his other critics. He went again in May but was again repulsed, and in turn defiantly refused to keep silence on the controverted doctrine, on which, he felt, the Scripture was unequivocal. 'I would rather that my tongue should be cut out,' he declared. Beza records that Zébédée, after Calvin's death, penitently recanted his objections to predestination. Johann Haller (1523–75), the leading minister of Bern, was favorable to Calvin but lacked influence with the magistrates.

The 1526 alliance of Geneva and Bern had been for a twenty-five-year period and had been renewed in 1551 for five years. Negotiations were begun by Geneva for its renewal before its expiration date, March 1556, but were not completed until much later. The hostility of Bern was at last overcome, but only after many sharp interchanges. The Bernese still championed Perrin. On 29 January 1557 Calvin helped to prepare a moderate but firm reply in the name of the Geneva councils to what was regarded as a threat of war. But on 10 August Emmanuel Philibert, duke of Savoy, with Spanish troops defeated the French at St. Quentin. Thereafter he menaced Geneva, where his ancestors had held sway. Alarmed but resolute, Geneva prayed, and armed against him. Late in October a fresh deputation was sent to Bern, where finally the sense of common danger overcame the antagonism of the previous years. John Knox exulted in the divine deliverance by which Geneva's old ally was taught to remember her duty. On 10 January 1558 Calvin wrote to François Hotman, the distinguished jurist: 'Yesterday, at last, after many bickerings, a perpetual pact with the Bernese was confirmed by oath.' He added realistically, 'However, I don't think the strife is over.' Beza informed Farel of 'incredible jubilation' in Geneva, quoting: 'Blessed be the Lord, who hath scattered the devices of the wicked.' The advantage gained, from Calvin's point of view, was that thereafter the points of disagreement were to be settled on equal terms by arbitration. Bern had, in fact, for the first time conceded equality to her neighbor and ally. The Perrinists were left without overt political support. The duke of Savoy prudently withdrew.

But the alarm was soon again sounded. France and Spain ended their last war of the century by the treaty of Cateau-Cambrésis, 2 April 1559, and a project to crush Geneva was entertained by both parties. Alva, the Spanish general who had fought against the Pope and would later ravage the Netherlands, was invited by the constable of France to conduct the attack, but he declined the task and advised his king, Philip II, against it. With great energy Geneva prepared her defenses. The duke of Savoy, however, began active negotiations to bring Geneva peacefully to submission. A Savoyard noble in Geneva presenting the duke's claims met only courteous but resolute rejection. On 1 September Amblard Corne, representing the Council, firmly told him: 'For the sovereignty of God and the Word of God, we will adventure our lives.' Another of the magistrates summed up the Genevan policy in the words: 'to recommend ourselves to God and keep good watch.' These spirited replies, phrased in the very language of Calvin, eloquently testify to the spirit of the reformed city that was to stand, prayerful and alert, through many a crisis. In December a gracious emissary of Savoy, a bishop-elect, was honorably received by the Genevese, but departed with no answer other than that they wished to be the duke's good neigh-

bors. It was forty-four years later that Savoy attacked. Meanwhile
the religious and moral transformation of Geneva proceeded
under the stimulation of an exposed position but with little sense
of immediate peril from her neighbors.

— II —

Since 1541, Geneva had already been changed in large degree.
With each of Calvin's battles the opposition to his policy had
been weakened, and now, while the discipline was still infringed
in detail, it was no longer challenged in principle. The attitude
of many of the people was like that of Amblard Corne, mentioned
above. In 1546 he had been a syndic and president of the Consistory, yet he was among those involved in the dancing case in
which the Favre family were the principals. He had then humbly accepted the censure of the Consistory and had thereafter
been a loyal supporter of the discipline. But in no small degree
the change in Geneva was due to the immigration of refugees
from persecution elsewhere. The years of Calvin's growing control correspond to the period of fresh severe repression in Italy
(1542), of the extensive and sanguinary persecutions of Henry
II in France (1547–59) and Mary Tudor in England (1553–8),
and of increasing severity against Protestants in the Netherlands,
which Philip II took over from Charles V in 1555. From many
countries frightened refugees poured into Geneva, more than
replacing in numbers the fugitive Libertines. Most of them came
in poverty, as new to them as their new environment. In the
period 1549 to 1559, not less than 5017 new *habitants* were admitted to residence in the city; of these Doumergue states that
1708 came in 1559. Roget places the number for that year at
1680 and remarks that of these 685 came in the month of May.
In 1559, however, only 58 refugees became citizens, of whom
Calvin was one. The policy of Geneva differed sharply from that
of Zurich, Bern, and Basel in its liberal admission of the refugees
to citizenship as well as to hospitality. This was Calvin's policy
and, as we have seen, its full adoption in 1555 was crucial for his
success.

Those who became citizens were prevailingly French-speaking,
since by language they could better than others participate in
the town life and politics. The distinction of a few of these —
such as the learned sons of the great Paris Hellenist, Guillaume

Budé; Nicholas and Leon Colladon from Berry; the Noyon official, Laurent de Normandie; Guillaume de Trie, merchant of Lyons — and the stimulation of industry and trade which the presence of the refugees induced led to their acceptance by the old inhabitants who remained. English and Italian refugee citizens numbered less than one fifth of the French. While the conduct of some of the newcomers exposed them to the tribunals of discipline, the great majority, whether citizens or not, thankful to be safe and willing to be disciples of Calvin, lived in good relations with Church and government.

The chief exceptions were scholarly members of the Italian colony. In 1542, when Protestants were being hunted in Italy, a small Italian congregation was formed in Geneva. The eminent former Capuchin, Bernardino Ochino (1487–1564) of Siena, preached there for three years (1542–5). He was in full sympathy with Calvin's reforms, of which he wrote with exaggerated admiration. He visited Geneva again in 1553, arriving the day after Servetus' death. Though he disapproved of this act, he continued to speak very favorably of Calvin, who reciprocated his friendly attitude. A devout and honorable man, Ochino lived and taught thereafter in England, Zurich, Poland, and Moravia. He wrote numerous books which show an increasing strain of liberal speculative mysticism, far removed from Reformed orthodoxy. Another noteworthy Italian, less fortunate in his relations with Calvin, was Peter Paul Vergerio (1498–1565). He had been ambassador of Clement VII and of Paul III to Germany and had been made an archbishop, but was converted to ardent evangelical views by Protestant contacts and literature and by witnessing the agony of soul of Francesco Spiera of Padua, who had turned from Protestantism through fear and died in despair (1548). Calvin was not favorably impressed by Vergerio's published account of Spiera. When he met Vergerio in 1550 he judged him to be in many respects praiseworthy but doubted his stability. Vergerio hoped to be employed in Geneva but went elsewhere, giving years of useful labor in the Grisons. He seems to have been both uncomfortably egotistical and sincerely zealous.

Others of the Italians were, or became, Anti-Trinitarian. Matteo Gribaldi (d. 1565), a former law professor of Padua, was an occasional visitor to Geneva from the estate on which he lived in the canton of Bern. He held views on the Trinity that Calvin thought dangerous, and he opposed punishment for heresy. In a letter of 2 May 1557 Calvin reveals his own suspicion, stiffness, and reserve in an interview with Gribaldi, whom he summoned before the Council. Calvin disavows all enmity toward him or desire to punish him for differing in opinion from himself. But Gribaldi was expelled from the city as a propagator of the heresy that Christ is of a different essence from the Father. Two months later Giovanni Valenti Gentile was imprisoned on charges of a similar sort. He added to the Trinity a fourth element, a 'divine essence,' and made the Son the 'image' of the Father. The Council would probably have sentenced him to burning but for Calvin. Gentile was sentenced to death by the sword, but recanted and performed a humiliating penance. He escaped from Geneva, renewed and developed his heterodox opinions in France, visited Bern, and was beheaded there on conviction of heresy, 10 September 1566.

In 1557 Giorgio Biandrata, a Piedmont physician, held conferences with Calvin in which his points of dissent from orthodox Trinitarianism were presented as doubts and difficulties. Another Piedmontese, Giovanni Paolo Alciati, made bold to say that Trinitarians 'worshiped three devils.' The Italian congregation, with Calvin and two magistrates, took action to exclude these opinions and imposed a Trinitarian statement as a test of membership, 18 May 1558. The two opponents left for Bern, where they were hospitably treated. Biandrata was to be one of the chief founders of the Unitarian movement in Poland and Transylvania. Lelio Sozzini (Socinus) (d. 1562) — uncle of Fausto Sozzini (d. 1604), the distinguished missionary of Unitarianism (Socinianism) in eastern Europe — paid several visits to Geneva between 1548 and 1558, and held friendly intercourse with Calvin. The doctrinal inquiries on many topics which he addressed to Calvin from other places exhibited a skeptical approach to dogma and disapproval of intolerance. Calvin did not fully trust him but in 1558 recommended him to the favor of the Polish statesman, Prince Raziwill. After a short visit to Poland, Lelio returned to Switzerland. Bullinger befriended him and protected him in Zurich until his death. The attitude of Calvin and the treatment accorded by Geneva to these Italian skeptics and heretics must be regarded as relatively tolerant for the time, and certainly much less harsh than might have been expected in view of the Servetus episode. But Servetus was a celebrated heretic long before he came to Geneva, and these men were, rather, religious inquirers.

The one eminent Italian resident in Geneva who became a true disciple of Calvin was a nephew of Giovanni Petro Caraffa, head of the Roman Inquisition and later Pope Paul IV. This was Galeazzo Caraccioli, marquis of Vico in Naples (d. 1586). He was married to the daughter of a duke, and Charles V had appointed him 'chamberlain.' He seemed to have before him a brilliant political career. But the preaching of Peter Martyr Vermigli and the persecution of Italians under the Inquisition made him a student of Protestantism and finally, after an inward struggle, a convert to it. In peril of the Inquisition he abandoned his rich estates and family connections and came to Geneva in June 1551. He overcame the strong suspicion of the magistrates, won the warm respect of Calvin, became a citizen (1555), and resisted efforts of his uncle and his family to induce him to return to Italy. His wife remained behind, and at a later meeting at Vico (1558) he failed to persuade her to follow him, with their nine children, though there was deep affection on both sides. Calvin then attempted to arrange for their reunion in a place where both Caraccioli and they could exercise their religion; but she declined. After this, the Council pronounced the marriage dissolved, and in 1560 Caraccioli remarried. He was a highly respected figure in Geneva, leading layman and elder in the Italian church, and active in charitable relief. Calvin dedicated his *Commentary on I Corinthians* (1556) to Caraccioli, eagerly praising his heroic sacrifice of worldly status and family comfort that he might betake himself to Christ's camp (*ut in Christi castra migraret*) and share 'our poverty.'

— III —

The government of Geneva was not fundamentally altered, but some changes were introduced, and of these Calvin was the principal author. In the sixteenth century the intimate association of Church and state was assumed to be natural and desirable by all but a small minority. The distinction was really not that of Church and state as we understand these today, but between the ecclesiastical and the secular government of the same com-

munity. The word 'theocracy' is often applied to the Geneva of
Calvin's time, but the word is now ambiguous to most minds.
Many confuse 'theocracy,' the rule of God, with 'hierocracy,' the
rule of the clergy. With reference to Geneva James Mackinnon,
indeed, suggests the word 'clerocracy.' 'Bibliocracy' and 'christoc-
racy' have been proposed by other writers. Certainly the system
was a theocracy in the sense that it assumed responsibility to God
on the part of secular and ecclesiastical authority alike, and proposed as its end the effectual operation of the will of God in the
life of the people. In principle, at least, it was not hierocratic.
Calvin wished the magistrates, as agents of God, to have their
own due sphere of action. But so intense was his consciousness of
vocation, and so far did his mental energy outstrip that of his
political associates, that he ultimately gained ascendancy to the
point of mastery.

To say that he ruled as a dictator is, in our generation, to raise
to the imagination a figure in the similitude of Hitler, Musso-
lini, or Stalin, living as chief actor in a drama of lawless power,
with secret police, armed guards, vainglorious titles and insignia,
massed demonstrations, and vociferous public acclaim. Calvin
used lawful means, went unarmed and unguarded, lived modestly and without display, sought advice from many, claimed no
authority save as a commissioned minister of the Word, assumed
no title of distinction or political office. It was not until Christmas Day, 1559, after he had been instrumental in the admission
of hundreds of refugees to citizenship, that he himself, on invitation of the magistrates, became a citizen. He had avoided seeking this privilege lest a charge of political ambition be raised
to add to his difficulties. Jean Schroder has done a disservice to
historical truth by exaggeration of Calvin's masterful ways, and
Schroder's inspirer, Stefan Zweig, carried the misrepresentation
to greater lengths. It is rather absurd, for example, to make a
point of the fact that men called Calvin 'master' rather than
'brother.' Men of learning were commonly so addressed. But if
we examine the greetings with which Calvin closes his letters we
find evidence of a truly brotherly spirit. Such phrases as 'Farewell, my ever honored brother,' 'Excellent and honored brother,'
'your humble brother' leap to his pen. 'I am overwhelmed,' he
writes to Bullinger, 6 September 1560, 'with grief for the death

of our excellent brother Macar . . . a most upright brother and almost the half of my soul.' The fact that those to whom, or of whom, he so expressed himself were very numerous suggests that in private conversation he used the same language. We may cite the words of his exposition of Deuteronomy 15:12, a passage on the liberation of a purchased slave, whose master is made to say: 'I am master but not tyrant; I am master, but it is on the condition that I am also brother.'

The sway Calvin exercised in Geneva was very real, and at some points unduly harsh. His ascendancy was not, however, acquired through worldly devices but resulted from an uncompromising devotion to principles that to his mind rested on an immoveable foundation, and his undiscouraged, eloquent advocacy of these principles from day to day and from year to year.

Soon after his return to Geneva, he was put to work with the secretary of the Little Council, Claude Roset, to set in order the laws and edicts of the city, which from frequent changes and additions were in a state of confusion. In January 1543 the resulting code was presented and substantially adopted. The task of Calvin in this was primarily that of an editor and compiler. At his suggestion certain constitutional changes were introduced, and these indicate a desire to obtain efficiency by increased centralization. The initiation of legislation now rested solely with the Little Council. Measures passed by it were to be acted upon by the Two Hundred before reaching the General Council. The latter ceased, too, to nominate the syndics: the names of eight candidates were presented to it by the Council of Two Hundred, and from these it elected four. The laws were again revised in 1568 by Germain Colladon. In the interval some further minor changes were made in the political structure of Geneva, tending to greater control by the Little Council. The danger of disorder and of attack made it natural to prefer a government that could act promptly, as only a small body could do. We shall see later how the aristocratic and democratic principles were conjoined in Calvin's political theory. In Geneva the citizen was still a voter; the secret ballot was used in the election of syndics and other officials, and Calvin did not seek to alter this. Even while he was promoting political centralization, he was seeking a more democratic basis of eligibility for the eldership.

Since in his view all authority in human society derives from

God, it was Calvin's aim to bring religious influences to bear upon the magistrates. On 2 February 1554, at his prompting, the Council of Two Hundred, with uplifted hands, together swore henceforth 'to live according to the Reformation, forget all hatreds and cultivate concord.' He later induced the Little Council to establish the custom of stated meetings of its members for mutual correction. This plan, manifestly imitative of the ministers' assembly, was brought into operation by the Council 10 December 1557. The minutes record a decision to hold meetings for this purpose, monthly or quarterly as may prove expedient. All must attend, prepared frankly to air their criticisms of one another but to guard carefully the spirit of charity and brotherly love, 'that the grace of God may be present with us.' A solemn pledge of secrecy was imposed; to reveal the transactions of the meeting would incur the penalty for perjury. In the record of a meeting of 2 March 1558, there is reference to fraternal correction uttered in love and charity, each man freely exposing the others' defects and faults. Calvin was trying to make of the magistracy a Christian fraternity or society for mutual criticism and improvement. This assembly for fraternal correction was called the *grabeau*. It is fully in accord with his statement in the *Institutes* (IV, xx, 8) that the state is safer when a number hold authority, rather than one, so that they may mutually help and admonish each other and no one be permitted to become overbearing. Mackinnon declares the *grabeau* to be 'unique as an attempt to apply the Christian spirit to the art of politics, to ensure the observance of rectitude in the conduct of government.'

Calvin attempted to call forth among all the citizens a political conscience and a sense of public responsibility. He adopted the practice of delivering a sermon annually before the February election of syndics and other officials. In these (e.g., 4 February 1558 and 4 February 1560) he pointed to the perils of the city — which without God's aid is less than nothing — in the midst of the convulsions of the world, and the necessity of choosing magistrates 'with a pure conscience, and without regard to anything but the honor and glory of God and the safety and defense of the republic.' God, he said, should be held 'the president and judge of our elections.'

— IV —

The restrictive and disciplinary elements of the theocracy were by no means relaxed when it became politically more secure. Rather they were enhanced. The Consistory came to enjoy an autonomy over against the magistracy that it had been denied before 1555. It obtained authority to call witnesses and examine them on oath; and its decisions were rarely challenged. Eligibility for election to the eldership was broadened in 1560, when it was made possible to elect them from the Two Hundred without requiring, as before, that half be members of the smaller councils. In 1558 the step had been taken of admitting refugee citizens to the magistracy. In that year four of the most eminent of these entered the Council of Two Hundred and one the Council of Sixty. The number of ministers had by 1560 reached eighteen, while the elders still numbered only twelve. The Consistory was thus becoming a more truly ecclesiastical court, and at the same time, in the eldership, more democratic. Calvin's aim was to have 'the most suitable persons' selected for the eldership. In 1561 it was agreed that the ministers should be consulted in the choice of elders (a provision of 1541 that had been neglected) and that the names of those chosen should be posted in the churches so that anyone might present objections before final action.

The Consistory advanced in constitutional power. The Ecclesiastical Ordinances were revised and, for the first time, published, in 1561. This revision, like that of the laws in 1543, was the work of Calvin and Claude Roset, the secretary of state. There were additions on marriage for which Calvin had vainly sought approval in 1545, and fresh provisions on excommunication that had been substantially adopted on 12 November 1557, by which the Consistory had explicit authority to admit to and exclude from communion. It is noteworthy that, 'in order better to distinguish between temporal and spiritual jurisdiction,' the syndic who presides in the Consistory must now lay aside the baton of his secular office. This is an acknowledgment, confirmed by a symbol, of the ecclesiastical authority and independence of the court. One is reminded of the insistence by the medieval Papacy on a comparable concession from the feudal powers — investiture of bishops by ring and staff. The Reformed Church was claiming, and would claim, immunity from secular interference in its discipline.

— V —

In Calvin's later years, and under his influence, the laws of Geneva became more detailed and more stringent. In the unreformed city, prostitutes had been licensed and adulterers had been very leniently treated. Calvin kept urging sterner measures. A source of corruption was removed when each of the two city bath houses was assigned to one sex only. In December 1556 the Two Hundred declined to adopt severe edicts proposed by Calvin on adultery and blasphemy — at the same time 'chastising' noisy protesters against his proposals. It was determined to leave penalties for these offenses to the discretion of the Little Council. Calvin favored the death penalty for incorrigible adulterers, and in one or two instances it was inflicted. Prostitution was ultimately stamped out by various means. Prostitutes, wearing a cap of shame, were sometimes made to walk through the streets and were expelled from the city; if they persistently returned they were liable to be drowned in the Rhone. Cases of adultery nevertheless continued to be numerous. Great was the grief of Calvin when the wife of his brother Antoine was found guilty of adultery with Calvin's hunchback servant; and the similar behavior of his now married stepdaughter, Judith Stordeur, still more poignantly wounded him. By the laws of Geneva the Council granted divorce in such cases, and also for desertion. They took action on proposed marriages and prevented the union of persons of widely different age. When sixty-five-year-old Guillaume Farel in Neuchâtel surprised everybody by marrying the daughter of a woman to whom he had given hospitality (1558), Calvin was so displeased that he ceased to correspond with his old friend until shortly before his death.

The tale of trials and penalties in Geneva after 1555 does not support Beza's pleasant suggestion that the devil had fled with the Perrinists. Roget can only regard as 'barbarous' some of the sentences pronounced by the Council. In 1561 a probably demented 'prophetess,' who thought herself the 'woman clothed with the sun' of Revelation 12, was whipped, while another deluded woman, who tried to persuade Calvin that he was her husband, was obliged to watch the act; both were banished. A man had his tongue pierced for 'blasphemy against the ministers.' A student who consigned the ministers to the devil was whipped at the college as an example. The death penalty was too frequently inflicted (eleven instances in 1561), often for offenses that are not capital in modern civilized nations.

After the 1557 elections the syndics ordered a reforming visitation of the city. Servants were to be admonished to attend church, and parents to send their children to school. Nurses of babies were warned not to go to bed with them. Rascals and scoundrels were to be arrested. No fires were to be permitted in rooms without chimneys, and chimneys were to be swept for safety. Latrines were to be provided for houses in which they were lacking, and the streets kept clean. Rooms were not to be let without police permission; and the night watch was to be duly performed by those appointed or by reliable substitutes. Such matters came within Calvin's care. He was also asked to sit in judgment on an invention for the cheaper heating of houses and on a painting to commemorate the peace with Bern. It was at his suggestion that railings were ordered for the balconies of houses for the safety of children, and it was he who brought about the strict enforcement of the law against recruiting mercenaries in Geneva. He also, as early as December 1544, prompted the Little Council to introduce the manufacture of cloth in order to provide a livelihood for the unemployed poor. The first dentist who appeared in Geneva was not licensed until Calvin had personally tested his skill. Dishonest or exorbitant practices in business were severely penalized.

— VI —

Notwithstanding the repressive discipline, harsh laws, and paternalistic controls, the positive and constructive elements of Calvin's system were becoming more and more effective. The people of Geneva listened to preaching several times weekly. A new generation was arising, trained in Calvin's Sunday School, instructed by his sermons, able to recite his catechism, to sing the Psalter, and to read the Bible with understanding. Possibly no community had ever before existed so well indoctrinated and broken to discipline.

The singing of the Psalms in French verse was in constant practice. Like the *Institutes* the Psalter grew through its numerous editions. Clement Marot had taken flight to Geneva in November 1542, and while there added 19 to his early 30 translated Psalms. In an act of self-abnegation, for the glory of God, Calvin in his Psalter of 1543 suppressed his own translations made for the 1539 Psalter (above, p. 148) and substituted Marot's texts. The other chief translator who served the Geneva church was Theodore Beza, then in Lausanne, who would later come to join Calvin and would become his successor. In 1551 there was a new but still incomplete Psalter, with no less than 54 psalms rendered by Beza. In 1562 the complete Geneva Psalter appeared. It made use of 125 tunes. The composers of most of these are not known with certainty. The Strasbourg musician, Mathias Greiter, had probably supplied much of the music for the Strasbourg book, and two of his tunes survived in the final revision. The man who apparently contributed most of the tunes of the Geneva Psalter was the gifted musician and teacher, Louis Bourgeois (d. 1561?), who gave nearly seventeen years of his life to the Geneva church (1541–57). He was at first associated with Guillaume Franc, who went to Lausanne in 1545. In 1547, with commendation by the Council, Bourgeois was received to citizenship, but despite Calvin's plea in his behalf he was meagerly paid. The Council stupidly imprisoned him in December 1551 for venturing to alter one of the familiar Strasbourg tunes. Calvin promptly saw that he was set free, and the alteration was adopted. Bourgeois undertook a full program of singing instruction and showed great versatility as a singing teacher of young and old. The children had long periods of psalm singing in school, and weekday afternoon gatherings in the churches were devoted to this exercise. To the gratitude of the people, he introduced the announcement of the psalm selections on bulletins in the churches. But while Calvin wished to confine the music to melody, Bourgeois was eager to employ harmony. In 1547 he published, not in Geneva but in Lyons, *Fifty Psalms of David* with music in four parts. It is supposed that his dissatisfaction with Calvin's refusal to admit harmony in church services caused Bourgeois to leave for Paris in 1557. His *Old Hundredth* (1551), first sung to a text by Beza, is unsurpassed as a musical treasure of the Reformation, a tune beyond praise for solemn strength and compelling beauty.

The leadership of Geneva in the period of reform came from minds trained elsewhere. Calvin's aim was to make the Church educationally self-perpetuating. We saw that the intention to establish a school for all the children had been declared, and Antoine Saunier appointed to head it, in the decisive meeting of the citizens, 21 May 1536. To this had been added, in 1537 and in 1541, declarations of the necessity of a college for higher education. The Ordinances of 1541 speak of 'the need to raise up seed for the time to come, in order not to leave the Church a desert to our children,' and of the obligation 'to prepare youth for the ministry and civil government.' So long as this objective was not realized, no permanence was assured for the work of reform.

Calvin urged his old tutor, Maturin Cordier, who had been in Geneva during Calvin's absence and was now with Farel at Neuchâtel, to come and lead the enterprise. Cordier apparently felt himself, at sixty-one, too old to attempt such a task; he recommended a young teacher of Bordeaux. Instead, Castellio was appointed, with the results already noted. The school in which he taught was the Collège de la Rive, which was begun under Antoine Saunier in 1536 and had ceased activity during Calvin's Strasbourg period. Though Castellio succeeded in reviving it (1542–4), it remained in a state of deplorable poverty and did not approach Calvin's conception of the kind of institution that would meet the need. A school for girls also existed, apparently in the house of one Pierre Joly: it was simply continued in 1541. There were numerous small and ill-managed schools for young children that required to be reformed. Calvin was intent upon a complete reordering of the teaching of the young. His correspondence shows that he was impatient to undertake this and critical of the council's hesitation through fear of the costs. He was in touch with Claude Baduel, who had established a school at Nîmes on a graded plan similar to that of Sturm's institute at Strasbourg. Baduel paid a visit to Calvin in 1550. But Geneva's tensions and tumults continued to delay Calvin's plans. It was the treaty with Bern in January 1558 that first relieved the pressure enough to present the opportunity he sought.

Before the establishment of the Geneva Academy, the private elementary schools were inspected and reorganized. They were reduced to four and were distributed into the four parishes (St. Germain having been added to the three parishes of 1541). These schools were now directed chiefly by the ministers. The abler pupils were set to studying Latin and moved on through the stages of the central system that was now being shaped. Calvin returned in October 1557 from a visit to Strasbourg, where he was received and applauded in Sturm's academy and witnessed its prosperous growth since he had known it. He was now determined to push for action, and immediately after the Bern treaty he secured from the Council a committee to select a site for the proposed institution. They reported favorably on a plot already selected by Calvin, on elevated ground with wholesome air and a view of the lake.

Many citizens shrank from the undertaking; for Calvin would not have a poor, impermanent building. It would require sacrifice if a city of 13,000, plus nearly half that number of refugees, most of them impecunious, were to shoulder the burden. Yet the Council took courage to break ground, and the building began slowly to appear. Roset, the secretary, in a lucid statement of the motives and difficulties involved, says: 'The enthusiasm [*bonne volonté et affection*] of the magistrates and the people rose above their poverty.' Money and teachers had to be secured. The money came as a result of Calvin's public appeals and personal canvass, from generous gifts by a number of the more prosperous burghers, and from legacies. Lawyers were expected, in drawing up wills, to appeal to the testator for a bequest to the fund, and by the end of 1559 twelve considerable sums had accrued to it from this source. A number of the refugees helped, and the patriotic (if not puritanic) Bonivard devoted the substance of his wealth to this good cause. A commodious building was completed by 1563, and the meager salaries of the teachers were increased.

The school was in existence before the building. A number of eminent teachers sought by Calvin declined to come. The most distinguished of those appointed came from Lausanne. It was fortunate for the Geneva Academy that in 1558 the ministers of Lausanne protested against Bern's assertion of secular authority in discipline and (January 1559) were deposed. First Theodore Beza and then all the other Lausanne ministers came to Geneva. He and Viret and at least three others were appointed to the new faculty, and Beza was chosen to be rector. The nominations were made by the Venerable Company, and accepted by the

Little Council, in May 1559. On 5 June an inaugural service was held in the cathedral, at which, before a great assembly, the statutes of the school (*Leges academiae genevensis*), which Calvin had prepared, were read by the secretary, Roset, and the new rector and professors were installed. Beza delivered a notable address in Latin, learnedly recounting high points in the history of education and congratulating the city on its provision for liberal studies free from superstition. Calvin presided, spoke briefly in French, and closed the meeting with prayer. It may seem surprising that he had not himself sought the office now entrusted to his new colleague. In the statutes he had set down the qualifications of the rector and, in more detail, of the principal of the gymnasium, or college, who served under the rector and directly controlled the lower grades. Besides piety and learning the latter must possess 'un esprit debonnaire,' a gracious personality, free from harshness and rudeness, 'that he may set an example to the scholars, and good-naturedly bear the trials of his office.' Apart from the decline of Calvin's health and the widening of his European interests, we may remember that he never deceived himself into supposing that he could be counted on to display these qualities. Beza was better equipped than Calvin to be a university president.

In Calvin's rules, attention was given to clean and tidy conditions, promptness, and disciplined behavior. Punishments were to be proportioned to offenses and must not be excessive or cruel. (In 1563 a teacher was dismissed and disqualified for brutally striking two young boys.) The pupils in the college, or *schola privata,* were divided into four sections according to residence in the four departments of the city, and classified into seven grades, from beginners (class 7) to the graduating class. These grades were not necessarily annual, since, on evidence of attainment, students might be promoted within the year. But ordinarily they awaited the annual celebration of 1 May, when, examinations over, awards and promotions were made. In class 7 the boys passed from the alphabet to fluent French reading and went on to get a taste of Latin. Class 6 was drilled in Latin grammar and simple composition. Vergil, Ovid, and Cicero followed, and, amid an ample diet of Cicero, Greek grammar was begun in class 4. Classes 3 to 1 had an abundance of Latin and Greek literature. On Saturdays the pupils listened for an hour to a reading from the desk of portions of the Greek New Testament. Rhetoric and dialectic were taught on the basis of classical texts. Reviews and disputations were prominently featured: debating exercises were conducted in groups of ten.

School work began at six in summer and at seven in winter, and closed at four. A recess, during which the pupils were escorted home, from nine to eleven daily, two hours of supervised recreation each Wednesday, and another break from twelve to three on Saturdays lightened the tension of classroom disciplines. There was a vacation of three weeks in the autumn. With respect to the predominance of the classics in the curriculum, the college was a typical Renaissance school. It was said, from their readiness in Latin declamation, that the boys of Geneva talked like Sorbonne doctors. Calvin, like Sturm, wanted to develop competence in Latin speech and writing on the model of Cicero. But another feature is not less marked: the Psalms were sung, not in Latin but in French; the hour from eleven to twelve daily was devoted to this exercise. The alumni of the Geneva school were nothing if not vocal in speech and song.

The Bernese, including Johann Haller, supposed the venture would fail for lack of students. But it began with an enrollment of 162, chiefly boys from France, and this number was multiplied by ten in about six years, most countries of Europe being represented. Many of the abler graduates of the college went on to study in the academy proper, or *schola publica*. The purpose of this advanced school was mainly preparation for the ministry, with law and medicine as secondary interests. Students also entered the academy from schools in other parts of Europe.

Calvin had been, in effect, a professor of theology from the beginning of his work in Geneva. He continued after 1541 the series of lectures that had been broken off in 1538 and lectured regularly twice a week on books of the Bible. Many of his commentaries are composed almost entirely of such lectures, as recorded by secretaries. Now Beza lent able assistance. When the academy was founded (1559) Calvin was fifty years of age, and Beza (1519–1605) was forty. A well-trained pupil of Melchior Wolmar, Beza was to be famous for his expertness as a Greek scholar and teacher, for his contributions to New Testament science, and for his leadership of the Geneva church for forty years after Calvin's death. He had taught for ten years in Lausanne, in association with Viret, who was now again at his side in Geneva and shared the teaching of theology with him and Calvin. Beza had spent a youth of careless ease, studied law, and written fashionable poetry. He had been converted to a firm evangelical faith and had long felt a desire to live in Geneva. In 1550 he published there a play of *Abraham's Sacrifice,* which was enacted at the Lausanne school exercises of May 1551 and has been called by his biographer, P. F. Geisendorf, the only successful example of the fusion of the two great traditions of Greek tragedy and the medieval mystery play. It points suggestively to the unfaltering sacrifice required of those who would live according to the Gospel. Beza remained, in his interests, still a man of letters. 'I have never been able,' he wrote late in life, 'to repent of my love of poetry.'

With the establishment of the academy, says its historian, Charles Borgeaud,

> Calvin had achieved his task: he had secured the future of Geneva . . . making it at once a church, a school and a fortress. It was the first stronghold of liberty in modern times.

— VII —

It was not only the future of Geneva but that of other regions as well that was affected by the rise of the Geneva schools. The men who were to lead the advance of the Reformed Church in many lands were trained in Geneva classrooms, preached Geneva doctrines, and sang the Psalms to Geneva tunes. But Calvin's impact upon Europe was by no means due to the academy alone. He had gained a European influence and become an ecumenical figure of first importance before the school was begun. He wrote numerous letters to kings and queens and others rulers, urging reform measures in their domains. His theological battles on the Eucharist, predestination, and other issues had reverberations over all Europe. His principal writings, and some of his minor ones, were beginning to be circulated in many lands. Translations into a number of languages aided greatly in spreading his doctrines; but since the age was one in which all educated people read Latin easily, it would be folly to regard the translations as the measure of his influence.

His efforts to promote the reform process in various nations will call for reference in chapters to follow. Here we may rather recall some of his fraternal contacts with Protestant churches. Although, as we saw, he thought more favorably of Luther than of Zwingli, he was led to form closer ties with the Zwinglians than with the Lutherans. Bucer, who was not exactly of either Protestant camp but sought to maintain fellowship with both, may have helped to lead Calvin to his similar position. But on occasion Calvin criticized Bucer's ecclesiastical diplomacy. On 12 January 1538 he wrote from Geneva to Bucer, whose colleague he was soon to become, complaining of Bucer's undue concessions to Luther and his failure to seek 'a sincere concord in the pure Word of God.' In Strasbourg he gained a fuller understanding of Bucer's thought and so far agreed with him as to make co-operation easy. In the same period he saw something of the problems of the German church in other areas and was greatly attracted to Melanchthon. His esteem for and substantial agreement with Melanchthon aroused in Calvin the hope of a unification of Protestantism. The union of the Swiss churches became an immediate concern, though never to the exclusion of the claims of the wider fellowship. In a letter to the pastors of Bern in February 1537, he called for 'a meeting of the brethren' to settle disputes, and a year later he again proposed, in a letter to Bullinger, a synod that would seek 'agreement among ourselves.' In March 1540 we find him seeking to draw Bullinger into more 'brotherly relations' with the Strasbourg leaders, and stressing the importance of the cultivation of friendship with all the ministers of Christ in order that the churches may faithfully agree: 'As for me, I pledge myself, so far as in me lies, always to labor to this end.'

This was no passing resolution. The principal purpose of his *Little Treatise on the Holy Supper* (above, p. 153) was to offer a basis of general agreement on that doctrine. He would have his readers reverence both Luther and Zwingli, though they had misunderstood each other and lacked 'patience to listen to each other.' Repeatedly he approved the variant version of the Augsburg Confession (*Confessio Augustana variata*) published by Melanchthon in 1540, in which the article (x) on the Lord's Supper states that 'with the bread and wine the body and blood of Christ are truly shown forth' (*vere exhibeantur:* instead of 'are truly present,' *vere adsint*). This was the form presented to the

Regensburg colloquy of 1541; but it was ultimately to be repudiated by the Lutherans. Occasions of strife between Luther and the Swiss kept recurring. After a violent pamphlet by Luther in 1544, Melanchthon wrote to Bullinger: 'I cease to hope for the peace of the churches.' Calvin, still calling Luther 'my revered father,' tried to soften the resentment of the Zwinglians and wrote to Melanchthon: 'I reverence him [Luther] but I am ashamed of him.' The opening of the Council of Trent (December 1545), with its prospect of a papal revival, made Calvin all the more anxious for Protestant unity.

When an open door for agreement remained, Calvin would enter it. He never allowed Bullinger to be alienated from him; and he now sought (1544-9) to reach a formal agreement with him whereby Geneva and Zurich would lay aside their differences on the Lord's Supper. 'If we could only talk together for half a day,' he wrote in November 1544, 'we would agree without difficulty.' 'Though I am conscious in myself,' he stated on 1 March 1548, 'of a greater communication of Christ in the sacraments than you express, we shall not therefore cease to be one in Him.' In 1548 he sent to Bullinger a set of twenty-four articles on the sacraments; the reply was cautiously favorable. Calvin was less encouraged by the response of Haller to a similar formulation for the church of Bern early in 1549. In May 1549 Calvin, sorrowing over his wife's recent death but encouraged by Farel, aroused himself to visit Zurich — Farel joining him on the way — for face-to-face negotiation with the Zurich magistrates and with Bullinger. The Geneva Council had commissioned him to seek the Zurichers' approval of the renewal of the Swiss alliance with France. He failed in this, but held a fruitful conference with Bullinger, out of which came the Zurich Consensus, ratified the following August. Bern and Basel were not pleased that an agreement had been reached in their absence; but after two years all the Swiss Reformed Churches were signatories of the Consensus. The document combines distinctly Zwinglian concepts with Calvinist ones. The sacraments are badges of fellowship and testimonies of grace: that which they figure forth Christ truly performs. They do not confer grace, but through them Christ communicates himself to us. Those who take literally 'This is my body' are 'preposterous interpreters,' and transubstantiation is a 'papist fiction.'

The reader of the Consensus will perhaps conclude that Calvin accepted phrases that he would not have chosen and that Bullinger drove a hard bargain. Nevertheless, the spiritual presence of Christ in the Eucharist was affirmed. Calvin, supposing that Melanchthon's opinions would prevail among the Lutherans, was hopeful that the Zurich Consensus would prove a basis of understanding with them. This hope was shared by some on the Lutheran side, as well as by Bucer and à Lasco. But Melanchthon failed to countenance the document, and Calvin's Lutheran opponents, especially the Hamburg pastor, Joachim Westphal, three years later opened a pamphlet war on him. Striking back powerfully, Calvin appealed in vain to Melanchthon to declare himself. Calvin was slow to realize that it was the anti-Melanchthians who were gaining position in Lutheranism. Even if Melanchthon had declared, as Calvin wished, that the *Augustana variata* was not opposed to the Zurich Consensus, fresh storms of controversy rather than peace would probably have resulted. The triumph of the rigorists was brought home to Calvin when he visited Strasbourg in 1557. The city was now fully Lutheranized. Calvin was given a gracious reception in Sturm's academy but was refused permission to preach.

Calvin took up the cause of the Waldensians when they were under special persecution in 1545, traveled and wrote to induce the Swiss states to intercede for them, got the refugees from massacre admitted in large numbers to Geneva, and raised money to help them. In 1555 they were again under stress and in 1557 Beza and Farel were sent to the Swiss cantons and Rhine cities, seeking to bring pressure to bear on the French in their behalf. Bullinger aided this effort. The commissioners went beyond their instructions, raised the issue of church union with ministers of Strasbourg and Heidelberg, and presented a form of agreement that surprised Calvin and displeased Bullinger, when it was disclosed to them, by its strongly Lutheran phraseology. Nothing came of this; but in the same year Beza and Farel went to the meeting of theologians and princes at Worms and presented a new statement to Melanchthon and the other Lutherans. Bullinger was unfavorable to any union on the basis of the Augsburg Confession, although Calvin and Beza, and now the Basel ministers, were willing to subscribe to it in its variant form of 1540. All that came of the negotiations was the sending by the

Lutheran princes of messengers to Henry II with a strongly worded remonstrance against his persecution of Protestants, who, it is declared, hold the doctrine of the Catholic Church as taught by the Apostles and by earlier celebrated Paris doctors.

But Lutheranism was not thereafter to make common cause with the Reformed Church. Grave troubles had arisen for the refugee French church of Strasbourg. Under the pressure of Charles V, it removed in 1549 to England, but fled thence from Queen Mary in 1554 to Frankfurt-am-Main. Its injudicious minister, Vallérand Poullain, was soon in trouble with both the congregation and the Lutheran magistrates. Calvin, though suffering from ague, went to Frankfurt to seek a pacification (September 1556). His efforts were unsuccessful. The French congregation was finally forced out in 1562, and its members took flight to various places, some going to Elizabeth's England. From 1554 to 1559 it shared the same church in Frankfurt with a congregation of English exiles, whose troubled history will be discussed in another chapter (below, pp. 295, 312).

Calvin's attempts to establish concord with the Lutherans were frustrated through the decline of Melanchthon's influence among them. The death of Melanchthon in April 1560 depressed him. He wrote with deep emotion of their former fellowship. But he was not discouraged in his labor for Christian unity. His warm response to Archbishop Cranmer's proposal for a consensus (1552) (he would cross ten seas if he could be of service), and his return to this project in a letter to Archbishop Parker (1560) suggesting the summoning of a meeting of Protestant clergy 'wherever dispersed,' are among many proofs of his constant readiness to promote the consolidation of the churches of the Reformation. Late in 1560 he proposed 'a free and universal council' to end the divisions and 'reunite all Christianity.' He even declared his willingness that the pope should preside in the council on condition that he undertake to submit to its decisions. Reformed Protestantism has never quite lost the ecumenical impulse it received from Calvin.

CHAPTER XIII

CALVIN AS WRITER AND THEOLOGIAN

— I —

THE topics stressed in Calvin's teaching can be listed and described without difficulty. It is not so easy to say with confidence precisely where his thought has its center or what he would have us regard as its dominant theme. Is the sovereign majesty of God the conception about which his whole message revolves? Or does it center, as is often popularly assumed, in the doctrine of election? Or is he really indifferent to the priority of any one major doctrine over another and primarily concerned to be an interpreter of the divine Book, the Word of God by which man obtains a knowledge of salvation? Not thinking that we should ask questions of this sort, Calvin did not answer them. Animated discussion arises when scholars of our time present their answers, leaving an impression that Calvin's theology is not so simple and explicit as his followers have often represented it.

Certainly he aimed at simplicity and clarity, and we read him chapter by chapter with no sense of obscurity. Yet even so great a Calvin specialist as Emile Doumergue, after many years of familiarity with his writings, dared not claim a full knowledge of his thought. It is a superficial judgment that regards him as a resolute systematizer whose ideas are wholly unambiguous and consistent and set in a mold of flawless logic. In dogmatic exposition, says Henry Strohl, 'Calvin did not seek harmonization; he was fond of tracing a middle way between two extreme solutions.' Thus, between asceticism and natural enjoyment he chooses the equilibrium of 'sobriety'; and while he urges meditation on the life to come, he no less insistently demands responsible activity in the present world. This is a valid judgment, and we may add to it a further complication. Sometimes the antinomy is resolved in an 'equilibrium,' and we detect the application of Aristotle's doctrine of the golden mean. At many points, however, Calvin does not hesitate to leave unresolved paradoxes and logical tensions. Numerous writers of our generation have stressed this dialectical character of his thought. Peter Barth has expressed it by condemning the attempt to make any one doctrine basic to his theology, which is rather to be thought of as an assertion of the Word of God in all its complex variety and hidden unity.

The simple effort to utter the truths of the Bible may have made Calvin hesitate to force its meanings to a consistent pattern. If we try to represent the sovereignty of God as the constitutive principle of his theology, we have difficulty with his views of sin and evil, and even of predestination and reprobation. If we attempt to make his thought begin and end with predestination, we have to contend with a constant stress upon human responsibility and a recurring anomalous recognition of free will. But it is no less true that if we make the declaration of the Word his primary concern, we are likely to be led to forced interpretations of his treatment of human reason and natural law. Indeed, so serious is the problem of harmony and primary emphasis in his theology that we have been invited by H. Bauke to understand it as essentially composed of inharmonious elements, a *complexio oppositorum,* or conjunction of opposites.

Calvin formerly stirred debate because people agreed or disagreed with his teaching. Recently men have been in disagreement with regard to what his teaching was. Under the sharpened academic treatment that he now receives, it is apparent that earlier the very clarity of his style had a tendency to distract attention from the variety and subtlety of his thought. This modern experience, however, helps to explain the fascination his books have had for the best minds in past centuries. The reader has always been rewarded by a continual sequence of fresh facets and surprises. It is difficult to define the quality in great books by which they awake in us a persistent sense both of worthfulness and of novelty. Much that Calvin wrote has this quality, and few theologians have it in equal degree. It springs from a resourcefulness that is not overmastered by an anxious consistency.

Too facile attempts to classify Calvin's mind are to be shunned. To say that he was a French lawyer who turned to theology is one of the most misleading of these. There is extremely little in his work as a theologian that is a product of his legal training. It is nearer the truth to say that he was a humanist man of letters who after conversion made the Bible his literary study. His whole study of the Bible reflects the humanist interest in words and their meanings. Yet this fact does not carry us far toward an understanding of the impact of his writings. His conversion is more significant than his literary equipment. Calvin's writings must be first of all thought of as the utterance of deeply felt religious convictions that resulted from the primary experience of a sudden conversion in which he felt himself arrested and redirected by God. The Scriptures were his guide, authority, and arsenal — as they were of men whose theology differed from his. Calvin was Calvin. To classify him with any group of his contemporaries does not explain him, nor do we gain much by associating him closely with any present-day theological school. It is mainly through a knowledge of his personality and experience of God that we should seek whatever unity is to be discovered in his thinking. 'God subdued my heart to teachableness.' This is the clue to his emphasis upon divine sovereignty and election. He is one whom God has made teachable, learning through the Scripture what to teach others of this God who has laid hold of his life.

— II —

A thoughtful reading of the *Institutes* enables us to realize the main doctrines of Calvin and creates a sense of their relative importance; but to know the full range and impact of his mind we need also to give attention to his other writings. Only a few of these can receive notice here. Mention was made above (pp. 148 ff.) of those of the Strasbourg period: the second edition of the *Institutes,* the *Reply to Sadoleto,* the first *Psalter,* the *Form of Prayers,* the *Commentary on Romans,* and the *Little Treatise on the Holy Supper.* The variety of these titles is indicative of the range of Calvin's entire production. His books may be classified as liturgical, exegetical, catechetical, systematic, and controversial. Outside this classification lies the large body of his letters, a rich treasury of the thoughts and opinions he shared with his friends and a record of his efforts to win influential support for the cause of reform.

The growth of Calvin's *Psalter* to its completion in 1562, has already been noticed. The Geneva editions of the *Form of Prayers* show a trend toward undue simplification. The absolution was omitted, and the metrical Decalogue gave place to a Psalm. Calvin's *Catechism* of 1541 in French, revised and translated into Latin in 1545, was drawn up with great care, in part on the basis of the Apostles' Creed, the Ten Commandments, and the Lord's Prayer — an outline utilized in many previous instruction books. The sections are Faith, the Law, Prayer, the Word of God, and the Sacraments. The dedication of the Latin edition, to the ministers of East Friesland, is remarkable for its ecumenical spirit; the book is set forth to help correct the divided state of Christendom and to unite in a common piety and instructional effort all 'who aim at the restitution of the Church.' The *Catechism* is a masterpiece of simplicity and condensation, free from polemic, laden with Christian knowledge, and informed with evangelical feeling.

Following the work on Romans, Calvin resumed the publication of commentaries in 1547, when that on Corinthians appeared. This was followed in four years by the remaining Pauline and other Epistles. By 1553 had come commentaries on the Acts, the Synoptic Gospels, and John. Meanwhile the Isaiah (1551) gave promise of a great series on the Old Testament books, which by 1564 included the Psalms, Hosea, the Minor Prophets, Deuteronomy, Samuel, Daniel, Job, Jeremiah, and *A Harmony of the Pentateuch*. Commentaries on Joshua and the twenty chapters of Ezekiel that he had time to treat were published after his death. A number of these commentaries, notably the ample and discursive *Sermons on Job,* took the form of expository sermons or lectures. After 1547 Nicholas des Gallars aided Calvin with his manuscripts, and from 1549 Dennis Raguenier, a skilled shorthand writer, took down many of his sermons and made careful copies. But when all allowance is made for this excellent secretarial help, it remains difficult to imagine how Calvin found time for the study and thought required to produce these works, no less luminous than voluminous, while under his heavy burdens of responsibility and in the midst of scenes of strife.

Every year many other writings, large and small, went to the press. A large proportion of these were directed against the Papacy and the champions of the Counter-Reformation, or against any concessions by the evangelicals to the distinctive practices of Roman Catholicism. His two long letters from Ferrara, to Duchemin and Roussel respectively, referred to above (p. 130), were followed by a *Little Treatise on the Duty of a Faithful Man Living among Papists* (1543) and *John Calvin's Excuse to the Nicodemites on the Complaint That They Make of His Too Great Severity* (1544). The latter castigates those who compromise with Roman usages because they have not the courage of their convictions, especially the delicate dignitaries of the Church (*protonotaires*) and the darlings of the court who talk pleasantly with ladies and call Calvin inhuman. In controversy with the Utrecht scholar, Albert Pighius, he wrote *A Defense of the Sound and Orthodox Doctrine of the Slavery and Deliverance of the Human Will* (1543), in which Calvin's role resembles that of Luther in his disagreement with Erasmus. The same year saw the first edition of the oft-printed *Address Showing the Advantages That Christendom Might Derive from an Inventory of Relics,* a mercilessly witty satire; the *Articles of the Sorbonne with the Antidote,* which, in the sections presenting mock proofs of the Sorbonne articles (1542) in support of the Papacy, is similarly sarcastic; and a much weightier work, *Of the Necessity of Reforming the Church,* a bold address to Charles V written in anticipation of the diet soon to meet at Speyer. Differences in policy between Charles and Pope Paul IV led Calvin to hope that the emperor and princes of Germany might be induced to sever relations with the Papacy and countenance or support the Reformation. The tolerance of Charles toward the Protestant estates called forth from Paul a severe reprimand, which Calvin incorporated in his *On Paul III's Paternal Admonition to the Emperor* (1545). The Council of Trent was now in prospect; Calvin points to the calling of church councils in early centuries by emperors and not Popes, and assails papal interpretations of Scripture.

The council met, and after its first period at Trent Calvin attacked its decisions, taking occasion to expose the personal life of the Pope, in *Acts of the Synod of Trent with the Antidote* (1547). After the First Schmalkald War, Charles pursued a policy unsatisfactory to both religious parties. His *Interim* of 1548 was a politician's compromise, repulsive to men of religious conviction. It drew from Calvin a violent and contemptuous assault upon the doctrines and abuses it left uncorrected and upon all who favored them: *The Adultero-German Interim with the True Method of Reforming the Church and Healing Her Dissensions* (1549).

To this general class also belongs the eloquent and thoughtful *Treatise on Scandals* (1552). As in the New Testament, a 'scandal' (*skandalon*) is here a cause of offense or of stumbling. Thus true doctrine is a scandal to the worldly-wise; the rise of sects and controversies in Reformed Churches and the evil lives of professed Christians are scandals of another sort. Calvin points to Scripture and history to show that the believer ought not to be disheartened by the distress and poverty of the Church. While Christ lay helpless in a manger, angels sang his praise. Calvin himself had feared too sweeping a victory in the Schmalkald War, lest it serve only moral disaster. We should know that in the present world the Church must endure adversity and fight 'under the cross.' The book was apparently in part a response to the charges of Protestant divisiveness, and it ends with an exhortation to unity. We may add here a mention of the vivid and rhetorical *Congratulation to the Venerable Presbyter Gabriel de Saconay* (1561). This Lyons cleric had written a preface to a new edition of Henry VIII's tract against Luther, assailing the Protestant parties. Calvin's rapid-fire counterattack does not fail to mention Petrarch's observation that Rome is the mother of heresies.

— III —

It is possible that these urgent or violent pamphlets against the papal church did a good deal to set limits to its recovery of strength. Most of them bear upon the unstable and menacing situation in Germany, and there Calvin fully associated himself with the imperiled cause of Lutheranism. He did not realize that the Melanchthonian Lutheranism with which he felt at home would give place to that of Melanchthon's irreconcilable opponents.

The progress of the Swiss churches and the Zurich Consensus of 1549 had an effect on Lutheranism opposite to that which Calvin desired. Melanchthon, assailed by violent critics and weary of strife, could not be induced to break silence in support of the Consensus and of Calvin's view of the Eucharist, and the victory lay with Joachim Westphal and Tilemann Hesshus. Against these rigorists of Lutheranism Calvin wrote a series of controversial tracts on the Lord's Supper, beginning with a moderate exposition and defense of the Consensus (1554). The series includes the extended *Second Defense against Westphal* (1556); the *Final Admonition to Westphal* (1557); and *On the True Partaking of the Flesh and Blood of Christ* (1561), against Hesshus. Although in these tracts Calvin resorts to violent invective, they bear also a consistent exposition of his sacramental doctrine and express his aspirations for the unification of Protestantism.

He also wrote, in defense of the doctrine of justification by faith, against Andreas Osiander, an opponent of Melanchthon whose conception of infused righteousness played havoc with that Lutheran doctrine and deeply offended Calvin.

Another class of Calvin's tracts consists of those directed against sectarians. The Anabaptists received his attention incidentally in numerous works, and his early book, *Psychopannychia* (1534, published in 1542), was written to combat an Anabaptist heresy of the soul's unconsciousness between death and resurrection. In *Against the Sect of the Anabaptists* (1544) he refutes seven of their typical teachings, including their detachment from civil government. In 1545 appeared *Against the Fanatical and Furious Sect of the Libertines Who Call Themselves Spirituals*. The 'Libertines' described in this vehement pamphlet are not to be identified with the political opposition party in Geneva. They are a widespread antinomian spiritual sect, whom Calvin regards as similar to those described in II Peter 2:12–15, and whom he charges with feigned ecstasies and abandonment of moral restraint. Two men protected by Marguerite d'Angoulême, one of whom had recently been in Geneva, are the personal objects of his arraignment. Learning that Marguerite was deeply offended by the tract, Calvin wrote to her (25 April 1545), yielding no point at issue and affirming his lofty indifference to courtly favors, while assuring the queen of his cordial good will and respect.

Calvin's principal tract against Servetus (1554) (above, p. 176) was followed by others designed to confute Anti-Trinitarians such as Giorgio Blandrata and Francesco Stancaro, Italians then in Poland. These are of no great distinction or significance.

Calvin's approach to science is perhaps best indicated by his *Admonition against the Astrology That Is Called Judicial* (1549). 'Judicial,' or fortune-telling, astrology is here clearly distinguished from 'natural' astrology, or astronomical science, for which he has only approval. He makes good use of Prophets, classical authors, and common sense to disprove 'this bastard astrology which the magicians have feigned,' and includes alchemy among related superstitious aberrations. He does not reject a possible influence of the stars upon human lives, but he denies all claims of those who make a profession of declaring its secrets. He cites the case of twins who may have very different qualities and careers. Calvin is here on common ground with Luther, who ridiculed Melanchthon's credulity of astrological predictions.

— IV —

Calvin begins his catechism for children with man's need to know God. It is this that is 'the chief end of human life,' and without it we are more wretched than the brutes. He begins the *Institutes* with the statement that our best wisdom consists in a knowledge of God and of ourselves; we cannot know either without some knowledge of the other. Throughout his thought a judgment of the nature of man accompanies the doctrine of God; theology is linked with anthropology. God is not for a moment conceived merely as the author and ruler of the universe, but always as Creator and Redeemer of man. God's resources answer man's need. When man, examining himself, considers his own endowments, he must gratefully attribute them to the bounty of God; when he realizes his own depravity, he humbly craves the redeeming grace of God. We cannot know God rightly without knowing ourselves. If we were not too indolent we should 'descend within ourselves' that we might find God. Yet we can know ourselves only when we have beheld the majesty of God. These two factors in knowledge are so intermingled that Calvin declines to say whether either of them precedes the other.

To know God involves for Calvin far more than intellectual comprehension. He repudiates the speculative elaboration of doctrines and discourages all curiosity that is not informed with piety. Piety is 'that reverence joined to love of God which a knowledge of His benefits induces.' God is to be known in order to be worshiped and obeyed. True knowledge of Him cannot be that which flits through the brain; it is that which takes root in the heart.

> It is necessary, therefore, that the principal care and solicitude of our life be to seek God, to aspire to Him with all the affection of our heart, and to repose nowhere else but in Him alone (*Instruction in Faith*, 1, Fuhrmann's translation).

Correspondingly, no unconcerned Epicurean deity would be worth man's seeking. God is the author, the director, the supreme fact of every man's life. Our knowledge of Him involves commitment and devotion. Calvin reproaches the scholastic theologians for their elaborate and fruitless speculations and discourages all the intellectualism for which God is merely a fascinating problem.

God makes Himself known to man in a twofold revelation. He is known as Creator, both through the outward universe and through the Holy Scripture: He is known as Redeemer through the Scripture alone. This distinction had such growing importance for Calvin that, according to E. A. Dowey, Jr., it controlled the structure of the *Institutes* in the final Latin edition. Man is himself a part of that created world through which God is made known. The ordered array of the heavenly host, the symmetry and beauty of the human body, the versatility and inventiveness of the mind are testimonies of God, and His acts of justice and mercy in experience and history invite us to acquire a knowledge of Him. Yet through the perversity of our natures we 'turn upside down' these intimations of God and set up as the object of our worship 'the dream and phantom of our own brain.' Not on the basis of the light of nature but through the revelation of the Word we gain a true and saving knowledge of God.

Calvin's world, from stars to insects, from archangels to infants, is the realm of God's sovereignty. A reverent awe of God breathes through all his work. God, transcendent and unapproachable in majesty and unsearchable wisdom, but also immanent in human affairs, righteous in all His ways, and merciful to undeserving men, is the commanding theme to which Calvin's mind ever reverts. The flame of worship to the eternal God is ever on the altar of his thoughts.

God is known, yet remains mysterious. 'If we should enter into His great majesty we should be overwhelmed.' The knowledge we have consists largely in faith, trust, love, acceptance. It is possible only to piety, which mingles reverence with love. What God is in the abstract is a question not to be pried into with audacious inquisitiveness: what we can know is what sort of Being God is to us ('Non quis sit apud se, sed qualis erga nos,' *Institutes* I, x, 2). Certain attributes, or perfections (usually called *virtutes*), are habitually distinguished, such as eternity, power, wisdom, goodness, truth, justice, and mercy — to quote one list he offers. Elsewhere he stresses spirituality, unity, and holiness, and (from Jeremiah 9:24) loving kindness, judgment, and righteousness. While we dwell upon the divine attributes, we are not called upon to penetrate the mystery of the divine essence. In lowly adoration and penitent obedience we experience that knowledge of God which is the chief end of our living. Nothing worse can happen to us than to miss this life-controlling knowledge of Him. Alienation from God is Calvin's hell, which is 'figuratively represented' in terms of fire and brimstone. 'How calamitous it is,' he exclaims (*Commentary on Luke* 12:47), 'to be alienated from all communion with God.' 'There is no unhappiness so great,' says the Catechism, 'as not to live according to God [*selon Dieu*].'

It is usually said that the conception of God, which Calvin deduces from Scripture, lays chief stress on the demands of His justice and on His abhorrence of man's sin. Since Adam's fall, all men are under the blight of sin and under the judgment of God. We are helpless in ourselves before the divine tribunal — utterly without resource or rightful claim. God might justly condemn us all eternally. That any should be saved is due to His wholly undeserved mercy. This mercy is extended to those whom, in His inscrutable will, He has eternally chosen to receive it. Others are excluded from the operation of His gratuitous saving grace, to suffer the consequences of their sin.

> Predestination we call the eternal decree of God by which He has determined with Himself what He would have to become of every man. For . . . eternal life is foreordained for some and eternal damnation for others. Every man, therefore, being formed for one or the other of these ends, we say that he is predestinated to life or to death (*Institutes,* III, xxi, 5).

The elect owe to God ceaseless gratitude and full obedience; the reprobate may not question the justice or wisdom of the 'dread decree' (*decretum horribile*) by which they are left in their state of alienation and damnation. That it is God's will is its justification; argumentative reason may not intrude. 'God hath mercy on whom he will have mercy, and whom he will he hardeneth' (Romans 9:18). Calvin knows that he is making statements that do not admit of moral explanation. God rules and overrules all that is, and He is both loving and just, in ways that escape our understanding. The very discussion of election is 'a perilous ocean,' and anxiety about it a temptation of Satan. It is to be mentioned only in the context of redemption in Christ. The essential meaning of election is discovered and verified in our progressive comprehension of Christ's sacrifice, which overcomes the malignity of sin. Beyond the Scripture itself, Calvin turns for support of the doctrine not to the masters of argument but to the devout and personal testimony of St. Bernard, who declares:

> It is enough for me to have the favor of Him against Whom I have sinned. O, place of true quietness, a chamber in which God is beheld not as if aroused by anger, where His will in this is proved to be good and perfect. This view [*visio*] does not terrify, but soothes, does not excite curiosity, but allays it . . . [condensed] (*Institutes*, III, xxiv, 4, quoting Bernard's *Sermons on Canticles*, xxiii).

Double predestination is a doctrine not to be rashly proclaimed. Calvin avoids it in his catechism for children, which teaches very simply that God is 'almighty and altogether good,' and that each of us 'should be assured that He loves us and wishes to be our Father and Saviour.' Nevertheless Calvin fought vigorously, as we have seen, against those who controverted his teaching on election and reprobation. In the midst of his controversy with supporters of Bolsec in 1555 he wrote to the Bernese Council:

> I know well enough that we ought to be humble and modest in the treatment of this profound mystery . . . [my] only object is to subdue the pride of the human spirit, and to teach it to reverence, in all fear and humility, the majesty of God.

The startling nature of this doctrine has led many to suppose that Calvin neglected the scriptural emphasis upon the divine mercy. On the contrary, this theme is constantly recurring and is given very great emphasis. He declares that 'while God is to be praised for all His works, it is His mercy that we should principally glorify.' (On Psalm 136). That He is 'merciful and gracious, slow to anger and plenteous in mercy is a summary of all that it is useful to know of God Himself' (On Psalm 103:8). While Calvin warns against assumptions of God's indifference to sin, he also points out the great difficulty men have in 'acknowledging that He is merciful' (ibid.). He deplores this frequently, and notes that while all confess that He might justly condemn any man, 'yet how few are persuaded of what the prophet now adds [there is forgiveness with thee, Psalm 130:4], that the grace of which they have need will be made available to them.'

The doctrine of double predestination is a forbidding one, and a ruthless emotional oratory may make it terrifying and damaging to tender minds. It would seem that such results did not follow from Calvin's own preaching. This may have been partly because he treated the doctrine with the reticence he recommended to other teachers. Another reason may well be the fact that he did not treat it in isolation from the body of his soteriology. He led men to wonder and worship before God's majesty, power, and grace, so that they escaped the psychological trap set by the mere doctrine of reprobation. It is false to say that his God is capricious will and power without justice and love. He tries to have us understand that though he does not know enough to expound the justice of God in reprobation, justice remains unviolated. This is not a philosopher's answer: it is the answer of a faith that is not quenched before the embarrassing dilemma of reason. Urgently he protests that

> One might more readily take the sun's light from its heat or its heat from its fire, than separate God's power from His justice. He who makes God capricious [exlegem] despoils Him of a part of His glory, since he tramples upon His righteousness and justice . . . For such is the symmetry and agreement between His mercy and His justice that nothing proceeds from Him that is not moderate, lawful and orderly (Opera, VIII, 361).

— V —

The saving knowledge of God is conveyed to us by the Holy Scripture. Calvin's great resource was his familiarity with the

Bible and mastery of its contents. It was impossible for him to know the origins of the books of the Bible as these are known to scholars today. But his talents, training, and religious feeling for the meaning of Scripture were such that much of his interpretation defies the acids of modern critical research. Both Testaments were for him the Word of God; yet he asserts and discusses 'the superior excellence of the New Testament over the Old.' The Hebrews were 'instructed in a manner suitable to their tender state,' and received the truth through images and shadows of what was to be fully revealed in Christ. From the Old to the New we pass from the covenant of bondage to that of liberty, and from the redemption only of Israel to the redemption of God's elect among all peoples (*Institutes* III, XI).

Revelation was for Calvin progressive. 'In the beginning, when the first promise was made to Adam, it was like the kindling of some feeble sparks.' Gradually the light diffused its splendor until, in the New Testament, 'the Sun of Righteousness illumined the whole world' (*Institutes* II, x, 20). Revelation is accommodated to man's stages of capacity to receive it. Thus the impression in Genesis is that the moon is second in size of the heavenly bodies. Astronomers know that this is not the case. Moses, Calvin thinks, had no quarrel with the useful science of astronomy but, having to teach the uninstructed, who merely followed the suggestion of 'common sense' by which the moon appears larger than Saturn, he 'descended' to language they could grasp (*Commentary on Genesis* 1:16).

Calvin's developmental concept of revelation, with its accompanying theory of accommodation, is allied with the argument of Lessing in his *Education of the Human Race*. It is surprising that the entire point has been missed by most interpreters of Calvin (Paul T. Fuhrmann is an exception). This may be because he does not adhere strictly to it but often cites from any part of the Bible without discrimination the passages that have a bearing on his argument. Habitually, however, he colors Old Testament passages with interpretations drawn from the Gospel. His reliance is really upon the New Testament. In the *Institutes* the numbers of quotations from the Old and New Testament have been counted by Ford L. Battles: they are respectively 2474 and 4330. (Letter to this writer, 18 March 1966).

The Scriptures set forth the promise of salvation on which faith rests, and the Gospel is peculiarly 'the Word of faith'

(Romans 10:8). 'Faith can have no stability unless it be placed in the divine mercy.' It is also said to rest on a persuasion of the truth of God, which the Scriptures reveal. It is briefly defined as 'knowledge of the divine will toward us perceived from His Word.' It is more than acceptance of the Gospel history and more than acknowledgment of the unity of God. 'God Himself would remain far off and hidden [*absconditus*] if the brightness of Christ did not illuminate us.' In the experience of faith 'God allures us to Himself by His mercy' (*Institutes*, III, II, 1, 6, 7).

— VI —

The doctrine of the Church was one to which Calvin gave high importance and which he labored to clarify. He holds with Luther that in the Apostles' Creed 'Catholic Church' and 'communion of saints' alike refer to the whole body of the redeemed of all times and places. This true universal Church is invisible; its members, the elect of God, are known to God alone. Of its membership, we can have no certainty; but 'by a judgment of charity' we regard as members those who by confession, example, and participation in the sacraments profess God and Christ. The visible Church, consisting of those who profess the faith, is also catholic, since it is extended through the earth and endures through history. It contains some whose profession of faith is hypocritical; but we may not therefore sever ourselves from it so long as it retains the marks (*notae*) of a true church. These are the true preaching and reverent hearing of the Gospel and the administration of the sacraments according to the institution of Christ. A third mark, subordinate but important for Calvin, is discipline, which maintains, as it were, the tone of the visible Church, correcting the behavior of the members and excluding from communion scandalous and obdurate offenders. Discipline is described as the 'nerves' or ligaments of the Church. It is held necessary in order to maintain inviolate the sanctity of communion.

Calvin notes that the phrase 'communion of saints' admirably expresses the reality of the Church, since in it the members mutually communicate all the benefits God confers upon them. This thought of communion and communication is strongly emphasized. Calvin has no tolerance for any solitary piety that detaches itself from this active interchange of spiritual values. The

Church is an indispensable agent in the divine plan of salvation. As Cyprian said, she is Mother to all to whom God is Father; and she remains the nurse of the Christian life in her children:

> since there is no way of entrance into life unless she conceive us in her womb, give us birth, unless, moreover, she keep us under her protection and guidance . . . For our weakness is such that we may not leave her school until we have spent the course of our life as her pupils (*Institutes,* IV, 1, 4).

Writing on Ephesians 4:13, Calvin makes this crisp statement:

> The Church is the common mother of all the godly, which bears, nourishes and brings up children to God, kings and peasants alike; and this is done by the ministry.

It is a grave sin to depart from the fellowship of a true visible Church even though its doctrine be defective at nonessential points. Calvin observes that none of us is free from ignorance, and he distinguishes between essential principles — 'such as, that there is a God, that Christ is God and the Son of God, that our salvation depends on the mercy of God' — and nonessential points. In the latter we should strive to have errors corrected, maintaining unity with those who hold them, and without disturbing the peace of the body. Every member, says Calvin, must exert himself for the common edification of all. Still more should we bear with faults of behavior and avoid schism from false notions of perfection. With insistence and vehemence Calvin denounces the schismatic temper, while he carefully distinguishes fraternal admonition from schism. Paul did not break fellowship with the Corinthian church, even though many in it were corrupt in both morals and doctrine. To alienate oneself from the communion of the Church is to desert religion and to deny God Himself (*Institutes* IV, 1, 10–12). Only where the true faith is subverted and the true sacraments fail does separation become a duty.

The Church is One, Catholic, and Holy. It is holy in the sense that Christ sanctifies and cleanses it so that it daily progresses toward a perfection not yet attained (Ephesians 5:25–7). Toward this its members 'aspire with all their souls.' Not alone, but in the fellowship of the Church that is becoming holy, men are zealously to be urged to seek perfection; but the persuasion that they have attained it is a 'diabolical invention' (*Institutes* IV, 1, 20). The saints are not yet sinless, and the Church is the society in which, by the goodness of God, the merit of Christ, and the sanctification of the Spirit, sins are continually remitted. When the Apostles received the power of the Keys it was not that they should absolve new converts only, but that they should exercise this function of absolution continually among the faithful.

> In the communion of saints, therefore, sins are continually remitted to us by the Ministry of the Church, when the presbyters or bishops, to whom this office is committed, confirm pious consciences.

It is only within the communion of the Church, through preaching and sacraments, that this pardon comes. On Ephesians 4:4 Calvin remarks that the unity of Christians ought to be such that they form one body and one soul, professing one faith and rendering every kind of assistance to each other. We should dread all 'animosity,' since it separates brethren and 'estranges us from the Kingdom of God.'

Calvin saw the Reformation as the restoration of the true Catholic Church that had been almost completely suppressed and undiscoverable in the previous era. With Luther, he regards it as a return from Babylon to Jerusalem. Commenting on Isaiah 66:8–10, Calvin observes that the prophecy was partly fulfilled in Israel's return from Babylon, and more brilliantly in the Gospel, and adds significantly:

> Have we not indeed in our own time seen the fulfillment of this prophecy . . . these thirty years in which the Gospel has been preached?

In his *Necessity of Reformation* he hails Luther as the beginner of this restoration, which he and others are helping to promote. In the preface to the final edition of the *Institutes* he solemnly avows: 'Never have I had any other purpose than the Church's advancement.'

— VII —

More than Luther, Zwingli, or Cranmer, Calvin was a high churchman, if by that term is meant one who reveres the Church as the one divine institution endowed with, and testifying to, the grace of Christ. He has a correspondingly high doctrine of the ministry and its authority. Those officers who are spoken of both as bishops and as presbyters in the New Testament are identified with the ministers of the Word and the sacraments. While he regards the original bishops and presbyters as the same persons and makes no place for a separate order of bishops, his treatment of the history of the Papacy shows clearly that he did not regard as an evil the development of the episcopal hierarchy during the early centuries, when 'the Holy Spirit guarded the ministers' from proud dreams of dominion. From the end of the age of Gregory the Great (604), Calvin sees the Papacy, with its overweening monarchical claims, as the agent of a general corruption of the Western Church, in which corruption the bishops share.

While insisting that the bishops and presbyters of the Apostolic Church constituted one order, Calvin would not reject all episcopacy in contemporary churches. For Poland, indeed, he recommended the establishment of an episcopally ordered reformed church, and the suggestion that this was intended as a stage preparatory to the elimination of bishops is without documentary support. In his respectful and fraternal letters to Archbishop Cranmer he proposes reforms but does not suggest that the primate should reform out of existence his own primacy — 'that high office which God has laid upon you.' The seventeenth-century Huguenot scholar, Jean Daillé, pointing to the Reformer's recognition of Anglican bishops, remarked:

> Calvin honored all bishops who were not subject to the Pope, and who taught the pure and sincere doctrine of the Apostles.

He is primarily concerned to guard against a condition in which one minister may lord it over others. The episcopacy that is admissible is that which is free from 'dominion,' 'principality,' or 'tyranny.' For St. Paul, he remarks, 'monarchy among ministers does not exist.' He holds that the early episcopate arose by delegation of the presbyters for special duties connected with discipline and the holding of synods. Any doctrine of a succession from the Apostles of bishops as a distinct order is, of course, remote from his view. Pastors, says Calvin, have the function of the Apostles (*Institutes* IV, III, 5).

We had occasion to refer above to the fourfold ministry as described in the Ecclesiastical Ordinances of 1541. The 'pastors,' Calvin sometimes states, are distinguished from the 'doctors' or teachers in that the former are busy with a local charge, while the latter's function is that of maintaining sound instruction in the Church at large. He gives much fuller attention to the duties and qualifications of pastors. (See especially the Commentaries on I and II Corinthians, Ephesians, Pastoral Epistles). While mildness and tenderness of spirit are repeatedly commended in ministers, they will have to expect 'no truce from Satan' and must have the courage to contend without flinching. To the preaching presbyters belongs the administration of the sacraments. The elders, who assist in 'ruling,' or in discipline and guidance, may be helpers but not principals in this ministry. The discipline is itself a means of protecting the sacraments from profanation.

Baptism is not to be administered where there is no evidence of faith. In infant baptism, which is stoutly defended, the conscious faith is that of the parents; but repeatedly Calvin declares that the consciousness of having been baptized is conducive to faith as one comes to responsible years. The practice is held to be a counterpart and continuation of circumcision, and is supported by Christ's blessing of children and by the evidence of the New Testament and the early Church Fathers. It is a symbol of our membership in the household of faith, an initiation into the fellowship of the Church. It does not effect salvation; Calvin frequently rejects the view that infants who die unbaptized are damned. Yet at times he seems to suggest that regenerating grace is conveyed to infants in the rite ('some portion of that grace of which they will ere long enjoy the full abundance,' *Institutes* IV, XVI, 19). In a short confession prepared by Calvin for the French church, he writes that God has 'adopted' the little children of Christians: to deny them baptism is to defraud them of their right.

The doctrine of the Eucharist was elaborated upon by Calvin in numerous tracts, but his view is most lucidly expressed in the *Little Treatise on the Holy Supper* (1540) and in the *Institutes* IV, XVII, XVIII). In his stress upon the spiritual presence of Christ's body he is nearer to Luther than to Zwingli; but he is as hostile as Zwingli is to the notion of the 'ubiquity' of the body. Christ ascended to heaven, and his body is in heaven, a place of whose location we can say only that it is separated by distance from earth. The sacrament brings an especially vivid moment of communion with Christ in which we are enabled, by a mysterious and incomprehensible intervention of the Holy Spirit, to partake spiritually of his glorified body. The sacrament is an extension of the Word and is not to be dissociated from it or celebrated without the words of institution. There is here, no less than in the Mass, a miracle; 'not a physical miracle but a spiritual one' (*Auguste Lecerf*).

It may be pointed out that this doctrine of the Eucharist is also a doctrine of the Holy Spirit, and that it corresponds to what Calvin says of the Spirit's 'testimony' to Scripture for the faithful reader. But the emphasis is on the celestial glory of Christ and communion with the heavenly Christ, whereby he sheds abroad in the heart a power of life which is the one thing needful. Jean Cadier, in a study of Calvin's teaching on the Lord's Supper, notes that 'an intense mystical fervor is revealed in all his pages, a profound love for the person of Jesus Christ.' This author has been surprised to observe that little is said of the communion of the faithful with each other, of Eucharistic thanksgiving, or of the memorial aspect of the sacrament, and that no eschatological concept of the rite emerges. Certainly, however, in other contexts thanksgiving, remembrance of Christ's death, and eschatological expectation (*meditatio futurae vitae*) are often stressed, and a spiritual and social mutuality (sometimes called communion) is a favorite emphasis.

In the section on the Visitation of the Sick in Calvin's liturgy, it is stated that the faithful pastor is not only to teach his people publicly but also 'to admonish, exhort, rebuke, and console each one in particular.' So greatly was this personal ministry emphasized by the Reformer that J. D. Benoit, in a book entitled *Calvin as Director of Souls,* regards him as even more pastor than theologian. We have noted the principal features of the Geneva system of discipline. It provided a framework for a variety of efforts employed in the cure of souls. This important province of practical theology was treated at some length by Calvin and received vivid illustration in much of his correspondence.* Here we dis-

---

* The subject is discussed in my *History of the Cure of Souls,* New York, Harper & Brothers, 1951, 1965, London, S.C.M. Press, 1952.

tinguish three aspects of Calvin's soul-guidance. First, the high doctrine of the ministry already noted is fully apparent in this field. The minister absolves penitent sinners. Yet, secondly, his authority is restricted in being subject to the Word of Scripture, and also restricted in relation to the private conscience. Nobody is compelled to confess sins to his minister or obliged to make a meticulously complete recital of all offenses. The penitent is the judge of what he ought to reveal for the relief of his conscience and the comfort of his soul. Thirdly, the cure of souls is treated for the most part as a mutual activity of Christians. The exercises of mutual confession, admonition, correction, consolation, and edification belong to the normal life of lay believers. Thus the ecclesiastical importance given to laymen by Calvin lies not only in the eldership, with its disciplinary authority, but also in the enlisting of all in a lively attention to each other's spiritual state and needs. Ministers and magistrates, too, had their work and conduct frankly reviewed in secret conferences. Calvin probably felt the influence of Bucer and the Strasbourg practices in all this; but like other Reformers he found in the New Testament the pattern of this mutual ministry. His letters are full of counsel for persons of high and low estate, urgent messages to men of power, rebuke and encouragement to those who falter, guidance for the perplexed, consolation for the bereaved, appeals for reconciliation of those alienated. The spirit in which he admonished friends with whom he disagreed is well illustrated by his letter to Melanchthon on concessions to Charles V's policy concerning ceremonies (18 June 1550).

> In frank admonition I fulfill the office of a true friend. Do not think it due to any lessening of my old good will and regard for you . . . I accuse you to yourself that I may not be forced to support those who condemn you in absence . . . [If what is reported is true] you extend too far the category of adiaphora [*res medias et indifferentes*].

Correspondents with whom he was on terms of intimacy received his confidences with his admonitions, and some of them, albeit deferentially, reciprocated with their criticisms of him. When Francis Dryander complained of his uncontrolled anger, Calvin replied that he had been more patient than his correspondent supposed, adding:

Still, I take it kindly of you to exhort me to moderation . . .
I am perfectly aware that my temper is naturally inclined to
be violent [November 1557].

The Church provides the environment in which mutual fraternal
correction without resentment or alienation becomes possible;
each helps his fellow as they move on together toward an unat-
tained perfection of faith and works.

— VIII —

From faith 'all good works spring.' The Christian life is not
only gladdened by faith and the knowledge of God: it is laden
with responsibilities, and these extend to every task and every
hour. There is no realm of life that is exempt from obligation
of service to God and man. H. Hauser has spoken of Calvin's
'laicization of piety.' The layman's calling is not secular or religiously indifferent. We are not our own: every Christian is to
live as one dedicated. 'In our entire life we have dealings with
God [negotium cum Deo].' Calvin makes much of humility and
the abandonment of assumptions of superiority and all self-love,
as basic to Christian behavior. In grateful response to God's love,
we love and serve our neighbor, who, good or bad, attractive or
repulsive, bears the image of God. 'The blessings we enjoy are
divine deposits,' to be 'dispensed for the benefit of our neighbors.'
Calvin would have us abandon all thought of seeking material
prosperity for ourselves. Whatever of worldly goods we handle
or possess, our function with them is one of stewardship. We and
our possessions together belong to God. This view involves the
hallowing of each man's vocation. It is 'the post assigned,' to be
faithfully exercised. It may be exchanged for another only for
God's glory; and no task is so humble that it is not very precious
in God's sight (Commentary on I Corinthians 7:20; Institutes,
III, x, 6).

A man's historical influence often appears ironically at variance with his own conscious aims. Calvin's insistence on diligence
and frugality, his horror of waste of time or of goods, his permitting interest on money under strict limitations of equity and
charity, and his similarly guarded permission of a change of
one's vocation are justly held to have contributed something
to the development of capitalistic industry and business. He
certainly laid great stress upon obligation in vocation, and

thereby has a part in such conscientiousness as is in evidence in the lives of many modern business men. Max Weber has convinced many that Calvin's doctrine of election led to a sense of 'unprecedented inner loneliness' and that, not in Calvin but in later Calvinists, this induced the quest of vocational success in order to allay anxiety regarding the divine favor. It is true that each soul has to do with God; but it should not be overlooked that for Calvin this is the basis of an industrious altruism, never of unsocial economic individualism. Nor can we safely follow with Weber the trend of Calvin's teaching by reference to Baxter, who was an Arminian, or to Franklin, who was a Deist. The now popular notion that Calvin held the prosperity of believers to be proof of their election is a perversion of Weber and an inversion of Calvin. 'For Calvin himself this was not a problem,' wrote Weber. 'The elect differ externally in this life in no way from the damned.' * Calvin was, indeed, most anxious to repudiate the view now attributed to him, as the following sentences suggest:

> Whenever prosperity flows uninterruptedly, its delights gradually corrupt even the best of us . . . The Israelites laughed at all reproofs because God seemed propitious, as though He manifested His favor by prosperity . . . This is a common evil (*On Deuteronomy*, 8:12).

> It is (spiritually) much more dangerous to be rich than to be poor (*On Job* 1:2-5).

> [Zophar's false opinion that the afflicted are wicked and] that when we see a man live at his ease we may know thereby that he is in God's favor . . . is the error of the Sadducees [who did not believe in the life to come]. This conclusion . . . proceeds from the devilish error that men's souls are mortal (*On Job* 21:7).

> For we see daily the state of the faithful is more miserable than the state of the despisers of God (*On Job* 42:7).

> Prosperity like wine inebriates men, nay even renders them demented (*On Hosea* 9:13).

> Prosperity [to the godly] is like mildew or rust . . . for our hearts are enfeebled by prosperity so that we cannot make the effort to pray (*On Zechariah* 13:9).

* Max Weber, *The Protestant Ethic and the Spirit of Capitalism*, translated by Talcott Parsons, New York, 1930, p. 110.

Therefore whosoever esteemeth this judgment of God by the present estate of men . . . he must needs fall away from the faith at length into Epicurish contempt of God (*On Acts* 23:8).

Calvin's commentaries are virtually flooded with statements of this sort. Success, plenty, and prosperity are an occasion rather than a cure of anxiety regarding the state of the soul, and it is the 'ungodly' who think otherwise. Where concession is made here to Old Testament suggestions of an equation between goodness and worldly prosperity, it is with an explanation that utilizes Calvin's accommodation theory. Offspring and cattle and length of life were given to help those who were not yet aware as we are 'that the Lord Jesus Christ hath opened the gate of paradise.' If God does not make us prosper in a worldly way we must not grieve: a better recompense than the 'ancient fathers' knew awaits us (*On Job*, 42). Commenting on Psalm 25:13, 'His soul shall dwell in good,' Calvin quotes I Timothy 4:8, 'Godliness is profitable.' A blessing in this life *(terrena benedictio)* is promised, he states, yet often the faithful are vexed with afflictions and troubles while the ungodly take delight. Nevertheless the former are happier than the despisers of God, since in their dire poverty *(extrema paupertas)* they are still assured that God is with them. The condition of the saints is the better one, since though they are not rich in goods they continually 'taste' the fatherly favor of God. Despite the popular error, and the tribute paid to it by some theologians of high repute, this is Calvin's constant refrain.*

---

* It is true that in his treatment of the providence of God, arguing against the notion of chance to explain the events of history, he speaks of good success as the mark of God's blessing and calamity as His curse; but the treatment does not bear upon economic ethics (*Institutes* I, xvi, 8). Continuing the topic of providence, Calvin makes it clear that the pious may be visited with adversity (I, xvii, 8). I have been unable to locate his declaration, introduced by Dr. Reinhold Niebuhr (*The Irony of American History*, New York, Scribner's, 1952, p. 51), 'that riches should be the portion of the godly rather than the wicked, for godliness hath the promise of this life as well as that which is to come.' The index of scriptural quotations provided by the editors of the *Corpus Reformatorum* edition of Calvin's works cites a number of references to this verse (I Tim. 4:8) without including this one. It would be of interest to

— IX —

The life of the Calvinist was designed on a pattern of neat efficiency in a vocation serviceable to God and neighbor, to church and community. Among the vocations, none is more honorable than that of the magistrate. The systematizer of Protestant theology took a positive attitude toward political order as resting upon divine authority and natural law. Calvin rejects both the Anabaptist view of Christian detachment from the state and the Roman claim of hierarchical authority over it. The moral law of Scripture, summarized in the Commandments, is an attestation of that natural law which God has engraved on all men's minds. The laws of nations may vary and yet be good if they rest upon this divinely given natural law. This endowment of natural justice and equity in man is impaired but not obliterated by sin: it does nothing for man's eternal salvation, but it makes him capable of civil morality.

Efforts have been made to show that Calvin was favorable to monarchy; but few writers have so freely and copiously denounced historical and contemporary kings for their godless pride and oppression. His doctrine of obedience to rulers, including kings, as vicegerents of God is strongly stated, however, and is supported from Scripture. If they are tyrannical, we can but pray for relief. God sometimes calls forth a deliverer and avenger of the oppressed. In some circumstances, too, another door is open. If magistrates such as the Spartan Ephors have been constitutionally appointed to protect the people from the license of kings, it would be a nefarious breach of faith for them to fail in this. Perhaps, says Calvin, the Three Estates in modern kingdoms may render this service (*Institutes* IV, xx, 31). In general, European parliaments, meetings of estates, diets, and conventions of notables had in Calvin's time an acknowledged place in government. The French Estates General had in an earlier century made a strong bid for power; but the kings had triumphed and had not called a meeting of the Estates in Calvin's lifetime. Evidently he would have welcomed such a meeting. Broadly, he holds the best defense against tyranny to lie in a

---

see it in its context. Discussion of this general topic is resumed below, p. 418.

form of government in which aristocracy (the rule of the best) is mingled with democracy. It is safest that a number should jointly exercise government so that they may help and correct each other (see p. 187 above) (*Institutes* IV, xx, 8). Government by lawful rulers is for Calvin 'a holy thing' and those who exercise it are to be held in honor and reverence as 'vicars and lieutenants of God.' They are, however, warned to do nothing unworthy of their office as God's ministers, and obedience to them is placed under the prior obligation of obedience to God. Election of rulers by general vote of the people is the most desirable system. 'Where men are born to kingship, this does not seem to be in accordance with liberty.' And he several times speaks of liberty as 'an inestimable good' and 'more than half of life.' In a pre-election sermon preached in February 1560 he urged the citizens of Geneva 'to choose [their magistrates] with a clear conscience, without regard to anything but the honor and glory of God, for the safety and defence of the republic.' Liberty, he declares in his *Sermons on Deuteronomy*, is to be used and defended by a people to whom God gives it 'as a singular benefit and a treasure that cannot be prized enough.' Rulers are reminded that they are under obligation at once to God and to men (*On Romans* 15:4). The combination of theocracy and elective government, often represented as opposites, offered no incongruity to Calvin since citizens and rulers alike were participating in what had been authorized by God. In his concept of aristocracy mingled with democracy he sees the best prospect of an ordered freedom under God:

> I freely admit that no kind of government is more happy than one where freedom is regulated with becoming moderation and is properly established on a durable basis . . . Indeed the magistrates ought to apply themselves . . . to prevent the freedom (whose guardians they have been appointed) from being in any way diminished. (*Institutes* IV, xx, 8, Library of Christian Classics XXI, 1494; related passages there cited, footnote 21).

He is far, however, from teaching that this ordered freedom is to be introduced by way of revolution. Some of those nurtured in his guarded and almost academic doctrine of republicanism were to give bolder advice.

CHAPTER XIV

CALVIN'S PERSONALITY AND HISTORICAL IMPORTANCE

— I —

CALVIN's seal of the flaming heart on the extended hand bore the Latin motto, *Prompte et sincere in opere Domini*. That he lived ever ready to act 'promptly and sincerely in the work of the Lord' can hardly be denied. Amid the excitements of Europe, and of Geneva, he could never experience a life of undisturbed routine. But whatever the day brought, it brought labor. Even while others slept or took their pleasure, he read and wrote and prayed. Although he began life with a normally healthy and active body, in manhood he never enjoyed robust health. In his thirties, he became a chronic sufferer from catarrh, asthma, indigestion, and headache. He begins one of his lectures on Amos with the explanation that a point was missed in the previous lecture because headache prevented his seeing the text. His letters occasionally refer to sickness and express commendation of physicians who have helped him. After 1558, when he had a long illness of quartan fever, he never recovered his strength, and his diseases multiplied. To those mentioned were added not only arthritis, ulcerous hemorrhoids, and calculus but also pleurisy leading to malignant tuberculosis. His body was ceaselessly wracked with pain. Well-disposed physicians of Montpellier volunteered to advise him. His letter to them of 8 February 1564 contains a long recital of his symptoms. It is the letter of a dying man objectively reporting his diseases, with no element of emotion except gratitude to his correspondents for their concern to prolong his life.

He did not cease to work to the limit of his strength. When his legs would not carry him to the cathedral, he was carried by others, and continued to preach until 6 February 1564. His last attendance at church was the following Easter Sunday, 20 April. He received the communion from Beza, who reports that Calvin afterward joined in the singing (the *Nunc dimittis*) with faltering voice but joyous countenance. On 27 April he bade farewell from his bed to the members of the Little Council and on the 28th to the ministers of Geneva, recounting to both his aims, his struggles, and his faults. 'My sins have always displeased me,' he said, 'and the fear of God has been in my heart.' He continued, with great composure, to dictate whenever possible to his secretary until his speech failed a few hours before his death. His will (25 April) contains a testimony of his personal faith. 'Farewell my best and most faithful brother,' he wrote to Farel (2 May), 'live in memory of our union, which as it was useful to the Church of God, the fruits of it will abide in heaven for us.' Thereafter his voice was heard only in prayer. His sufferings were prolonged until 27 May. Beza, who saw him die, writes:

> On that day, with the setting sun, the brightest light that was in the world for the guidance of God's Church, was taken back to heaven.

In Geneva, citizens and strangers mourned for him, while the Little Council in special session declared: 'God marked him with a character of singular majesty.'

— II —

It is not easy to evaluate a great personality who has been spiritedly attacked and defended through four centuries. The fact that thousands of pens have been busy about him is itself evidence that he is not to be casually estimated. Some historians may prefer to ignore or belittle him, but with a certain insistence this frail, earnest Frenchman comes back to haunt their researches. At his own request, no stone marks his place of burial, but little of him was really buried there. His fame endures, and his influence will continue to defy time and oblivion.

'Nothing extenuate, nor set aught down in malice.' Few have tried to treat Calvin with this even justice. Prejudice and admiration alike have blundered. He was no paragon with the mind of an archangel, nor was he a finished saint. Nor yet was he a malicious and inhuman tyrant, but, rather, a highly gifted and unreservedly dedicated man, whose moral greatness was marred by serious defects. Some of these defects he himself saw. He particularly deplored the unconquered 'wild beast' of his hasty and violent temper. Beza seems to regard this as a result of his loss of health: but his best-known fit of anger occurred in 1539, when he was only thirty. 'I sinned gravely,' he wrote the next day; and he frequently speaks apologetically of this weakness. Something must be allowed to a man harassed, afflicted, and overwrought as he habitually was. But his fault was more than a native ill-temper, and greater than he acknowledged. His judgments were often uncharitable and harsh, his language in controversy intemperate and abusive. Passages of assertive dogmatism and of repulsive vituperation mar his compositions and alienate the sensitive reader. He was not uniformly intolerant, but on an issue that he felt to be crucial his intolerance could be relentless.

Calvin's intolerance has usually been exaggerated and the range of his tolerance has been overlooked. Here again he might claim, and sometimes did assert, that he was assailing not his private enemies but adversaries of the Gospel. In controversy he ordinarily reveals no doubt that the truth is on his side. Earlier adverse judgments of Calvin, when not manifestly the product of ecclesiastical antipathies, have usually been based either upon certain expressions used by him on the doctrine of predestination or upon his connection with the prosecution of Servetus. These matters have been referred to above. Many would be glad to damn and dismiss Calvin by a reference to Servetus; but no man ought to be judged solely by his worst acts. The advocates of tolerance do not always exercise that virtue (as Benedetto Croce bids us do) 'even toward the intolerant of the past' — to whom nineteenth-century liberalism was a thing wholly unknown. For his severity, Calvin is forever blameworthy; but less so than the great majority of men in places of responsibility during his disturbed age. It was an age of mass burnings and of mass butchery for religion. On persecution he shared the views of those gentle Englishmen Thomas More and Thomas Cranmer, though, with characteristic zeal, he became more prominent in the prosecution of the victim, so leaving the latter's death linked with his name. It is commonly forgotten that he sought for Servetus 'a more merciful death' than the flames, while More did not ask for such mitigation for any of those Protestants burned when he was Lord Chancellor, nor did Cranmer for the Maid of Kent.

Calvin was capable of considerable forbearance toward those suspected of heterodoxy who were not dangerously hostile to his system. He argued against narrow definitions of the doctrinal terms of communion so as to exclude diversity of opinion on nonessentials, since we are all ignorant on some points. He favored a liberal practice of intercommunion between churches, even where minor divergences existed in doctrine, discipline, and worship. In 1554 he besought the English refugees at Wesel not to desert the communion of the Lutheran Church there because of dissatisfaction with its worship. Fellowship with Lutherans, Anglicans, Waldenses, Bohemian Brethren, as well as with the national branches of the Reformed, was cherished by him. Along with Bucer, he cultivated, as Karl Holl has observed, an interconfessional toleration. He unhesitatingly admits that some within the Church of Rome are God's elect. His passion for ecumenical unity induced an ecclesiastical tolerance that was unusual in his day and is still distasteful to many who profess themselves Christians.

— III —

Among the most hostile present-day critics of Calvin is Oskar Pfister, who has created a diversion by attacking from the standpoint of a Freudian analyst. He condemns Calvin and certain modern exponents of his teaching for insisting on what he calls an 'ecclesiastical monopolizing of the cure of souls' to the exclusion of the medical psychiatrist. It is, however, quite possible that Calvin would have proved more receptive of psychiatry than those Barthians (G. Thurneysen and W. Kolfaus) with whom Pfister quarrels. Certainly Calvin showed no prejudice against the medical profession as he knew it. He secured the services of physicians for the hospitals and for the poor, regarding them as co-workers with the church officers. By analogy, he might have favored psychiatric workers within the Geneva system, had they been available. He would undoubtedly have judged their work from the standpoint of his theology of redemption, and would have opposed their functioning in secular rivalry with church ministries. In this sense there would have been 'ecclesiastical monopoly': for Calvin the Church is the matrix of all beneficent activities.

Pfister regards Calvin as the pitiable victim of a compulsive neurosis that compelled him to reshape the message of Jesus and the Apostles, producing a harsh substitute for the Gospel, and drove him to acts of cruelty. This characterization is illustrated by evidence of Calvin's intervention in the witch trials at Peney in 1545, on which Pfister rejects the view of Doumergue, who as usual defends Calvin. The reader of Pfister must be impressed by this evidence, but he may well remain unconvinced by the generalizations that accompany it. Pfister's treatment of Calvin is not unlike that of Luther by Father Hartmann Grisar — a hostile interpretation utilizing a psychological argument. The psychological approach is legitimate enough, but it may very readily become a too facile way of disposing of a historical figure. In order to make Calvin appear to have omitted love from his version of the Gospel, so much of his message and personal record has to be ignored that the reader familiar with the Reformer's work as a whole finds Pfister describing a man who was not there. It is likely that Calvin research will increasingly utilize psychological data and produce a more balanced account of Calvin's personality than this scholar has presented.

Calvin was one of those scholarly and highly sensitive persons whose talents mark them for prominent leadership, and who shrink from but dare not shirk the duties involved. Such persons may become assertive even in overcoming an inclination to retirement. 'God,' he said, 'thrust me into the game.' The game proved to be a series of battles in which hard blows were dealt and suffered. Calvin's intensity arose from a sense of mission and was not more psychopathic than that felt by other men dedicated to a cause. His confidence was in God; through all crises he doubted not that God was with him. 'Believe me, I am undone [*fractus*] unless God stretch forth his hand,' he wrote to Viret (14 December 1547) after confronting an armed mob. He was prepared for defeat and often came near to despair regarding his work, but God, Whom he served, would not be defeated.

Under stress, the timid student became unduly combative and was usually ready to retaliate upon a censorious adversary with a torrent of abuse. Yet he rarely, if ever, so far loses perspective as to offer no possibility of reconciliation. When Westphal complains of his reproaches he not only points out that Westphal has begun the quarrel, and that on the example of St. Paul and of Jesus severe language may be used where the truth of Christ is at stake: he adds somewhat wistfully that if his adversary will acknowledge the truth he will hasten to embrace him as a brother. This assumes that the truth is certainly on his side: meanwhile angry words flow, deepening the cleavage.

Most of those who are admirers or adherents of Calvin's theology would be happier if the sarcastic sentences and bitter epithets that lower the dignity of his thought had been exscinded from his pages. Such passages no doubt reflect his familiarity with humanist and other predecessors who cultivated a skill of invective; but they reveal something of his own personality that is unlovely and unworthy of his own ideals.

In Calvin's last letter he exhorts his old friend, Farel: 'Live mindful of our union.' It is true that his friendships were for the most part tied up with his sense of mission; but he could be gracious to an early companion (Daniel) from whom he was ecclesiastically parted. To regard Calvin as a man incapable of friendship is utterly erroneous. His letters throughout show him warmly attached to a variety of persons of marked individuality. He prized these associations, and rarely severed a friendship. When, exiled from Geneva he declines Du Tillet's invitation back to France and to the Roman church it is with no less kindness than resolution; and in his breach with De Falais, who had joined his opponents, sadness mingles with his anger. Countless friends and strangers made his house their hostel. One of these wrote him afterwards: 'Your hospitality in the name of Christ is not unknown to anybody in Europe.' One cannot deny Calvin's austerity, but he was not 'the great black phantom' described by his calumniators.

— IV —

In nothing, perhaps, has Calvin been more misjudged than in the view that he lacked any aesthetic sense. Such a statement should not be made of so good a writer as he. Critics of different religious preferences have joined in admiration of his style, both in Latin and in French. While his thoughts flow, the words in which he clothes them are chosen and sifted with a trained sense of artistic fitness. We see in his writing both a scriptural simplicity and a Ciceronian eloquence. He boasts unduly of his 'rudeness' and 'brevity': these are not practiced at the expense of elegance, nor do they prevent the effective use of imagery. He observes closely the varieties of style of the Bible writers; and in his school regulations he calls for studious attention to the formation of style. He likes to praise an apt expression, using words such as 'beautiful,' 'elegant,' 'splendid.' He delights in bringing to notice impressive scripture similes, metaphors, antitheses, and hyperbolic or ironic phrases. References to Latin and Greek poets are fairly abundant in his works, and he loves the Psalms as poetry. The 'majesty' of the language of a Psalm arrests the reader and stirs him with a burning desire to learn it (On Psalm 78:3). Calvin confessed to Bucer's former secretary, Conrad Herbert (19 May 1557), 'a natural propensity to poetry,' which, however, he had not followed since he was twenty-five, save for his *Epinicium* of 1540 (above, p. 148). Calvin had not a high opinion of his own verses; and this judgment has not been seriously disputed even by warm admirers of his prose.

There are in Calvin's work numerous passages of striking beauty in appreciation of the forms of nature. He praises the front and rear gardens and the exceptional view of a house he has hired for De Falais in Geneva (25 February 1547). Few have written with equal admiration of the beauty of sun and stars, of birds and flowers. He is one of those who in the contemplation of nature feel 'a presence that disturbs us with the joy of elevated thoughts.' When he describes the exhilaration of beauty, he habitually speaks of it as an intimation of the bounty, and of the presence, of God. The living creatures are witnesses of God to men:

> The little singing birds are singing of God; the beasts cry unto Him; the elements are in awe of Him, the mountains echo His name; the waves and fountains cast their glances at Him; grass and flowers laugh out to Him. Nor indeed need we labor to seek Him afar, since each of us may find Him within himself, inasmuch as we are all upheld and preserved by His power dwelling within us (Preface to the New Testament, 1535).

The glory of God, he observes (looking, says Doumergue, from his window), reveals itself everywhere: the stars of heaven are 'a living picture [*peinture vive*] of the Majesty of God' (On Job, 12). In the *Institutes* (I, XIV, 20) he enjoins us not to be slow to take delight in 'the manifest and familiar works of God in this most beautiful theater,' the created world.

— V —

Calvin took himself very seriously. Fritz Büsser, in course of a work on *Calvin's Judgment of Himself,* notes the evidence of his consciousness of leadership. With his very high regard for Luther went the realization that he himself was Luther's successor, with a responsibility connected with the whole Reformation struggle. We cannot doubt that this represents only a just appraisal of his own talents. He occupied an awful eminence, and he labored in the knowledge that even with able and loyal men about him he was in a sense alone. Yet he was not distrustful of, or detached from, his associates. He visited in their homes, aided the marriage arrangements of their young people, shared their jokes and laughter, and according to Beza was a refreshing dinner companion. He not infrequently joined in a game of quoits; a chance visitor reported that John Knox, calling at his house once on a Sunday, found him playing bowls. Another game he enjoyed — an excellent one for ready relaxation, as those who have played it will agree — consisted of tossing a bunch of keys so that they slide over a table and approach as closely as possible to the farther end of it without falling to the floor. But it is likely that an hour of recreation was exceptional for him, especially in later years. No ascetic in theory, he was in practice stern with himself, and the mind preyed upon the body. He continued stoutly to assert that 'we are not forbidden to laugh or to drink wine,' and that we should receive with joyous gratitude the good and beautiful things about us as gifts of God and testimonies of His love. But what men chiefly saw in him was the intense concentration that arose from his basic conception of the Christian life as self-denying labor and a whole-hearted embracing of the divine will.

— VI —

Calvin undoubtedly felt that his work would have permanence. It comforted him to know that though childless he had an uncounted number of spiritual sons. He spoke with a sense of authority on the course of the Reformation. Believing it instituted by God, he was confident that it could not fail. But he had no clear idea of his own uniqueness, or of the fact that no reforming leader of equal stature would follow him as he had followed

Luther. Yet so well did he express his concept of true doctrine and of the Reformation of the Church that many in later days were content to be his disciples and imitators. The *Institutes* became for three centuries the essential textbook of theology in the Reformed churches. It remains for the historian the readiest key to the thought of the Reformation, and for the theologian a still invigorating treatise. His other works have exerted a secondary formative influence upon modern Christianity. All that follows in this book, and indeed all modern Western history, would have been unrecognizably different without the perpetual play of Calvin's influence. His vigorous and orderly affirmation of an evangelical faith secured the Protestant cause against forces that might otherwise have destroyed it. His teaching affected, in ways still not fully clear, both the political and the economic development of the West. His educational interests bore fruit in an immeasurable advance in lay intelligence and in the preparation of a well-instructed ministry. The energies that flowed from his strange devotion, mingling with other elements, produced in the realms of society and culture some results that he would have deplored. He would never have countenanced the secularization of the state, and the exclusion of religion from education would have seemed to him madness. On the other hand, the development of representative government, advanced in some degree by his own teaching, would have his general approval; and the tyranny of fascist or communist dictatorships would call forth his wrathful condemnation. Racial supremacy in any form is excluded by his doctrine of man. 'We behold as in a mirror' he wrote (in a *Sermon on Gal.* 6:9-11), 'our own face in those who are poor and despised . . . even though they be utter strangers to us.' Even a Moor or a Barbarian is 'our brother and our neighbor.'

If after four centuries Calvin were to revisit our world he would be no less shocked by our secularity and inhumanity than astonished by our material achievements. We can imagine such a man as he laboring with utmost energy among us, playing a leading role as a learned, impatient, prophetic leader in the Ecumenical Revival, an eager participant in all Christian thought and action directed toward meeting human need in our troubled age.

PART III

THE SPREAD OF REFORMED PROTESTANTISM
IN EUROPE AND EARLY AMERICA

Calvin's system of doctrine and polity has shaped more minds and entered into more nations than that of any other Reformer. In every land it made men strong against the attempted interference of the secular power with the rights of Christians. It gave courage to the Huguenots; it shaped the theology of the Palatinate; it prepared the Dutch for the heroic defense of their national rights; it has controlled Scotland to the present hour; it formed the Puritanism of England; it has been the basis of the New England character; and everywhere it has led the way in practical reforms. His theology assumed different types in the various countries into which it penetrated, while retaining its fundamental traits. — Henry Boynton Smith, 'Calvin' in Appleton's *American Encyclopedia,* New York, 1858.

CHAPTER XV

THE REFORMED CHURCH
OF FRANCE

— I —

AT THE opening of the sixteenth century France was the greatest
of national powers. The Valois kings had entered upon a contest with the emperors for the control of northern Italy. The
governmental system already bore the aspect of a royal absolutism, and this was to become its fixed character. Earlier efforts
to make the Estates General a counterpoise to the monarchy had
signally failed, and while the nobility might resent the increasing
domination of the king, the resistance they offered proved ineffective. Louis XI (1461–83) practiced the policies later thought
of as Machiavellian, and ruled with so little advice that men
said: 'The King's Council sits on the King's mule.'

The Church alone had retained through the fifteenth century
a measure of independence of the throne. By the terms of the
Pragmatic Sanction of Bourges (1438) the French Church secured
a largely autonomous position in relation both to the king and to
the Pope. Important elements of papal taxation were discontinued; the authority of ecclesiastical councils was affirmed; and
the prelates were elected by due process of canon law. This concordat, though repudiated by Pope Pius II (1460), yet remained
in large part operative and was reaffirmed (1499) by Louis XII
(1498–1515) as a measure of resistance to the Papacy. This ruler
behaved toward his subjects with such considerateness that he
was gratefully called 'the father of his people.' His Italian am-
bitions clashed, however, with those of Pope Julius II (1503–13),
the 'Warrior Pope,' and in defiance of Julius he fostered a movement to obtain a general reforming council. The effort failed,
but it made necessary the countermove that produced the Fifth
Lateran Council (1513–17) (see p. 13).

It was left for Francis I (1515–47) to subdue the Church of
France and co-ordinate it completely with the absolutist system,
which could not be made secure while the Church was free. We
have noted in general terms the situation in France in the beginning of his reign, when in an hour of triumph in the Italian
wars he formed with Leo X the Concordat of Bologna (1516)
(above, pp. 95 f.). This agreement was as injurious to the Church
as it was advantageous to the monarchy. An early historian remarked that by it the spiritual power secured a temporal advantage and the temporal power usurped the spiritual sway. The
authority of Church councils was no longer affirmed, and canonical election of bishops gave place to royal appointment. The ten
archbishops, 83 bishops, and 527 heads of religious houses then
in France became appointees of the king, who thus held in his
hands the disposal of vast and much coveted ecclesiastical benefices. All who looked to service and promotion in the Church
would now be inclined to study not the will of God so much as
the pleasure of the king. The need for reform was pressing, but
the royal domination of the Church seemed to forbid it. Whereas
in Luther's Germany local princes could defeat the policies of
the emperor, in France all centered in the king and no voice that
was not pleasing to him would long be heard.

The Concordat was for him a secular triumph of the greatest
magnitude. The Sorbonne theologians looked back from it to
the better days of the Pragmatic Sanction. The spirit of the
Reformation would seek a fundamental reorientation and admit
no concordat with the Pope on either the old or the new pattern.
Regarding the Church as an unrivaled instrument of the monarchy, Francis would not be likely to favor any change that would
imperil his control of it. If he showed at times a disposition to
tolerate advocates of reform, it was largely that thereby he could
humiliate the old theologians who had opposed the Concordat.
Francis also had a genuine appreciation of the new learning of
the Renaissance, which was now entering France through contacts formed in Italy. He encouraged humanist scholars and favored their scriptural as well as other studies. He is said to have
enjoyed reading the Bible in French. Still he remained largely
obtuse to the spiritual. He early fell into licentious habits from
which his adoring mother, Louise of Savoy, did not, and his devout sister, Marguerite of Angoulême, could not, restrain him. It

was natural that churchmen who were favored and promoted by such a king should themselves lack the qualities requisite for the pastoral office. Many of the higher French clergy of the Reformation era were, in fact, worldly, greedy, and profligate. Some of them, under royal favor grasping numerous benefices, were fantastically rich and lived in splendor and indulgence far from their proper fields of labor. This deterioration was to be challenged, but not soon overcome.

Francis was ill-fitted, too, to meet the political opportunity his position afforded. Had he devoted his talents to the higher duties of kingship he might have made France a prosperous and happy nation. But he seems to have felt no urge to bestow upon this elementary duty any constructive thought or serious effort. Superficially brilliant, and pleasure-loving, he wasted the revenues, replenished the treasury by reckless sale of offices, drew to his side advisers who were self-seekers, and increased taxation in order to maintain a system of waste. Those elements of misgovernment that in the eighteenth century would become intolerable were already making their appearance in his reign.

— II —

In 1519, when the Sorbonne finally consented to the concordat, Luther was beginning to be known to Paris scholars. In July of that year his debate with John Eck took place at Leipzig, as a result of which the Sorbonne was asked to give judgment on his doctrines. Earlier, in defense of his attitude toward the Pope, Luther had cited, and imitated, the Sorbonne's appeal for a council (1518) against the Concordat of Bologna. The Sorbonne doctors, after long delay, declared the Reformer's writings heretical, 15 April 1521, the day before Luther entered Worms to appear at the imperial diet. On 9 November, the faculty also condemned the works of the most original and forward-looking of Paris scholars, the veteran teacher of the Bible, Jacques Lefèvre of Etaples (above, p. 96). In his *Commentary on St. Paul's Epistles,* Lefèvre anticipates Luther's doctrine of justification and shows an aroused expectation of reform. Taking the new discoveries of lands and peoples as a good omen of a new era for the Church, he observes: 'We must hope that God will visit his Church and raise it from its degradation.' His further indiscretions, and the increased alertness of his Sorbonne opponents after

Luther's voice was raised, brought his work in Paris to an end (1521).

Before his condemnation Lefèvre had already responded to the invitation of his friend Briçonnet, bishop of Meaux, and found temporary safety in this diocese. The work of Lefèvre, Farel, Gérard Roussel, and other teachers associated with Briçonnet proved the beginning of an evangelical movement. In the preface to his *Commentary on the Gospels* (1522), Lefèvre writes enthusiastically of 'the Word of God, the gospel of peace, of liberty, of joy, the gospel of salvation, redemption and life.' His translation of the New Testament followed: it was eagerly bought and read. Briçonnet zealously promoted the movement until, through the attacks of friars, the hostility of the Sorbonne, and the irresponsible behavior of some of the reform party, he timidly began to retract his own utterances and disown his associates. In 1525 he finally yielded to an inquisitorial commission of the Sorbonne and ceased his reform activities. The evangelical preachers were scattered. Farel went to the Dauphiné and later to Basel; Lefèvre and Roussel to Strasbourg. At this time King Francis, having been taken prisoner at the lost battle of Pavia, was being held by the emperor in Madrid, and his mother was acting in his stead. On his return (March 1526) he showed favor to Lefèvre. The latter, now aging and dispirited after a period at Blois, during which he completed his translation of the Bible, found a haven at Nérac under the protection of Marguerite d'Angoulême (1530). The converts of Briçonnet's preachers remained to meet the shock of persecution. Noël Beda induced the Sorbonne to condemn French translations of treatises of Erasmus and to order the burning of Lefèvre's New Testament (1525).

The translator of Erasmus was Louis de Berquin, a nobleman of devout life, high courage, and unusual learning. While Erasmus wrote with cutting sarcasm to Beda, he warned de Berquin in his own interests to desist. De Berquin was not the man to take advice of this sort. He had been under charges of heresy in 1523, when he was commended by the Paris students in an enacted farce replete with satire on the Sorbonne. He had welcomed Luther's writings and translated some of them into French. He possessed a copy of the radical *Defensor Pacis,* by Marsilius of Padua, a book condemned by Rome in 1327. During the king's absence, de Berquin was imprisoned and condemned to burn for heresy, but before the planned hour of execution the king returned, and de Berquin was released by royal command. Later he assailed his opponents in vigorous language, charging Beda himself with numerous heresies. In April 1529, he was again under trial on charges of Lutheranism, before the Parliament of Paris, and on 17 April he was burned at the stake. Any fresh intervention of the king was forestalled by the haste of the judges. De Berquin's religious convictions are not to be stated with assurance: he was a student of the Bible and was deeply influenced by Luther. There had been numerous resolute martyrs for the new doctrines before him, but none of such distinction.

— III —

Francis had lost some of his mastery of France through his defeat and imprisonment abroad. The clergy, who possessed great wealth, were slow to respond to his financial needs until he met their demands for suppression of the evangelicals. He consented to acts of violence and began to issue edicts of persecution. We had occasion above (pp. 111 f.) to note the significance of the incident of Nicholas Cop's rectorial address, 1 November 1533. This incident is connected with the Sorbonne's condemnation of Marguerite d'Angoulême's *Mirror of a Sinful Soul,* a book reflecting the new emphasis on faith, which had been republished earlier that year. The king's anger flared at this act of the Sorbonne; but he soon afterward felt it advantageous to ally himself with the reactionaries. His diplomacy called for a marriage between his son Henry and Catherine de Medici, a niece of Pope Clement VII, and at the very time of Cop's address king and Pope were conferring at Marseilles. This negotiation may have determined the king's mind. On 20 October he wrote to reject the Bernese Council's plea for immunity for Farel, declaring: 'We have nothing in the world more at heart than the extirpation of heresies.' The crisis of 1533 severed Francis completely from the cautious and tolerant reforming group favored by Marguerite.

After the Cop incident, and the numerous arrests, flights, and burnings that followed it, extremists in the evangelical ranks called down fresh violence upon their fellows. On the morning of 18 October 1534 Paris citizens awoke to find their houses, public buildings, and churches placarded with crude broadsides against the Mass. The daring distributors of these sheets reached the king's bedchamber at the Château de Blois and left one in the receptacle in which lay the royal handkerchief! Startled and angered, Francis, having hastily consulted with the cardinal of Tournon and other ecclesiastics, introduced severe measures. The persecution was indiscriminate. Large numbers were imprisoned, and not a few were burned. Ingenious and savage tortures were invented, including the *estrapade,* a machine for the intermittent roasting of the victim. Among the sufferers were Calvin's Paris friend Etienne de la Forge and one of the printers of Marguerite's *Mirror.* The king was induced, indeed, to prohibit printing altogether for a short time in 1535. Marguerite retired to her own domains, and in Nérac and Béarn she received numerous fugitives from her brother's severity.

While many evangelicals suffered without wavering, there were also those who felt the appeal of Biblical religion but were not prepared to embrace it at such cost. We have mentioned the service to the Reformation of the poet Clément Marot (above, p. 130). Marot did not actively join the Protestant movement, although his poems exhibit an evangelical view of God, sin, and grace. After the incident of the placards he took flight, and he could not afterward make his home in France. Nor did he find the discipline of Geneva congenial. From a fruitful period there, he retired to Turin, where he died in 1544, leaving to the Reformed Church the enduring legacy of his French Psalms. The popular satirist, François Rabelais (d. 1553), whose *Pantagruel* (1533) had been condemned by the Sorbonne, mingled his coarse jests at the 'Sorbonacles' with evidence of respect for the Bible. During the persecution he prudently obtained the favor of Cardinal du Bellay, visited Rome, begged pardon for his 'apostasy,' and was absolved (1535); he then became a beneficed cleric and lived in relative safety. No such worldly success was the lot of Etienne Dolet, satirist of monks and theologians, advocate of liberty to study and print, and himself the publisher of works of Lefèvre, Rabelais, and Marot. Having once abjured 'Lutheranism,' he was again arrested and after a long trial courageously went to the stake (1546). On his way thither he is said to have punned: 'Non dolet ipse Dolet' — 'Tis not Dolet who's doleful.

— IV —

It would be easy to turn this history into a 'book of martyrs.' A mounting toll of burnings for what was usually called 'Lutheranism' marks the late years of Francis and the reign of his son Henry. The theory of monarchy was summarized in the phrase, 'One law, one faith, one king.' Unity of faith and church was to be maintained by force and terror. There were, however, periods of relaxation. As in the days of the early Christians, the steadfastness of the persecuted was a persuasive to their beliefs. Terror itself challenged heroic testimony. The 'extermination of heresy' proved a task beyond the power of government. There is some reason to think that Pope Paul III warned Francis to desist from his inhumanities. The number of fugitives was giving France a bad name. In the Edict of Coucy, 15 July 1535, Francis offered conditions to those who would return, and ordered that the prosecution of all except the Zwinglians be discontinued.

Since Francis was entangled in a Continental policy in which hostility to the emperor was basic, he at times courted the emperor's Lutheran opponents. While his Protestant subjects were being hunted down, his agents were negotiating with the Lutheran princes. He sought to induce Philip Melanchthon and Martin Bucer to aid him in bringing a religious peace, with the co-operation of the Pope. Bucer, always excited by any hope of unity, was eager to help. Melanchthon sent a conciliatory statement, containing preliminary terms of negotiation. John Sturm, then in Paris, and Cardinal John du Bellay urged the German theologians to come to Paris, and in June 1535 the king personally invited Melanchthon. The Swiss were also consulted; but Bullinger warned Bucer that Protestants would die rather than yield to the Pope. At the end of August the Sorbonne flatly condemned Melanchthon's proposals, while Melanchthon, forbidden by his prince to leave Saxony, politely declined the king's invitation.

It was at this time that Calvin's *Institutes* went to press, bearing a strong appeal to King Francis on behalf of the persecuted. When the book appeared, March 1536, French-speaking Protestants had a reasoned exposition of their faith by which to confute misrepresentation and to indoctrinate converts. We see in this the beginning of a new and decisive stage in the movement.

It had hitherto had no theological unity or firmness but had been a recovery of the Gospel and a piety based on the Bible. Short statements of the evangelical faith by William Farel (1525) and François Lambert (1529) had been published abroad, but they seem to have had little influence in France. There was loss as well as gain in this passing from the earlier free and indeterminate Biblicism to Calvin's firm organization of thought and church. The transformation was effected not by his book alone but also by his guidance and by the educational strength of Geneva, which became the seminary of French Calvinism.

The liberal Edict of Coucy brought little response from the distrustful exiles, and Francis resumed his attack on the growing groups of Protestants. More ample legal machinery for trials and executions was provided (1540). In April 1545, through the devices of Cardinal François de Tournon, the peaceable Waldensians of Mérindol and neighboring villages were massacred to the number of 3000, a few making their escape to Switzerland. The king had been falsely informed that they were in armed revolt. In 1546 a Protestant church was formed in Meaux but was at once suppressed. Fourteen of its leaders were tortured and burned, and others were variously punished. At Nîmes another effort to organize was crushed at its inception. While Francis lived we find no evidence of such a congregation maintaining itself. But meetings were quietly held, literature was circulated, and the evangelical fraternity grew under the stimulus of danger. Though no longer demonstrative, the movement did not wholly 'go underground,' and everybody knew that its numbers were considerable in virtually all the cities of France.

— V —

For Henry II (1547–59) 'extermination' was still the policy, and he hoped to succeed where his father had failed. He provided the Parliament of Paris with a new inquisitorial court, commonly known as 'the burning chamber.' The parliaments of the provinces also took on new activity in persecution. Prisons were filled and deaths by fire were frequent. Henry's Edict of Châteaubriand, 1551, was designed to speed proceedings and prevent delaying appeals. Books on the Scriptures and all books from Geneva were prohibited. The tongues of victims were cut out to silence them at the stake. Yet their silent testimony continued to be persuasive.

The forces of repression began to lag. Secular courts resisted the royal and ecclesiastical demands. Urged by Charles de Guise, cardinal of Lorraine, the king moved to counteract this by establishing the system of the Spanish Inquisition (1555). But the law scholars of the Parliament of Paris dared to oppose so complete a negation of human rights. The Parliament could not veto, but it could discuss and delay, the royal edict. Its spokesman, Pierre Séguier, boldly reminded the king that the Emperor Trajan had refused to take such a method 'against the early Christians, persecuted as the Lutherans now are.' Two years later Henry, with authorization from the Pope, brought forward a similar plan, but this measure, too, was halted by the Parliament and never became operative. Instead, by the Edict of Compiègne (1557), the judges, charged with having been 'moved by pity,' were strictly forbidden to exercise leniency.

France was now at war with Spain. While one French army defended the papal states from the Spaniards, another was crushed at St. Quentin on the Netherlands frontier (10 August 1557). The national calamity was charged to the Protestants. Hatred was fanned by malicious falsehoods resembling those spread by pagans against the Christians in the second century. When large numbers of Protestants attended a communion service in Paris they were set upon by a mob. Those of them who had swords protected the others as well as they could until peace was restored by the soldiery. In this vivid incident lay the sinister forecast of civil war. Far from being intimidated, Protestants gathered in thousands at Pré-aux-clercs to sing the Psalms, and it was observed that there were nobles and notables among them.

With increasing numbers and rising confidence came the organization of churches. A considerable number of these, meeting in houses, came into existence about 1555. Protestants declined, where possible, the services of priests in the sacraments, and felt the need of pastors to administer Baptism and the Lord's Supper. Amid great dangers, a congregation was organized in Paris in September 1555. Soon this example was imitated in Meaux, Poictiers, Bourges, Tours, and other centers. Pastors trained in Geneva began to take leadership of existing lay groups. Recruits to Protestantism now included some nobles of repute. The names of François d'Andelot, Gaspard de Coligny, and Louis de Condé brought prestige and a political potential. The hope of a Protestant France was aroused. But there appeared no way to effect this by constitutional means. France had no parliament in the English sense. The Estates General had last met in 1506. Any profound change would have to be instituted by the king, who had every wish to extinguish the new movement. The worshiping groups in Lutheran Saxony and in Reformed Swiss cantons were the old parish units. In France they were congregations of converts assembling in defiance of government, without security and without traditions. Yet the church polity they produced was a notable and admirable one.

Antoine de Chandieu, a minister of Paris, visited the church of Poictiers where the pastors had drawn up 'Articles of Polity' for nation-wide church organization (1557). Returning to Paris he planned a general meeting to frame and adopt standards of faith and order. Representatives of about fifty churches were gathered in Paris, in late May 1559. Working rapidly and in full agreement, they adopted a form of discipline and a confession of faith. With respect to church polity they were under the influence of Geneva; but a single city could not furnish a model adequate for a church as broad as France. The Reformed Church was given a guardedly representative structure. The elders and deacons were to be in the first instance elected by the people and thereafter co-opted by the consistory with the consent of the people. Elders sat with the minister in the local consistory which ruled the congregation. The pastor and one elder attended the colloquy, which supervised a number of congregations, its bounds being set by authority of the national synod. It was to meet, if possible, quarterly, and after deliberation to close with 'fraternal admonitions.' The colloquy was made subject to the provincial synod, which met once or twice a year and was attended by each minister with two elders. The supreme authority in the government of the Church was the annual national synod, made up of two ministers and two elders from each of the provincial synods. The system is comparable to the carefully framed representative plan of the Dominican order, with its pyramided 'chapters,' conventual, provincial, and general. But here we have a government not of learned friars but of common Christians and their pastors. The elective process extends to the lay membership of the congregations, and elders vote with ministers in each assembly.

The functions of the officers are described in terms similar to those of the Geneva Ordinances. Numerous matters of authority and discipline were laid down, and these were to be amplified in later national synods. Simple scriptural preaching is called for; those on whom God has bestowed the gift of writing are to exercise it modestly. To forestall ingratitude, pastors' salaries are to be paid in advance! Provisions for the discipline of offenders are marked by moderation. All faults acknowledged are to be erased from the records, and private confessions of penitents are to be kept secret. Games involving scandal, waste of time, lotteries, and dueling are subject to censure, but attending weddings of Roman Catholics is a matter of indifference. No one is to be called before the consistory without good reason.

— VI —

Six weeks after this meeting King Henry was dead. His feeble son, Francis II, husband of Mary Queen of Scots, succeeded. About this time the Protestants came to be commonly called 'Huguenots.' The origin of the name is uncertain. It has been connected with the Swiss *Eidgenossen,* or confederates, and also with a jest made in a sermon against Protestants at Tours, likening them to the night-walking ghost of King Hugh (Hugo) Capet, who had been lay abbot of the monastery of St. Martin there. They were now to become not only a Church but also a political party. Their greatest enemies were Queen Mary's uncles, the Guises, scions of a noble family of Italian origin that was never loyal to the Valois kings. Francis II died 5 December 1560; but even his short reign was significant for the Protestant movement, which was rapidly taking on a political and military character.

It would not be profitable to recite in detail the bitter struggles of the decades that led up to the stage of temporary relief reached in the Edict of Nantes (1598). During that period the Reformed Church seemed sometimes on the eve of a general success, at other times on the verge of extinction. The liberal chancellor of Catherine de Medici, Michel de L'Hôpital, whose wife was a Huguenot, attempted to secure toleration. In 1560, a meeting of the Estates, the first in fifty-four years, was held. A conference on religion met at Poissy (1561), where Beza, Peter Martyr, the Jesuit Laynez, and prelates of France held high debate without the slightest measure of agreement. The edict of toleration issued by Catherine as regent in January 1562 embodied L'Hôpital's policy. But he was a pioneer in an unpopular cause, and his plans were soon defeated by the violence of the Guises and the headlong zeal of the Huguenots in resistance to it (1562).

France was now torn by a series of wars, with intervals of armed peace. The Peace of St. Germain, 1570, was so favorable to the Huguenots as to make their opponents unhappy. Gaspard de Coligny, eminent Huguenot layman, supported a policy of aid to Netherlands Protestants against Spain. Catherine secured the betrothal of her daughter Margaret to Henry of Navarre, the young heir to that kingdom still under Spanish occupation. Henry's mother was Jeanne d'Albret, daughter of Marguerite d'Angoulême, and she had brought him up a militant Protestant. The marriage was celebrated on 18 August 1572, thousands of Huguenots sharing in the celebration in Paris. Catherine also tried to marry first her elder son, Henry of Anjou, and later her younger son, Alençon, to Elizabeth of England. Elizabeth, here as always in similar cases, made the most of the wooing politically, but would not be won. When Catherine realized that she had enraged Spain without winning England, she consented to the plan of the Guises to appease Spain by the murder of Coligny.

Coligny survived the attack of an assassin; whereupon, on persuasion of the Guises and in a desperate effort to escape the political impasse created by her maladroit and unscrupulous policy, Catherine gave the frightful command to slay the assembled Huguenots en masse. On the eve of St. Bartholomew's Day, 24 August 1572, the savage butchery began, in which in Paris and other centers of Protestantism about 70,000 Huguenots were put to the sword. The 'slaughter of the Huguenots' was gleefully celebrated in Rome; and Catherine thought them virtually exterminated. But the survivors were numerous. They took arms and within a year wrested new concessions from the government.

The bourgeois class was increasingly affected by Protestantism, and the leadership of the nobility was passing. The massacre stimulated political thinking, and writers such as François Hotman, Hubert Languet, and Philippe du Plessis Mornay advocated representative government and constitutional limitation of monarchy. Hotman's *Franco-Gallia* (1573) treated French history as illustrating the triumph and decline of these principles. Languet and Mornay apparently shared the authorship of the more fundamental work, *A Defense against Tyrants* (1579), a treatise of great importance in the history of political theory, especially for its doctrine of the right of resistance. In some areas the Protestants were now in control of local governments and held political assemblies of their own.

The struggle continued. King Henry III (1574–89), driven to desperation by the domineering conduct of Henry, duke of Guise, had the latter slain in the royal apartment (August 1588). A year later he was himself assassinated by a fanatical monk. There remained as heir Henry of Navarre, who had been spared in the massacre of St. Bartholomew and was now thirty-six, able, daring in war, supple in diplomacy, and attached to the Protestant cause. A third party had now arisen, known as the Politiques. They were men of L'Hôpital's opinion, patriots favorable to toleration in the interests of peace. In order to defeat the pro-Spanish and pro-papal Guises, they at times made common cause with the Huguenots. In fact, numerous Protestants were themselves Politiques, though most of them entertained less tolerant views. Henry of Navarre was already looked to by both as their leader. But he had to fight and bargain his way to the throne. France was weary of a long strife that had cost hundreds of thousands of lives. In the interests of peace and unity Henry abandoned the religion of his mother and was received into the Roman communion. He was crowned at Chartres (27 February 1594), entered Paris, pardoned those of his enemies who yielded to him, and proceeded to reduce the remaining opposition and give peace to his country.

The noblest figure among the Huguenots of this period was Philip du Plessis Mornay, warrior, lay theologian, and resourceful leader. In his wife's memoirs we read that Mornay received in a private interview the king's explanation of his conversion: he had found himself politically 'on the brink of a precipice' and had no alternative. Mornay still urged him to break from the Papacy. But in the end the policy of Henry's choice was that of the Politiques rather than that of the Huguenots. It took shape in the Edict of Nantes, 13 April 1598. Mornay and other Protestants were consulted on its terms, though it by no means represents all that they desired.

— VII —

The edict embodied the provisions of pacification agreements made in 1570 and 1576, in intervals between wars, and spelled out in detail the privileges of those of 'the allegedly [*prétendue*] reformed religion.' Complete freedom to profess this religion was permitted in about 200 towns and in the castles of about 3000 nobles. Synodical meetings of the Reformed Church were permitted without interference. Law cases affecting its members were to be tried in bipartisan courts. The secular Huguenot organizations were continued, and 150 places of security, including five garrisoned towns, were retained in their possession. Henry was informed from Rome that Pope Clement VIII was 'disconsolate' over the edict since by it 'liberty of conscience is granted to everyone, the worst thing in the world.' He had now to withstand much pressure from the Pope and the French prelates to have it revoked. This he constantly refused, though he did permit some serious infringements of its provisions. The edict did not produce all the results hoped for by the king. In essence it was a treaty of peace between belligerents who had merely lost hope of victory and remained at heart mutually distrustful and hostile. As for the Huguenots, they made the most of their new opportunity for peaceable advance.

Their interest in education was intense. Provision was made for this in the edict, and funds supplied by the king were employed in the establishment and maintenance of schools and colleges. Shortly after 1598 existing academies were transformed into the universities of Nîmes, Montpellier, Montauban, Saumur, and Sedan. When, after Henry's death, the royal grants were reduced and then withheld, retrenchment was unavoidable; but the Protestant ministers did not cease to be well trained, and they included in their ranks not a few eminent scholars. Some of these, such as the Scot, John Cameron (d. 1623) of Saumur, and his pupil, Moïse Amyraut (d. 1664), were sufficiently radical in theology to be charged with heterodoxy. Amyraut's view of election ('Amyraldism') was an attempt to avoid some of the harshness of Calvinism by affirming a 'hypothetically universal' predestination: Christ's atonement was sufficient for all, though efficient only for the elect. Pierre Dumoulin (d. 1658), pastor of the great church the Protestants had built at Charenton and later professor at Sedan, wrote his *Defense of the Reformed Churches of France,* an able and well-informed book. David Blondel (d. 1655), one of the most gifted of historians, distressed his colleagues, who had made him a sort of itinerant professor, by disproving the legend of 'Pope Joanna' and thus forcing the abandonment of a favorite anti-papal argument. His other historical studies, however, more than compensated for the rejection of this ficti- tious scandal. Another Charenton pastor, Charles Drelincourt (d. 1669), wrote in the field of pastoral theology (e.g. *Consola- tions against Death*), while his friend Jean Daillé (d. 1670) is celebrated for his treatises *On the Use of the Fathers* and *On Auricular Confession*. In a manner not typical of earlier Re- formed opinion, Daillé exposes the disagreements and errors of the Church Fathers in order to disparage their authority. The titles here cited are merely examples of an extensive literature of thought and research.

— VIII —

So long as Henry IV lived, and for some years thereafter, the national synods and political assemblies of the Huguenots con- tinued to meet and, despite a good deal of internal discord, to maintain the unity of the Reformed communion and its organs of defense. After Henry's assassination, 14 May 1610, disagree- ments among Protestant nobles gravely disturbed the Reformed Church. Mornay, as moderate as he was brave and steadfast, was unable to dissuade them from courses that led to war. The most eminent and sincere of these contentious men was Duke Henri de Rohan (d. 1638), whose adventurous career took him far be- yond France. When the restoration of Roman Catholicism in the territory of Béarn, Protestant since 1563, was brought about with cruel violence, Rohan led a revolt that ended unfavorably to the Huguenots; and when the treaty that ended it was violated by Louis XIII, Rohan renewed the strife. While he was vainly trying to arouse the dispirited Protestants elsewhere, La Rochelle, their maritime stronghold, fell after a year's siege to the army of Cardinal Richelieu (October 1628). The remaining military forces of the Huguenots were soon after exterminated.

Deprived now of political and military defenses, the French Protestants were exposed to constant pressure to renounce their religion, a pressure exercised alike by government, clergy, and religious orders. Elie Benoist (d. 1728) later in exile compiled the story of their sufferings in five quarto volumes (1695). Their church services were interrupted, their synods were rarely per- mitted to meet, their fraternal relations with foreign churches were cut off, and they were increasingly deprived of personal rights. For some years during Louis XIV's minority, his minister, Cardinal Mazarin, practiced a more generous policy; but a strong reaction followed and the position of the Huguenots became pitiable indeed. Their national synods were suppressed after 1659, the year in which Louis assumed the functions of kingship. They had hoped that Louis, assured of their loyalty, would return to the enforcement of the Edict of Nantes: instead the remaining elements of toleration provided by the edict were gradually chiseled away.

From 1665 the Huguenots were obliged to surrender their children to be educated as Roman Catholics. By 1679 the law courts in which they had been represented were all abolished. Efforts to convert them were redoubled, and they had no respite from the unwelcome persuasion. In many parts of France bands of dragoons were billeted in their houses with instructions to humiliate and oppress them so that they would seek immunity by conversion. Though forbidden to emigrate, thousands of them made their escape from France. Finally, on the pretense that no Protestants remained, Louis resorted to the Revocation of the Edict of Nantes (17 October 1685). The king's decision was reached on the advice of Mme de Maintenon, whom he had secretly married a year earlier, of his minister of war, the ruthless Louvois, and of the eminent bishop of Meaux, Jacques Bénigne Bossuet.

— IX —

Although French Protestantism had lost its visible organization, its pastors and its properties, and large numbers of its people, it did not cease to exist. Even in France an uncounted number survived, to welcome now and then the visits of some daring fugitive pastor, or to meet under the leadership of elders. Indeed, twenty years after the Revocation there was a serious Protestant revolt in the Cévennes. Antoine Court (d. 1760) was later to effect the peaceful organization of 'the Church in the Desert.' But the strength of the French Reformed Church was now outside of France. Despite frontier precautions, some 400,000 of the proscribed religionists found their way to Holland, Germany, England, Switzerland, and other lands, bearing everywhere valued contributions in character, education, and industry.

As in the case of twentieth-century oppressions, the refugees numbered in their ranks some of the ablest minds and finest spirits of their nation.

We have noticed a tendency toward divergence from original Calvinism in the theology of the French Reformed schools. The influence of the philosopher Descartes (d. 1650) was felt by some of their teachers and resisted by others. But amid the changing points of view, the most marked change was in the field of political theory. The favor of Henry IV and the unwarranted hope that his successors would enforce his edict had tended to produce assent on the part of the Huguenots to the prevailing doctrine of royal absolutism. The royal authority was asserted, even under persecution, in strong terms. But the royal heart was hardened; and when there was nothing to hope for from the king, the Huguenot writers returned to the literary fight against absolutism that had been waged in the days of Hotman's *Franco-Gallia* and the *Defense against Tyrants*. Both these works are reflected in the theories of Pierre Jurieu (d. 1713). As a refugee in Rotterdam, Jurieu assailed in various writings the tyranny of the French system and affirmed the rightful authority of the Estates against the assumptions of the king. Other distinguished exiles included the historians, Jacques Basnage (d. 1723) and Elie Benoist, and the able preacher and writer, Jean Claude (d. 1687). Claude had personally debated on equal terms with Bossuet, who after Claude's death published his celebrated attack on the Reformation, *The Variations of Protestantism*. Claude shared with Bossuet the gift of eloquence as a preacher. His *Composition of the Sermon* became a widely used textbook on homiletics and marks a stage in the development of pulpit rhetoric. Unlike the other scholars of the dispersion, who in general remained closely attached to a cautious scriptural Protestantism, Pierre Bayle (d. 1706), on leaving Sedan for Rotterdam, cultivated a critical and skeptical rationalism. Typical of his legacy to posterity is his *Historical and Critical Dictionary,* in which brilliance of expression lights up the realm of historical learning.

The tragedy of the Huguenots was the tragedy of France. The nation lost their service and their moral strength. The triumph of their enemies was the triumph not of faith but of intolerant power. The refugees carried away with them much of the soul of France. So far as their own country was concerned their heroic testimony and bitter losses seemed at the time to have been largely in vain. Even martyrdom did not prove invincible. The defeat of the Huguenot party was no doubt due in part to its own mistakes. Yet the innocent believers could not prevent the Huguenot church from being laid hold of by influential nobles and led into political embroilments. It was natural, too, that later, grasping for security, they put their trust in princes and accepted for a time the claims of absolutism so far as to yield the doctrinal basis of resistance. But when we see their Church on the broad canvas of history we recognize the importance of its spiritual testimony. In their sufferings the Huguenots are comparable to the Waldensians and the Hussites, the suppression of whom also approached extermination on the native soil. But in all these cases, the last word is not of the loss and anguish of persecution. The Christian Church everywhere stands enriched by their example. Of the resurrection of their cause among their compatriots we shall speak later.

CHAPTER XVI

THE REFORMATION IN THE NETHERLANDS

— I —

CALVINISM, by common consent, was a powerful formative influence in the national existence of the Netherlands and has continued to be a distinctive factor in the life of the Dutch nation. Yet it may be said that there the modern era in religion began not with Calvin's or Luther's influence but with the brotherhood movements of the fourteenth and fifteenth centuries, especially the Brethren of the Common Life. This important religious fraternity was founded by Gerard Groot and Florentius Radewins in 1378 and from its cradle at Deventer moved into many towns, and made an impression in most of the universities, of northern Europe. Its profound and mystically based charitableness was expressed with special effect in education, in which classical and Christian learning flourished together. As schoolmasters the Brethren had no rivals, and they brought literacy and intelligence to a high point of development. They were interested in New Testament Greek and other Biblical studies and, for a century before Erasmus, had contended and labored for the circulation of the Bible in the spoken language. *The Usefulness of Reading Sacred Scripture in the Common Speech* is the title of a treatise by Gerard Zerbolt (d. 1398), a companion of the founders. The Brethren were pioneers in the use of the printing press for this and other religious purposes. Their theology was Augustinian. Like other writings of Groot and his circle, the popular devotional classic, *The Imitation of Christ* (mainly from his pen, though expanded by Thomas à Kempis), bears the stamp of Augustine's emphasis on the divine initiative in salvation. The teaching of the Reformers, as Karl Ullmann and Albert Hyma have shown, has much in common with that of the Brethren before them. John of Goch (d. 1445) left numerous books, such as his *Grace and Faith* and *Liberty of the Christian Religion,* that contain opinions later made familiar by Luther, and the parallels between Luther and John Wessel Gansfort (d. 1489) are equally obvious. For editing Goch's works (1521), Cornelius Graphaeus, Antwerp official and friend of Erasmus, was imprisoned and banished.

The Renaissance discoveries were bringing a new commercial prosperity to the maritime towns of Flanders, Zealand, and Holland, while Renaissance humanism was expressing itself in a vigorous development of art and in the 'chambers of rhetoric' that cultivated drama and oratory. The sixteenth century opened hopefully, amid the evidences of a colorful civilization marked by freedom, intellectual achievement, and a progressive spirit.

The seventeen provinces of the Netherlands which the prince who later became the Emperor Charles V inherited in 1506 occupied the areas of the present Netherlands Kingdom, Belgium, Luxembourg, and a populous strip of territory now within France. The southern ('Walloon') provinces were French-speaking, but in the others the language was Dutch. Since the rule of Charles the Bold of Burgundy, who had begun to hold meetings of the 'states general' in 1465, a sense of unity and nationhood had been arising, which would reach full development in the sixteenth-century war of liberation. On the death of Charles the Bold, his daughter Mary, wife of Maximilian I of Germany, was obliged to grant the 'Great Privilege' of 1477, which, together with similar provincial charters, reduced the authority of the prince and affirmed that of the states and their representative council.

Charles V was the grandson of Maximilian. His father, Philip the Good, died in 1506, and his mother, Joanna the Insane, daughter of Ferdinand and Isabella of Spain, was incapable of rule. Charles was a child of six. Maximilian was nominated regent, but he appointed his daughter, Margaret of Austria, widow of a duke of Savoy, to govern for him, She was the first of three Hapsburg ladies to fill this office. Mary of Burgundy, sister of Charles and widow of Louis II of Hungary, became regent in 1530, and gave place to the personal rule of Philip II in 1555. In 1559 Philip, on leaving the country, appointed his illegitimate half-sister, Margaret of Parma, who held office until

1567. Thus, in a period of great problems and changes in the Netherlands, government was in the hands of the aunts and sisters of its absent kings. Though they were all women of ability, their success was limited, and only the first of the three can be said to have won the loyalty of the people.

— II —

Luther's early treatises promptly appeared on the bookstalls of Louvain, Ghent, Antwerp, and other Netherlands cities. Despite their condemnation in February 1520 by the university of Louvain, Henry of Zutphen, who was prior of an Antwerp house of Augustinians and who knew Luther personally, was reported some months later to be diligently spreading them. In 1521, Jerome Aleander, papal nuncio, passed through the Netherlands seizing and burning stocks of the offending books. Dissatisfied with the results, he proposed to the emperor the burning of some Lutherans instead. In 1522 Charles induced Pope Adrian VI to appoint two inquisitors for the country. Two of the Antwerp Augustinians, Henry Voes and John Esch, were burned at Brussels, 1 July 1523. Luther's first published verses were inspired by the martyrdom of these Dutch disciples. Henry of Zutphen had been snatched by the populace from a like fate. A series of edicts by the emperor and the appointment of a new inquisitional council by the Pope slowed but failed to prevent the growth of Lutheranism. Inquisitorial measures were hampered by the attitude of magistrates, and even of the vice-ruler, Margaret of Savoy, who was inclined to moderation. We have noted above (p. 46) the important contacts of the Dutch scholar Hinne Rode with Luther and Zwingli. Rode introduced to them the views on the Eucharist of Cornelius Hoen, a representative (then imprisoned) of the school of Wessel Gansfort. The agreement of Rode and Zwingli is the first evidence of direction toward a Reformed, and away from a Lutheran, trend in the Netherlands.

Meanwhile a widespread Anabaptist movement was receiving more attention and yielding more victims than Lutheranism. This movement found its adherents among the town working classes. Its first stage was marked by intense conviction and enthusiasm. Under the pressure of peculiarly inhuman persecution, this zeal became wildly fanatical and culminated in the sanguinary Münster episode of 1534–5, in which the leading roles were played by Dutch Anabaptists. From 1536 to his death in 1561, Menno Simons was able under great difficulties to reorganize the remnants of the movement and impart to it a gentle and reasonable spirit.

From 1540 to 1550 Charles promulgated edicts laying down severe penalties for the circulation of foreign-language books on religion and Dutch and Latin editions of the Scriptures. His attempt in 1550 to establish a genuine, efficient inquisition on the Spanish model met with such resistance as virtually to nullify it. The regent Mary was regarded as sympathetic with the Lutherans, and is known to have urged Charles to avoid depopulating the provinces by wholesale slaughter of Anabaptists (1543). Persecution was severe but irregular. The new movements were native to the country; the oppressive forces were Spanish and Roman and were indifferently supported by Dutch magistrates. The aged and gouty emperor was finally beaten. On 25 October 1555, in a moving scene at Brussels, he abdicated in favor of his son Philip II, who had spent some unhappy months in England as consort of Mary Tudor.

A zeal against heretics burned in the bosom of this resolute and patient Hapsburg. Charles, by birth and upbringing a Netherlander, had been liked by many of the people. Philip, an uncongenial Spaniard, was seemingly indifferent to the good will of his subjects, and to their sufferings. They resented his heavy and arbitrary taxation, as well as his repressive ecclesiastical policy and the presence of Spanish troops in the provinces. The period of Philip's personal rule in the Netherlands was disturbed by war with France and with Pope Paul IV, in the course of which his attention was drawn away from the Protestants. But he undertook a reorganization of the hierarchy in order to increase the ranks of the Netherlands bishops, and to withdraw the bishoprics of Cambrai, Arras, Tournay, and Utrecht from the foreign jurisdiction of the archbishops of Rheims and Cologne. The reorganization added no less than fourteen sees and erected into archbishoprics Cambrai, Mechlin, and Utrecht. Philip's hope was to use the bishops in the suppression of heresy: he would rather, he said, die a hundred deaths than be a king over heretics. In the manner of Francis I, he secured the royal control of episcopal appointments; but he demanded that bishops be theologians. Opposition was voiced by many of the nobles, by the wealthy abbots, whose property was seized for the support of the new sees, and by the townsmen of Antwerp, who did not want a bishop in their midst; but the opposition was overridden. The bishop of Arras, Antoine de Granvelle, a native of Besançon, was made archbishop of Mechlin and primate of the Netherlands. While this plan was coming into effect the war with France ended with the Treaty of Cateau-Cambrésis, February 1559. But conditions in Spain called Philip thither and he departed in August 1559.

Within the Council of State which now assisted the regent, Margaret of Parma, strong disagreement had arisen. Lamoral, Count of Egmont, hero and victor in the recent war, and William, Prince of Orange, trusted adviser of Charles V, were unwilling to co-operate with the policy of Granvelle and the other two members. They presently found themselves in the leadership of an opposition party which represented popular sentiment against the new bishops, the severities of persecution, and the presence and insolent behavior of the king's Spanish mercenaries. The views of these leaders may be compared with those of the French Politiques: they were patriots who favored a liberal religious policy. But in this instance the reigning policy was determined by an absent, alien, and unpopular king.

A dramatic and bitter political struggle was now beginning, and at the same time a new religious force that would ally itself with the cause of the patriots and invigorate the national movement made its appearance in the Netherlands.

— III —

John Calvin's wife was of Walloon origin. She had come with her first husband as a refugee from Liége to Strasbourg. They were then Anabaptists and were converted to Calvin's doctrines under his preaching. In Strasbourg and later in Geneva many other French-speaking Netherlanders learned Calvinism or were confirmed in it. From Emden in East Friesland also, the teaching of John à Lasco was having an influence in the Netherlands. It was 'to the faithful ministers of Christ throughout East Friesland' that Calvin dedicated his Latin Catechism of 1545. He states his reasons for this. Some of those addressed had expressed their love for him and approval of his writings, and had requested him to write the work in Latin. And what he had learned about them from good men had bound him to them with all his soul. The church established by à Lasco in London in 1550 was attended for the most part by Dutchmen engaged in merchandise, who kept up intercourse with the Dutch ports. The literature of the Reformed Churches could not be excluded from a land accustomed to trade across all its frontiers by land and sea. It was to little avail that Charles V's edict of 1550 expressly penalized with death by fire the printers or possessors of 'any book or writing made by Luther, Oecolampadius, Zwingli, Bucer, Calvin, or other heretics reprobated by the Holy Church.' The infiltration was greatest in the French-speaking provinces. There, in the very years of Philip's personal reign, Calvinist units of organization arose and multiplied.

The year of Philip's departure, 1559, was, as we have seen, the year of Calvin's final edition of the *Institutes,* and of the adoption of the French confession of faith. At the beginning of that year, an important resolution had been silently formed in the mind of William of Orange (1533–84). During the negotiations between Philip and Henry II of France he learned the intention of the negotiating princes to destroy heretics, and saw in this such a menace to justice and liberty in the Netherlands that he then deeply resolved 'to drive the Spanish vermin from the land.' William was not at the time a Protestant. In 1561 he married a Saxon Lutheran princess. It was not until 1573, when Calvinism had already become widespread in the Netherlands, that he became a Calvinist. 'We improve as we grow older,' he explained. His later confession of the secret resolution of 1559 caused him to be called William the Silent — a misleading sobriquet, since, unlike his enemy Philip II, he was ordinarily rather outspoken.

Numerous Walloon and some Dutch congregations were now being organized on the Reformed model. In 1561 Guy de Brès, a native of Mons who had associated with Calvinists in France, Switzerland, and England, wrote a confession of faith 'for the faithful who are everywhere scattered through the Netherlands.' It was sent about the Reformed churches for comment. Calvin liked it but thought its adoption unwise, since the French had just issued their confession. In 1562 it was published in French and Dutch and was sent to Philip II with a bold request that, having learned their beliefs, he would either increase his burnings and tortures or become the support and refuge of his loyal subjects. Its author paid with his life for his faith, at Valenciennes in 1567. Meanwhile the confession had been adopted by a synod held in Antwerp in 1566: it was to become, with modifications, the principal doctrinal standard of the Netherlands Calvinists. We know it as the Belgic Confession.

The records of the early Reformed synods of the Netherlands offer evidence of thoughtful provision for numerous matters of organization, discipline, and worship. The earliest was held at Turcoing, 26 April 1563. In the years following, local and general synods met frequently at various places. A number were held in Antwerp. The first general synod met at Wesel in 1568, the second at Emden in 1571, both outside the borders of the country. The synods exhibit the growth of the authority of representative assemblies in 'the churches under the Cross' (as they were designated) from a period before the development of a revolutionary national organization to free the Netherlands from Spanish rule. They dealt with countless details regarding the duties of pastors, elders, and deacons, marriages, the reception of strangers in a congregation, the administration of the sacraments, *etc*. The Synod of Emden, 1571, states that:

> No church may pretend to domination or preeminence over the other churches, nor minister over other ministers, elders over elders, deacons over deacons.

The principle of equality is carried further and is associated with the practice of fraternal correction. The Synod of Dort, held in June 1578, requires that before a communion service the ministers, elders, and deacons 'censure one another . . . and receive in charity Christian admonitions.' The Emden synod adopted a scheme of government for all the Netherlands churches, uniting them in effect into a national church. The Belgic Confession of Guy de Brès was adopted; the Geneva Catechism was to be used for the French-speaking churches, the Heidelberg Catechism for the Dutch. The framework of church government comprised local consistories, meeting weekly; classes, consisting of groups of the consistories (and corresponding to the French colloquies and Scottish presbyteries), meeting quarterly; synods meeting annually in three areas; and, over all, biennial national synods. No national synod could be held on Netherlands soil before that of 1578 at Dort: this synod, with other modifications of the polity, ordered that the national synod meetings should thereafter be triennial. Actually the national synods were allowed to lapse during the years 1586 to 1618.

— IV —

From 1566 to 1578 the country was ablaze with war, and the patriots under William of Orange won substantial victories. Some historians would give the impression that the war of independence was motivated by secular concerns. If we examine the Reformed Church organization, however, we see that it antedated the corresponding political development. It is to be remembered, too, that on 2 October 1565 Francis du Jon (Junius), a French Calvinist, instituted with prayer an organization of twenty nobles at Brussels to plan the campaign of national liberation. The boldness of the Reformed encouraged the resistance to the king. From 1566 they ventured to hold outdoor meetings for preaching and psalm singing, under voluntary armed guard. A Dutch metrical version of the Psalter was supplied by Peter Dathenus, a prominent pastor formerly at Frankfurt, and great assemblies gathered to sing the Psalms to the Genevan tunes.

The Protestant cause suffered by the destructive violence of anti-clerical mobs who took the opportunity to loot and desecrate churches. In 1566 they wrecked the interior of the Cathedral of Antwerp. Philip II tried in vain to have the decisions of the Council of Trent enforced in the Netherlands. Concerned equally over heresy and rebellion, he sent the steadfast and ruthless Alva, who had once fought for him against the Pope, to destroy heretics and crush resistance. Alva's dictatorship (1567–73) cost many thousands of lives but failed to bring submission. In 1575 the provinces of Holland and Zealand were united under the prince of Orange, and in 1576 these states together with those of the southern Netherlands agreed, in the Pacification of Ghent, to join under William in opposition to Philip, without prejudice to Roman Catholicism. When this provision was used as a basis of negotiation with Philip, the northern provinces independently formed the Union of Utrecht (January 1579). William was induced to accept this action which precipitated the Netherlands declaration of independence (26 July 1581). Brabant and

Flanders united with Utrecht, Guelderland, Holland, and Zealand in abjuring their allegiance to Philip and constituting an independent state.

Somewhat ineptly, William sought to share the Netherlands rule with a French prince, the incompetent Francis, duke of Alençon and later of Anjou, and brother of Henry III. A resulting conflict opened the way for Philip's new governor, the Prince of Parma, to recover Flanders and Brabant and secure the Spanish position in the southern provinces. Philip had put a price on William's head, and the prince survived several attempts on his life. Finally he was assassinated by a fanatic on 10 July 1584. His son Maurice succeeded him. By able generalship he ultimately secured the independence of the new republic. Its provinces, Guelderland, Utrecht, Friesland, Overyssel, Zealand, and Holland, constituted a rich land extending from the German duchy of East Friesland to the mouth of the Scheldt. In the war these provinces had suffered less devastation than Flanders and Brabant, and commerce and prosperity now moved from Antwerp to Amsterdam. In 1609 Maurice concluded a twelve-year truce with Spain, which in effect meant the final establishment of the Dutch Republic.

— V —

Before this state of outward security was reached, the life of the Reformed Church was greatly disturbed by theological strife. The contest arose out of the teachings of Jacob Arminius (d. 1609), who, having earned distinction in his studies in Geneva, was made a minister of Amsterdam and later became the successor of Francis Junius in the university of Leyden (1603). Despite his interest in the anti-Aristotelian, Peter Ramus, whose views were rejected by Beza, Arminius had been a theological disciple of that rigorous Calvinist, whose supralapsarianism added something to Calvin's doctrine of election. The decree of election, according to Beza, preceded the fall of man and contemplated man's fallen state as part of the eternal plan of God. A liberal thinker, Dirk Coornhert (d. 1590), had challenged this position, and Arminius found that he could not defend it. He later engaged in a long correspondence with Junius, who had been the chief reviser of the Belgic Confession, over this doctrine, and wrote against William Perkins of Cambridge, who was of Beza's opinion. His great opponent, Francis Gomarus, a Leiden colleague, was a brother-in-law of Junius and a defender of the confession. This typically Calvinist statement stresses man's loss in the Fall of all but 'little traces' of his original goodness, thereby becoming 'the slave of sin' (XIV). It further states that God mercifully saves those whom, 'in His eternal and unchangeable council, of mere goodness' He has elected in Christ, and justly condemns the others. This is most naturally interpreted as supralapsarianism. Although Arminius had clearly rejected that doctrine, he argued that he could still accept the confession. An opposing view, infralapsarianism, represented the divine decree of election as subsequent to the Fall. Arminius moved away from this doctrine also and introduced one of co-operation of the human will in salvation. The atonement wrought by Christ is sufficient for all. The decree of election embraces only those who repent, believe, and persevere, and the decree of reprobation applies only to the impenitent.

After Arminius' death, his disciple Simon Episcopius (d. 1643) wrought his master's doctrines into a system, notably in his *Confession and Declaration* (1622). This is a treatise in defense of the basic document of the Arminian party, the celebrated *Remonstrance* of 1610. The chief framer of the *Remonstrance* was John Uytenbogaert, chaplain to Prince Maurice. Briefly this document states (1) that the eternal decree of salvation refers to those who shall believe and persevere in the faith; (2) that Christ died for all men, though believers only are benefited; (3) that man can do nothing truly good until he is born again through the Holy Spirit; (4) that grace is not irresistible; and (5) that the faithful are assisted by grace in temptation and are kept from falling if they desire Christ's help and are 'not inactive.' These are the Five Points of Arminianism. A *Counter-Remonstrance* was promptly issued by the Gomarists. Controversy was now intensely waged among the learned, and even entered the common life. A blacksmith with a red-hot iron chased Episcopius in the street. Ministers were driven from their posts by magistrates favorable to the Remonstrants. Riots were occurring, and there was danger of civil war. The Advocate of Holland, John Oldenbarnevelt, had strongly supported the Remonstrants. Maurice became alienated from him, and although he 'did not know whether predestination is blue or green,' he decided to favor the Gomarists. The young scholar, Hugo Grotius, also belonged to the Arminian party. The States General finally called a synod to meet at Dort. When it met, Maurice had already put Oldenbarnevelt and Grotius in prison.

The Synod of Dort held 154 sessions during the period from 13 November 1618 to 28 May 1619. Its Dutch membership was prevailingly of the Gomarist or rigorous Calvinist persuasion, but theologians from the churches of England and the Palatinate tempered the rigor of its decisions. The French delegates were not permitted by Louis XIII to leave France. The canons of the synod assert: (1) that election is founded on God's purpose 'before the foundation of the world'; (2) that the efficacy of Christ's atonement extends to the elect only; (3) that the Fall has left man in a state of corruption and helplessness: his gleams of natural light are of no value for salvation; (4) that regeneration is an inward renewal of the soul and of the will and is wholly a work of God, 'powerful, delightful, astonishing, mysterious, and ineffable'; (5) that God so preserves the elect, ever renewing their repentance, patience, humility, gratitude, and good works, that, despite their sins, they do not finally fall away from grace. We have here the Five Points of Calvinism — unconditional election, limited atonement, total depravity, irresistible grace, and the perseverance of the saints.

The Remonstrants had asked in 1610 for a synod to be called by the states but had opposed the calling of this synod of theologians. Episcopius and a few of his party attended some of its early sessions. He spoke with great boldness; but he and his friends were treated as persons suspected of heresy and obligated to clear themselves, and were finally dismissed by the president in an angry speech (16 January). Shortly before the conclusion of the meeting, the aged Oldenbarnevelt was convicted on a trumped-up charge of treason and was beheaded at The Hague. Maurice, who desired a monarchical authority which the republican statesman had opposed, was responsible for this execrable deed. Grotius, through a stratagem of his resourceful wife, was carried out of prison in a box, and lived to write the weighty books on religion and government by which his fame endures. The Arminians who declined to accept the decisions of Dort were exiled, but on the death of Maurice (1625) they were allowed to return, establish congregations of the 'Remonstrant Church,' and teach freely.

— VI —

The Dutch Church was rich in learning and produced a considerable body of theological writing. The baron Philip van Marnix (d. 1598), one of the first leaders in the revolution (1565), had studied under Calvin in Geneva and came to be a close adviser of William of Orange. He was the author of satires and Calvinist treatises and the translator of parts of the Old Testament into Dutch. His *Treatise on the Sacraments* appeared after his death. Francis Junius was considered one of the ablest of the theologians, and he wrote voluminously. In his *Theological Theses* (1584) he covers amply in short, numbered paragraphs the principal topics of theology. He appears to advantage in his *Eirenicum, or the Peace of the Catholic Church* (1592) addressed to the Landgrave of Hesse, which takes the form of 'Meditations' on Psalms 122 and 133 and warmly urges the cultivation of a spirit of peace and unity in the churches. Arminius wrote an oration of similar intent in the midst of his controversies, *On Reconciling the Dissensions among Christians* (1600), which contains specific proposals for bringing unity through conference.

The seventeenth century was to see the free development of theology and philosophy in the Netherlands. René Descartes (d. 1650) wrote most of his works during a residence of twenty years there. A minority of Reformed theologians felt strongly the influence of his rationalism. At Franeker and Leyden, John Cocceius (d. 1669), a German from Bremen, elaborated his doctrine of the covenants of works and grace, in which he had been anticipated to a great extent by Swiss, Scottish, and English writers. *His Doctrine of the Covenant and Testaments of God* (1648) changed the emphasis in Calvinism, bringing into the foreground the divine undertaking in the covenant of grace prefigured in the Old Testament and fully revealed in the New, and relegating to the background the concept of unilateral decrees. Like Arminianism and Amyraldism, it tended to modify the harshness of Calvinism.

Perhaps the most authoritative, though not the most original, of the Dutch Calvinists of his generation was Gisbert Voet (d. 1676) of Utrecht, whose long life of intense study bore fruit in a variety of learned works. He defended old-fashioned Calvinism against Arminians, Jansenists, Lutherans, Cocceius, and Descartes. He exercised, too, a notable influence in the development of the devotional life, through a mystical piety that was partly fed by the *Imitation of Christ*. In this he was associated with William Teelinck (d. 1629), who was under English Puritan influence, and Jodocus van Lodensteyn (d. 1677). With these devout men he introduced a Dutch pietist movement that anticipated the German Pietism of Spener, and he was like the latter indebted to both medieval and English Puritan devotional literature. A strongly individualistic pietist was Jean de Labadie (d. 1674), a French convert from Roman Catholicism who at Geneva influenced young Spener and was later associated with Voet at Utrecht. After a pastorate at Middleburg, he broke with the Reformed ministers and founded the Labadist sect at Amsterdam. Among his disciples was the highly gifted Anna Maria Schürman, a former pupil of Voet. The Labadists advocated a spiritual and prophetic church on the model of the first Christian community in Jerusalem.

The seventeenth century saw the flowering of the Calvinist republic. It was a wealthy nation and a colonizing power. It was a land of relative freedom and the refuge of free minds. After the separation from the southern Netherlands, says the historian Pieter Geyl, 'Holland had suddenly become fertile soil for all the activities of civilization.' Dutch art reached a new vitality in the original and versatile Rembrant van Rijn (d. 1669), whose powerful brush employed light and shadow in a way suggested probably, as Leon Wencelius holds, by the contrast of sin and grace in Calvinist thought.

The free culture of the Netherlands can be ascribed only in part to Calvinism. The orthodox Calvinists were far less tolerant than was the prevailing spirit of the country. When Balthasar Bekker of Amsterdam exposed the folly of belief in witchcraft (1691) he was suspended from the ministry, but his salary was continued by the magistrates until his death.

CHAPTER XVII

CALVINISM IN GERMANY AND EASTERN EUROPE

— I —

It was chiefly in the 1560's that the Reformed type of Protestantism entered the Rhineland. Before that decade there had been frequent religious intercourse between the Rhine cities and Zurich, Basel, and Geneva. The Reformation in Strasbourg under Bucer's leadership showed, indeed, some of the characteristics of the Reformed discipline, and the church system was such that Calvin felt entirely at home in it. From the period of his work there, Calvin was known to many up and down the Rhine. From that area several replies were written to his *Treatise on Relics* (1543), in which he showed an extraordinary knowledge of the shrines of Treves and Cologne. No German city became Calvinist, however, in Calvin's lifetime. Strasbourg was attached to the Lutheran Schmalkald League. After Charles V's *Interim* (the brief enforcement of which had driven Bucer out in 1549) proved unworkable, and the city was free to return to Protestantism, it became strongly Lutheran and anti-Calvinist. The pastor of Calvin's former congregation of French refugees was expelled (1555), and the Calvinist professor, Jerome Zanchi (d. 1590), though supported by the venerable John Sturm, after a struggle found it necessary to withdraw; he was to spend his late years with distinction as a professor at Heidelberg.

Luther had visited Heidelberg in 1518, and it was then that Bucer, a young Dominican, hearing the Reformer discourse in the Augustinian cloister, cast in his lot with the new movement. The Rhenish or Lower Palatinate, under the elector Otto Henry, had adopted a Lutheranism so moderate that it tolerated expressions of Zwinglianism and Calvinism. By the late 'fifties, however, the university of Heidelberg had become the scene of a bitter quarrel, in course of which the Lutheran rigorist, Tilemann Hesshus, assailed those of Melanchthonian and Reformed persuasion and introduced forms of worship and ceremonial that were highly resented as idolatrous by the opposing groups. The angry outbursts of Hesshus, no less than his principles, alienated Otto Henry and his successor, Frederick III (1559–76).

Sincerely and intelligently religious, Frederick made himself familiar with the disputed points in doctrine and worship. He was inclined to Calvinism by his distaste for elaborate ceremonies such as the new anti-Calvinist Lutheranism demanded. The decline of Melanchthon's influence and his death in April 1560 made impossible the continuation by Frederick of the liberal Lutheranism of his predecessor, especially since other German princes were now supporting the rigorist party. At the time of the marriage of his daughter to the Lutheran duke of Saxe-Weimar (June 1560) a five-day Latin disputation was held at his court, in which the Calvinist doctrines were so convincingly presented that Frederick, already favorable to Calvinism, began to move in the direction of its adoption. The theologian who, in Frederick's view, won the argument against the court preachers of his new son-in-law was the little-known but able French Calvinist, Pierre Boquin, whom Otto Henry had recently appointed to a Heidelberg chair.

The following January a conference of princes met at Naumburg to consider Protestant unity, but its effect was to divide Lutherans from Calvinists more hopelessly than before. The elector now proceeded to promote Calvinism in his domain. The Calvinism introduced was, however, no simple product of Geneva but was tinged with a Melanchthonian spirit. He found it necessary to invite new leaders. One of those sought as professor of theology was Peter Martyr, the Italian Reformer, who was then in Zurich, and had reached an age that justified his declining the invitation. But he had a brilliant German pupil, a native of Breslau, whom he recommended for the post. The studies of Zacharias Ursinus (Bär; d. 1583) had ideally fitted him for co-operation in Frederick's policy. At Wittenberg he had spent nearly seven years under the tutorship of Melanchthon, to whom he was greatly attached. He had traveled to other Reformation centers and had listened to Calvin in Geneva. He had been forced from his ministry in Breslau by the Lutheran reaction there

(1560) and had turned to the teachers of Zurich, where Peter Martyr led him to explicit Calvinism, as far at least as the doctrine of man's sinful state is concerned. At the age of twenty-seven Ursinus was a highly trained scholar, fond of the classics and of poetry, and familiar with the whole field of theology. At the elector's wish he came to Heidelberg early in September 1561.

The man who was to be his co-worker, Caspar Olevianus (Olewig, d. 1585) of Treves, had preceded him. Like Calvin, Olevianus had studied law at Orléans and Bourges (1550–57). While at Bourges he became known to the future elector when he tried in vain to rescue Frederick's young son from drowning. He became a Calvinist in this period, later studied for a year in Geneva, in close relation with Calvin, at whose prompting he attempted to preach in Treves. He soon found himself accused of being a disciple of Calvin and was imprisoned. He obtained his liberty through the vigorous intervention of Frederick, who at once brought him to Heidelberg, in January 1560. He was two years younger than Ursinus, more eloquent and less scholarly.

— II —

Frederick utilized the services of both these young men in the College of Wisdom, the theological school he created from what had been an academy; but Olevianus became chiefly a preacher and Ursinus a professor. It was planned to prepare and authorize a catechism to replace the conflicting catechisms of Luther, Brenz, and à Lasco that had been in use. The two scholars, both in their twenties, co-operated in the framing of the Heidelberg Catechism, finished in January 1563, one of the most remarkable of all statements of faith both for its content and for the extent of its circulation in many languages. It quickly obtained formal assent in virtually all the Calvinist churches, and in both the German and the Dutch Reformed churches was made the basis of 'catechetical preaching.'

This great document is a confession in 129 questions and answers. The answer to Question 1 contains the affirmation, 'I am not my own'; under Question 2 we are given the outline of what follows — 'my sin and misery,' 'how I am redeemed,' and 'how I am to be thankful.' Man's depravity and God's displeasure are confessed in solemn language (3–11); the plan of redemption is unfolded with a discussion of the Apostles' Creed, but without reference to election (12–85). The concluding section on thankfulness as the basis of good works (86–129) embodies a treatment of the Commandments and the Lord's Prayer.

The Catechism is remarkable for the use throughout of the first-person pronoun, often in the singular, a feature that gives a warm, personal quality to its evangelical testimony. Here is the definition of faith (21):

> It is not only an assured knowledge whereby I hold as true all that God has revealed to us in His Word, but also a hearty trust, which the Holy Spirit works in me through the Gospel, that not only to others, but also to me, forgiveness of sins, everlasting righteousness and blessedness are freely given by God, of mere grace, only for the sake of the merits of Christ.

God the Father is said to be 'my God and my Father'; Christ 'took upon himself the curse that lay upon me.' The interpretation of the 'descent into hell' in the Creed as a figurative representation of Christ's anguish on the Cross is peculiar to this Catechism among other confessional statements; but it is in fact a view borrowed from Calvin. Ursinus in his lecture notes later published by his eminent pupil David Pareus (*Exposition of the Catechism*) uses the phrase, 'today . . . with me in paradise' (Luke 23:43), to support the view that Christ did not literally descend into hell. The 80th question, on the difference between the Lord's Supper and the Mass, is an insertion 'added on command of his Electoral Grace' after the first printing; and a clause condemning the Mass as 'an accursed idolatry' was further added to this by Frederick in response to the decrees of the Council of Trent.

The third part of the Heidelberg Catechism suggestively interprets the Christian life as the thankful response of the believer to the blessings of God. Sorrow for and hatred of sin, and a heartfelt joy in God, are the marks of the new life. Simple details of morality are stressed by means of brief, penetrating interpretations of the Commandments. Envy, hatred, and anger are called secret murder, and theft includes deceitful tricks, covetousness, and waste. '[I must] labor faithfully that I may be able to help the poor.' The treatment of prayer stresses its importance as 'the chief part of thankfulness,' and sustains through a condensed interpretation of the petitions of the Lord's Prayer the sense of 'filial reverence' for God as Father and an awareness of His 'heavenly majesty.' It is hardly too much to say that this section constitutes a little classic of the devotional life.

— III —

After the Naumburg conference the fate of Melanchthonianism was sealed. Confusion reigned in Lutheranism until the adoption of the Formula of Concord (1580), a statement designed to exclude the Calvinist positions. At Wittenberg the doctrine of Melanchthon, defended by his son-in-law, Caspar Peucer, remained in favor until 1574, when its exponents were expelled or imprisoned. The designation by which the views of Peucer and his colleagues were known among their opponents was 'Crypto-Calvinism' — Calvinism in disguise. There was nothing dishonestly concealed in their teaching, but on the doctrine of the Lord's Supper it approached Calvin's position closely, as indeed did the teaching of Melanchthon. An important point in all this was the fact that by the Augsburg Treaty of 1555, which settled the territorial issues of Lutheranism and Roman Catholicism in Germany, no provision had been made for Calvinism. Only those of the Augsburg Confession and of the 'old Religion' had rights by the terms of the treaty. Duke Christopher of Wurtemberg and other Lutheran princes brought pressure to bear on Frederick to have him repudiate the Heidelberg Catechism. Instead, Frederick proceeded to introduce a church order containing a liturgy with the Catechism, which was equally unsatisfactory to his critics. The Palatinate Liturgy is partly dependent on that of Calvin. It provides for a bimonthly celebration of the Lord's Supper in large towns, elsewhere (as in Geneva) at Christmas, Easter, Whitsuntide, and the first Sunday in September. After the preparatory service and before communion any who wish to speak privately with the minister may do so. Discipline is to be administered by the pastor together with 'honest and Godfearing men' elected by the people. At the Sunday morning service the prayer of confession is followed by a declaration of divine grace (quoting John 3:16) to the penitent and a declaration of judgment for the impenitent. The sermon is followed by a prayer 'for all men in the whole world,' and for the persecuted:

Be pleased O Father of Grace . . . to strengthen the persecuted with victorious stedfastness and the power of Thy
Holy Spirit that they may joyfully receive these sufferings
from Thy hand and in the midst of tribulation experience
that peace which passeth all understanding.

Services are included for the visitation of the sick and of prisoners, and for funerals.

The issue of Calvinism in the Empire was now acute. Even the
emperor, Maximilian II, who was not ill disposed toward Protestantism in its Lutheran forms, warned Frederick to abandon
the Heidelberg Catechism and adopt the Augsburg Confession.
The elector had (like Calvin) no objection to that confession in
the edition published by Melanchthon in 1540 — the *Augustana
variata* (see above, pp. 197 ff.) — and had so declared at the Naumburg conference; but he was determined to hold to the Catechism. In May 1566 he was called to account before the imperial
diet at Augsburg. The plan of his accusers was to have him deposed as a violator of the Treaty of Augsburg, and some of his
subjects even feared for his life. But he made before a hostile
diet so eloquent and impressive a defense, committing his life to
God and the Catechism to the test of Scripture, that no punitive
action was taken against him. The effect of this incident was to
give an opportunity to Calvinism within the Empire, although
there was no formal decision securing its status.

Frederick and his theologians now proceeded to organize the
Church more fully, in order to give it permanence and security.
The local consistories were already coming into existence, and
the elector urged their formation in every congregation. He also
promoted the establishment of classes (or presbyteries) representing groups of neighboring parishes. Through the zeal of Olevianus, a firm discipline was established in which the Church acted
independently of the civil power. A prominent Swiss Zwinglian,
the physician Thomas Erastus (d. 1583), a professor of Heidelberg and member of the elector's council, favored a system like
that of Zurich, in which discipline was left for the most part to
the secular government. At this period the university of Heidelberg, with a distinguished faculty that included Ursinus, Boquin,
Erastus, Zanchi, and the Jewish Christian Biblical scholar
Emanuel Tremellius, attracted advanced students from many

countries. Controversy was aroused over the defense of a thesis on church discipline presented for the doctorate by George Wither, an English Puritan minister, in June 1568. Erastus, in objection to Wither, assailed the system that Olevianus and Ursinus, with the elector's favor, were establishing. He prudently reserved from publication, however, his *Seventy-five Theses on Excommunication;* which appeared posthumously in 1589 in London. This book gave rise to the common use of the word 'Erastianism' in the sense of the control of the Church by the state, a concept much more far-reaching than Erastus' own thought on discipline.

The elector and his theologians were embarrassed by the appearance of Anti-Trinitarian theology in the Palatinate. The Servetus of the electorate was a pastor named John Sylvanus, who led a small group of pastors to the same opinions. One of these fled to Turkey and became a Mohammedan. It was at the wish of the Calvinist ministers that Sylvanus was beheaded in Heidelberg in December 1572. Unitarianism was still for Calvinists outside the pale of toleration, and the death penalty was their remedy. In this they were fully supported by the Lutheran and Roman Catholic opinion of that age, and the execution of Sylvanus helped Frederick's position in the empire. On the other hand, he made enemies by supporting the Netherlanders against Spain. His young son Christopher, commanding a Palatinate contingent in aid of the Dutch, fell in battle against the Spaniards.

On 26 October 1576 Frederick died. He was succeeded by his son Louis VI, who had ruled the little state known as the Upper Palatinate and had resisted all efforts of his father to admit Calvinism there. Louis now undertook to extinguish the Reformed Church of the Rhenish Palatinate. Calvinist professors and pastors to the number of 600 were deposed and expelled.

— IV —

During this period the Lutheran Formula of Concord was in preparation; it was finally adopted by a large number of Lutheran states in 1580. Its definitions were wholly unfavorable to Calvinism; its effect was less so. In some of the states it was repudiated: King Frederick II of Lutheran Denmark threw into the fire the handsome copies sent to him. A Melanchthonian reaction against it can be seen in some areas, and the resistance tended to become allied, or identified, with Calvinism. John Casimir, spurred by the policy of Queen Elizabeth I of England and the zeal of her young emissary, Sir Philip Sidney, worked up a political association of Calvinist and pro-Calvinist powers, and in September 1577 there occurred at Frankfurt a meeting of representatives of Elizabeth, Henry of Navarre, and the Reformed of the Palatinate, the Netherlands, France, Poland, and Hungary. Its project for a common confession of faith failed to mature. Instead there appeared (1581) the *Harmony of Confessions,* prepared by Beza and Jean François Salvard, then one of Beza's Geneva colleagues. This book, written to promote Church unity, exhibits the similarity in doctrine of fifteen Protestant confessions, and is a landmark in ecumenical history. Meanwhile the international Huguenot scholar, Hubert Languet, who had been in the service of the elector of Saxony at the imperial court and was later to give valuable service to William the Silent, was engaged in an itinerant mission to prevent the adoption by princes of the Formula of Concord, and to affirm the claims of Calvinism. This Reformed campaign against the Formula of Concord was continued by Rudolph Hospinian of Zurich in a large and learned treatise, *Discordant Concord (Concordia discors,* 1607), which describes the history of the Formula and points out its 'errors, divergences from the Augsburg Confession, contradictions, unjust condemnations,' and so on.

The Calvinist exiles from the Palatinate made their influence felt in the states to which they were scattered. As far as possible they were replaced by Lutherans, and a great effort was made to suppress Reformed worship and establish Lutheran worship. All the university theologians were soon forced out.

The Calvinist refugees from the elector Louis were soon active elsewhere. Olevianus fled to Berleberg, Tremellius to Sedan; the other Reformed teachers found a refuge in Neustadt, where John Casimir, brother of Louis, ruled. This prince was no less a Calvinist than his father, Frederick III, had been, and while acting as a guardian of his brother's nine-year-old son, Frederick, and ruler of the Palatinate after his brother's death in 1583, he restored the status of Calvinism in that state as it had been in Frederick III's reign. Hundreds of Lutherans were now dismissed and Calvinists took their places.

John Casimir's successor, Frederick IV (1592–1610), continued the policy of favor to the Reformed Church and strengthening of its organization. He led in the formation of the Protestant Union of Lutheran and Reformed princes (1609). He allied himself with Henry IV of France against Emperor Rudolf II; but his death followed Henry's in the same year, 1610. The outstanding figure in the Palatinate Church in his time was David Pareus (d. 1622), a loyal pupil of Ursinus. As professor of Old Testament and later of New Testament theology, Pareus attracted students to Heidelberg from distant parts of Europe; his numerous treatises reveal the trends of Calvinist thought. At least one of his works assumes new importance in our century, the *Irenicum* (1614–15), in which he presents at length a proposal for Protestant Union by means of a universal synod, the members of which would be 'the best and weightiest men from every province and nation of the Christian world.'

— V —

Meanwhile other German states and cities were adopting Calvinism. In Nassau this change was due to the influence of the Palatinate preachers driven out by Louis VI, together with that of those Melanchthonians who came in 1574, having been forced out of Wittenberg by their prince. The combination of these elements is seen in the decision made at a synod held in 1578 to use the 1540 *Augustana variata* of Melanchthon instead of the 1530 form of the Augsburg Confession, and to introduce a Reformed discipline. The Heidelberg Catechism was adopted in 1581, and Olevianus was called (1582) from Berleberg to help institute the new Reformed university of Herborn. The Nassau organization was formed in some measure under the influence of the Netherlands synods. The theologian, educator, and encyclopedist, John Henry Alsted (d. 1638), a native of Herborn and a professor there, from whom John Amos Comenius gained suggestions toward his educational theories, was the most distinguished of Nassau Calvinists. His *Encyclopedia of All Knowledge* (1630), a celebrated reference work which Cotton Mather called 'a short cut or Northwest Passage to all sciences,' was the product of his own research.

After his escape from prison (1522) the Antwerp Augustinian, Henry of Zutphen (above, p. 257), introduced Lutheranism into

Bremen. The Calvinist movement there began when Albert Hardenberg, a friend of John à Lasco, who was the principal preacher in the cathedral, published a confession of faith that showed a Reformed strain and started a controversy on the Eucharist. Hardenberg and his party denied the high Lutheran doctrine of the ubiquity of Christ's post-Resurrection body. An intense clerical antagonism to him was generated, and, though still in favor with the people, he was forced to leave the city (1561). The Formula of Concord, however, proved unacceptable to the magistrates, who called in the Melanchthonian, Christopher Pezel (1582). Later, as superintendent and professor of theology, Pezel drew up the *Consensus of the Bremen Ministers* (1595), a document that is essentially Calvinist. The Heidelberg Catechism and the doctrinal works of Calvin and Bullinger were approved, and Reformed practices in discipline and worship were introduced. Lutherans were not excluded from the city, however, and in 1638 they were given the use of the cathedral for their worship.

Wesel, on the lower Rhine, was a Lutheran city and received many refugees from Holland and England, most of whom were Calvinists. In 1545, the fugitives were required to sign the 1540 variant version of the Augsburg Confession in order to be permitted to remain; Calvinists did not object to this Melanchthonian document. Charles V succeeded in gaining partial obedience to his *Interim* of 1548, but Lutheranism was afterward restored. We have seen the importance for the Dutch Reformed Church of the synod held in Wesel in 1568. A classis for the Walloon Calvinists of Wesel was formed, which received into membership a German congregation in 1579. The German Reformed element rapidly increased, and when the Netherlanders departed a German synod of Jülich, Cleves, and Berg was left. Though this synod was formally a part of the Dutch Church, the Netherlands influence was largely replaced by that of the Palatinate. The Heidelberg Catechism was in use, and the language of the churches was German. In 1610 these Lower Rhine Reformed classes held a general synod which marked their severance from the Netherlands Church.

It was the insistence of the Lutherans upon the acceptance of the Formula of Concord that brought on a Calvinist trend in Anhalt and Hesse. Melanchthon's son-in-law, Caspar Peucer, after a twelve-year imprisonment in Saxony, in 1586 became a resident of Dessau and helped to confirm the opposition to the Formula. In 1595 the prince of Anhalt, John George, married a daughter of John Casimir, and thereafter pressed for the introduction of Calvinist worship on the Palatine model. While the *Augustana variata* of 1540 was subscribed, the Church also acknowledged (1616) the Heidelberg Catechism and became essentially Calvinist. The pattern of development in Hesse, one of the first strongholds of Lutheranism of a conciliatory type, was similar. Even in the time of the celebrated Landgrave Philip (d. 1567), the influence of Bucer and Calvin colored the Melanchthonian theology of Marburg university. The most influential teacher there was Andreas Hyperius (d. 1564), a widely traveled scholar who became an admirer of Bucer and leaned toward Calvinism, and whose works on theology, preaching, catechesis, and pastoral care were read by many later generations of students. In the late 'seventies a controversy developed when Landgrave William of Hesse-Cassel, with the support of the clergy, persistently refused to sign the Formula of Concord. His successor, Maurice (d. 1605), introduced a Reformed system, without resistance; but when Marburg and Upper Hesse came also under his sway, Calvinism was somewhat arbitrarily established only after riotous scenes and the imposition of martial law. The confession that was adopted in 1607 affirms Calvinist positions against those of the Formula on the five disputed points: the Commandments (especially the second), abolition of pictures, the alleged ubiquity of Christ's body, election, and the participation of the unworthy in the Lord's Supper. By 1610 the polity of the Church had become typically Reformed, from consistory up to general synod; worship, too, with slight concessions to Lutheranism, followed the Reformed practice.

— VI —

The situation in Brandenburg was altered by the expansion of that Lutheran state to include territories affected by Calvinism. In 1609 the elector, John Sigismund, claimed as his inheritance by marriage the duchy of Cleves, which included the territories of Cleves, Jülich, Berg, Mark, and Ravensburg. The ensuing quarrel with the Count Palatine of Nauburg was attended by the conversion of the latter from Lutheranism to Roman Catholicism and of John Sigismund to Calvinism (1613). The elector had been influenced by attacks on the Formula of Concord and by the attitude of numerous Brandenburg ministers who had moved in the same direction. His brother, Ernst, had preceded him in espousing Calvinism. His public aim was to establish a Melanchthonian-Calvinist compromise, with the recognition of what he called 'the improved Augsburg Confession.' But in the end he adopted a system not of unity but of mutual toleration and equality between Lutherans and Calvinists (1614). The new system was violently resisted: a court preacher in Berlin was mobbed and his goods were plundered. Distinctly Calvinist congregations became numerous, however, and enjoyed the elector's favor. Yet Lutherans remained in the great majority, and not until the migration of exiled Huguenots in 1685 did Calvinism become strong in Brandenburg. The refugees came on the invitation of Frederick William, 'the Great Elector,' whose gifted and devout first wife, Louise Henriette (d. 1667), had been a great-granddaughter of Coligny and a granddaughter of William, prince of Orange. At that time thousands of French Protestants found refuge in other Calvinist states of Germany, bringing with them manufacturing skills, military knowledge, experience in trade, educational attainment, and scriptural devotion — valuable contributions to a nation recently stripped and degraded by a protracted war.

The Thirty Years' War (1618–48) brought immeasurable disaster to Germany. In common with other German states, those that had established or permitted Calvinism suffered irreparable losses. No part of Germany endured more devastation and misery than the Palatinate, whose elector, Frederick V, was put forward as king of Bohemia and was utterly defeated near Prague, while his principality was overrun by Bavarian and Spanish armies (1620–23). It was the Great Elector of Brandenburg who successfully insisted, during the negotiations leading to the Peace of Westphalia, that Calvinists should have the same status as Lutherans in the Empire. For the first time the Reformed churches had unequivocal legal recognition by the imperial power. Papal condemnation of the treaty did not prevent its operation. The Upper Palatinate was retained by Bavaria and was forcibly sub-

jected to Roman Catholicism, while the Rhenish or Lower
Palatinate was restored to the heir of Frederick V and continued
as a Calvinist territory.

Later in the century (1688–93) this area was to be ruthlessly
devastated by the armies of Louis XIV. Destitute refugees escaped in large numbers down the Rhine to the Dutch Netherlands. Those who remained were deprived of most of their pastors and were subjected to persecution and persuasion to become
Roman Catholics. The elector John William (1690–1716) himself adopted that faith and attempted a systematic destruction of
Calvinism. After protests by Frederick I, king of Prussia, son of
the Great Elector, the Emperor Francis Joseph I himself intervened to halt the persecution. However, much Reformed Church
property was transferred to the Roman Catholic clergy, and a
divided population remained. The German Reformed body in
America had its beginings in this period. Their principal colony
consisted of refugees from the Palatinate led by George Michael
Weiss in 1727. By 1732 this pioneer group had been so swollen
by fresh migrations that there were 15,000 of the Palatine refugees
scattered through several counties of Pennsylvania.

— VII —

Poland, under a line of kings who were the rulers also of
Lithuania, was a proud kingdom that had often shown indifference to the wishes of Popes. John Ostrorog, law scholar and humanist, interpreted the prevailing view of his countrymen when
he wrote in an academic treatise of 1473: 'The Polish king recognizes nobody's supremacy save that of God.' He recommended
not only that the king should appoint the bishops but also that
the possessions of the Church should be used for public needs.
The disorderly lives of the clergy before the Reformation encouraged a widespread anti-clericalism. Waldensians, Wycliffites,
and Hussites here and there carried on their scriptural propaganda. Luther's early works sold widely in Poland. In 1520 at
Thorn a papal legate was driven with stones from the fire in
which he was burning Luther's books and picture. The Lutheranizing of East Prussia, whose ruler was a vassal of the Polish
king, and the continuous frontier intercourse with Bohemia
rendered impossible the exclusion of Reformation literature and
ideas. King Sigismund I (1506–48) did what he could to suppress

Protestantism. But obedience was not a great virtue among the Poles, and nobles and towns often disregarded the royal edicts. At the opening of the reign of Sigismund II (Augustus) (1548–72), many of the Bohemian Brethren found refuge from their persecuting king, Ferdinand, by flight to Greater Poland and East Prussia.

About the same time Calvinism made its appearance among Polish priests and nobles. Humanists, of whom the brilliant satirist Nicholas Rey was chief, leaned strongly toward Calvinism. Despite strict prohibition by the bishops, many priests introduced elements of Calvinist worship and doctrine. King Sigismund was in correspondence with Calvin and read the *Institutes* with admiration. Calvin presented to him a project of Polish Church reform under an archbishop and bishops of evangelical spirit (5 December 1554). Nicholas Raziwill, Lithuanian prince and chancellor of Sigismund, frankly adopted Calvinism and gave it his support. But the king himself never undertook to initiate the radical reform urged by Calvin or to establish a Reformed Church for Poland.

In the section known as Lesser Poland, Calvinist churches became numerous in the 'fifties. Clerical and lay superintendents were appointed in 1560 to supervise the local churches in matters spiritual and temporal. The Calvinists of Lesser Poland were in brotherly relationship with the Brethren of Greater Poland. A joint synod of these churches was held in 1555 at Kozminek, where they adopted as their common statement the confession edited by the leaders of the Brethren twenty years earlier, which had been printed and circulated in the West. They confirmed their federation by celebrating the Lord's Supper together, and continued to practice intercommunion. Most of them, however, were located in different areas of the country, and they did not coalesce.

About 1550 a general hostility to the bishops on the part of the nobles was aroused in connection with the resolve of a priest, who was also a noble, to be married. Protestant influence became strong in the national diets. Repeatedly they demanded a meeting of a national council for church reform. A diet at Piotrkow in 1556 adopted a resolution in nine points for reform of the Polish Church. The items included permission to priests to be married and the rejection of the legal authority of bishops in civil suits. The initiative in this effort was taken by nobles of Little Poland and Lithuania, led by Raziwill. Poland's great Reformer, John à Lasco, had lived in various Western lands most of the time since 1523. A Protestant since 1538, he had formed contacts with the leading Reformers, had served important churches in Emden and in London, and enjoyed the full confidence both of Geneva and of Zurich. With his own special and original emphases, he was in fact a Calvinist. On invitation of a Polish Calvinist synod, he now returned (December 1556) to Poland. He had suffered harsh treatment from Lutherans in Denmark and Germany; but he now began a zealous effort to unite the Reformed not only with the Brethren but also with the Lutherans in Poland. He appealed to the Lutherans of East Prussia for co-operation in this, but learned that no union was possible except on the basis of the unaltered Augsburg Confession of 1530. He assisted also in the preparation of a Bible in Polish (1563), in which eighteen scholars co-operated. He was the author of numerous statements of doctrine, including the Emden Catechism (1554) used in East Friesland, the *Confession of the Frankfurt Community of Foreigners* (1554), and the *Whole Form and Method of Church Service in the Church of the Strangers* (1550 and 1555). The last of these, usually cited as *Forma ac ratio,* is an ample description of the discipline and worship of à Lasco's London congregation of Continental refugees (1550–53), which fled with him from England early in Mary's reign. Through no fault of his own, à Lasco was defeated in his aim to organize a united national Protestant Church of Poland. His work served to strengthen the Reformed Church, but without the desired union it was not long able to withstand the forces of repression that were coming into play.

The royal secretary, Andreas Fricius Modrevius (Modrzewski), an early friend of à Lasco who had studied under Melanchthon but remained a humanist with an inclination toward Calvinism, had long urged a national or general council of the Church for reform. He was strongly opposed to the methods of the Council of Trent. The completion of the work of Trent and the rising strength of the Counter-Reformation under Jesuit leadership halted the growth of Polish Protestantism and prepared the means of its collapse. Confronted by the new danger, the Lutherans consented with Calvinists and Brethren in the adoption of the Consensus of Sendomir (April 1570). This agreement actually served as a pledge of mutual forbearance rather than as a basis of union. It contains, however, a statement of the Eucharist that is confessedly in accord with the teaching of Melanchthon — with whom, we recall, Calvin always affirmed his essential agreement on this doctrine. When Henry of Anjou (later Henry III of France) became king of Poland in 1573, he was obliged by the nobles to declare his assent to an agreement of mutual religious toleration known as the *Pax Dissidentium* (Peace of the Dissidents). This document states that 'neither Catholics nor any other dissidents shall shed blood over diversity of cult . . . they shall not mutually punish or injure or imprison or exile any for religion.' The tolerant policy here affirmed was to be abandoned slowly. The Counter-Reformation was gradually organized in Poland. Jesuits entered (1564) and became very active. Under their influence King Stephen Batory (1575–86) abandoned Protestantism at the time of his election. The long reign of Sigismund III (1587–1632) saw the virtual extinction of the Reformed Church as an organization. Only a small remnant of Calvinists survived to the eighteenth century, and the boon of toleration came only with the partition of their country among powerful neighbors (1772–95).

— VIII —

In Bohemia, too, Calvinism had wide acceptance followed by suppression. After 1526 the country became a part of the Hapsburg domains and was ruled by Ferdinand, brother of Charles V. The old Hussite Church had long been divided into two rival communions: the Utraquists, who followed the agreements (*Compactata*) arranged at the time of the Council of Basel (1433) and practiced communion in both kinds and some other ceremonial variations from Roman usage; and the Unity of Brethren, the radical Hussite Church formed through the efforts of Peter Chelčický in 1471. Luther had formed contacts with both these Churches. The Utraquists gradually became Lutheran (Neo-Utraquists). John Augusta (d. 1572), of a Utraquist family but a member of the Brethren by choice, wrote, and revised at Luther's suggestion, a notable confession of faith (1535), which was presented to King Ferdinand but was ultimately rejected by him. It was this confession that Polish Calvinists accepted in their agreement with the exiled Bohemian Brethren in Poland (1555).

The numerous Czech students at German and Swiss universities were now turning from Wittenberg to Strasbourg and Geneva. In 1540, at dinner in Strasbourg, Calvin met Matthias Červenka, a youthful minister of the Brethren, and questioned him closely on his Church and nation. Calvin followed this by correspondence with Augusta, in which he made friendly criticism of the Brethren's rule of clerical celibacy. Bucer exchanged numerous fraternal letters with Augusta (1541-2), and his book *On the True Cure of Souls* was published in a Czech translation (1545). It was due to Augusta's policy that the Brethren refused to support the Hapsburg cause in the Schmalkald War. In retaliation Ferdinand began in September 1547 to imprison and exile them. Augusta himself did not escape to Poland but was imprisoned; he remained in confinement, and under pressure to recant, for fourteen years. He attempted in vain to direct from prison the course of the Church. He was misrepresented and distrusted. John Blahoslav (d. 1571), an opponent of his policy, became the chief leader and bishop of the Unity. A better scholar than Augusta, he produced a history of the Brethren, with a companion source book; a work entitled *The Faults of Preachers,* a treatise on music; and a translation of the New Testament from Greek to Czech.

The strictly Calvinist influence was brought in by returning students of noble families who had studied in Geneva, Strasbourg, Heidelberg, Leyden, and other Calvinist centers. Prominent among these were Václav Budovec, a widely traveled scholar who labored for Czech freedom and was executed in Prague in 1621; and Karel Žerotín, who was known at the courts of Queen Elizabeth and Henry IV and corresponded with Philip du Plessis Mornay and other persons of distinction, and who died in exile in 1636. The effect of this foreign study was a continuous Calvinist influence upon the Bohemian nobles, many of whom established Reformed worship on their estates.

Under the Emperor Maximilian II (1564-76) Lutheranism and Calvinism had large freedom in Bohemia. Before a diet held at Prague in 1575 a confession was presented which was later known as the Bohemian Confession. It may be described as Melanchthonian rather than typically Calvinist. Fear of suppression through the Counter-Reformation induced the Lutherans, Calvinists, Neo-Utraquists, and Brethren to frame and adopt this confession jointly. It was favorably received by the emperor, who verbally assured its signers of religious liberty. Maximilian remained faithful to this pledge. His son, the Emperor Rudolf II, was induced by the Calvinist Žerotín and the Bohemian estates to issue a charter (*Maiestätsbrief*), which made explicit the immunity from persecution of adherents of the confession of 1575 (9 July 1609). The incompetent Rudolf was succeeded by his ambitious brother Matthias in 1612. Five years later his cousin, the Archduke Ferdinand, was designated king of Bohemia. At his coronation Ferdinand confirmed the Bohemian charter, which he had no intention of maintaining. The Calvinist nobles, exasperated by the infringements of their immunities, held a general assembly in Prague and, after long deliberation, resolved on resistance. On 23 May 1618 three detested agents of Ferdinand were hurled from a high window of the castle of Prague. This 'Defenestration of Prague' started a new chain of events that rapidly plunged Europe into the Thirty Years' War, during which Bohemia was devastated, its population reduced to one fifth of what it had been, and its Protestantism virtually extirpated by the Hapsburg power and the zealous Jesuit 'converters.' The luckier victims survived in exile. Among these was John Amos Comenius (d. 1670), bishop of the Brethren, educator and versatile genius, whose *Bequest of a Dying Mother, the Unity of Brethren* (1650) pathetically recalls the extinction of his own Church in its homeland. In the writings of Comenius we see the fruits of his early association with John Henry Alsted and with the Reformed schools of Herborn and Heidelberg (above, p. 276). It was only under the 'Enlightened' Emperor Joseph II that Calvinism was permitted in the Austrian Empire (1781). In the present century it showed reviving strength and promise before the revolution of 1948.

— IX —

When Louis II of Hungary fell in the battle of Mohács (1526) the crown went to John Zapolya of Transylvania but was claimed by Ferdinand of Hapsburg. Ferdinand was able to reduce Zapolya's sway to Transylvania, where he ruled by permission of the Sultan. Lutheranism had already entered the country. In 1523 Lutherans had been made subject to the death penalty, but this measure was not rigorously enforced. The aggression of the Turks caused internal political confusion, and politically, though not culturally, separated Transylvania from Hungary. In both areas Calvinism made headway, but its strength was greater in Transylvania.

One of the beginners of the Reformation in Hungary was Matthias Biro Dévay (d. 1545), a native of Deva in Transylvania, once a student residing in Luther's house but later to some degree under the influence of Bucer and perhaps of Calvin. He was present at the synod held at Erdöd in 1545, which adopted a statement mentioning favorably the Augsburg Confession, and he was the author of numerous minor practical treatises. There was an active trend toward reform, motivated in part by dissatisfaction with the old clergy. But many Magyars, especially in Transylvania, looked unfavorably upon Lutheranism as associated with the German masters of Hungary. Calvinism had no such antinational implications. There is evidence that in 1551 the works of Bullinger were receiving much attention. Calvin's influence asserted itself later. His very limited correspondence with Hungarian admirers includes a letter written from Wittenberg by an otherwise unknown Francis Caphrophontes, assuring Calvin that his doctrine of the Eucharist prevailed in Hungary (26 December 1561). As in Bohemia and Poland, Hungarian students in the Western schools moved from the Wittenberg conceptions of reform to those of Zurich and Geneva.

Because of his Calvinist propaganda Martin Kálmáncsehi (d. 1557), an early companion of Dévay and pastor of Debreczen (on the Hungarian side of the border), was obliged to take flight to Transylvania (1554), where he continued to spread the Swiss doctrines, apparently under Bullinger's influence rather than Calvin's. A controversy with Lutherans followed, and Melanchthon was appealed to: his answer satisfied neither party but urged peace.

In Debreczen now appeared Peter Melius (Juhasz) (d. 1572), an able preacher and a former pupil of Stephen Kis at Tulna, from whom he learned Calvinism. In 1559, with Francis Dávid (whom he had converted from Lutheranism and who was soon to turn to Unitarianism), he drew up a confession of faith. Its circulation caused fresh conflict. Several efforts were made to end the quarrel, but finally a Lutheran majority expelled the Calvinists from their Church. The government continued to promote negotiations for agreement and gave people freedom to go to the pastor of their choice. A new Reformed confession was drawn up by Melius and his friends; called the 'Catholic Confession,' it was adopted by synods in both parts of the country (1562). Its doctrine of the Lord's Supper is one of commemoration together with the spiritual presence. Calvinism had fresh successes thereafter, as many Transylvanian Lutherans adopted the new confession. By an edict of June 1564, permission was given for the separate organization of the Reformed who had hitherto been in confused relations with the Lutherans in local churches. In 1566 and 1567, Calvin's Catechism and the Second Helvetic Confession were adopted in Hungarian synods. A system of Calvinist discipline was locally coming into effect.

Along with Melius, Stephen Kis of Szeged, a doctor of theology at Wittenberg, gave important service to the Reformed cause, both as a scholarly writer and as an evangelist. His *Commonplaces of Theology* gave a fresh statement of Calvinist thought. He was also instrumental in framing the polity of the Hungarian Reformed Church, which developed from the action of a synod of 1576. The work of ministers was carefully regulated. Above the local church councils with their pastors and elders, but much under the influence of the local magistrates, were the *seniorates;* above these the *superintendencies.* The superintendents, or bishops (ultimately five in number), were active throughout their wide districts. The seniorate had two chief officers, clerical and lay, and the superintendent likewise had his lay *curator* at his side, who, like his superior, was chosen by the church councils of the superintendency and was responsible to these. In this instance Calvinism adopted a constitutional episcopate, the episcopal eminence being one of jurisdiction, not of order. The sovereign ruling body was a synod of the whole Church; it ordinarily met only once in ten years.

The growth of Unitarianism in Transylvania is a phenomenon of the period after 1560. It was vigorously combated by Melius, with indifferent success. It obtained, with Roman Catholicism, Lutheranism, and Calvinism, the protection of the law (1564). This liberty was possible because of Turkish influence. In Hapsburg Hungary the Counter-Reformation was at this time triumphant and Protestantism was greatly weakened.

The Turks, without ruling directly, impoverished and humiliated the Christians with complete impartiality, though not equally in all areas. The Emperor Rudolf also menaced the oppressed nation and announced his intention to repudiate his pledges and exterminate Hungarian Protestantism. A Transylvanian hero, Stephen Bocskay, arose to deliver the nation. He was a Calvinist, and is so recognized in the Reformation Monument in Geneva. By fighting and diplomacy, he was able to secure, in 1606, the year of his death, favorable treaties with the emperor and the sultan. Equal rights for the various communions in Hungary were assured. His successor, Gabriel Bethlen (or Bethlen Gabor), an ardent Calvinist, confirmed his policies. But half a century later new disasters befell the Magyars. After long anguish, the Turks were repelled and the Hapsburgs ruled the land. Their attempts, with Jesuit support, to extinguish Calvinism were cruel but never fully succeeded; and Joseph II's Toleration Edict of 1781 was followed by a decade of rapid growth of Calvinism. Unfortunately this emperor later tried to impose the German language to the exclusion of Magyar, and alienated the Calvinists. Anti-Protestant measures were again severe under the Emperor Francis I, though they were relaxed before his death (1836). The celebrated patriot, orator, and revolutionary leader of 1848, Louis Kossuth, was trained in a Calvinist academy, and it was in a Calvinist church that he proclaimed Hungarian independence. Through Russian intervention, the movement perished. But during the last hundred years the Hungarian Calvinists have been a numerous element in the population, and between the two world wars they became influential in the nation's life.

— X —

For the most part Calvinism in eastern Europe has not shown the energy it possessed in Switzerland, France, and the Netherlands. Where it was able to secure its existence it did so by availing itself of the aid of small political lords who opposed a hostile central government. The early Christians under the Roman government had a much better chance to propagate their faith and increase their numbers than had the Protestants in Poland, Bohemia, and Hungary during most decades of the seventeenth and eighteenth centuries. The heavy tread of the Hapsburg power, with its menace to liberty in religion, was seldom out of hearing. Save for a generation or two in Transylvania after 1564, and another generation in all Hungary after 1781, the Reformed Church was gravely handicapped in preaching, teaching, and printing, and at times suffered appalling losses from persecution. The circumstances forbade any impressive growth of religious literature and thought. There was, however, great activity in translation, not only of the Bible but also of Western Reformation literature. This continued in the age of Puritanism and Pietism. For example, Lewis Bayly's celebrated *Practice of Pietie* became 'a household book' (says E. Révész) of Magyar Protestants. (It was perhaps equally popular in the Czech translation.) F. A. Lampe, in his *History of the Hungarian Reformed Church* (Utrecht, 1728), shows evidence of considerable learning among the pastors during the age of persecution. The Hungarian Psalter, edited by Albert Molnar in 1607 at Herborn, significantly affected the rise of Hungarian poetry; the Psalms were sung to the Geneva tunes.

During the early years of the seventeenth century Calvinism made entrance even in the realm of Eastern Orthodoxy. Its principal representative was Cyril Lucar (Loukaris) (1572–1638), a native of Crete who traveled widely in Europe and fell under the influence of Geneva. He became a bishop in Volhynia, a Russian province bordering Poland and Hungary, and was afterward made Patriarch of Alexandria (1602) and of Constantinople (1621). He was in intimate correspondence with Western Reformed leaders, and felt especially the influence of Antoine Leger, a Geneva minister who went to Constantinople. It was Patriarch Cyril who presented the important New Testament *Codex Alexandrinus* to King James I. From a printing press that he imported from England he issued his Catechism (1629), in which typical Calvinist doctrines regarding Scripture, justification, and predestination are frankly set forth. Opposition to his reforms, and the intrigues of Jesuits in Constantinople, resulted in his deposition and death by strangling. His doctrines were officially repudiated in three synods, of which that of Jerusalem in 1672 represents the virtual extinction of Eastern Calvinism, which had never been the conviction of any considerable number in the Eastern Church.

CHAPTER XVIII

THE REFORMATION IN
SCOTLAND

— I —

THE CHURCH OF SCOTLAND was reformed as a result of a dramatic struggle in which French and English interests played a part and in response to the impact of forces of the Continental Reformation. The relations of Scotland with England during the Middle Ages were, normally, hostile. English kings attempted to reduce Scotland to vassalage, while the Scottish rulers contended for full national autonomy. France was the natural ally of England's northern enemy, and the alliance was maintained even after it became burdensome to the Scots. The relations of Scotland to the Papacy were ambiguous. Pope Alexander III recognized the independence of the Scottish sees from the archbishops of York (1176); but Boniface VIII took the English side in the political struggle (1302). Robert Bruce had been excommunicated (for a wicked deed) by Clement V before his decisive victory over Edward II at Bannockburn (1314), and John XXII long withheld recognition of Bruce's title as king. In 1320 an assembly of Scottish nobles addressed to this Pope an eloquent declaration, affirming the injustice of the English claims and their own resolution to fight with Bruce 'for that liberty which no good man loses unless with his life.'

The structure of the medieval Scottish Church was established before the time of Bruce. St. Andrews had long held a primacy of honor among the bishoprics when it received metropolitan rank (1472) and it retained the primacy after Glasgow became Scotland's second archbishopric (1492). By papal decisions provincial councils for Scotland were held (1225+), at first annually and afterward less frequently. They were instituted to correct the 'very many enormities' prevailing, but they failed to establish good discipline, and conditions deteriorated further.

A surprising number of religious houses, representing many orders of monks, canons, friars, and nuns, were spread over Scotland. The Celtic monasteries established in the early period of Irish missions had given place to Continental types. In the early sixteenth century most of these communities were scandalously ill governed. John Major, philosopher and historian, writing in 1521 attributes their decline to their undue wealth and the influence of 'worthless sons of our nobility' who gain control of them, so that 'under a wicked head all the members lead an evil life.'

The Scottish bishops included a few worthy and eminent men, with others utterly unqualified. Distinguished among the former were James Kennedy (d. 1465) of St. Andrews, and William Elphinstone (d. 1514) of Aberdeen, both of whom made notable contributions to education and also took important parts in politics and diplomacy. In the fifteenth century the universities of St. Andrews, Glasgow, and Aberdeen were founded, and higher education was advancing. Nevertheless the evidence of a deplorable state of clerical life is irrefutable. It does not rest upon the satires of William Dunbar (d. 1520), a friar turned court poet, or of Sir David Lindsay (d. 1555), whom Sir Walter Scott commended for his 'satiric rage' that

> Branded the vices of the age
> And broke the keys of Rome.

But these writers apparently do not exaggerate the 'profane lewdness' and 'crass ignorance' charged against the clergy in a national synod (1549), or 'the unhonestie and misrule of Kirkmen' that certain acts of the Scottish parliament of 1540 sought to correct. Lindsay's *Satire of the Three Estates,* first enacted in 1540, ingeniously mingles allegory with broad humor and is designed not only to entertain but to arouse. Its author was one of those who, a few years later, urged John Knox to mount the pulpit.

— II —

The fifteenth century saw Scotland's turbulent nobles tamed and the kingdom unified as never before. Across the border the

Tudor house arose in Henry VII (1485–1509), who planned an end of the feud with Scotland by the old device of marrying his daughter to his enemy. Margaret Tudor became the Queen of James IV of Scotland. The marriage resulted in a quarrel over the dowry of the princess, and the Scots met their worst disaster in the battle of Flodden Field, where James fell with the flower of Scottish chivalry (1513). The death of his successor, James V, followed another humiliating defeat of the Scots by an English army, at Solway Moss (1542). James V, not without reason, distrusted his uncle, Henry VIII, and disappointed him first by marrying a daughter of Francis I of France and on her death by renewing the French bond in a marriage with Mary, sister of the duke of Guise. When James died his heir was a baby girl a week old: she is known as Mary Queen of Scots. A treaty by which the Scots lords sought to use the crisis for a change of allies and promised the infant in marriage to Henry's son Edward, aged six, was nullified by her mother and Cardinal David Beaton, who contrived to have her taken to France for her upbringing. Henry was so angered that he sent an army to ravage Scotland. The ruins of Melrose and Dryburgh abbeys still attest his fury — though the devastation has sometimes been falsely attributed to Oliver Cromwell.

That Scots should have desired such a marriage marks a rising dissatisfaction with the long-standing but costly French alliance. This new attitude was to be associated with Protestantism. Those who spirited the princess away were the enemies not only of England but also of Protestantism, which had already made its appearance in Scotland. England had severed the tie with the Papacy; France had retained it. The Reformation in Scotland was to be associated with the reversal of the old alignment with France against England, yet without the subjection of the country to the rule of the Tudors.

Protestantism in Scotland had its forerunners. The Wycliffite English priest James Resby was burned at Perth in 1407, and the Czech physician and Hussite missionary Paul Crawar suffered at St. Andrews in 1433. An inquisitor was then employed to search out Lollards, and he probably found a considerable number. Thirty from Ayrshire were brought to answer before King James IV in 1494 but were set free as being harmless. In 1520 Murdock Nisbet, a Scottish Lollard, reworked Wyclif's New Testament into Broad Scots; it remained unprinted until 1901. It was only after Tyndale's New Testament in English reached Scotland (1526) that Scottish Protestantism became a movement.

Patrick Hamilton, son of a noble knight and descendant of a king, learned of Luther when a student in Paris. Later, quietly studying in St. Andrews, he was cited to appear before the archbishop, James Beaton. He fled to the Continent, and at Marburg, in association with François Lambert (above, p. 34), he published a short set of distinctly Lutheran articles of faith (*Loci communes*), later translated into English by Tyndale's friend, John Frith, and known as *Patrick's Places*. With a martyr's resolution, he returned to preach in Scotland. At Kincavel he received from Beaton an invitation to St. Andrews. He was tried there and burned, under Beaton's eyes, 27 February 1528, affirming in the slow fire with heroic constancy his scriptural faith. He was only twenty-four. Many were led to think well of the doctrines that could call forth such a testimony. Beaton was advised to burn other heretics in deep cellars, 'for the reek [smoke] of Patrick Hamilton has infected all that it blew upon.' John Knox in his *History* notes that after Master Patrick's death 'the knowledge of God did wondrously increase within this realm, partly by reading, partly by brotherly conference . . . but chiefly by merchants and mariners.' Despite all vigilance, prohibited religious books and new ideas came with the ships from the mainland.

James Beaton was succeeded (1539) by his nephew David Beaton, a worldly prelate with political talents which he devoted to maintaining the ties with France and Rome. About this time there began to be circulated numerous ballads about church matters, many of which were later published in a book, *Good and Godly Ballads*. They ranged from broad satire to sincere piety. Some of the most unkind concerned Beaton. He was made a cardinal and a papal legate, but was so busy in Scotland that he declined to attend the Council of Trent.

In his zeal to destroy Protestantism Beaton gave it an eminent new martyr. This was George Wishart, formerly a teacher in the Academy of Montrose, the first school in Scotland in which Greek was taught. Charged with teaching the Greek New Testament, he fled to England and later to Switzerland. He translated into English the first Swiss Confession and was a Zwinglian in his conceptions of reform. He taught for a time at Corpus Christi College, Cambridge, where one of his pupils noted that he was tall, black-bearded, comely, courteous, ascetic, devout, learned, and charitable. It is possible that he was the Wishart who is known to have been connected with an English plot against Beaton's life; but no such charge was made at his trial. He re-entered Scotland, preached in Montrose, Dundee (where he tended the plague-stricken), and parts of Ayrshire, and was touring East Lothian when he was arrested near Haddington by the Earl of Bothwell. He had been guarded by a sturdy priest of thirty-two named John Knox, who bore a two-handed sword. Seeing the inevitable outcome, Wishart dismissed Knox with the words, 'One is sufficient for one sacrifice.' Bothwell, perhaps for a reward, handed him over to Cardinal Beaton. On 1 March 1546, having celebrated communion with a few friends in the castle of St. Andrews, where Beaton held him, the saintly Reformer, as he had foretold, 'suffered gladly for the Word's sake.'

Anger flamed against the cardinal, who had also incurred private enmities. On 29 May a small band of armed nobles entered the castle, aroused him from his bed, and confronted him with drawn swords. One of the intruders — the only one known to have been a Protestant — solemnly charged him with the murder of Wishart, 'which,' said he, 'we from God are sent to revenge.' Minutes later, they hung his lifeless body from a window. His last words, according to Knox, were, 'All is gone.' The old Church regime and the French alliance were doomed, and that, says A. R. MacEwen, 'before Knox had preached a single sermon.'

— III —

We first encounter Knox in February 1546, bearing a claymore for the protection of Wishart. The facts of his early life remain obscure. Apparently he was born not (as formerly supposed) in 1505 but about 1514, in or near Haddington. He probably attended the university of St. Andrews, where very likely John Major was among his teachers, and where, we know, St. Leonard's College was affected by the new leaven. He had become a priest and an 'apostolic notary' and a tutor to the sons of a nobleman. The slayers of Beaton held the castle of St. Andrews and were joined by Protestants and others who had opposed the cardinal. A year later, Knox and his pupils, weary of seeking safety elsewhere, joined the company. On the urging of the leaders in a highly emotional scene, Knox was induced to preach. This he did with startling effect: 'Others,' it was said, 'cut the branches of the Papacy, but he strikes at the roots.'

French cannon were turned upon the castle and it became untenable. Knox was among the captives taken when it fell, and he spent nineteen months as a prisoner in the French galleys. Then, religiously unshaken, he got to England, where for five years (1549–54) he made his influence felt by his ministry in Berwick, sermons in London, and contact with Archbishop Cranmer. In his congregation at Berwick, communicants sat about a table, in what he thought was the scriptural manner. His objections to kneeling in receiving the elements led Cranmer to insert in the Second Prayer Book a highly Protestant explanation of kneeling, commonly called the Black Rubric. Some months after Mary Tudor's reign began, Knox took flight, and was soon among the English exiles at Frankfurt, where he introduced a 'compromise liturgy' to allay Anglican-Puritan dissension. But when the Frankfurt authorities were informed that he had called the emperor 'a Nero,' he was obliged to leave the city. He became minister of the community of English exiles in Geneva. But his work there was soon interrupted by a visit to Berwick, where he was married, and to Scotland, where for nine months he preached with great daring. Mary of Guise was now regent of Scotland for her young daughter, who remained in France. Knox appealed to her to show 'motherly pity' to her evangelical subjects but got no reply.

Back in Geneva, Knox published a liturgy (1556) based upon Calvin's *Form of Prayers* (above, pp. 150 ff.). This *Genevan Service Book* was later used in Scotland and by some English Puritan groups. When he first reached Geneva his opinions were probably still, like Wishart's, essentially Zwinglian. But observation of the Geneva system and contact with Calvin made him in most respects a Calvinist. Calvin was by this time molding Geneva to his pattern, and to Knox the city was 'a perfect school of Christ.' Because of its peaceableness he afterward referred to it humorously as 'a den of ease.'

There was to be little enough of ease for him in the years ahead. He was still in touch with affairs in Scotland, where, in December 1557, a few Protestant nobles formed the First Scottish Covenant. It was a solemn pledge 'before the majesty of God' to commit their whole power, property, and lives to the cause of 'the Word of God and his Congregation.' The term 'Congregation' had reference to the Scottish adherents of the Reformation as a body. In 1557 the Scottish lords flatly refused the regent's demand that the country aid France in war against England. In April 1558, however, the Princess Mary was married to the dauphin (crown prince) of France, Francis, eldest son of Henry II and Catherine de Medici. For seventeen months, from Henry II's death to that of Francis II (December 1560), Mary Stuart was queen of France.

Meanwhile on the death of Mary Tudor and the succession of Elizabeth (17 November 1558) the course of the Reformation in England was resumed, and most of Knox's Geneva congregation returned to their homeland. He had just published the most indiscreet of political tracts, *The First Blast of the Trumpet against the Monstrous Regiment of Women* (1558). Designed as an attack on the government of Mary of Guise and Mary Tudor, it was just in time to offend Elizabeth. It begins with the generalization that the government of a woman is 'repugnant to nature and contumely of God.' It is understandable that the author was now refused admission to England, where he had expected to renew his influence. Abandoning hope of this, he sailed directly from Dieppe to Leith and reached Edinburgh on 2 May 1559.

— IV —

Knox found the Congregation engaged in a half-hearted fight against the regent. Presently his preaching aroused in them the spirit of victory. Thomas Randolph, Elizabeth's ambassador, reported that Knox's voice could 'put life into them more than 500 trumpets.' Knox himself indicates that in his traveling about he was eluding enemies charged to kill him, and was in need of a better horse. At Dundee and Perth his preaching was sensationally effective, and Perth became the scene of riotous destruction of images by what he calls 'the rascal multitude.' In defiance of Archbishop John Hamilton's warning, Knox preached once more in St. Andrews Cathedral (11 June 1559), thus fulfilling a hope he had entertained in the French galleys.

Elizabeth might have disliked Knox but she wished him well. She and her minister Cecil knew that if his party should be crushed England would not long be spared from attack. Francis and Mary had been proclaimed sovereigns of England. Elizabeth determined upon a judicious intervention, which she hoped would not involve a declared war with France. A plan was formed and was carried through without a hitch. By the Treaty of Berwick (February 1560) England took Scotland under her protection. The treaty mentioned not religion but the 'liberties' of the Scots. When it was signed, an English fleet was already in the Firth of Forth, and soon afterward an English army peaceably joined that of the Congregation at Prestonpans and marched against the French troops concentrated at Leith. The Lords of the Congregation demanded of the regent that she restore the ancient liberties and dismiss the French soldiers. She became ill and, calling the reforming nobles to her side, now sorrowfully proposed that both French and English soldiers be withdrawn. It was the Protestant, John Willock, who ministered to her at her death, 11 June 1560. The helpless French, with little Scottish support and no possibility of reinforcement, capitulated. The Treaty of Edinburgh, 6 July 1560, secured the withdrawal from Scotland of both French and English forces. On the 15th, the French sailed, and the English marched, for home. On the 19th, John Knox led a great public service of thanksgiving in St. Giles Cathedral, remembering in his fervent prayer 'our confederates of England, the instruments by whom we are now set at liberty.'

The new treaty did not mention church reform but actually cleared the way for it. The necessity of reshaping the Scottish Church was the more pressing because episcopacy had almost ceased to function. Archbishop John Hamilton (1546–71) had held a series of three national councils (1549, 1552, 1559). As an expression of the Counter-Reformation, these councils, planned to reform abuses, served rather to expose them to criticism. After the second of these synods there appeared *A Catechism of the Catholic Faith,* called 'Hamilton's Catechism' but probably written by John Winram, which shows concessions to Protestantism. Hamilton left his see in 1559: he and his fellow bishops were overwhelmed by the tide of events.

Scottish parliaments had sometimes enacted bold ecclesiastical measures, and the treaty provided for a meeting of parliament to deal with the crisis. A committee of nobles and burgh commissioners was already at work placing able preachers in many of the churches. In St. Giles, Edinburgh, Knox expounded the book of Haggai, the prophet of reconstruction after the captivity of Israel. He so presented the challenge of the hour that one noble-man mockingly complained: 'We must forget ourselves and bear the barrow to build the houses of God.' The privy council set another committee to work preparing basic documents of church reform. The estates assembled and sessions began on 1 August. Taking advantage of a hitherto neglected privilege, many of the lesser landholders came to this parliament, increasing its Protestant slant.

The continued absence of a royal head during the critical months following the regent's death gave to the nation the aspect of a republic rather than a kingdom. Not awaiting the judgment of the absent queen, parliament boldly gave the people what they seemed to crave. Without much debate or excitement, and with no violence, far-reaching reforms were promptly enacted. The few who registered opposition were secular-minded nobles rather than convinced defenders of the old regime.

Parliament received a 'Supplication' assailing the errors and abuses of the hierarchy and calling for reform in education and relief of the poor. The committee to prepare a book of discipline and a confession of faith consisted of six Johns — Knox, Willock, Spottiswood, Winram, Douglas, and Row. They were all notable personalities. John Row, the only one of them younger than Knox, was a doctor of laws of Padua and had observed conditions in the Italian Church. Willock, a former Franciscan, who was praised by Knox for his 'faithful labors and bold courage,' had become acquainted with leading Reformed personalities and Churches on the Continent. Winram, presumed author of Hamilton's Catechism, had been called upon while an Augustinian sub-prior to examine Knox for heresy (1547), but even then had sympathized with the accused, who was alleged to have taught that the Pope is an antichrist and the Mass idolatry.

— V —

Their joint product, the 'First Scottish Confession,' was read in parliament and passed without delay, 17 August. There was in the *Good and Godly Ballads* a versified Protestant confession based on the Apostles' Creed, but it had no authority. Knox's

Geneva Liturgy also contained a brief expansion of the Creed. But the confession of 1560 is an extended statement in twenty-five articles, written in popular language and with a highly interesting preface. It begins:

> Long have we thirsted to have notified to the world the sum of that doctrine which we profess, and for which we have sustained infamy and danger.

The framers undertake to alter any part that may be shown to be 'repugnant to God's Holy Word.'

The confession affirms Calvinism with a simple fervor. The doctrine of eternal election out of 'mere grace' is closely tied to that of the mediation of Christ. Reprobation is not asserted, save that in a subordinate clause there is incidental mention of 'the reprobate.' By grace we become the sons of God and are not afraid to call Him our Father. Good works flow unfailingly from Christ's indwelling spirit; stress is laid on their importance 'for the profit of our neighbors.' There is a lively description of the one true Church — catholic in that it contains the elect of all ages, realms, and races, and invisible since 'God alone knows whom He has chosen.' It is, however, not so invisible as not to be 'discerned' from the false church, 'the Kirk Malignant,' by its 'notes' or marks. These are the true preaching of the Word, the right administration of the sacraments of Christ, and ecclesiastical discipline in accordance with the Word. Scripture is to be interpreted in obedience to the Holy Spirit, not to the church authorities. Councils are useful but fallible; and ceremonies are to be changed when they foster superstition. The section on the Eucharist affirms a mystical presence: believers so eat the body and drink the blood of Christ that He remains in them and they in Him. The confession speaks highly of the honor due to civil magistrates: they are 'lieutenants of God in whose sessions God Himself doth sit and judge.'

The Book of Discipline had been prepared earlier, but it never received state sanction. It contains some elements that belong to doctrine rather than to discipline and is somewhat disorderly in form. Idolatry in worship is said to consist of 'all honoring of God not contained in His Holy Word.' This is the 'negative Scripture rule' that we have seen in Continental Reformed Churches. In the admission of ministers a high standard is set. The candidate is publicly examined, by ministers and elders, for ability to teach and defend the Gospel. Ministers are settled in congregations on election by the people; if this is neglected the superintendent and his council take action. Where fully qualified ministers are not available readers are to be appointed to read the prayers and Scripture. The office of reader was an interim provision until enough ministers for the parishes could be recruited and trained. It is possible, too, that the office of superintendent was designed to be temporary only; but the plan for it is carefully framed. Ten districts of Scotland are marked off and referred to as 'dioceses of the superintendents.' These have a recognized relation to the thirteen medieval dioceses. The superintendents are warned not to live like the idle bishops of the past. They were in fact overloaded with work, having duties in parishes of their own together with administration, supervision, and travel in their dioceses. Actually only five were appointed, and with their death or retirement the office was discontinued.

Noteworthy in this book is the design for a fundamental reform of education. In rural places the minister or reader was to teach the children; in every town parish there was to be a schoolmaster; each town of a superintendent was to have a college with an adequate and well-paid staff; and the universities were to be reformed, each according to an elaborate plan that included estimated costs. The patrimony of the Church is to be drawn upon for the schools as well as for the support of ministers and the poor. A plea is made, however, for relief from tithes ('*teinds*') of those 'poor brethren, the laborers and manurers of the ground.' The greed of oppressive landlords and the private seizure of public properties of the Church are vigorously condemned. Professor Hume Brown employed the term 'Christian socialism' to describe these features of the Book of Discipline. The lords of the Council, led by William Maitland of Lethington, were unwilling to commit themselves to a scheme that denied them the possibility of aggrandizement from the possessions of the Church.

While they declined to authorize the book, the lords were not unfavorable, apparently, to the sections on the discipline of offenders. In these the secular power is accused of negligence in proceeding against those guilty of blasphemy, adultery, murder, and perjury. Among lesser offenses, punishable by the Church, oppression of the poor is again mentioned. Excommunication is the ultimate penalty, to be employed only after a series of steps designed to secure repentance have failed. Excommunication is a grave matter, since it shuts off the offender from business and social life and the sentence is 'published throughout the realm.' All are subject to the same discipline, 'as well the rulers as the ruled.'

Explicit directions are given for the conduct of the congregations, including preaching, catechetical instruction, examination for admission to the (quarterly) celebration of the Lord's Supper, prayer, and teaching in the home. Once a week in every town 'that exercise that St. Paul calleth prophesying' is to be held. The reference is to I Corinthians 14:29–31, 'Let two or three prophets speak . . . for you can all prophesy.' The Reformers here urge the importance of the 'exercise' for the Church of God in Scotland, though with certain cautions against doctrinal error, over-curiosity, and the use of invective in the free discussion:

> For thereby shall the Church have judgment and knowledge of the graces, gifts and utterances of every man within their own body; the simple and such as have somewhat profited shall be encouraged daily to study and proceed in knowledge . . . and every man shall have liberty to utter and declare his mind and knowledge to the comfort and edification of the Church.

Such was the 'group method' in Scotland four centuries ago, following models in the Reformed Churches abroad. But since business had to be done for the churches participating, the exercises naturally tended to assume administrative duties and ruling authority in these parishes. This was soon to lead to the formation of presbyteries, with specified districts and powers.

— VI —

Scotland had not rejected her absent queen. On her husband's death (4 December 1560) Mary Stuart was urged, by some Scottish nobles hostile to the Reformation, to return with an army and undo it all. Such a plan could not have succeeded: the new order was surprisingly acceptable to all but a few. She returned peaceably, reaching Leith on 19 August 1561. On the following

Sunday she had the Mass said in Holyrood Castle. Knox thundered against this from his pulpit in St. Giles, and the battle between the Reformer and the Queen began.

Mary's French uncles, the Guises (above, p. 247), were then beginning their role as the most ruthless enemies of the Huguenots. In no position, and with no desire, to imitate their cruelties, she planned to overthrow the Reformation by methods of ingratiation, for which her familiarity with the corruption and intrigue of the French court had prepared her. England trembled lest she should subdue Scotland to France and the Pope. She was beautiful, gracious, brave, and clever; but she lacked stability of character and could not understand the intractability of men of conviction. Knox, on his part, failed to make allowance for her youth, and by denunciation lost the possibility of persuading her.

Five interviews between these antagonists are recorded. In the second, shortly after the massacre of Vassey (1562) by soldiers in the service of Francis, duke of Guise, Knox denounced Mary's uncles as enemies of God, who spilled innocent blood. When, without seeking her consent, he took to himself as his second wife a distant cousin of the queen (1564), Mary was deeply offended. The question of Mary's marriage was of no less interest to Knox, because of its importance for the nation and Church. In their fourth meeting (1563), after he had assailed the proposal that she should marry a Roman Catholic, she exclaimed, 'I have sought your favor by all possible means . . . I vow to God I shall be revenged.' In tears of exasperation she called forth from him a reply that has since been often quoted:

> But what have you to do (said she) with my marriage? Or, what are you within this Commonwealth? A subject born within the same (said he) Madam; and albeit I be neither Earl, Lord, nor Baron within it, yet hath God made me . . . a profitable and useful member within the same.

Here the Reformer rests his right to speak of a matter of public concern not upon his position as a minister of Christ but upon his birthright as a subject of the realm. This is a basic democratic concept that assuredly he did not invent, but it was supported by a religious certainty that set him free from fear.

In consonance with this assertion of the freedom of the subject to advise the ruler was Knox's insistence upon the corporate freedom of the Church to assemble and determine its own policy. The General Assembly had been summoned to its third meeting, that of December 1561, when Maitland, now secretary of state, questioned its right to meet without the queen's permission. Knox stoutly replied: 'Take from us the liberty of assemblies and you take from us the Gospel.' It was of the greatest significance for the Kirk that the assemblies continued to meet and to direct the process by which the presbyterian polity was developed. In 1562 the provincial synods were established, to meet twice a year.

In this year also Knox's liturgy was in part adopted: in 1564 in revised and expanded form it became the authorized standard of worship. A great deal of the *Book of Common Order,* as the revised Geneva book came to be called, is taken up with services for discipline and the cure of souls — excommunication, public repentance, absolution, visitation of the sick. The Form of Public Worship followed substantially the pattern of Calvin's *Form of Prayers.* At the communion service the communicants sat about a table — a practice continued until the early nineteenth century. The prayers are long and in some instances verbose. There was no intention that they should be used without variation or to the exclusion of extemporaneous prayer.

Psalm singing in Scotland as elsewhere was a mark of the Reformed Church. In the volume containing the liturgy, the metrical Psalms were habitually included. A collection of fifty-one Psalms was in use in Knox's congregation in Geneva. The General Assembly provided for the completion and printing of the entire Psalter in 1564. The Geneva tunes were favored, but the Scots frequently sang them in harmony; and soon there appeared editions written in four parts. The texts lacked poetic quality. Out of a variety of later translations came the much superior version of the second Scottish Psalter of 1650.

Mary's course was almost run when, in 1567, after the murder of her husband, Lord Darnley, and under the influence of her new husband, the Earl of Bothwell, she adopted a new policy. She gave a bounty to the Reformed Church ministers and at the same time, in violation of the law, ordered the restoration of Archbishop Hamilton to his jurisdiction. Knox roused the country to a realization of the trap involved in this ambiguous policy: the old episcopate would have made short work of the Reformed

Kirk. It was Mary's marriage to Bothwell, and the refusal of the nobles to permit this worthless adventurer to become king, that brought about her defeat and imprisonment (June 1567). A month later her infant son, James VI, was crowned at Stirling — Knox being present to preach about the boy king, Joash (II Kings 12). In December he preached at the opening of parliament. It was an important session, for it ratified with new safeguards the legislation of 1560; made it obligatory on all future kings that they should take oath to maintain the Protestant religion; and recognized the liberty and authority of the assemblies of the Church.

The queen's half-brother, James, Earl of Moray, was made regent. Until his assassination in 1570 the government lent willing support to the ministers, by whom Moray was called the 'Good Regent.' Queen Mary was now confined in an English castle, while the humanist George Buchanan (d. 1582), advocate of popular sovereignty, tutored the boy king and wrote a weighty book, *Law of the Scottish Kingship* (1579). In the atrocious massacre of St. Bartholomew, the Guise faction had its way in France. Knox had enough strength left to assail anew the imprisoned queen along with her French relatives. He now sought to bring her to trial for her life in Scotland. But just two months later, 24 November 1572, the Scottish Reformer died. The earl of Morton, who was then regent, declared over his bier: 'Here lies one who neither feared nor flattered any flesh.' We know from Knox's own letters that he did not so estimate himself. But he had stedfastly contended for what he deeply believed, and laid the foundations of the enduring structure of Scottish presbyterianism.

— VII —

It was Morton's policy to reintroduce episcopacy, though in a condition of subservience to the state. Bishops would yield to the government the greater share of the ample incomes still paid to the deposed bishops, who would soon all be dead. (Hamilton himself had been put to death (1571) for complicity in Darnley's murder). Such a plan had been earlier suggested by Cecil, who wanted to see the Scottish Church less unlike the English. Morton secured the appointment of John Douglas as archbishop of St. Andrews, bargaining with him for most of the revenue (1572), and followed this by other similar appointments. The

new prelates were nicknamed '*tulchan* bishops': the Gaelic word
means a stuffed calf-skin used to induce the mother cow to yield
her milk.

The history of the Scottish Church from the year of Knox's
death to the Westminster Assembly (1643-9) can be written for
the most part with reference to the question of the episcopate.
Of grave importance also was the issue of public worship. With
these issues, that of the relation with the Church of England is
closely involved.

Knox himself did not absolutely reject episcopacy: for England his proposal was that each diocese should be divided into
ten, so that the bishops might be bishops indeed to their flocks.
A new champion of presbyterianism arose, whose opposition to
all prelacy was uncompromising. This was Andrew Melville, who
returned to Scotland from studies in Geneva in 1574, was exiled
by James VI (James I of England) in 1607, and died at Sedan
in 1622. At his prompting the General Assembly stated in 1576:
'The name of bishop is common to all who are appointed to take
charge of a particular flock.' Six of the *tulchans* were present, but
spoke not a word. In 1581 the Assembly finally adopted the document known as the Second Book of Discipline, which declares
'bishops,' 'pastors,' and 'ministers' equivalent terms. These ministers are to be appointed only after 'the lawful election and assent of the people.' The functions of teachers (doctors), elders,
and deacons are explained. The state is required to aid in ex-
tirpating abuses and in furthering the establishment of presbyteries and the reform of parishes. A chapter on Church assemblies indicates the four sorts of these — local, provincial,
national, and of 'all and diverse nations.'

The young king was now assuming the government, and was
taking advice from men hostile to the Kirk, who instructed him
in royal absolutism. Melville led the ministers in a written protest against the king's assumption of the 'spiritual sword,' and
when challenged by the Earl of Arran in the words: 'Who dares
subscribe these treasonable articles?' answered, 'We dare,' wrote
his name, and was followed by the others. Later the young king
was snatched from his favorites and held for months in Ruthven
castle. In 1584 a series of measures called the 'Black Acts' was
put through parliament. They made objection to the king's authority treason and attempted to replace the Church's assemblies

by a return to episcopal rule. Melville had to flee abroad; but the fight went on, and he soon returned.

It was unfortunate for the cause of episcopacy in Scotland that it was associated first with the scandal of the *tulchan* appointments and then with the claims of royal absolutism, a political doctrine alien to the Scottish mind and repudiated alike by the scholastic John Major, the humanist George Buchanan, and the Reformers, Knox and Melville. The Spanish Armada (1588) led James to a greater appreciation of the Kirk, and during his absence to obtain a bride in Denmark (1589–90) he left a staunch Presbyterian, Robert Bruce, entrusted with high responsibilities. In May 1592 Bruce was moderator of a General Assembly that laid down terms of settlement with the king. These were substantially adopted by parliament a month later in an act that constitutes a veritable charter of liberty of the Kirk, affirms fully its presbyterian constitution, and annuls all contrary earlier legislation.

Bruce is reported to have preached to James VI and I on the text, James 1:6, 'He that wavereth . . .' James was soon again in a quarrel with Melville and the ministers. In 1596 this reached a crisis, when he wished to condone the treasonable negotiations with Spain of certain Roman Catholic lords and called the Assembly's commissioners seditious for holding a meeting on the matter. The old issue of freedom of assemblies was thus renewed. In one scene, Melville took his majesty by the sleeve and calling him 'God's silly [i.e. feeble] vassal' told him with vehement emphasis: 'King James is the subject of King Jesus . . . You are not the head of the Church.' James was confirmed in his hostility to presbyterianism as a form of religion that made the ministers of the Church censors of the government. His policy appears more tolerant than that of Melville, but it was one of appeasement rather than of generous toleration. He was intent upon securing recognition of the divine right of kings to rule without consulting Church or people. He wanted authority to appoint the masters of the Church, and he saw his way to this through a restoration of the episcopate. Although he reiterated his promises to the Kirk when he became king of England (1603), his determination had been formed to bring the Scottish Church into agreement in policy and worship with the Church of England. The sequel of this belongs in another chapter.

— VIII —

The Reformed Church of Scotland had already achieved much that would prove enduring. No established church of the Reformation outside of Switzerland was more deeply rooted in the life of the people. The opposition to it was among the aristocracy; the people as a whole welcomed it and, though they sometimes winced under the severity of its discipline, felt for it a growing loyalty. Its pulpits, as H. T. Buckle wrote,

> stirred up the minds of men, woke them from their lethargy . . . and excited that inquisitive and democratic spirit, which is the only effectual guarantee the people can have against the tyranny of those who are set over them.

Its documents took note of the needs of the poor and stressed the duties of the rich. At the turn of the century it had already done much to improve education, from the parish school to the university. Melville was himself probably the most learned Scot of his generation. He had brought from the Continent the anti-Aristotelian philosophy of Peter Ramus (pp. 263, 391), but he knew his Aristotle well in Greek. He wrought a transformation, in turn, of the universities of Glasgow, Aberdeen, and St. Andrews, introducing a system of departmental specialization.

The ministry of the late sixteenth and early seventeenth century included a good many men of sound scholarship and excellent preaching talent. John Craig (d. 1600), a former Dominican, who because of a riot had escaped burning as a Protestant in Rome, was the author of the so-called 'King's Confession,' a short statement required of ministers for the security of presbyterianism (1581), and of 'Craig's Catechism' (1592), long highly regarded in the Kirk. In 1583 the university of Edinburgh began its distinguished history. Its first principal, Robert Rollock (d. 1599), was admired by Beza as a theologian and was the author of numerous Latin works. His *Treatise on Effectual Calling* (1597) was widely read in Latin and English, and stands as one of the earliest systematic discussions of the Covenants, anticipating the later development of the 'Covenant Theology.' Robert Bruce (d. 1631), who had early studied law in France, was led to the ministry by Melville. He was in favor with the king and might have had any bishopric in Scotland had he not opposed episcopacy in principle. James VI had him dismissed from Edinburgh, but despite much hardship he preached in various places, often with profound effect. *The Way to True Peace and Rest* is a compilation of his sermons.

These learned men preached in a dialect the hearers readily understood. The ministry of Patrick Simson (d. 1610) in Stirling was celebrated and was described at the time as 'wonderfully comfortable to his people.' The Glasgow principals, Patrick Sharp (d. 1615) and Robert Boyd (d. 1627), trained capable ministers, and John Cameron (above, p. 250), a Glasgow alumnus, returned from France to lend his talents to that university as principal for a year (1622–3). Boyd was a brilliant exegete, celebrated for his work on Ephesians. One of the finest spirits of the Scottish Church was David Dickson (d. 1662), a pupil of Sharp and Boyd and long the minister of Irvine, where his spiritual counsel was sought by many distressed souls. Besides commentaries and treatises, Dickson wrote a work of casuistry, *Therapeutica sacra* (1656), the product of his experience in dealing with cases of conscience.

All of these men, and others like them, were in some ways involved in the episcopal-presbyterian controversy. The strength of the Presbyterian cause lay in the fact that it had many learned and able spokesmen who were also faithful and devout ministers, beloved and admired by the common folk.

CHAPTER XIX

CALVINISM IN ENGLAND
AND IRELAND

— I —

Historians have noted that the word 'Calvinist' first appears in printed English in 1579; they seem to have overlooked the earlier use of its equivalent, 'Calvinian' (1566), and of 'Calvinism' (1570). About the middle of Elizabeth's reign these terms began to be found convenient and to replace 'Helvetic' or 'Zwinglian' where reference was made to the doctrines of the Swiss Reformed Churches. Yet most of what was embraced by the word 'Calvinism' had been introduced to the English mind through the influence of Bucer and Bullinger. The contribution of Peter Martyr Vermigli and John à Lasco, who like Bucer were refugee scholars protected and consulted by Archbishop Cranmer in Edward VI's reign, led in the same direction.

The first notable manifestation of what was later called Puritanism in England is seen in the scruples of John Hooper over the vestments prescribed in the [First] Book of Common Prayer. Hooper had lived about eight years in Zurich and had become a great admirer of Bullinger. Appointed (1550) to the see of Gloucester, he protested against the pontifical garments; it was only after imprisonment and much persuasion that he consented to wear them at his consecration on condition that he should not be required to wear them afterward. On this compromise his Continental well-wishers took divergent views. Bucer and Martyr, both of whom had stiffly refused to wear the surplice, thought well of the solution, while à Lasco and Bullinger were disappointed in it. Calvin, too, followed the case with interest and evidently shared Bucer's view, for he wrote to Bullinger expressing admiration for the imprisoned Hooper's firmness but regret that he had carried his objections too far (12 March 1551)

On another matter even Knox appears less rigid than Hooper. Despite his preference for sitting at communion, when once the explanation of the Black Rubric (above, p. 295) had been adopted Knox thought it better in the interests of peace and charity to accept the kneeling position, and he wrote to his former Berwick parishioners disapproving Hooper's continued opposition to it. It was to be characteristic of the English Puritans that they were more unyielding on points of worship and ceremony than their instructors, Calvin, Bucer, and Knox.

The influence of Bucer on both Anglicanism and Puritanism has long been recognized and has been justly stressed by W. Pauck and A. Lang. Lang gives John Bradford (d. 1555), one of the noblest victims of Mary's persecution, a prominent role in the transmission of Bucer's teaching. Bradford's discussion of the Lord's Supper, however, may be held to reflect Zurich doctrines. C. D. Cremeans, in his study of Calvinistic thought in England, seems to regard both Bradford and Hooper as followers of Calvin in their teaching on election. This may be questioned: Hooper, at least, gives expression to an unfavorable judgment of Calvin. But, in agreement with earlier scholars, Cremeans observes that in Edward's time it was not Calvin but Bullinger who was 'probably the most respected' of the Reformers. This ascendancy of Bullinger for English Protestantism was maintained during the period of Bucer's stay in England and was later enhanced by the generous hospitality of Zurich to the Marian exiles and by their personal contacts with Bullinger. His correspondence with many Englishmen is voluminous and intimate; and from about 1550 a number of his writings were circulated in English. These included his celebrated *Five Decades of Sermons,* a work already well known when Archbishop Whitgift in Convocation made it required reading for a large class of the clergy (above, p. 71) .

— II —

It is misleading, however, to assume that the English response to Bucer or to Bullinger can be sharply separated from Calvin's English influence. These men were not Calvin's rivals but his heralds. A few Englishmen had, indeed, made Calvin's acquaintance very early in his career (1537), and the Reformer took an interest in English affairs. In June 1548 he dedicated to the Pro-

tector Somerset his *Commentary on I Timothy,* and four months
later (22 October) he addressed to him a long letter of advice on
the essentials of a thorough reform of the Church, in preaching,
worship, and discipline. In 1550 Bucer, then at Cambridge, was
informing Calvin of English conditions in order to engage his
prayers and make effective his own admonitions to the Protector.
In that year an English version of Calvin's catechism appeared
in London. In 1551 Bullinger commended to Richard Cox, Dean
of Westminster, Calvin's defense of the Consensus of Zurich
(above, p. 199). Nicholas des Gallars was, so to speak, Calvin's
envoy in England. Returning to Geneva in June 1551, he reported very favorably on the reception of Calvin's letters to
Somerset and to Edward. What most delighted Calvin was that
Cranmer himself had sent him word that he could 'do nothing
more useful than write to the king frequently.' In the same letter
(15 June 1551) he expresses 'the deepest anguish' over the death
of Bucer, who 'would have been of great advantage to England.'
In March 1552 Cranmer sought Calvin's aid toward a conference
of theologians to frame a consensus on the Eucharist. Calvin responded warmly (above, p. 200), but the death of King Edward
ensued, and the conference was never held.

The reversal of policy involved in Edward's death and Mary's
succession (July 1553) altered the nature of Calvin's influence
but did not interrupt it. Instead of urging on to more advanced
reform those in authority in Church and state who were receptive of his views, he was now to aid and guide refugees from the
hostile government that restored England to the Roman obedience. In this role he was still surpassed by Bullinger so far as
personal kindness to and friendship with the exiles is concerned.
As it turned out, Zurich, which in doctrine and worship seemed
farther from Anglicanism than Geneva, was thereafter more in
favor with certain Anglican leaders, and with Queen Elizabeth,
than Calvin's city. One reason for this undoubtedly was that
the state control of the Church admitted in the Zurich reform
was congenial to Anglicanism, while Geneva had set up a system
of church autonomy that made Elizabeth shudder.

It is not without significance, however, that Geneva provided
for the exiles, as Zurich did not, an opportunity to organize and
conduct their own church. The English congregation, led by
John Knox, Christopher Goodman, William Whittingham, and

Anthony Gilby, flourished in the disciplined city. It proved a training ground in scriptural worship and church order and fostered a desire to see the system imitated in England. Whittingham, before seeing Geneva (1553), had studied in Orléans and Paris and visited German universities. He attempted (1555) to gather the refugees into one community in Frankfurt. *The Troubles at Frankfurt* is his own narrative of the conflict there that sent him back to Geneva, with Knox and a large portion of the Frankfurt colony. (The statement that his wife was a sister of Calvin is erroneous.)

So close was the association of these scholars that it is impossible to assign to each his part in the preparation of the Geneva Bible (1560) — to which Miles Coverdale also contributed — but Whittingham was undoubtedly foremost in this important labor. His New Testament had appeared in 1557 and was later revised; it was largely dependent on Beza's Latin text. The Geneva Bible far surpassed in circulation all other English versions of the period: there were sixty editions by 1603 and ten later. Knox's Service Book also probably owed much to his co-laborers.

The friendship of Calvin toward them all and their admiration for him and his system are well attested. Friendship and admiration did not, however, involve full agreement with him. It is always a mistake to assume that one who chose to sojourn in Calvin's Geneva was, or became, in all things a disciple of Calvin. Both Knox and Goodman embarrassed and annoyed him by their tracts on political resistance, and Whittingham was implicated through his preface to Goodman's *How Superior Powers Ought To Be Obeyed*. This radical work is of the same date (1558) as Knox's unfortunate *First Blast* (above, p. 296), to which Goodman wrote a preface. The marginal notes in the Geneva Bible also attest, in their headlong and sweeping rejection of unscriptural rites and ceremonies, and their animus against episcopacy, a practical radicalism that is in contrast with Calvin's conciliatory attitude in his correspondence with Anglicans.

In some degree the leaven of Calvin's doctrines affected the exiles in other centers. John Jewel in Zurich, John Foxe and John Bale in Basel, David Whitehead in Frankfort, John Ponet and Edmund Grindal in Strasbourg gave a general assent to his teaching. Of these all but Ponet — author of the weighty *Short Treatise of Politik Power* (1556) — lived to return to England.

Grindal, the most thoroughly Calvinist of them, was to become bishop of London and, after Parker, an unsuccessful Archbishop of Canterbury (1575–83). The other Geneva men would have little opportunity in the Anglican Church. Whittingham obtained a modest eminence as Dean of Durham, a task hardly worthy of his talents. Jewel, the most influential of the Marian exiles in the Elizabethan Church, owed far more to Bullinger than to Calvin.

— III —

The exiles had suffered a fundamental cleavage in the Frankfurt 'troubles,' and they never reached any over-all agreement. Anticipating Mary's death, Knox had sent William Kethe to visit their various communities, urging them to 'hold fast together,' but had received disappointing replies. They returned to England dispersedly, and with no concerted program.

Calvin was prompt to resume his counsel of the English government, and in January 1559, writing to arouse the lagging zeal of Cecil, he makes it clear that he has already admonished Elizabeth to pursue the right path. In the same month Knox put forth his *Brief Exhortation to England for the Speedy Embracing of the Gospel*. Knox's *First Blast* had, as he said, blown from him his English friends; and the frustration of his desire to work again in England was a blow not only to him but also to Calvin's own influence. Calvin explained to Cecil that Knox had published the offending tract without his consent. Cecil in his reply (22 June 1560) accepts the explanation and credits himself with 'the warmest zeal for the evangelical profession.' Grindal, newly appointed bishop of London, applied to Calvin for a minister for the French congregation there. Nicholas des Gallars was induced by Calvin to accept this pastorate in April 1560 and was most cordially received by Grindal, as was his successor three years later.

Calvin had few years to live after the exiles returned. After his death, Beza shared with Bullinger the confidences of the aggrieved Puritans, and these two leaders exchanged some interesting letters, which show their distress over the controversy. Calvin's works were now speaking for him through translation as well as in their originals. His Catechism was a university textbook. In 1561 Thomas Norton, parliamentary leader and gifted dramatic author, presented an admirable translation of the *Institutes*. No less than twenty-seven collections, large and small, of Calvin's sermons had appeared in English by 1592. These included the great tomes excellently done by Arthur Golding, translator of Ovid and Caesar, of the *Sermons on Job* and the *Sermons on Deuteronomy*. Golding also translated the *Commentary on the Psalms* and several other works of Calvin.

The Calvinist struggle for England seemed victorious so far as doctrine was concerned. The Thirty-nine Articles of the Church may be fairly interpreted as capable of a Calvinist interpretation, even though it was Bullinger's thought that had been chiefly incorporated in them when they were promulgated in Edward's reign as the Forty-two Articles. Article xvii, on predestination, is so obviously Calvinistic that at the queen's wish it was suppressed after adoption; it appeared only with the edition of 1571, after the papal excommunication of Elizabeth. Students at the universities learned Calvinism from able theologians, including John Reynolds of Oxford, William Whitaker and William Perkins of Cambridge. When Peter Baro introduced Arminian doctrines at Cambridge, Whitaker and others with Archbishop John Whitgift framed and issued a statement in nine paragraphs (the Lambeth Articles, 1595) of the most downright Calvinist predestinarianism. The works of Whitgift against Presbyterian Cartwright are replete with quotations from Calvin in which the Geneva oracle is made to controvert essential positions of the Puritans. During Whitgift's episcopate (1583–1603) Richard Hooker (d. 1600) wrote his great exposition of Anglicanism, the *Laws of Ecclesiastical Polity*. While Hooker took exception to Calvin's doctrine of the authority of Scripture, he, too, paid the Reformer remarkable deference. It was only after the Synod of Dort (1618–19), and chiefly in the 1630's, that Arminianism gained assent in anti-Puritan Anglicanism.

— IV —

On questions of worship and polity, however, the invasion from Geneva was repelled. But here it is well to avoid confusion at the outset. There is no evidence that either Calvin or Beza would have favored what the Elizabethan Presbyterian party attempted. Calvin had reverentially addressed Cranmer and in his case made no scruple of the prelatical office. In 1560 he similarly greeted Elizabeth's new archbishop, Matthew Parker, urging him to take the initiative in a project to unite the evangelical churches. Parker referred the matter to the royal council, where action on it was indefinitely postponed, apparently because of Elizabeth's unfounded suspicion that an attack on episcopacy was involved. The Huguenot interpreters of Calvin, such as Pierre du Moulin and Jean Daillé, are justified in their insistence that he honored all bishops of evangelical principles, such as Cranmer and his colleagues of the English Reformation, and wished to live in communion with their successors. Beza corresponded in a fraternal spirit with Parker, Grindal, and Whitgift. To Whitgift he wrote in March 1591:

> I have always impugned the Roman hierarchy, but I have never had the intention of opposing the ecclesiastical polity of your Anglican Church. I wish and hope that the sacred and holy society of your bishops may continue and maintain forever the right and title to the government of the Church with all Christian equity and moderation.

It is true that in his controversy with Adrian Saravia, friend of Hooker, and in his defense of the ministry of the Scottish Church, Beza created the impression of hostility to an episcopal polity; but basically his position was that episcopacy, while not necessary to the existence of a true church, was permissible and sometimes desirable. When the Scottish superintendents and ministers, led by Knox, sought relief for English Puritans troubled about the vestments, they addressed 'the bishops and pastors in England' as their 'brethren' (1566).

Within England itself criticism of the episcopate took various forms. There arose through the teaching of Bucer (1551) and Knox (1559), and from the opinions and practice of à Lasco, a concept of reform by what came to be called the 'reduction of episcopacy.' Bucer's proposal was that suffragan bishops, each with a council of presbyters, be set over areas of twenty parishes, to maintain efficiency in preaching and discipline. Knox would be rid of 'proud prelates' with their 'great dominions,' and, in the interests of effective preaching and pastoral care, would divide the dioceses 'so that for every one as they be now (for the most part) be made ten.' A Lasco's Church of the Strangers in London, including French, German, Dutch, and other language

groups each with its own preacher, exhibited a modified episcopacy in the superintendency, along with presbyterianism in
the council of ministers and elders.

At the same time there grew up an uncompromising and exclusive presbyterianism, resembling that of Andrew Melville
rather than that of Knox, which proposed the abolition of episcopacy and the lodging of church authority wholly in councils
of presbyters — consistories, classes, and synods. The chief advocates of this radical presbyterianism were Thomas Cartwright
(d. 1603), Walter Travers (d. 1635), and John Field (d. 1588).

The hope of many of the Presbyterians was that the Church
of England, like the Church of Scotland, might be transformed
into a presbyterian structure by parliamentary action. This
seemed no idle dream. It was (and still remains) uncertain
whether Cecil (Lord Burleigh) was in favor of the change. Sir
Francis Walsingham, the great diplomat and adviser to Elizabeth, showed kindness to some of the Presbyterians and on occasion lent support to their cause. The Earl of Leicester, who long
enjoyed the queen's favor, gave encouragement to the party.
Arthur Golding, Calvin's translator, had access to these men.
He was a friend of Sir Philip Sidney (above, p. 275), who had been
in Walsingham's house in Paris during the St. Bartholomew massacre, an event that confirmed his zealous Protestantism. Sidney
was Leicester's nephew, and he married Walsingham's daughter.
He maintained a warm friendship with Hubert Languet, Huguenot theologian and envoy, who traveled with him in Germany
and visited him in England; and with Philip du Plessis Mornay,
the great Huguenot leader, who was also his guest in England.
The principal parliamentary spokesman for the Presbyterians
was Peter Wentworth, whose wife was Walsingham's sister. In
literature, not only Thomas Norton and Sidney but also the
celebrated Edmund Spenser favored the Calvinist discipline. *The
Shepheards Calender* (1579), which Spenser dedicated to Sidney,
contains elements of Puritan Calvinist propaganda clothed in
transparent allegory.

— V —

A new controversy over vestments disturbed the 1560's and
occasioned numerous expulsions of ministers. But the effort to
presbyterianize the Church began in earnest in 1572. The pre-

vious year Walter Strickland had proposed alterations in the Prayer Book and Peter Wentworth had shocked Archbishop Parker by a bold assertion of the right of Parliament, as over against the bishops, to determine standards of discipline. In 1572 a new bill was introduced to modify the Prayer Book in accordance with Dutch and French Reformed practice. It had majority support but was suppressed by the queen's intervention. Wentworth then suffered the first of his three imprisonments for questioning the royal authority. On 8 March 1576 he delivered in the Commons a daring oration claiming the right of free debate in Parliament: 'Without this it is a scorn and mockery to call it a parliament house.' It is, he affirmed, the duty of the members to maintain this freedom. In Wentworth we see that Presbyterian-Puritan affirmation of the freedom and authority of Parliament which was to become effective in the 1640's.

The *Admonition to Parliament* of June 1572 censures the clergy, the liturgy, and the polity of the Church, and assumes the authority of Parliament in reform measures. John Field and Thomas Wilcox were imprisoned for writing it. But a second *Admonition* soon appeared, provocatively written, bearing suggestions for the reordering of the Church. The author was probably not, as formerly thought, Cartwright, and cannot be named. Amid further efforts in Parliament, a pamphlet war proceeded in which Cartwright led the forces of presbyterianism against Archbishop John Whitgift. Cartwright, dismissed from the Lady Margaret professorship at Cambridge, had taken safety in flight. He visited Geneva but did most of his writing in Amsterdam. Melville tried in vain to obtain his services in St. Andrews university. His chief associate was Walter Travers, an Oxford scholar, who, having returned from the Netherlands in 1580, at the Inner Temple, London, preached 'Geneva' against Hooker's 'Canterbury' and promoted the presbyterian cause by his pen.

Some writings of the presbyterian movement acquired a certain authority with its supporters. Travers published in Latin a treatise that Cartwright translated as *A Full and Plain Declaration of Ecclesiastical Discipline* (1574). It is a militant assertion of Presbyterian principles, demanding tests to exclude 'unable' ministers, the abolition of prelacy, and the adoption of church government by means of elected elders and graded synods. *A*

Directory of Presbyterian Government was the English title of a later brief book of polity, also first written in Latin (1584).* This is a plain, uncontroversial outline of a presbyterian establishment. The ministry, discipline, and polity are specifically described. In the consistory, the local governing council of elders and minister, the majority decides. This body controls the services, keeps the records of the congregation, and deals with major matters of discipline. A stubborn offender, on the lapse of four weeks after the first warning in public services, is to be excommunicated, 'that his spirit may be saved in the day of the Lord.' Provision is made for a graduated series of assemblies — consistory, classis, provincial, national, and ecumenical synods — and the functions of each are indicated. For a classis, which is comparable to the Scottish 'presbytery,' a district embracing twelve churches is suggested; a provincial synod would comprise twenty-four classes.

While the Presbyterians hoped, and repeatedly attempted, to gain their ends through Parliament, a provisional presbyterian organization began to take shape. This grew out of conferences of leaders and adherents of the party. These meetings had the favor of Leicester and Walsingham and were skillfully promoted by John Field, a London minister. Before the conferences, there had widely appeared the voluntary meetings or associations called 'exercises,' or 'prophesyings,' comparable to the types of group-discussion meetings we saw in Zurich, Strasbourg, Geneva, and Scotland. In England the 'exercise' was commonly a weekly two-hour session of ministers and qualified laymen, with a sequence of speakers appointed in advance and with open discussion of Scripture passages by the members. At Northampton (from 1571) the Monday morning exercise, Tuesday and Thursday afternoon meetings of the people for lecture and mutual correction, and a Sunday afternoon school for children (using Calvin's Catechism) were features of an active religious program that enjoyed the favor of Edmund Scambler, bishop of Peterborough. As in Geneva, special visitations preceded the quarterly communion service, and the ministers met quarterly for mutual

* The English version, found in Cartwright's papers and published in 1644, has been edited by P. Lorimer (London, 1872); the Latin text is appended to A. F. S. Pearson's *Der älteste englische Presbyterianismus*, Edinburgh, 1912.

admonition and censure. The exercises, with their enrolled membership, gained stability and authority. They met a need for brotherly association and scriptural instruction and were favored by a number of evangelical-minded bishops.

There was nothing more calculated to alarm the queen than free discussion of religious matters among her subjects; and as the 'prophesyings' spread and flourished she determined to extirpate them. In Archbishop Parker's last year she induced him to demand that John Parkhurst, bishop of Norwich, suppress the meetings in that diocese, and when convocation sought a reconsideration of this measure, she commanded their prompt suppression. The appointment of Grindal to succeed Parker (1575) was designed to satisfy Protestant feeling. Though Grindal opposed the radical presbyterianism of Cartwright, his sympathies were with the scriptural reformers and he continued to approve the 'prophesyings.' A personal command from Elizabeth drew from him a nobly indignant refusal to suppress the exercises by an injunction:

> Bear with me — I beseech you, Madam, if I choose rather to offend your earthly Majesty than to offend the heavenly Majesty of God.

Grindal was 'sequestered,' and the queen herself commanded all the bishops to cause the prophesyings 'to cease and not be used' (7 May 1577). Spenser, in the July eclogue of *The Shepheards Calender,* alludes most favorably to Grindal ('Algrind'), who has been 'long ypent' (confined). But the bishops acquiesced in the suppression. It is well that they did not respond to the queen's former suggestion to Parker that preaching be confined to the reading of the Book of Homilies.

— VI —

That there was something Calvinist in the exercises is generally recognized. Dr. A. F. S. Pearson calls them 'embryonic presbyteries'; but many of their members and favorers may have thought them quite consistent with continuing episcopacy. This cannot be said of the series of conferences that followed their suppression. We owe much of our information on these to the ablest assailant of presbyterianism, Richard Bancroft. In his *Dangerous Positions and Proceedings* . . . (1585) Bancroft regards English presbyterianism as originating in Geneva and mediated through Scotland: his memorable phrases are 'Scots genevating' and 'English scottizing.' Another source of information is the minute-book of the Dedham classis, which held eighty meetings in the years 1582–9.

In London, conferences that bore some resemblance to the forbidden exercises took place in private houses, but these were only preliminary. Whitgift's attempt in 1583 to secure from ministers assent to the statement that the Prayer Book 'contains nothing contrary to the Word of God' called forth resistance and increased the activity of conferences. Some of the meetings in London and in Cambridge (1584–7) were of the nature of national synods. In 1584 Andrew Melville and other Scots visited Oxford and Cambridge in the interests of the cause. At the same time, new efforts were made in Parliament to institute a presbyterian system, apparently on the basis of Knox's Liturgy. But the conferences, acting on principles of the Travers-Cartwright Discipline (which they revised, adopted, and again revised), began, without waiting for parliamentary action, to take the shape, and perform some of the functions, of a national presbyterian organization. From 1587 they actively circulated the Discipline: it is likely that some 500 ministers subscribed it by 1590.

But now the tide turned against the Presbyterians. The Dedham meetings, says their scribe, were 'ended by the malice of Satan.' He does not specify the means employed by the fiend; but we can assign some probable reasons for the virtual collapse of the movement. Prominent among these were the deaths of Field and Leicester, both in 1588. That year also saw the appearance of the scurrilous Marprelate Tracts, the authorship of which is still uncertain. Martin Marprelate's opinions of prelacy bore a basic resemblance to those more decently expressed by known Presbyterians, and his bad manners injured their reputation. One of their ministers, John Udall, died in prison, after brutal treatment, on unjust suspicion of the authorship. England's great deliverance from the Spanish menace is of the same date (1588). The queen had been resolute against the Presbyterians; her prestige was enhanced by the victory over the Armada, while the fear of Roman Catholicism, which filled Puritan propaganda, receded. The numerous measures employed by Whitgift, his writings against Cartwright, and the pamphlet counterattack led by Bancroft were also bearing fruit. Bancroft gives the impression that his description of presbyterian efforts is the exposure of a vast subversive plot. Patriotism now repudiated presbyterianism and acquiesced in the imprisonment of its leaders and the silencing of its spokesmen in Parliament. Save in some parishes exempt from episcopal jurisdiction, the presbyterian organization rapidly disintegrated.

— VII —

At the Hampton Court Conference held in the presence of King James in January 1604, John Reynolds of Oxford, spokesman for the Puritans, proposed a fresh translation of the Bible, and, in the same speech, advocated the revival of the exercises. James welcomed the first but vigorously rejected the second of these proposals, as smacking of 'Scottish presbytery which as well agreeth with a monarchy as God with the devil,' since it allows 'Tom and Will and Dick' to censure the king. A Calvinist in theology, James was a great enemy of the presbyterian polity, as a dangerous challenge to that royal absolutism which he did his utmost to inculcate. The Calvinists, defeated on that front, also lost ground in doctrine during his reign. The participation of his emissaries in the Synod of Dort was featured by the assertion of episcopacy by one of them and the rejection of intolerant Calvinism by another. From his experiences at Dort, John Hales decided to 'bid John Calvin goodnight.' The Arminian doctrines were not embraced by him, but he represents a latitudinarian reaction to the dogmatic spirit of English Calvinism. The adoption of Arminian doctrines by the High Church opponents of Puritanism was to follow. While predestinarian Calvinism rapidly declined in Anglicanism, it retained the adherence of most Puritans through the seventeenth century.

In the (episcopal) Church of Ireland, however, the Geneva doctrines prevailed. Their chief exponent was James Usher (d. 1656), Irish by birth and education, a Dublin professor and a prolific and learned writer, who became bishop of Meath and later archbishop of Armagh. The 104 articles adopted by an Irish convocation in 1615, incorporating the nine Calvinist articles of Whitgift (above, p. 314), were written by Usher.

In 1641 Usher drew up a proposal for 'the Reduction of Episcopacy to Synodical Government' in the Church of England.

The scheme is essentially a return to suggestions made by Bucer and by Knox. Suffragan bishops, each with his own synod, for districts corresponding to those of the rural deans, and representative diocesan and provincial synods, with governing powers, were features of the scheme. Usher declined to attend the Westminster Assembly, and he died before the Restoration — at which time Richard Baxter submitted Usher's plan to Charles II as a basis for ecclesiastical peace (1660).

The 'Plantation of Ulster,' with settlers from England and southwestern Scotland, began about 1606. The Scottish settlers were Calvinist Presbyterians. Some of their early ministers, including such gifted men as Robert Blair, Josias Welsh (a grandson of John Knox), and John Livingston, held parishes within the established Church of Ireland. But after 1633, when William Laud became Archbishop of Canterbury and Thomas Wentworth Lord Deputy of Ireland, the leading Scottish ministers were deposed and expelled. A violent insurrection, attended by the massacre of many Protestants (1641), brought to Ireland Scottish and English Puritan soldiers, who helped to form the first unit of presbyterian organization, the presbytery of Carrickfergus (1642). The Scottish ministers now returned, and the parishes of Ulster came largely under presbyterian control. But the vigorous opposition of Irish Presbyterians to the execution of the king (29 January 1649) brought upon them reprisals that involved the expulsion of many of their ministers. After 1653, however, a favorable policy was followed by Cromwell's government. At the Restoration (1660) the clergy of the Church of Ireland numbered many who were presbyterially ordained. Charles II's bishops, including Jeremy Taylor, bishop of Down and Connor, were expected to correct this: in 1661 Taylor deposed thirty-six of them in his diocese who declined reordination at his hands. Presbyterianism in Ireland outside the establishment, adhering to a rigid Calvinism in doctrine and polity, survived the later measures designed to suppress it.

— VIII —

The last great effort to establish a Calvinist system in England is associated with the work of the Westminster Assembly of Divines, 1643–9. The provocation of the Scottish Presbyterians by the policies of the Stuarts culminated in 1637–8 when Charles

I attempted by mere royal authority to impose a new liturgy upon the Kirk. Resistance was resolute and effective. Led by Alexander Henderson, representatives of all classes of the people signed at Edinburgh the National Covenant, which renewed the King's Confession of 1581 and was a solemn pledge of mutual support in maintaining 'the true worship of God' (28 February 1638). This is the covenant of the 'Covenanters,' whose tenacious adherence to it was to cost them dearly through the age of the later Stuarts. The following November in Glasgow the General Assembly, with Henderson as moderator, repudiated all episcopacy as well as the innovations in worship that had been introduced under James and Charles.

This successful rejection of the royal policy encouraged the hopes of the Puritans in the Church of England, many of whom were, or now became, presbyterian in their views of church order. An intense pamphlet controversy on the presbytery versus episcopacy theme suddenly arose. This literature exhibits an emphasis on 'divine right' claims. This type of argument had been anticipated in some of the utterances of Melville and Bancroft and by the high doctrine of 'divine right of kings' expounded by James I. The ecclesiastical parties were not disposed to compromise on such a plan as that of Usher; *The Danger of Limited Prelacy* is the title of a treatise written by Henderson at the request of London Presbyterians (1641). The same ground was taken by Stephen Marshall and four collaborators in pamphlets which from the initials of their names they ascribed to 'Smectymnuus.' The acquiescence of the Church of England in the gross misgovernment of Charles I, and the cruel sentences of the Court of Star Chamber, of which Laud was a member, had produced a mounting hostility toward the bishops. The abolition of episcopacy was proposed in popular petitions, and compromise proposals (including Usher's) were rejected by the bishops in Parliament; the bishops were insulted in the streets by hostile crowds. In November 1643 episcopacy was abolished by the Long Parliament; the civil war had begun a year earlier.

The attitude of the Scots in their intimate negotiations with leaders of the Parliament affected this outcome. The Puritan leaders looked for Scottish support not to the Scottish parliament but to the General Assembly of the Scottish Church, which had led the nation in the contest against Charles. The abolition of episcopacy was designed to prepare the way for presbyterianism. The Scots who had rejected the attempt to extend the Anglican system to Scotland now hoped to assist in transforming the Church of England into the likeness of the Kirk.

Parliament's attempts in 1642 to secure a meeting of scholarly ministers were frustrated by the king. After the war began, his wishes were disregarded. In June 1643 the Assembly of Divines was called, to meet on 1 July in Henry VII's Chapel, Westminster Abbey. (It later removed to the Jerusalem Chamber.) From this date until 22 February 1649, the assembly held 1163 sessions; thereafter it continued informally and through committees for about three years.

The Assembly was the creature of the Parliament and was never able to escape from Parliamentary supervision. Its 151 original members were nominated by Parliament. Of these 121 were described in the call as 'learned, godly and judicious divines.' The others represented the two houses of Parliament. The task laid upon them was to reform church government and doctrine in a manner

> most agreeable to God's Holy Word, and most apt to procure and preserve the peace of the Church at home and nearer agreement with the Church of Scotland and other Reformed Churches abroad.

Shortly after it was opened, the Westminster Assembly received and adopted a document called the Solemn League and Covenant, already agreed to between the Scottish General Assembly and an English deputation sent to Scotland. This was not merely another Scottish covenant but a league for 'the peace and safety of the three kingdoms,' in which the signers pledged 'the preservation of the reformed religion in Scotland' and 'the reformation of religion in England and Ireland.' The agreement was solemnly adopted by both the Westminster Assembly and the Parliament, 25 September 1643. The Church of Scotland now sent five commissioners, of whom Henderson (d. 1647), George Gillespie (d. 1648), and Samuel Rutherford (d. 1661) furnished real leadership, while Robert Baillie used his talents for diplomacy and recorded events in his letters. The Scottish commissioners had a consultative role and did not vote as members. The 'Reformed Churches abroad' were not represented, although numerous letters from them were received and answered.

The far-reaching plans of the Presbyterians were not to be fulfilled. The work of the Westminster Assembly was carried on with increasing difficulty, not from episcopacy but from the rise of a new party, the Independents, who had gained control of Parliament and as a united minority prolonged the debates in the Assembly of Divines. The Scots were unfavorable to the English presupposition, shared even by many Presbyterians, that the state may have controlling authority in the Church. The authority that had been assumed by the kings was now in large measure exercised by Parliament. A few scholars in the assembly, forming what is called the Erastian party, carried this principle so far as to exclude church authority in discipline. There were also considerable variations of opinion among the presbyterian majority. Yet the debates were conducted throughout with admirable dignity and patience.

In the absence of the former church authorities, action on many transient matters consumed the time of the divines. But they slowly accomplished the tasks of restating doctrine and discipline. They began with an examination of the Thirty-nine Articles, but Parliament peremptorily ordered them first to prepare a book of discipline. After much argument, chiefly over eldership, ordination, and the authority of synods, the *Form of Presbyterial Church Government* and the *Directory of Public Worship* were finished in 1644. *The Confession of Faith, The Larger Catechism,* and *The Shorter Catechism* were completed respectively in April, October, and November 1647.

The Form of Government describes the functions of pastors, teachers, and 'other church governors' — a term ambiguously chosen through difference of opinion regarding the status of those whom 'Reformed Churches generally call elders.' The Directory regulates the outline of morning worship in some detail and includes in the communion service the 'fencing of the tables,' or warning to the unworthy, which points up the Calvinist sense of discipline and the awful sanctity of the Eucharist.

The Confession follows largely the outlines of Usher's Irish Articles of 1615 but is superior to this model in the impressiveness of its language and the adequacy of its content. It is, with its companion, the Shorter Catechism, a classic of Calvinism. It brought Calvinist theology up to date by the formulation of the doctrine of the Covenants of Works and of Grace, to which numerous Scottish and Puritan writers had given attention. Edward Fisher's *Marrow of Modern Divinity* (1645) is based on the covenant theology; the celebrated work of John Cocceius of Leyden on this topic did not appear until 1648. The word 'reprobation' is avoided in the Confession, but double predestination is expressly taught. It affirms a truly Calvinistic doctrine of the majesty and sovereignty of God and of the authority of 'the Holy Spirit speaking in the Scripture' to determine doctrine. The section on repentance (xv) contains the statement:

> As there is no sin so small but it deserves damnation; so there is no sin so great that it can bring damnation upon those who truly repent.

On Christian liberty (xx) the watchword is uttered: 'God alone is Lord of the conscience.' The Shorter Catechism, an epitome of the Larger, remains a masterpiece of literary economy and clarity. The bold sentence with which it begins — 'Man's chief end is to glorify God and to enjoy Him forever' — admirably reflects Calvin's message. God is not only to be glorified but to be enjoyed — a central insight of the Reformation, which many a Calvinist has failed to grasp.

— IX —

It was in Scotland, not in England, that these documents of the Westminster Assembly were to have lasting influence. The Scottish General Assembly adopted them all, with carefully stated conditions, by acts of 1645 and 1647. The conditions were such as to conserve Scottish practice in worship and the Scottish view of the Church's autonomy vis à vis the secular power. In adopting the Westminster Standards the Kirk did not repudiate its previous constitutional documents or notably alter its ways, although it is probably true that the Shorter Catechism became the layman's guide to religious knowledge as no previous book of instruction had been.

In England presbyterianism was defeated through Cromwell's ascendancy. The forcible exclusion of the presbyterian members from Parliament (Pride's Purge, 6 December 1648) made possible the execution of Charles I (29 January 1649), an act at which Scottish Presbyterians were appalled. Some English presbyterian protesters against it suffered as traitors. Christopher Love, a London minister, was executed on Tower Hill, the first of the 'Covenanter martyrs,' and two weeks later Cromwell crushed the Scots in battle at Worcester (3 September 1651). What Queen Mary had failed to do Cromwell accomplished by force, when in July 1653 his soldiers broke into a meeting of the General Assembly in Edinburgh, marched the ministers out of the city, and dispersed them with warnings not to reassemble. David Dickson, the moderator, was no John Knox.

Cromwell's antagonism to the Presbyterians was on the ground of their intolerance. The charge was voiced by Independents such as Philip Nye (who had been the chief spokesman for the Solemn League and Covenant in 1643) when it was evident that the Presbyterians desired an established church with a system of synods and a unified discipline. The position of the opposing party and of Cromwell was that there should be no superior to the local church except the government. Milton's angry rhetoric, 'New presbyter is but old priest writ large,' and Samuel Butler's brilliant doggerel:

> They prove their doctrine orthodox
> By apostolic blows and knocks

helped to fix this concept of presbyterianism in the English mind. The English revulsion to persecution had brought the ruin of Laud and Charles; it was now turned upon the exponents of the presbyterian system. Evidence for the justice of this charge is supplied from the teachings of some Presbyterians; but it should be weighed against a record largely free from persecuting acts and in marked contrast to the severities of the Laudian decade. On the principle of compulsion the Presbyterians were not in agreement. Their co-operative manifesto, *Divine Right of Church Government* (1646), accords to the state coercive power only 'about' and not 'in' the church; while the *Vindication of Presbyterial Government and Ministry* (1649) declares: 'We abhor an over-rigid urging of uniformity.'

Feebly and late, Parliament took action to establish presbyterianism. In March 1646 it authorized the election of elders in the parishes. In October 1647 further steps were taken. The 137 parishes of London were to be formed into 12 classes, and county committees were set up to plan similar districting of classes, or presbyteries, everywhere. Funds needed to initiate the new church order were not provided; but at the time of Pride's Purge London had become presbyterian, Lancashire had 9 classes, Essex 14, and Suffolk 14. Local synods were held, and the normal life of presbyterian churches was in evidence. The *Form of Church Government* was issued for circulation in England and Ireland.

But Cromwell had no intention of permitting a presbyterian triumph. Pride's Purge, which split Puritanism in two politically and reduced Parliament to a subservient 'rump,' the king's death, and the execution of Christopher Love disheartened the Presbyterians. A new theocracy under a lay ruler was in the making. The decade of the 'fifties was the era of Cromwell and the Independents — Calvinists (as were also many of the Baptists) in doctrine but not in polity. After 1654, Cromwell's Triers and Ejectors probably helped to raise the quality of the ministry. But the Church was torn by controversy and sectarianism. Ecclesiastically the best the times afforded consisted of the 'associations' formed by Richard Baxter in Worcestershire (1653) and later extended into at least eight English counties and into Ireland. In these, many tolerant ministers, abandoning the controverted issues, fraternized and co-operated in frequent meetings, framing and following common rules for discipline and the sacraments. Whatever promise these voluntary associations held for religious peace and unity was swept away at the Restoration, along with most of the surviving fragments of presbyterianism. In May 1560 there was a new king upon the throne, who had willingly signed the Covenant to win the Scots, but whose considered opinion it was that 'Presbyterianism is not a religion for gentlemen.'

The true attitude of Charles II to presbyterianism and the Covenant was soon apparent. The Recissory Act put through the 'drunken Parliament' of 1661 canceled all legislation favorable to the Kirk since 1633. When synods protested, they were silenced or disbanded. Alexander Campbell, Marquis of Argyle, whose hands had placed the crown of Scotland on the head of Charles in 1651, for his resolute support of the Covenant was beheaded as a traitor. The reign of Charles saw the heroic resistance of the Covenanters through scenes of battle, imprisonment, torture, and martyrdom. Richard Cameron, a covenanting minister, rode into the town of Sanquhar, Dumfriesshire, and posted a declaration of war against Charles as a perjured tyrant and an enemy of Christ (22 June 1680). Though Cameron and his friends suffered death, the opposition continued. The majority of Scots tamely submitted to a new imposition of episcopacy and the fresh assertion of royal absolutism. The Covenanters were often extreme in their opinions and violent in their methods; but it stands to their credit that they alone had the courage to challenge the oppressive policies of the later Stuarts long before James II so antagonized all Britain as to bring on the Great Revolution of 1688. The Revolution was attended by the resurrection of the Scottish Kirk and was followed by its full legal recognition (1690). The covenant to which William III assented was not that of 1638 but a political bill of rights that abolished royal absolutism and tied the king's power to that of parliaments freely elected and free to debate.

The union of parliaments of England and Scotland (1707) proved rather unfavorable to the Presbyterian Church of Scotland, since it was followed by the Patronage Act of 1712. This measure gravely impaired the presbyterian system by withdrawing the right of parishes to choose their ministers, and occasioned dissension and schism in later decades.

In England the resettlement of religion under Charles II involved the Great Ejectment of St. Bartholomew's Day, 1662, by which, with those previously expelled since the king's return, some 2400 ministers who had been presbyterially ordained were dismissed and later subjected to diverse restraints and penalties. Many Episcopalians had suffered similar treatment during the Puritan ascendancy, but a larger proportion of able and devoted ministers was here affected. Presbyterianism and Independency lived on feebly, though the heroic services of their ministers during the Plague year (1665) did something to raise them in public estimation. With the Toleration Act of 1689 they began to take heart again and to make common cause. In 1690 they established a joint fund for the education of ministers, and in 1691 carried further their co-operation in the London area by adopting the Heads of Agreement, a plan for ministerial common action, especially in ordinations. They failed to maintain long the 'happy union' planned, and their achievements in the eighteenth century are not impressive. The most admirable phase of their history in that era consists of the 'Dissenting Academies,' a series of schools of respectable learning conducted under great handicaps, by which they maintained an educated ministry and perpetuated Puritan educational ideals.

CHAPTER XX

CALVINISM IN AMERICA

— I —

EARLY in the era of British colonization in America, George Herbert wrote in *The Temple* (1633):

> *Religion stands on tiptoe in our land,*
> *Redie to pass to the American strand.*

The lines might have been written much earlier, and not only in England but also in Spain, France, or Holland; for in all these countries the idea of colonies as Christian communities nurturing the Church and propagating the faith had found ample expression.

The first Calvinists in the New World were not from the British Isles. It was a utopian dream of Gaspard de Coligny to plant across the sea a settlement as a place of refuge for Huguenots. In 1555 he brought about the expedition of Nicholas Durand de Villegagnon to Rio de Janeiro. A year later, on its leader's request to Coligny for 'divines' from Geneva, Calvin and his colleagues dispatched fourteen young men to the colony, of whom Pierre Richier and Guillaume Chartier were the first Protestant ministers to cross the Atlantic. The first Protestant service of worship in the New World was conducted by Richier, 10 May 1557. But the whole effort was a tragic failure. Villegagnon abandoned his Protestantism (or pretense of it), shipped the Calvinists back to France under charge of heresy, drowned the few who escaped back to land, and soon after abandoned the enterprise.

Coligny made other futile attempts at Protestant colonization. The company sent under Jean Ribaut to the Florida coast (1562), after a series of misadventures, was savagely exterminated by the Spaniards (1565). Although the main Huguenot migrations followed the Revocation of the Edict of Nantes (1685), a considerable number arrived earlier and established small

churches in New Netherlands, Massachusetts, and South Carolina.

French Canada awaited settlement long after its first exploration by Jacques Cartier. The real beginnings were made largely
on the initiative of a Huguenot nobleman, Pierre du Guast, Sieur
de Monts, a friend of Henry IV. De Monts was designated governor of 'Acadie,' which included, before the English colonies
were planted, the whole of New England and most of New York.
The plan was formed in 1598, but not till 1604 did the expedition of de Monts reach the Bay of Fundy and take winter shelter
on the island of St. Croix, whence it later moved to the mainland
and established Port Royal (Annapolis, Nova Scotia). It was a
mixed community, and had a Calvinist minister and a Roman
Catholic priest, whom Samuel de Champlain describes as en-
gaging in fist fights to settle their controversies, encouraged by
the 'savages' and the French on both sides. At the direction of
de Monts, Champlain founded Quebec in 1608. Champlain also
served under the de Caens, uncle and nephew, who had control
of trade in New France. The nephew, Emery de Caen, sought to
establish Huguenot practice in prayer and psalm singing and
showed hostility to the Jesuits on their arrival at Quebec (1625).
The formation of the Company of One Hundred Associates for
the government of New France in 1627 brought the attempt,
only partly successful, to exclude Huguenots from the country. It was under a Huguenot commander of Scottish ancestry
that the English fleet took Quebec in 1629, and after the war it
was Emery de Caen who officially received it back to French
control. But the Huguenots had no liberty to worship and organize, and their religion survived only in a few families, to the
English conquest of 1759. The historian Parkman thought it
probable that if they had been permitted to settle in New France,
the French occupation would have been, through their numbers
and energy, expanded over the areas that were, instead, to be
slowly peopled by the New England Puritans.

— II —

Very different was the attitude of the English government on
the migration of disaffected religious minorities. Any attempts
to keep them in England were halfhearted and ineffective. When
James I in 1604 boasted that he would 'harry them out of the

land' he was not thinking of their destination once expelled. If
for a time Virginia excluded Puritans, they had their opportunity
in New England. Some of them had already attempted to sail to
American shores: it was the sea and not Elizabeth that thwarted
the projected migration of Brownists in the ships *Hopewell* and
Chancewell, 1596. James I seemed willing to have them go
whither they would out of England, and the same attitude prevailed through most of Charles I's reign. When opportunity
came, many of those who found shelter in the Dutch Republic
sought the western wildernesses to which England laid claim.

Richard Hakluyt, clergyman and lawyer, was one of the principal founders of the British colonial empire. His thoughts sprang
from maps and narratives of exploration, and took shape in
colonial projects. He had undergone in youth a conversion to
geography when his older cousin and namesake laid before him a
map of the world and a Geneva Bible and directed him to read
Psalm 107:23-4: 'They that go down to the sea in ships, and
occupy by the great waters, they see the works of the Lord.' The
Discourse of Western Planting, which he presented to the queen
in 1584, was prepared at the request of Sir Walter Raleigh. It
amply exhibits the Elizabethan Protestant patriotism that motivated men such as Walsingham, Sidney, Raleigh, and Gilbert.
The queen is urged, as the foremost of Reformed princes, to aid
in spreading the Gospel by settling colonies among the savages
of the New World. Those (Puritans) who grow contentious over
ceremonies will in colonial conditions give their attention to
central matters of faith. The planting of colonies would, he argued, provide a refuge for those everywhere persecuted for the
truth of God's Word. His great political aim was the defeat of
Spain; this he hoped to see achieved through establishing strongholds in America and intercepting Spanish trading ships. He
shortly afterward found, among Huguenots in France, and published René de Laudonnière's account of the Huguenot expedition to Florida, with a preface urging colonization on the motive
of 'the glory of God and the saving of souls.' In a dedication to
Sir Philip Sidney of his *Divers Voyages* (1582) Hakluyt attributes
the failures of certain English colonizers to 'a preposterous desire of seeking rather gain than God's glory.' Louis B. Wright
in *Religion and Empire* holds that Hakluyt's *Principal Naviga-
tions . . . of the English Nation* (1589, 1598) captured the Eng-

lish imagination and 'found a place beside Foxe's Book of Martyrs and the Bible' as a good Englishman's required reading.

Dr. Wright's examination of a great variety of evidence supports his view that the religious motive was a powerful factor in English exploration and colonization to the end of the reign of James I. This period saw the beginnings of Virginia and New England. English concern for the Gospel was coupled with intense anti-Spanish and anti-papal zeal. Professor W. W. Sweet points out that it was revived in the policy of Oliver Cromwell and appears in the sermons of Jonathan Mayhew a century later.

The Anglican Church was established in Virginia at a time when its ministry in England was prevailingly Calvinist in theology. The first charter of Virginia (1606), to explain the purpose of the venture, employs phrases that have a Calvinist flavor, such as 'the glory of the Divine Majesty.' No Puritan code is more severe in the penalties for blasphemy, adultery, Sabbath-breaking, and sacrilege than the early laws of this colony.

The contribution of Virginia to democratic institutions has been connected by a careful historian, G. W. Brydon, with the influence of Sir Edwin Sandys, the author of the early charters and 'a man who dreamed a dream of human freedom in a tyrannical age.' Sandys so admired the Swiss Republic and the city of Geneva that he said in 1623, 'If ever God did constitute a form of government it was that of Geneva.' He did his utmost to get the Pilgrims of 1620 to settle in Virginia. Confessing his dislike of monarchy he confided to John Bargrave his ambition to make of Virginia 'a free state.'

The so-called 'Apostle of Virginia,' Alexander Whitaker, was the loyal son of William Whitaker of Cambridge, the chief framer of Whitgift's high Calvinist Lambeth Articles. His labors in the James River Settlements, cut off by his death by drowning after six years (1611–17), gave an impulse to Virginian Anglicanism and may have given it the Low Church direction it later exhibits. He was eager to evangelize the Indians, and it was he who baptized Pocahontas. Like his father, Whitaker was a conforming Puritan. In 1614 he wrote to a Puritan cousin in England, William Gouge:

> I much muse [wonder] that so few of our English ministers that were so hot against the surplice and subscription come hither, where neither are spoken of.

In other letters he complained of the failure of ministers of his persuasion in England to volunteer for the hard tasks of the colonies.

'The surplice and subscription' came to be more of an issue, and Virginia resisted the pressure of English Puritanism. Criticism of the Prayer Book was sharply forbidden. There were some who were grieved in their consciences by this. When their friends were rising to power in England they invited the elders of Boston to send them Puritan ministers. Three were sent, but they were forbidden to preach, and when many people resorted to them for conference, they were not permitted to remain in the colony. A strict prohibition of the entrance of opponents of the Prayer Book followed (1642). Some Puritans were banished, and over three hundred accepted an invitation to settle in Maryland. Cromwell never secured complete obedience in Virginia. Shocked by the execution of Charles I, the 'ancient and most loyal Dominion' offered asylum to Charles II. The commissioners afterward sent by Cromwell conceded the use of the Prayer Book with the omission of prayers for the king. There is nothing theological in the tensions of this period, and presbyterian polity was not an issue.

— III —

When Calvinism in early America is mentioned, thought turns naturally to the Plymouth and Massachusetts Bay colonies. Different as these were, both were definitely Calvinist. The Pilgrim Fathers were loyal disciples of John Robinson, their pastor at Leyden, whose counsel ruled their lives and solved their disagreements. R. G. Usher says:

> They no doubt followed Robinson in his espousal of conservative Calvinism, accepting fully the doctrine of the Elect, of Predestination, and all that they involved. They also championed the right of investigation in the Scriptures for all individuals.

Robinson was a great defender of the ultra-Calvinist doctrines of the Synod of Dort. It is questionable how far any of the Pilgrims grasped the details of his theology; but they could not miss the *un*-Calvinist element of his church polity. They were Separatists on principle, who held the complete autonomy of the local church. In 1617 they had stated in a document presented to the English government:

> We believe that no synod, classis, convocation or assembly of ecclesiastical officers hath any power or authority at all but as the same is by the magistrate given unto them.

In this they were as far from the Calvinist model as were the Anglicans with their Prayer Book and their prelates. Yet they were true Calvinists in their devout obedience to the Scriptures, in their thought of God and conscience, and in their courage to live by their religion. The principles of mutual edification and fraternal correction which had been earnestly inculcated in the Reformed Churches had entered into the habits of life in the Leyden congregation, and enabled them in all their trials to avoid fatal contention. When complaints against them were made to the Merchant Adventurers in London, Governor Bradford could say in 1623 that there had been among them no religious 'controversy or opposition public or private.' Edward Winslow, who had sat under Robinson's preaching for three years, recalled that Robinson welcomed to communion members of the French, Dutch, and Scottish Reformed Churches. When the Pilgrims formed their *Compact* and instituted their own government, they were following literally Robinson's advice given on their departure that they should elect to rule them 'such persons as do entirely love and will diligently promote the common good' — phrases that might have come from one of Calvin's pre-election sermons. They had affirmed that synodical power rested in the magistrate, but in New England they elected their own magistrates. It was reported that Robinson also charged them in these words:

> The Lord has more truth yet to break forth from His Holy Word. I cannot sufficiently bewail the condition of the reformed churches who are come to a period in religion and will go at present no further than the instruments of their reformation. Luther and Calvin were great and shining lights in their times, yet they penetrated not the whole counsel of God . . . Be ready to receive whatever truth shall be made known to you from the written word of God.

Calvin himself would have approved this teaching. The Pilgrims, seeking a better country, were reminded also that they should not shrink from seeking a better theology.

In 1628–30 a new and far larger colony was begun at Massachusetts Bay. Its people had not been exiles from England; nor had they separated from the Church of England. But they had been made uncomfortable within it by the absolutism of the king and the anti-Puritan zeal of William Laud. From the time of Charles I's accession Laud had countered the influence of Archbishop George Abbot, a Calvinist, who for opposing the extreme monarchical views of clerics was sequestered from his jurisdiction in 1526. As Bishop of London and Archbishop of Canterbury (1633) Laud pursued a repressive policy that convinced many Puritans of the necessity of emigration. Shiploads of them now streamed into New England. The proclamation, initiated by Laud, prohibiting the departure of any but certified conformists (May 1638) may have prevented Cromwell and John Hampden from embarking, but it did not long halt the main migration. By 1640, when the Long Parliament took away the motive for flight, more than 20,000 had reached Massachusetts. That hardly anybody came in the 1640's is the best evidence that the motive of the colonizers was religious.

These fathers of much of what is America represent the Calvinist Puritanism with which Charles I was constantly in combat. It was their party in Parliament that had produced the Petition of Right (1629), which, invoking Magna Charta, assailed arbitrary government and taxation without consent. They had cried out against 'Arminianism and popery,' and looked for religious fellowship to the Reformed Churches of Scotland and the Continent. They did not intend a separation from the communion of the Church of England. Francis Higginson, the founder of the Salem colony, as their ship passed Land's End (1628), addressed the passengers in these words:

We do not go to New England as Separatists from the Church of England, though we cannot but separate from the corruptions of it; but we go to practice the positive part of Church reformation, and to propagate the Gospel in America.

They brought with them the learning of the university of Cambridge of the days of Perkins and his disciples, the 'spiritual brotherhood' vividly portrayed by William Haller in *The Rise of Puritanism*. In 1638 some forty or fifty Cambridge graduates were among the settlers, and these included the great majority of the ministers. Oxford was much less numerously represented. The most scholarly of the ministers of the 1630's — John Cotton, Thomas Hooker, and John Davenport — had earned distinction at Cambridge colleges. These three were later invited to be members of the Westminster Assembly. Had they attended, they would have disagreed with the majority, and at some points with one another. Basically they were all Calvinists, but their Calvinism was not a rigid and static system. They did not hesitate to seek with Calvin 'the truth wherever it appears' and had no thought of making any Reformer their sole master. They had moved away from the letter of the *Institutes* and the *Ordinances* of Geneva, as indeed had John Preston, one of their chief English advisers before his death in 1629. Alienated from the episcopal system, they did not rest with the presbyterian alternative, but were prepared for a fresh adventure in church order. The strange occasion of their new departure in church polity was an epidemic of scurvy.

The Salem colony was visited by this disease early in 1629, and the Plymouth folk sent to their stricken brethren Samuel Fuller, physician and deacon. The letter of gratitude sent by Governor John Endicott on 11 May suggests that the results were even more important ecclesiastically than medically: Fuller had persuaded them 'touching the outward form of God's worship.' In August the Salem church was formed in avowed imitation of the Plymouth model. Boston and the other communities adopted a similar congregational plan. Yet they continued to exhibit some of the presuppositions of Anglicanism and some of the elements of Presbyterianism.

In Massachusetts, in accord with English rather than with Genevan practice, the political suffrage was until 1647 confined to communicants. Thomas Hooker disapproved of this disfranchisement of freemen. He wrote to John Winthrop:

On matters which concern the common good, a general council chosen by all, to transact business which concerns all, I conceive most suitable, and safe for the relief of the whole.

Addressing the General Court of Connecticut at its formation (1635) Hooker expounded his view that 'the foundation of authority is laid in the free consent of the people.'

Roger Williams, after conferring with Cotton and Hooker in England, preceded them to America (1631). He so accentuated the Calvinist doctrine of the separate spheres of Church and state that he found himself unacceptable in Boston, and his teaching at Salem brought upon him expulsion by the General Court of Massachusetts (1636). The action was taken unwillingly; but Williams was in effect challenging the authority the court exercised in church matters. After great sufferings in a winter flight, during which he owed his survival to the Narragansett Indians, Williams founded at Providence the colony of Rhode Island, as 'a shelter for persons distressed for conscience.' This was in 1636, a year that saw another notable beginning, the foundation of Harvard College.

This was also the time of Mrs. Anne Hutchinson's 'antinomian' teaching in Boston, in which the Covenant of Works was assailed and direct inspiration apart from Scripture was affirmed. In 1637 a general synod of ministers met in Cambridge, at which her doctrines were rejected. She was soon afterward banished and found refuge in the Rhode Island 'shelter.'

— IV —

Thus New England Calvinism was producing its own critics and reformers. Its accepted theologians, too, show considerable variety of emphasis. Thomas Shepherd of Cambridge stressed the responsibility of man; John Norton of Ipswich the goodness of God: 'the elect's seeking God is the effect of God's seeking them.' Thomas Hooker implied, without systematically expressing, the entire Calvinist pattern of theology, with some elaborations of his own. The soul, he argued, must be so 'at God's disposing' as to be content to be damned if God wills it — a doctrine advanced by St. Francis de Sales and Fénelon. In defense of the congregationalist church system and against Samuel Rutherford's *Due Right of Presbyteries* (1644), Hooker wrote *A Survey of the Sum of Church Discipline* (1645), claiming for each congregation the power of excommunication and denying that synods have such power.

Synods for 'consociation' and the healing of controversies had a recognized place; Hooker himself was moderator of the Cambridge Synod of 1637. The important synod of 1646–8, also held at Cambridge, was to some extent the American counterpart of the Westminster Assembly. It was convened on invitation of the General Court of Massachusetts. It brought forth the Cambridge Platform, a document of authority in New England until about 1760. In its preface the claim is made of doctrinal agreement with 'all the reformed churches of Christ in Europe,' and the desire is expressed not to vary in teaching from the churches in England. The Westminster Confession is adopted bodily, with the exception of certain sections dealing with polity and discipline. These matters are regulated in a 'treatise' that lodges authority primarily in the local church. Representative synods, however, while given no disciplinary authority, have the functions of 'determining controversies of faith, and cases of conscience' and clarifying from the Scripture matters of worship. Their directions are to be received with 'submission' not only for their agreement with Scripture but also 'for the power whereby they are made.' This all indicates a limited measure of hospitality to presbyterian views. Presbyterian principles appear in John Eliot's *Communion of Churches* (1665), which describes an ideal church system, with councils of twelve or more churches and provincial, national, and ecumenical representative synods.

Cotton Mather, too, indicates the acceptance of essentially presbyterian views of the ministry. In *Magnalia Christi Americana,* Book v (1702), he points out that in New England the imposition of hands in ordination is by the 'presbytery,' not the 'fraternity' as a whole, since the New Testament 'mentions the former expressly but not the latter.' The right of nature as well as of Scripture requires the holding of synods 'to consult and conclude things of common concernment.' Since synods are of apostolic example, and 'a necessary ordinance,' their judgment is to be 'taken as decisive.'

The New England clergy largely controlled the country. They gave it schools, they framed its laws, they shaped the character of its people. From John Cotton to Jonathan Edwards, New England Puritanism passed through an epoch of greatness and produced a type of human being that no just and informed mind can think of without admiration. The laws were severe as compared with ours of today but not by standards of that age. The number of capital offenses was smaller than in other regions. The 'Blue Laws' of Connecticut were fabricated in the Revolutionary period to defame the colony. Actually the sumptuary and restrictive laws of Virginia were at some points harsher than those of Massachusetts. The worst blot on New England's name is the Salem witch-hunt of 1692, when nineteen persons were hanged and one was crushed to death for alleged witchcraft. The execution of witches, often by burning, was still for a century to be prevalent in most areas of Europe. This was the last of it in America. Even at the time many were deeply shocked by the fanaticism and by the activity of Cotton Mather and other ministers in the prosecutions. Earlier charges of witchcraft in Plymouth had failed in the courts. E. H. Byington credits the Pilgrims with a kindlier spirit than that of the Puritans — a gentleness 'learned in the hard school of adversity.' Perhaps, too, they had learned lessons of tolerance in Holland.

Apart from the Rhode Island colony, the refugees from Charles I had no idea of making their land a place of refuge for other religious minorities than those of their own kind. Baptists were arrested and tried in Boston; Obadiah Holmes was publicly whipped (1651). But the embarrassing result was the conversion of many to their views, of whom Henry Dunster, the president of Harvard, was the most distinguished. Quaker missionaries suffered imprisonment, and four of them were hanged, before Charles II commanded Governor Endicott to send them instead to England for trial. By 1665 Baptists had a church in Boston and Quakers were freely admitted to the colony.

The second and third generations saw a disquieting change of temper. The ideal of a church of the regenerate was faced with a condition of increasing indifference and the failure in many of evidence of conversion. A concession to this condition was made in the Half Way Covenant (1662), which without admitting the unregenerate to communion permitted the baptism of their children. The new plan called forth controversy but was at length generally adopted. It may have led to the weakening of the religious life that was characteristic of the early eighteenth century in New England as elsewhere. The 'Reforming Synod' of 1679 listed the marks of the prevalent moral and religious decay, and attempted to institute a revival. In 1680 the synod adopted the English Congregational Savoy Confession (1658), a revision of the Westminster Confession, not less Calvinistic but expounding the church order of congregationalism. The lost ground in religion was not regained, however, until the Great Awakening and the New England theology introduced by Jonathan Edwards.

— V —

After Henry Hudson, an English explorer employed by the Dutch, went up the Hudson River in 1609, a tiny Dutch community began to form on Manhattan Island. Fourteen years later a company of Walloon Calvinists, who like the Pilgrims had found refuge in Holland, settled near Albany (1623). Others of this type settled with the Dutch in Manhattan and in Staten Island. Although the aims of the Dutch settlers were economic, they and their backers were also motivated by the desire to see their Calvinist faith prevail against Roman Catholicism in the New World. Organization of the Manhattan colony was advanced in 1626 when Peter Minuit, a Huguenot, was made director, and again in 1653 when New Amsterdam was incorporated as a city. Worship was conducted by laymen until 1628, when Jonas Michaelius, a Leyden graduate, organized a church. He was preceded, and aided, by officers known as Comforters of the Sick, who undertook a variety of minor pastoral duties including those ordinarily attached to the office of deacon. In 1642 a church was formed in Albany under Johannes Megapolensis, who later served effectively in New Amsterdam and made an effort to bring the Gospel to the Mohawk Indians.

In 1640 it was formally declared that only the Reformed Church was to be permitted in New Netherlands. This did not mean persecution for opinions or restraint upon home worship. But a Lutheran minister who came to organize a church was sent back to Holland. The number of churches increased, following settlements in Long Island, Bergen, New Jersey, Harlem, and Kingston. They were still under the Amsterdam classis, while the secular government of the colony was under the Dutch West India Company. A Quaker whom the director, Peter Stuyvesant, refused to admit and shipped away to Amsterdam secured from the company a communication to Stuyvesant reversing this exclusive policy and laying down the principle of freedom of conscience (1663).

But the policy of planting settlements under proprietors (patroons) proved unsuccessful: contention and disaffection arose within the colony, and growth was slow. In 1664 armed English ships sent by Charles II trained their guns on New Amsterdam, and Peter Stuyvesant had no choice but to surrender. In 1673 by a similar action the Dutch recovered the town; but the next year it became English again by treaty. New Amsterdam was now New York. Dutch immigration ceased, and the ministers, left without state support, were impoverished and discouraged.

Nevertheless, under English rule the Dutch remained the majority for about a century. On the whole their liberties were respected, including 'the liberty of their conscience in divine worship and discipline,' as promised in the surrender of 1664. But in the reign of James II (1685–8), who as duke of York had already received from his brother, Charles II, authority in the colony, there was increasing fear of losing religious freedom. To guard it, the Dutch steadfastly declined to receive support for their ministers from the colonial government. In the reign of the Dutch king of England, William III, the autonomy of the Church was finally won, and a charter of 1696 incorporated 'the ministers, elders and deacons of the Dutch Church of the City of New York,' together with all who should be admitted to their communion. Anglicanism was now the Church formally (though somewhat ambiguously) established in New York City and in the counties of Richmond, Westchester, and Queens (1693), but no attempt was made to coerce the Dutch Reformed.

After the massacre suffered by the Waldensians of Piedmont in 1655, a shipload of the survivors reached New York harbor, only to be stranded off Staten Island, where many of these people found a home and were later merged in a Huguenot community. About the same time began the flow of Huguenot refugees that was to culminate after the Revocation of the Edict of Nantes. Many settled in New Paltz near Kingston, New York, where they obtained an able pastor, Pierre Daillé (1683). He later removed to Boston, where also the French refugees were entering in considerable numbers. The New England Puritans generally showed toward them less hospitality than they met from the colonial Dutch. They were given land and had an organized congregation in Boston, but it was not until 1716 that they were permitted to erect a church. The forty-five families that settled on Narragansett Bay in Rhode Island, after a prosperous beginning, were obliged through 'the lawless conduct of their neighbors' to leave their farms and dwellings and go to New York (1699).

The eighteenth-century revival of religion first affected the Calvinist churches through the preaching of a minister of the Dutch Reformed Church in America, Theodore Jacob Frelinghuysen (d. 1748). Born in Westphalia, the son of a pastor in the Reformed Church, he felt the influence of German Pietism. Having served as pastor in Emden and in East Friesland, he responded to the appeal voiced by a Long Island minister for the help of an 'evangelical and pious man,' and was appointed for American service by the classis of Amsterdam. In January 1720, he began work in settlements on the Raritan River, New Jersey. Frelinghuysen preached with evangelical passion, called his hearers to repentance and renewal of life, charged his colleagues in the ministry with being unconverted, warned the ill-disciplined and careless from the Lord's Supper, and pronounced damnation upon hardened sinners. His methods were calculated to arouse opposition: he was accused of Labadism and Quakerism, and when churches were closed to him, he was forced to hold his growingly popular meetings in barns. The Amsterdam classis, however, pronounced him orthodox and exhorted the parties to peace. Frelinghuysen's co-operation with Gilbert Tennent, Scotch-Irish Presbyterian leader of the Great Awakening, was to have important consequences; these we shall discuss in another chapter.

— VI —

Some of the 10,000 Scots taken prisoner by Cromwell were sent to New England (1651) and 'sold' into servitude for six to eight years. Their condition was really that of indentured laborers. John Cotton informed Cromwell that they were being well treated. They succeeded so well that six years later they (characteristically) established 'the Scots Charitable Society' of Boston, with member payments of sixpence quarterly, for the relief of one another or 'any of Scottish nation' needing their help.

Cotton Mather, whose trans-Atlantic correspondence was variously significant, sought to promote 'good Scotch colonies' to guard the northern frontiers of New England and to occupy Nova Scotia. Mather, who was sadly misguided on witchcraft, had a shrewd estimate of the Scotch-Irish. He lived to see a fair number of them in New England, where they were to fulfill some of his rather utilitarian expectations.

About 1710, large numbers of the Ulster Scots, who had suffered economic distress and political and religious disabilities under Queen Anne's government, began to arrive in New England and Pennsylvania. Before the Revolution they were to be found throughout the thirteen colonies, their greatest strength being in Pennsylvania. They established congregations and built churches near Portland, Maine, and in Londonderry, New Hampshire (which they founded). Forcibly prevented from building a church in Worcester, Massachusetts, they moved away to form new frontier settlements in New Hampshire, Massachusetts, and Vermont. In accordance with the hopes of Mather, who befriended the newcomers, they became a shield to the earlier inhabitants against incursions by French and Indian enemies.

The Scotch-Irish were now pouring into eastern Pennsylvania, whence some of them fanned out into Virginia, North and South Carolina, New Jersey, Delaware, Maryland, and later into western Pennsylvania. Many emigrant ships from Ireland came directly to the Carolinas, a few to New York. In most of these colonies some English-speaking Presbyterians had preceded them. Some of the first pastors were men who had parted company with New England Congregationalism. Francis Doughty, whose Presbyterianism was his offense in Massachusetts, preached to English hearers in New Amsterdam, 1643–50, and later labored in Maryland among Puritan-Presbyterians who had fled from Sir William Berkeley's harsh regime in Virginia. At Hempstead, Long Island, Richard Denton, after pastorates in New England, formed in 1644 a distinctly Presbyterian congregation, made up for the most part of incomers from Connecticut; this claims to be the oldest surviving congregation in America always called 'Presbyterian.'

A Scotch-Irish minister, educated in Glasgow, who preceded the migration of his brethren, takes the most important place among Presbyterian founders in America. Francis Makemie

(1658–1708) crossed the ocean in 1682 to Barbados. A year later he began an itinerant ministry in Maryland and Virginia. In a visit to London he obtained support and ministerial recruits. In 1706 he secured the attendance of seven ministers at a meeting in which the Presbytery of Philadelphia, the first American presbytery, was formed. Because of its combination of Scotch-Irish, Scottish, Southern Irish, and New England Puritan membership this Presbytery has been called by Charles Augustus Briggs 'a miniature of the entire history of American Presbyterianism.'

Makemie possessed some wealth, apparently through his marriage to a Virginia heiress, and was able to evade the Virginia law by preaching in houses that were his own property. In Maryland he and his associates formed churches, while Samuel Davies and others made Presbyterian beginnings in Delaware and in Philadelphia. In 1707 Makemie was imprisoned for preaching in a house in New York City. He claimed the benefit of the Toleration Act of 1689, and told the hostile governor, Lord Cornbury that as a minister of the Gospel he could not give bond that he would not preach. He was acquitted of any breach of the law but was unjustly forced to pay the costs of the trial. The publicity given to the case was favorable, both to Presbyterianism and to freedom. The Presbytery of Philadelphia was soon followed by three others, and these were grouped under the Synod of Philadelphia (1717). The Synod in 1729 adopted the Westminster standards with a liberal qualifying phrase — 'in all the essential and necessary articles.'

William Tennent, a former Irish Episcopalian, gave to Presbyterianism in America its first educational institution, the Log College of Neshaminy, Pennsylvania (1727). Here he trained able young men for the ministry. His death in 1746 was the signal for an effort to make fuller provision for education. The College of New Jersey was founded at Elizabethtown (1747) but removed to Newark and then to Princeton (1755). It was soon supplying well-trained preachers to all the Middle Colonies.

Some devout English settlers in Hanover County, Virginia, in search of edifying reading came upon a book that greatly attracted them, though they knew nothing of its origin. It was the Westminster Confession of Faith. In 1747 they obtained the services of Samuel Davies (1723–61), son of Welsh settlers in Delaware trained in a log college conducted by Samuel Blair. Davies contended for the right to preach not only in Hanover but wherever he might have opportunity, and for the recognition of this right for others, in accordance with the Toleration Act. This permission was officially secured only for his successor when he left to become president of the College of New Jersey (1759). One of the most eloquent of preachers, Davies made a lasting impression on American life.

John Witherspoon (1722–94), educated in Edinburgh, had become an eminent Scottish minister when he was with difficulty induced to accept the presidency of the college (1768). Samuel Davies, when in Scotland (1754), had read and delighted in Witherspoon's *Ecclesiastical Characteristics,* perhaps the cleverest satire ever written by an evangelical. Witherspoon had later written learned and able works expounding a Calvinist theology and assailing the Moderate Party and its submissive attitude to the state in church matters. His coming to America was rightly regarded as a notable boon to American Presbyterianism; at the time no one could have thought him capable of the political role he was to play. Witherspoon was the ablest of the clerical supporters of the American Revolution, and the only clergyman among the signers of the Declaration of Independence.

— VII —

Presbyterianism in the colonies was pretty solidly with John Witherspoon in this attitude toward Church and state. The great majority of its members were Scotch-Irish, who had no loyalty to England. Their fathers had gone from Scotland to Ireland before the union of the Scottish and the English parliaments (1707), and though London later became their political headquarters it was in the era when Parliament and bishops exasperated them by harsh treatment. Most of those Presbyterians who had come directly from Scotland were also disaffected by the results of the Patronage Act (1712), in which the right of parishes to call ministers was withdrawn, and by the worldly and indifferent ministers fattened with government favor, whom Witherspoon had tossed on his horns in *Ecclesiastical Characteristics.*

There was, moreover, in Calvinism itself not only a desire for church autonomy as against the state but also an element distinctly congenial to republicanism, an element brought to full expression by the Revolution. Calvinism had been born in Switzerland, a nation that had always been a republic. In France it had failed to make terms with kingship. In Scotland it was established in the absence of a monarch and thereafter was almost constantly in tension with the Stuarts. Its opposition to Cromwell was to a greater enemy of the Covenant than the king had been, and not to a republic based on free elections. It was then seeking a solution on the basis of a responsible monarchy with an elective parliament. Something like this seemed to be promised under William III, with the Bill of Rights and the Toleration Act. But the tendency to arbitrary government under the Hanoverians deepened the discontent of Scotland. Scottish Presbyterians in America were almost as anti-monarchical as the Scotch-Irish. With extraordinary alacrity presbyteries and synods declared for resistance and supported the Continental Congress on the ground that it 'consists of delegates chosen . . . by the body of the people.' Ministers sat on Revolutionary committees and thousands of Presbyterians hastened to join the Revolutionary forces, where they proved the most steadfast of Washington's soldiers.

In 1774 the Hanover Presbytery, allied with Baptists who made similar appeals, petitioned the Virginia government for 'the religious liberties of all dissenters in the colony.' They spoke as representatives of a world-wide 'church neither contemptible nor obscure,' and affirmed their concern for 'American liberty.' Their insistence on this principle, in common cause with Baptists and other 'dissenters,' brought the Virginia Bill of Rights of 1776, by which 'all men are equally entitled to the free exercise of religion.' This was in reality the implementation of the principle of the Confession of Faith xx, 2, 'God alone is Lord of the conscience.' But those who framed these words, and Calvin, whose language they paraphrase, would not have favored such an application of them as the bill provided. The constitutional separation of Church and state in the United States of America was a natural consequence of this and similar acts in the rebelling colonies. After long experience in a position of dissent in Ireland and America, Presbyterianism had ceased to demand a position of establishment and, without losing its religious character, had become committed to the principle of religious freedom.

— VIII —

Attention was called earlier to the migration of Calvinists from the stricken Palatinate after the ravages of Louis XIV's armies (above, p. 280). The decades that brought the Scotch-Irish migration saw also the arrival of thousands of Germans, many of them Palatinate Calvinists. William Penn, the liberal Quaker founder of Pennsylvania, whose mother was Dutch Reformed, and who had spent years under the instruction of the liberal Calvinist, Moïse Arryraut, in Saumur, had encouraged these people to migrate to the free colony. The first comers were aided by Dutch Reformed ministers. A congregation formed of both groups in Philadelphia (1710) soon afterward became Presbyterian. In 1720 came John Philip Boehm, who was to become a traveling minister and organizer through six counties of Pennsylvania. He met with the displeasure of the next minister, George Michael Weiss, for having long preached, and occasionally administered the sacraments, without ordination; but when he was ordained the two co-operated fruitfully.

They sent frequent reports to the Church of Holland, and in 1746 the Dutch Church sent Michael Schlatter, a Swiss scholar and pastor, to superintend the expansion of the Reformed congregations in America. A great traveler, Schlatter sought out the German Reformed wherever they had settled (he even paid an extended visit to Nova Scotia), established congregations, and brought the church of the German settlers to vigorous life. He had been commissioned to set up a governing convention, or coetus, and this was duly organized, and approved by the Dutch authorities in 1747. It consisted of the regular minister and two elders (later only one) from each congregation. In 1748 it formally adopted the Heidelberg Catechism and the Canons of the Synod of Dort. Unfortunately, Schlatter's energetic methods were resented; the 'charity schools' that he promoted with British support were unsuccessful, and he withdrew from the fellowship of the coetus, of which he was the chief founder.

The New York Dutch coetus also formed in 1747 soon fell into contention; the part of it affected by the revival of that time continued to meet, while an opposing group who wanted to maintain control from Holland formed what was called the *con-*

ferentie (1754). It was John Henry Livingston (d. 1825), born near Poughkeepsie, New York, and a Yale graduate, who was instrumental in restoring unity among the Dutch Reformed (1771). With the approval of the Amsterdam classis the American Dutch Church was now free to ordain ministers and to govern itself in all things, and was entering upon a stage of new vitality. Some of the abler ministers were already training young men for ordination. In 1784 Dr. Livingston became the founder and head of a seminary in New York, which removed to New Brunswick, New Jersey, in 1810.

PART IV

CALVINISM AND MODERN ISSUES

There is no fact better worth impressing on the modern liberal churches than this: that they have come to be what they are through a development out of the Calvinism they are only too ready to undervalue and to despise. — Ephraim Emerton, Professor of History in Harvard University, 'Calvin's Four Hundredth Anniversary,' *Evening Post*, New York, 10 July 1909.

Etre calviniste, ce n'est pas s'attacher à reproduire servilement les détails de cette grande pensée de Calvin qui nous déborde et nous entraîne dans son cours puissant. Etre calviniste, ce n'est pas faire le rêve de s'installer aux paysages où jaillaisait la source, il y a quatre siècles; mais c'est entrer dans le courant qui emporte avec lui non le mirage révolu d'un site initial, mais l'énergie d'un fleuve intarissable, et dont le mouvement ne s'arrête plus. — Henri Clavier, *Etudes sur le calvinisme,* Paris, 1936, p. 151.

CHAPTER XXI

THE FRAGMENTATION OF CALVINISM

— I —

DURING the eighteenth century and the first half of the nineteenth most of the Calvinist churches were torn asunder through a series of controversies. The causes of this divisive trend lay not in basic theological differences but largely in the varied response made by ministers and members to the impact of state power. The response was in turn conditioned by the influence of the new Evangelicalism that now stirred and challenged the churches, assailing the inertia and indifference to belief and conduct that had pervaded them. We must bear in mind these four elements that characterize the period for Calvinism: Erastian pressure on the churches; rationalistic elements in the environing culture that prompted acquiescence in this as a condition of ecclesiastical safety; the new evangelical forces; and the tensions and secessions that ensued.

It is in Scottish Presbyterianism that this pattern of events is most vividly exemplified. In Switzerland and the Netherlands, where Reformed Churches also were politically established, the history was similar. The small Presbyterian and Congregational churches of England became strongly affected by the secularity and rationalism of the age; the wave of Evangelicalism stirred them in a limited degree. On the Church of England the Evangelical Movement had a powerful effect, one aspect of which was the re-emergence of Calvinism to prominence within it. In Ireland and the British colonies the Scottish movements were reflected. Calvinism in the United States was agitated by a series of revivals; it imported some of the divisions created elsewhere, advanced in organization and education, and painfully adjusted itself to the demands of a moving and tumultuous frontier.

Christianity was widely confronted by the aggressive secularism of the Enlightenment, which asserted or assumed the supremacy of the state over churches and its right to coerce them. Persecution of individuals for their religious convictions gave place to subjection of the churches and their ministers to state policy. In Roman Catholic countries the system of state control was known as Gallicanism or Febronianism (from 'Frebonius,' the pen name of Nicholas von Hontheim, who advocated it in a work of 1762). Protestants came to use the term 'Erastianism,' from the *Theses* of Erastus (above, p. 273), written against the Puritan George Wither at Heidelberg, 1568, published in London in 1589, and translated into English in 1659, just before the Restoration. Erastus merely held the magistrates responsible for discipline and exempt from excommunication, but Erastianism came to mean the supremacy of the prince or state in all ecclesiastical matters. The position was developed in Holland during the Arminian controversy, especially in the writings of Hugo Grotius, and the subject was widely debated in treatises of the seventeenth century. The secular Erastianism of Thomas Hobbes (*Leviathan*, 1651) proved alarming even to churchmen who were not Calvinists. The Scots of that era, as disciples of Knox and Melville, were in general stout resisters of Erastian principles, but the eighteenth century brought a different spirit.

— II —

'Moderation is what religion enjoins, neighboring churches expect from you and we recommend to you.' From these words in King William's message to the Scottish General Assembly in 1690 the name 'Moderates' came to be applied to the party favoring co-operation with, and even submission to, the state. The first great Moderate was William Carstares (d. 1715), dubbed 'Cardinal Carstares' with a not unfriendly allusion to his adroit diplomacy. His vigilant leadership brought the Kirk safely through the difficult crisis of the Revolution. Educated in Edinburgh and Utrecht, he had been William's chaplain and confidant in Holland. Later he protected the Assembly from William's poorly conceived policies. Once he rode in haste to Kensington and thrust himself into the royal bed chamber at midnight to implore the rescinding of a command imposing a mischievous loyalty oath that would have flung away Scottish good will toward the king.

Guided by Carstares, the Kirk and the king came to agreeable terms. The Scottish parliament repealed the laws favoring Episcopacy, adopted the Westminster Confession, and fully approved the Presbyterian system. Many of the Episcopal ministers were now expelled: already in the Covenanting area of the southwest the curates had been 'rabbled,' or hustled out, by the populace. Ministers of Presbyterian conviction, including the survivors among those 'outed' in 1661, formed a corps of pastors that had yet to become numerically sufficient. The broken structure of the Church was soon fully restored. A notable advance in democratic procedure in ecclesiastical legislation was made in the Assembly's 'Barrier Act' of 1697, which required that measures involving the constitution of the Church must be approved by the presbyteries before final enactment by the Assembly.

A small body of irreconcilable Covenanters, declining a settlement that did not restore the Covenant, remained out of communion with the Kirk, and later found ordained ministers to lead them. They organized their 'Reformed Presbytery' in 1743. A number of Episcopal clergy (some of them supported by Carstares) also continued to gather congregations, and the Scottish Episcopal Church was able to survive in modest strength.

The reign of Queen Anne (1702-14) saw the unfortunate Patronage Act, which restored to lay patrons (heirs of the original donors of church property) the right to present ministers to parishes. This was a violation of the Act of Security (1707), which safeguarded Presbyterianism as it existed when the parliaments were united. The medieval system of patronage had been discarded in 1649, restored in 1661, and again abandoned in 1690. Its restoration by a London Parliament was an affront to alert Presbyterians, who prized the congregational 'call' in the settling of ministers. In vain did the aging Carstares journey to London to petition the House of Lords against the measure, and in vain did Scottish Assemblies protest it thereafter. The Moderates generally came to acquiesce in patronage. An act of the General Assembly of 1732 attempted to modify it but accepted it in principle — over the protest of a small minority of ministers.

Specifically it was patronage that was the primary point of

disagreement in the secessions that followed. But there existed also an emerging alienation in thought. The Moderates felt the influence of a new liberalism, which their opponents called Arminianism or Socinianism, though it was a temper of mind rather than a system of thought. Over against this there appeared a Biblical, evangelical element, somewhat affected by the spirit of the Covenanters that was freshly nourished by one popular book. Thomas Boston (d. 1732) found in his parish of Simprin a copy of Edward Fisher's *Marrow of Modern Divinity* (above, p. 326) and James Hog of Carnock republished it (1717). The book, written in the form of a lively dialogue, was at once assailed for its startling emphasis upon the wideness of God's invitation to mercy and the assurance of salvation, doctrines supported by quotations from Luther. In fact the *Marrow*, while essentially Calvinist, brought to rigid Scottish Calvinism a fresh stimulus from Luther's early triumphant message of faith and its fruits — a fact brought out prominently in some of Boston's notes, supplied in most editions. In 1720 the Assembly condemned it, to the dissatisfaction of a determined minority. Ebenezer Erskine of Portmoak with eleven other ministers ('the twelve apostles') asked for a reconsideration of this action, and when rebuked by the Assembly (1722) continued to teach the *Marrow* doctrines. The party had a sense of living in a crisis. Nothing like this, said one of them, 'has happened in any Reformed Church since Calvin's days.' At the same period (1729) Francis Hutcheson began to impart to Glasgow students his anti-Calvinist philosophy of the moral sufficiency of man.

Boston's numerous works include his popular *Human Nature in Its Fourfold State* (1720), an impressive treatise, marked by scriptural certainty and evangelical individualism, on the progression from original righteousness through depravity and regeneration to eternal bliss or doom. He sternly protested the mild sentence imposed by the Assembly on Professor John Simson of Glasgow, who was retired with salary for his Anti-Trinitarian errors (1729). After Boston's death Erskine (d. 1754), having removed to Stirling, still more boldly led the protesting minority on the patronage issue. The practice of patronage was becoming more objectionable in this period, and popular sentiment against it was easily aroused. Erskine's growing group denounced the acquiescent policy of the Moderate majority in the

Assembly; the protesters were deposed and formed a presbytery of their own (1733). Their deposition caused so much agitation that it was revoked. They were zealous and irreconcilable; the Assembly was patient and considerate toward them, willing to make minor concessions but fixed in its main policy. Their refusal to make terms was evident enough before they were finally deposed in 1740.

Their numbers still increased. Ebenezer Erskine's gifted brother Ralph, of Dunfermline, already added luster to their ranks. By 1745 they formed a synod of three presbyteries. Two years later internal strife split the synod into two sections. The issue was the Burgess Oath affirming 'the Protestant religion presently professed.' If this meant the Kirk of the Moderates, some consciences said no. The Erskines were 'Burghers'; that is, they voted to accept the oath. But Ralph's son and Ebenezer's son-in-law supported the 'Anti-Burgher' motion to excommunicate their senior relatives. The divided secessionists spread to Ireland, to Canada, to the United States. In 1799 came a further schism of the Burgher synod, and in 1806 the Anti-Burghers followed their example. There were distinguished scholars among the ministers in all camps. Thomas McCrie's still useful historical works will be better understood if it is remembered that he was of the Anti-Burgher branch and the founder of its Old Light wing, which in 1806 refused to revise the Westminster teaching on the civil magistrate.

How far would this fragmentation go? The First Secession of 1733–40 was followed by the Second in 1752, when Thomas Gillespie, a convert of Thomas Boston's preaching and an alumnus of Philip Doddridge's academy at Northampton, was deposed from his pastorate at Carnock for opposition to patronage. Among those who joined him was Thomas Boston, Jr. They formed the Presbytery of Relief in 1761. Without declaring for any standard of faith, they used the Westminster documents and practiced free communion. The Relief Church was the most progressive branch of Calvinism; but its growth was slower than that of the earlier secession. Gillespie felt the influence of Doddridge and English Congregationalism.

The divisions among the seceders were not attended by differences in matters of faith. Accordingly they were not to be permanent. Early in the nineteenth century there was something to encourage the hope that the trend toward schism would one day be reversed. A movement was begun for reunion of the severed fragments, and in 1820 most of the seceders were gathered into the United Secession Church. Their experience in separation from the state Church, however, had convinced them of the advantages of voluntary support, and their leaders taught the principle of 'voluntaryism,' condemning all church establishments.

— III —

With some justification, the view has been expressed that the secessions prolonged the evil of patronage by leaving its supporters in greater relative strength in the Kirk. The era of the undisputed sway of the Moderates is associated with the leadership of William Robertson (d. 1793) and Hugh Blair (d. 1800). Robertson, unsurpassed as a historian in his age, was the principal of Edinburgh university and for more than thirty years a powerful figure in the General Assembly. His excellent personal qualities were not expressed in any zeal for needed church reforms. Under his leadership the Assembly was content with annual formal appeals against patronage, and in 1784 even these were abandoned. It was ministers of the Kirk who in this period — at least in the opinion of Robertson's friend, Alexander ('Jupiter') Carlyle — led the world in history, literature, and the sciences. Blair's sermons were highly commended by Samuel Johnson, as were Robertson's histories by Edward Gibbon. John Home, whose tragedy of *Douglas* created a hot controversy in Scotland, was one of the few dramatic writers of his age. But the interests of these men were more cultural than theological and more ethical than religious. They were children of the Enlightenment, with its Erastianism and horror of enthusiasm. Hushing new voices in the Church, they fed the secessions, and fearing ecclesiastical innovation they fell behind the times.

Some vocal Evangelicals remained within the Kirk to trouble the majority. John Witherspoon did not become a seceder. In his *Characteristics* (above, p. 347) he mocked the deistic spirit of those whose creed began, 'I believe in the comely proportions of Dame Nature,' and ended by affirming the perpetuity of Francis Hutcheson's philosophy. Alexander Webster, despite his tippling habits, was an Evangelical stalwart and a practical man, who used his mathematical learning to frame the first tables of life-expectancy and fathered the first general plan for annuities to minister's widows. John Erskine (d. 1803), Robertson's ecclesiastical opponent and personal friend, became the admired leader of the Evangelicals. He opposed the war against the American colonies and advocated the cause of foreign missions.

Evangelicalism in Scotland meant more than the secession of zealots and a rising tide of opposition to Moderatism in the church courts. There is abundant evidence of 'revivalistic' phenomena in Scottish (and Ulster) parish life from the seventeenth to the nineteenth century. A glow of devotion and a remarkable intelligence of faith marked Scottish religion. The Bible reading in 'The Cotter's Saturday Night' was in fact more than a weekly exercise. In the Highlands and Islands, and other areas not previously much penetrated by the Reformation, religious progress was marked, especially after the founding of the Scottish Society for the Propagation of Christian Knowledge (1709). The great revival centered at Cambuslang (1742), begun under William McCulloch and aided by George Whitefield, was anticipated by numerous similar awakenings, chiefly in the Highlands. From 1730, for example, John Balfour of Nigg was the instrument of a fairly widespread movement in Rosshire. The Highland ministers were sensitive to the new thought of the age. Dr. Johnson found in the Hebrides ministers whom he begrudged to Presbyterianism. At the time of the Simson trial the Presbytery of Gairloch discussed in Latin the question 'whether Christ is true and supreme God.' The intrusion of ministers under patronage aroused a resistance that rested upon the Gospel and the Confession. John MacInnes has supplied ample data regarding the often quiet and sometimes animated expressions of evangelical fervor in the North during the days of Boston and the Erskines. He remarks that throughout the Moderate ascendancy 'the central Evangelical tradition was the most confident, aggressive and fruitful element in Scottish religion.'

This 'fruitful element' was growing in strength. It was generally more tolerant and ecumenical in spirit than were the Erskine seceders, who rejected the services of Whitefield for his participation in the Cambuslang revival and identified the cause of Christ in Scotland with their own organization. It fell to Webster to write a warm defense of the 'Cambuslang wark.'

But the Erskines organized numerous societies of lay folk for prayer and mutual edification. Evangelicals founded missionary societies in Edinburgh and Glasgow and narrowly failed to gain the Assembly's support for the missionary enterprise (1796). Actually the Church of Scotland was to be (in 1829) the first national church to give corporate authorization and maintenance to foreign missions. English Evangelicalism, chiefly Calvinist, was affecting the trend in Scotland. The numerous preaching journeys of John Wesley to Scotland were not without importance. It was an English Methodist in Monymusk, Thomas Channon, who first startled and fascinated the Scots by the performances of a trained choir, beginning a new development in choir singing. But the theology of Scotland was little affected by evangelical Arminianism. The courteous if not very enthusiastic reception of Wesley in Scotland and the response to the message of Charles Simeon of Cambridge in a preaching tour (1797) indicate an absence of prejudice against English voices. James Haldane, a young sea captain who underwent a typical conversion experience in 1794, was Simeon's Scottish companion. After a period as a Congregationalist, he was to be the chief founder of the Scottish Baptist churches, as Calvinist in theology as the Presbyterians. His elder brother, Robert, a retired naval officer who possessed some wealth, was also converted in 1794. He had entertained utopian hopes of the French Revolution, and he now turned his utopianism to the founding of the Society for the Propagation of the Gospel at Home (1797) and the inception of a notable revival in Geneva and southern France (1816 +) (below, p. 369).

The Church of Scotland was still to experience its greatest division over patronage and the rejection of it by the Evangelicals. The nineteenth century brought the leadership of Thomas Chalmers, a Moderate and an intellectual, who after painful struggles became an eager Evangelical and the energizing personality of the movement within the Kirk. His original efforts to overcome pauperism in Glasgow constitute the most effective early reaction of Christianity to the evils attendant on the Industrial Revolution. As professor in St. Andrews and Edinburgh he lectured, preached, and wrote with mounting popularity and influence. During the 'Ten Years' Conflict' (1833–43) he became the director of the campaign against patronage. The Assembly's Veto Act of 1834 gave to 'a majority of the heads of families in full communion' the right to reject a patron's nominee. Did this decision of the Church conflict with the patronage law of the state? A presentation to Auchterarder parish was rejected by the heads of families. The case went to the House of Lords and was decided in favor of the patron. The Evangelicals found such state control intolerable. An attempt was made to get the Veto Act approved in Parliament, but Parliament was dissolved without passing the measure (1841). The Assembly of 1842 adopted the 'Claim of Right,' affirming in high terms the inherent jurisdiction and autonomy of the Church on the basis of the Confession of Faith, and calling to witness

> the Christian people of this kingdom, and all the churches of the Reformation throughout the world who hold the great doctrine of the sole Headship of the Lord Jesus over His Church.

In January 1843 the 'Chapel Act' of the Assembly, authorizing the giving of full status to churches for unchurched areas as constituting parishes *quoad sacra,* was also declared invalid. The tide of feeling rose and reached a crisis at the 1843 Assembly, which met in St. Andrew's Church, Edinburgh. After prayer the Moderator, Professor David Welsh, read a formal protest against the conditions imposed by the government upon the Church. He laid the manuscript on the table and walked out, followed by about half the membership of the Assembly. Down George and Hanover Streets they marched three abreast to Tanfield Hall, where they elected Chalmers Moderator of the Assembly of the Free Church of Scotland. The Free Church embraced, says Lord Balfour of Burleigh, 'the majority of the most zealous and active among both clergy and laity.'

— IV —

In America, the stages of the Evangelical revival were also attended by strife. We saw that Theodore Frelinghuysen's aggressive pietism called forth strong opposition, which was, however, overcome. He was associated with Gilbert Tennent, leader of the 'New Side' Presbyterians who defended revivalism. Tennent was strongly influenced by George Whitefield, and formed fruitful contact with Jonathan Edwards, the Puritan philosopher and theologian. A little later Jonathan Dickinson, first president of the College of New Jersey, was urgently calling men to conversion, and Samuel Davies in Virginia was preaching with a similar evangelical fervor. These were men of intellectual distinction and not one of them was a narrow confessionalist. Dickinson, born in Massachusetts and a graduate of Yale, opposed the movement for 'strict subscription' in New Jersey designed to counter the flexible terms of the Adopting Act of 1729. He was the author of books on *The Reasonableness of Christianity* and *The Five Points of Calvinism*. Gilbert Tennent's New Side, or revivalist, Presbyterians separated from the Philadelphia Synod to found the Synod of New York (1745), but a book of Tennent's on ecclesiastical peace led to the resumption of fellowship in 1758.

Edwards (d. 1758) must be regarded as the most eminent of American Calvinists. As a boy he was gifted with remarkable powers of observation and experienced mystical states. 'We are to conceive of the divine excellence as infinite, general love,' he wrote at the age of sixteen, and at seventeen, 'Absolute sovereignty is what I love to ascribe to God.' At twenty, he resolved 'diligently to look into our old divines concerning conversion.' These are typical themes of his preaching. Having graduated from Yale at seventeen, he briefly served a Presbyterian church in New York, was for two years a tutor at Yale, and became the colleague and successor of his grandfather, Solomon Stoddard, in Northampton, Massachusetts. He preached the wrath as well as the love of God, and his tall, almost motionless form and pale, grave face lent impressiveness to his clear message. In his theology and in his treatment of the emotions he added humane elements to Calvinism, but in his preaching he elaborated the theme of hell as John Calvin never did. For Calvin, hell was alienation from God; for Edwards it was endless physical torment pictured in realistic detail. Yet he never lost his deep sense of the essentially loving nature of God. Even his lurid warnings were uttered in compassion, and his object in all preaching was to lead sinners to grace.

His works *On the Religious Affections, On the Freedom of the Will, On Original Sin,* and *On True Virtue* are still of more than historical interest and reflect a free handling of Calvinist doctrines against Arminianism in the light of what he had learned from the Cambridge Platonists, Newton, Locke, and other writers. Sin for him, as for Zwingli, is rooted in self-love. Man is morally free to do as he pleases, but what he pleases is determined by motives of which he is not master. True piety lies in love to man as well as love to God. Some of his more incidental writings are important for the light they shed upon religion in his times. They contain descriptions of the Great Awakening in Northampton and other Connecticut Valley towns (1735-44), which brought thousands to repentance and church fellowship. He edited the *Memoirs of David Brainerd,* that young missionary's moving account of his labors, supported by the Scottish S.P.C.K., with the Susquehanna Indians. The book had wide influence in Britain as well as in America.

Edwards himself was to become a missionary to Indians. Through opposition to his strict rules of conduct and admission to membership, he was obliged to leave his church (1750) and went to minister to the Housatonic Indians at Stockbridge in the Berkshire Hills. But unlike Brainerd, who wore himself out with travel, Edwards remained in one spot and there wrote his chief books. He was made president of the College of New Jersey — where presidents' terms were strangely short. A month after his inauguration on the first day of spring, 1758, he died, the victim of a clumsy vaccination for smallpox. His talented, devout, and charming wife, Sarah Pierrepont, briefly outlived him. They had nine children; and sociologists have noted the unusual quality of their numerous descendants. Edwards awakened the mind and soul of New England and left a spiritual legacy to Protestantism.

The new life of the Great Awakening spread through the reunited Presbyterian synod of New York and Philadelphia. With the aid of funds liberally subscribed in Scotland, England, and Ireland, religious literature was distributed and Indian missions were promoted. There were minor disputes, chiefly in New England, and in New York and Philadelphia Burgher and Anti-Burgher secessionists established congregations. Their unification in one presbytery remained incomplete through resistance from Scotland. There was also a small body of Reformed Presbyterians (Covenanters) who formed a presbytery. Dr. Briggs gives statistics to show a total of 247 Presbyterian and Reformed ministers in the colonies in 1776, and remarks that with the Congregationalists they 'had the ecclesiastical control of the American colonies.'

This numerical advantage they have since lost. But they had much to do with the formation and support of the early republic. The synod of New York and Philadelphia, embracing the great majority of Presbyterians, reorganized with a constitution that included not only the Confession of Faith, as before, but also, though in significantly altered form, the Catechisms and the Form of Government. The changes made explicit the toleration of other churches and freedom from state controls. This constitution was drafted in 1787 and adopted in May 1788 at Philadelphia, where at the same time the Constitution of the United States was also being framed (1787). The broad resemblance of the federal Constitution to that of Presbyterianism has been seen by many historians. The resemblance is not accidental; but other church polities of the period show resemblances as well. It may here be mentioned, however, that the Secretary of the Continental Congress, 1774–89, was Charles Thompson, a Presbyterian minister whom John Adams called 'the life of the cause of liberty.' The Church now possessed a General Assembly, four synods, and fifteen presbyteries, and was spread widely in the nation. The Assembly was convened under Witherspoon's chairmanship in 1789.

— V —

The relations of Presbyterian and Congregational Churches have always been difficult to define. The London Heads of Agreement of 1691, the views on polity of John Owen, Thomas Hooker, John Eliot, Cotton Mather, and Jonathan Edwards, the Cambridge Platform of 1648, and the Saybrook Platform of 1708 (which adopted the Heads of Agreement and a system of 'consociations' for Connecticut), all suggested a conciliatory attitude on the part of Congregationalist leaders. Increase Mather, Cotton Mather's father, while on a mission to England, had participated in the framing of the Heads of Agreement, and he later sought the adoption of this plan in Massachusetts. His dissatisfaction, shared by many, with the polity of the Massachusetts General Court and the liberal innovations at Harvard led to the foundation of Yale College (1701). It was first located at Saybrook, and to it delegates of the Connecticut churches came to frame their new church organization. The consociations, says William Warren Sweet, 'functioned more and more like presbyteries.' Indeed, in 1799, the Hartford North Association declared that the Connecticut church order contained 'the essentials of the Church of Scotland or of the Presbyterian church of America.'

The churches of America had now to answer the call of the frontier. Conditions in settlements in New York led to the proposal of a 'Plan of Union' by the General Association of Connecticut which was agreed to by the Presbyterian General Assembly of 1801. By this plan congregations could be formed of both denominations and ministers could interchange their ministries without losing denominational status. The plan was later adopted throughout New England, but its effects were felt chiefly in states farther west, especially where migrating New Englanders settled in mixed communities. In general the operation of the Plan of Union tended to aid the growth of Presbyterianism, since the Congregational system lacked the connexional strength needed to match the rapidly growing and changing frontier communities. In Ohio, Illinois, Michigan, and Kentucky, Presbyterianism had taken firm hold by the end of the eighteenth century.

The life of all the churches of Calvinist origin in America at that period presents two notable phases, revivalism and concern for education. In 1797, Logan County, Kentucky, saw the beginnings of a widespread revival, under the ardent preaching of James McGready, who had been active in Pennsylvania and North Carolina. In 1800 he instituted the 'camp meeting,' with great numbers from distant settlements attending. Relays of preachers kept up an intense religious excitement which found expression in prostrations, shrieks, sudden laughter, trances, and other symptons of hysteria, and gave occasion to licentious behavior. Nevertheless the revival, and its sequel in a series of such movements in western Pennsylvania and New York, produced a deepening of religious life and a growth of church membership. It was accompanied by the establishment of numerous colleges, through which Presbyterianism assumed educational leadership on the frontier. Dr. Sweet in his volume on the Presbyterians, in *Religion on the American Frontier,* briefly tells the story of this astonishing development, in which from 1782 to 1850 twenty-eight colleges sprang up in frontier states, including those as far west as Wisconsin and Texas.

Theological training was given under difficulties by able ministers such as John McMillan of Cannonsburgh, Pennsylvania, who started a log college in 1776 (the origin of Jefferson College) and gave instruction to about one hundred young candidates, and Samuel Doak, whose log college gave place to Washington College (1795) in Holston County, Tennessee. It became usual for synods and presbyteries to institute seminaries. Both Princeton Seminary and Union Seminary in Richmond, Virginia, began in 1812, Auburn in 1818, Western near Pittsburgh in 1827. In 1829 at South Hanover, Indiana, the institution began which in 1859 was McCormick Seminary in Chicago. The origins of Lane Seminary, Cincinnati (1829), were connected with the life of Joshua Wilson, pastor there for thirty-eight years and leader of the Old School Presbyterians. Union Seminary, New York, was founded (1836) by men of the New School as an institution that would be 'free from party strife,' and was (like Auburn) open to students of all denominations.

Presbyterianism was visited with new and injurious divisions, which again grew for the most part out of revivalism, and opposition to it, both in the ministry and in the seminaries. The northern part of Kentucky was the scene of the New Light Movement led by Barton W. Stone, which resulted in the suspension of five ministers for erroneous views on election and their foundation of the Springfield Presbytery and later of the 'Christian Church' (1803). In another area of the state, the Cumberland Presbyterian Church took its rise (1810) through the plea of revivalists for the admission of untrained ministers to evangelize the new settlements, and the rejection of this by the Assembly. At the same time Thomas Campbell and his son Alexander, who had come from Ireland, broke from the Anti-Burgher presbytery of Chartiers in Pennsylvania over the practice of free communion, which the presbytery forbade. In the course of their ecclesiastical pilgrimage the Campbells were for seventeen years connected with a Baptist Association, during which period Alexander (d. 1866) formed a seminary at Bethany. Thereafter he became the founder of the Disciples of Christ, which resulted from the union of his followers with the 'Christian Church' of Barton W. Stone (1832). These secessions, and the rivalry of the denominations to which they gave rise, cut sharply the growth of Presbyterianism on the frontier.

A new theological liberalism out of New England began to challenge the Westminster Confession's teaching on original sin, affirming in strong terms the moral freedom of man. Nathaniel W. Taylor of Yale, its chief promulgator (1828 +), and Albert Barnes, a minister in Philadelphia, were charged with Arminian doctrines. Barnes was repeatedly examined by the Assembly, and others of similar opinions were tried before presbyteries. It was in protest against the 'New Haven theology' of Taylor that Hartford Seminary was founded in 1834. There was dissatisfaction, too, with the organization of many congregations under the Plan of Union, in which elders were not elected, especially when officers of societies in the churches were sent instead of elders as commissioners to the church courts. These facts were among the causes of the schism of 1837. The Plan of Union was then abandoned, and four synods that had been instituted under it were abruptly exscinded from the Assembly. The New School Presbyterians, who favored the Plan of Union and the New Haven theology, in confutation of charges laid against them put forth the Auburn Declaration (1837), a brief positive statement of Calvinistic doctrines. Most of the Scotch-Irish Presbyterians belonged to the Old School. The two branches of the Presbyterians were reunited in 1869, after the Old School had accepted the Auburn Declaration.

Lyman Beecher, a Congregationalist, who had been made president of Lane Seminary, was attacked by the watchful conservative, Joshua L. Wilson of Cincinnati. Many students had gone to Lane under the spell of the evangelist Charles Finney. One of these, Theodore Dwight Weld, began to agitate for the abolition of slavery. The Assembly of 1818 had declared slavery 'totally irreconcilable with the gospel of Christ'; but a demand for its immediate abolition was disturbing. Weld and his 'Lane rebels' were expelled and went to Oberlin, which became the center of the religious abolitionist movement. Abolition was not debated in the divisive Assembly of 1837, for the reason, as Dr. Sweet explains, that men of the Old School who favored abolition, such as Wilson, did not wish to make it a church issue or to ally themselves with New School supporters of the abolition party. In 1857, after the New School had reiterated earlier Presbyterian pronouncements against slavery, its southern synods were severed from the northern.

The German Reformed in America felt the influence of the Pietist movement. Count Nicholas von Zinzendorf's visit to the German settlements in Pennsylvania (1740) made little permanent impression; but William Otterbein's introduction of Pietist group organizations in Baltimore (1776) and his association with Francis Asbury, the Methodist pioneer bishop, led to his withdrawal from the Reformed Synod (which had replaced the coetus in 1792) and to the formation, by an adherent, of 'the United Brethren in Christ' (1805). Elements of Pietism and revivalism were present in this movement; and in the first half of the century revival activity was endemic in the synod itself. For some years it was disturbed by disputes over the use of English in worship and by unfruitful proposals for union with the Dutch Reformed and (following the Prussian Union of 1817) with the Lutherans. A secession over the project for a seminary with instruction in English produced the Free Synod (1822), which had a separate life of only fifteen years.

The seminary was opened in 1825 at Carlisle, Pennsylvania; it was moved to Mercersburg in 1838. The 'Mercersburg theology' taught there by Frederick A. Rauch (d. 1841), John W. Nevin (d. 1886), and Philip Schaff (d. 1893), the eminent church historian, was, like the 'New England theology' of Edwards, a modernization of Calvinism (see below, p. 398). It caused widespread controversy within the denomination, and some secessions from it; it also apparently prevented a proposed union with the Dutch Reformed. Yet the most important result was an enrichment of theological thought in American Calvinism. The school removed to Lancaster in 1871.

— VI —

The secessions from Calvinist churches in Holland and Switzerland were also not without significance. Toleration for Arminians (1625) and other minorities became the rule in the Netherlands; but a remarkable controversy developed (c.1658) between the followers of Gijsbert Voetius and those of John Cocceius regarding such matters of conduct as Sabbath observance, plainness of dress, and avoidance of popular amusements, the pietistic Voetians taking the more austere view. The conflict was renewed in the eighteenth century but gradually gave place to mutual understanding.

The liberalism of that age called forth a strong reaction voiced by the poets Willem Bilderdijk and Isaak da Costa — the latter a convert from Judaism. Bilderdijk may be compared to Kierkegaard both in his personal misfortunes and in his contempt for a government-controlled Christianity softened by indifference. His clerical disciple, Hendrik de Cock of Ulrum, gave offense by extending his pastoral care into neighboring parishes and by his criticism of the hymnal. After being deposed, he led in the formation (1839) of the Christian Reformed Church. This evangelical church affirmed the system of the Dort decisions in an infralapsarian sense. A sterner theology was adopted by Abraham Kuyper, politician and founder of the Free University of Amsterdam (1880), who with the theologian Herman Bavinck instituted the 'Reformed Church' (*Gereformeerde Kerken*) (1896), asserting a hyper-Calvinist supralapsarianism together with an emphasis upon regeneration.

Robert Haldane (above, p. 360) carried his evangelical zeal to Geneva, where he discoursed on Romans to students and others. Under his leadership a group that was dissatisfied with the dry rationalism that had held sway there for two generations became the agents of an evangelical revival (the '*Réveil*') which affected French Switzerland and France. The prominent names are the pastor César Malan and the historian J. H. Merle d'Aubigné. Malan formed the separate 'Church of the Testimony' in 1824, and after some years of struggle a wider organization, the *Société Evangélique,* arose (1831) and established a theological school of its own. In Lausanne the eminent Alexandre Vinet was the leader of the Free Church of the Vaud (1847), the origin of which in some respects parallels the Scottish Disruption, since it was the result of a religious protest against injurious measures taken by the cantonal government.

Louis XIV attempted to scourge out of existence the Protestant remnant in France and, with the merciless suppression of the Camisard revolt in the Cevennes, he seemed to have succeeded. In 1715 he proclaimed Protestantism 'abolished.' Nevertheless, led by Antoine Court (d. 1760), Paul Rabaut (d. 1793), and other heroic 'Pastors of the Desert,' the Reformed Church began to recover its organic existence, and after the Toleration edict of

1787 it gradually gained strength. In accordance with Napoleon's settlement of 1802, its ministers were paid by the state, but freedom of assembly was for the most part denied and synods of national extent were not allowed. Under the influence of the spreading revival that had begun in Switzerland, and of Vinet's teaching on separation from the state, evangelical protests were uttered and worshiping groups were formed. These efforts led to the formation, under the leadership of Frédéric Monod and the scholarly Edmond de Pressensé, of the Free Evangelical Synod in 1849. Meanwhile, in the revolutionary movements of 1830 and 1848, government control was relaxed. In Languedoc, where the Pastors of the Desert had chiefly served, the English Methodist, Charles Cook, was instrumental in an extensive revival (1818–34) which gave new force to Protestantism.

— VII —

Here we may return for a brief reference to Calvinism in England, where the Presbyterian and Congregationalist nonconformists carried its banners but weakly in the eighteenth century. Congregationalism was best represented by Isaac Watts, the eminent hymn writer (d. 1748) whose Calvinism was not strictly orthodox, and Philip Doddridge (d. 1751), whose *Discourses on Regeneration* and *Rise and Progress of Religion in the Soul* anticipate the emphases of the Evangelical Movement. After the death of Matthew Henry (1714), author of an exceedingly popular Bible commentary, Presbyterian leadership was undistinguished. A tincture of rationalism and Socinianism entered the nonconformist academies, and many of the Presbyterian ministers rejected the Westminster standards and doctrines. Joseph Priestley (d. 1804), trained in a Congregationalist academy and teaching in a Presbyterian one, was the ablest promoter of the heterodox opinions. Those who remained orthodox were in general dull and ineffective ministers. The result was a decline in numbers and significance. This decayed Presbyterianism was restored or, more accurately, replaced by the activity of Scots in England, including both those of the Kirk and those of the secessions. A Scots presbytery was instituted in London in 1772, and in 1839 the Scottish Assembly recognized 'the Presbyterian Synod in England in connection with the Church of Scotland.'

This synod was broken asunder as a result of the Scottish Disruption of 1843.

The real force of Calvinism in England is seen in the Evangelical revival and its influence in Anglicanism. John Wesley, the greatest leader of the revival, was the only eminent personality in it who was not a Calvinist. Even Wesley's Arminianism retained (as did the teaching of Arminius) a great body of Calvinist doctrine, as is shown, for example, by his revision of the Westminster Shorter Catechism. His doctrine of the ministry, though not learned from Presbyterians, is in accord with that of the Reformed Churches, and much of his teaching has an affinity with that of Baxter and of Doddridge. The word 'Methodist' was applied in his time to manifestations of evangelical piety whether Wesleyan or not. George Whitefield, who was firmly Calvinist, carried that label, as did the Welsh evangelists whose efforts resulted in the foundation of the Calvinist Methodist Church — Howel Harris (d. 1773) and Daniel Rowlands (d. 1790). The Welsh revival began at the same time as the movement under Jonathan Edwards (1735), three years before Wesley's conversion. Numerous evangelical societies for mutual edification began to appear. Whitefield associated himself with the movement and co-operated in the formation of a union of these groups (1743). The benevolence of Lady Selina Huntingdon aided in giving permanence to the Welsh Methodist body, especially through her gifts to the academy at Trevecca.

Many Evangelicals of Calvinist persuasion became prominent within Anglicanism. The conversion after a bitter struggle of John Newton (d. 1807), formerly a degraded sailor, and the very different conversion experience of Thomas Scott (d. 1827), who had been a proud intellectual without doctrinal conviction, gave to the Church of England a co-operating pair of notable religious leaders who had widely different talents but were one in their Calvinist piety. After Scott had followed Newton to London, his sermons were attended by William Wilberforce and Henry Thornton. These are great names in the history of philanthropy and Christian social action. Both were prominent in the distinguished group called facetiously by Sidney Smith 'the Clapham Sect' and soberly by John A. Patten 'the Clapham Team.' The circle included also such men of affairs as Charles Grant,

Zachary Macaulay, Granville Sharp and James Stephen, with
Henry Venn, rector of Huddersfield, and his son, John Venn,
rector of Clapham. All of these held Calvinist views of salvation,
though not with the aggressive insistence of Augustus Toplady
or with William Romaine's excessive emphasis on the security
of the elect. Their theology was rather the presupposition behind
the social betterment and missions schemes in which they found
their religious vocation. Notable books of these Evangelicals in
Anglicanism are Newton's *Cardiphonia,* a collection of spiritual
letters, Scott's *The Force of Truth,* a moving spiritual auto-
biography, and Wilberforce's *Practical View of the Prevailing
Religious Conceptions of the Higher and Middle Classes . . . as
Compared with True Christianity,* a challenge to a serious faith
that honors God and serves mankind. Wilberforce took leadership in many new 'good causes.' His undiscouraged effort as a
member of Parliament to secure the suppression of the slave
trade was successful in 1807, and the longer fight for the emancipation of slaves throughout the British Empire was crowned
with victory while he lay on his deathbed (1833). Wesley's last
letter was written to Wilberforce, exhorting him to 'go on in
the name of the Lord.' The story of the Claphamites involves
much more than can be noted here. As a record of constructive
co-operation on the part of devout and gifted men of wealth, it
remains unique in history.

To these names many others might be added. Charles Simeon
(d. 1836) of Cambridge became a power for evangelical religion
in all Britain, but was only the foremost of a score of eminent
preachers who stirred the flame of religion in his day and in the
Victorian era. The cause of missions was promoted primarily
by Calvinist Evangelicals; and John Henry Newman felt that
he 'almost owed his soul' to the writings of Thomas Scott, which
he read at the age of sixteen.

— VIII —

In the era of controversy and revival that has been reviewed
in this chapter, Calvinism became ecclesiastically splintered. It
was viewed by observers at the middle of the last century, with
consternation or contempt, as demon-ridden by a schismatic
spirit. Yet when James Bannerman, a Scottish Free Church professor, wrote his learned volumes on *The Church of Christ* (1848)

he did not hesitate to stress the principle of unity. For him as for his predecessors, the Catholic visible Church embraced all its particular manifestations and separated parts: 'The local and accidental differences are merged in the higher and essential oneness that belongs to them.' Virtually all Calvinists would have agreed with this view. The fact is that Calvinism was disrupted over differences that were accidents of the age without becoming essentially sectarian. Intercommunion between the fragments of the Church was practiced and cherished, and the hope of visible and organic union not only of the Reformed family but of the whole Church of Christ was never abandoned. The pangs of separation would intensify the desire for reunion. The union of the Scottish seceders had already raised an ensign of hope.

CHAPTER XXII

REUNION, EXPANSION, AND
ECUMENICITY

— I —

In the broken Presbyterianism of Scotland the ideal of Christian union was voiced with almost pathetic insistence. In 1843, at the bicentenary celebration of the Westminster Assembly, Robert Balmer, of the United Secession Church, made an arresting plea for the promotion of unity. The address gave rise to the publication of *Essays on Christian Union* (1845), eight extended papers by a Scottish Independent, an English Presbyterian, and Scottish Presbyterians of four varieties. In the first essay Thomas Chalmers advocated 'co-operation leading to incorporation.' In the second, Dr. Balmer made good use of the Westminster Confession phrases on maintaining holy fellowship and communion, and remarked of the prevailing dismemberment of Christianity:

> These divisions have no doubt been overruled so as to produce some good; but in themselves . . . they are an evil of colossal dimensions and deadly malignity.

All the writers deplored the condition of schism, but not without hope. They were agreed in the recognition of the Westminster Standards and in the view expressed in one essay that 'all Scottish denominations of any magnitude are equally attached to Calvinistic principles.'

The restoration of unity in the Church of Scotland was a cumulative process. The first stage was reached in 1820 with the reunion of the New Light Burghers with the New Light Anti-Burghers to form the United Secession Church. Most of the Old Light remnants of these groups coalesced in 1827 as the Synod of Original Seceders, and a still separate Burgher element returned to the established Church in 1839. The Free Church, formed in 1843, was joined in 1852 by the Original Seceders and

374

in 1876 by the main body of the Reformed Presbyterian Church in Scotland (Covenanters).

We saw that the Relief Church was formed by Gillespie and his friends for reasons similar to those that prompted the earlier secession of the Erskines. By 1847 the Relief and the United Secession Churches were drawn together: they became the United Presbyterian Church, and for the first time the word 'Presbyterian' entered the title of a branch of the Scottish Church.

The repeal of the Patronage Act by Disraeli's government in 1874 removed the major cause of all the secessions; the measure was designed by its sponsors to promote reunion of the severed churches with the Kirk. But the long experience of freedom and growth in separation from the state had led the secessionists to prize that condition and to voice the principle of 'voluntaryism.' The founders of the Free Church had stoutly opposed this view. 'We quit a vitiated establishment,' said Chalmers, 'but we would rejoice in returning to a pure one . . . We are not voluntaries.' But later Free Churchmen began to adopt voluntaryism and to voice a demand for the disestablishment of the Kirk; this led to an angry controversy. The Free Church therefore shrank from reunion with the establishment and negotiated instead a union with the United Presbyterians, whereby the United Free Church was formed (1900).

A small minority, dubbed the Wee Frees, protesting against the 'godlessness' of voluntaryism, remained out of the union and claimed the name and property of the Free Church. Under the law of trusts, this claim was upheld; but to remedy the obvious absurdity of bestowing large endowments on those who could not use them, a parliamentary commission was appointed to make an equitable allocation of the properties in question.

While this was being effected, the United Free Church adopted a declaration of its corporate right to alter and define its own laws and subordinate standards (confessions and catechisms) and to unite with other churches (1905). This far-reaching affirmation of the Church's autonomy was in effect a friendly challenge to the state and the Kirk. The challenge was generously met. The principle of the declaration was incorporated, along with a recognition of the headship of Christ in Church and nation, in the Churches of Scotland Act of 1921. Negotiations had been active in the intervening years, though they were delayed by the First World War. The toil and thought that entered into these and the parts played by individuals cannot here be shown; but every advance toward reunion was costly in effort and involved concessions on the part of many as they sought, to use a phrase of Chalmers, 'the Christian good of Scotland' rather than the victory of a single section of Presbyterianism.

Scotland's rapidly growing population was being alienated from the fragmented Church. Thoughtful leaders, such as Lord Sands and John White in the Kirk and Alexander Martin and Archibald Henderson in the Free Church, drew men's minds away from the old divisive issues to the basic principles on which all professed agreement, and to the religious needs of the nation. The terms of the Act of 1921 had been agreed upon with a view to union by the general assemblies of the Free Church and the Church of Scotland. Another act of Parliament (1925) placed the church endowments on a new basis, leaving large discretion to a board of trustees, who were free to administer the teinds (tithes) in the interests not only of the parish that was their source but of the wider community in which it lay.

These enactments of 1874, 1921, and 1925 represent the triumph of principles voiced by the sixteenth-century Reformers who had proclaimed the Church's autonomy and right to control her properties. The Reformers had, of course, demanded an enforced unity in the national Church; the twentieth-century conception of unity was of a thing wholly spontaneous. The abandonment of Erastian claims by the state could hardly be more specific than it is made in this legislation. Disestablishment lost its appeal when it could add nothing to the Church's freedom, and the general desire for unity triumphed over the minor impediments remaining. The goal was the complete reintegration in a church at one established and free, and save for very small minorities that objective was realized. On 2 October 1929, St. Giles Cathedral, Edinburgh, was the scene of an event of great significance and promise: as the sun broke through rainy clouds, the members of the two general assemblies meeting in procession entered, through the psalm-singing ranks on the crowded line of march, the great church that had echoed to the voice of John Knox, and engaged in a service of prayer and thanksgiving preparatory to the act of union. John Buchan, vividly portraying the emotional experience of the occasion, says:

Yet in our hearts the chief joy was to behold how religion, so long a disruptive force in Scotland, was now a uniting power.

St. Giles was far too small for the crowds desiring admission to the reunion ceremony, which took place in the afternoon of the same day in a hall in the New Town, where 12,000 held numbered seats. Eloquence and devoutness marked the service. The duke of York (later George VI) represented the king. The new moderator, Dr. White, spoke realistically of the Church's tasks, including that posed by the 'churchless million' in the land. Delegates at the evening session included the aged Archbishop of Canterbury, Randall Davidson, who, looking toward fuller unity, reminded the Assembly that he was a Scot and a son of the manse. 'I come back,' he remarked, 'with unalterable veneration for the Church of my fathers.' Greetings were heard from many Reformed Churches of the world, and from Methodists and Baptists. Lutherans were represented by the primate of Norway.

Under new influences, including those of Scots in England and of fresh revival movements, an orthodox Presbyterianism, shaking off Unitarianism and affirming the Westminster Standards, grew up in nineteenth-century England. As a result there was formed a union between this English Presbyterianism and the Scottish elements in England that had united to form the United Presbyterian Church. By this union, solemnized in the Philharmonic Hall, Liverpool, 13 June 1876, the Presbyterian Church of England was formed. The basis of union, in five articles, accepts the Westminster Confession and Catechisms but expressly repudiates anything in these documents savoring of intolerance.

In the United States little has been accomplished that gives token of a reunion of the churches of the Reformed and Presbyterian order, but there has been much negotiation and expectation of such an outcome. The division occasioned by conditions of the Civil War in 1861 led to the union of the Southern branch of the New School Presbyterians with the Presbyterian Church of the Confederate States to form the Presbyterian Church in the United States (1863). The New and Old Schools in the Northern states were united in 1869, and in 1882 friendly correspondence was resumed between the Presbyterian Church in the U.S.A.

and the Presbyterian Church in the U.S. Efforts to heal the breach of 1861 have not been lacking and have become very active since the Second World War.

— II —

Meanwhile churches of Calvinist origin had grown to strength in the British dominions. The story of these churches in Canada is marked from the beginning by a trend toward union rather than division. At the foundation of Halifax (1749) Presbyterians and Congregationalists worshiped together. Ministers of these denominations united to ordain a pastor for German Reformed settlers in Nova Scotia (1770). In both Nova Scotia and Upper Canada Burgher and Anti-Burgher settlers were numerous, and soon had their own pioneer ministers, some of whom were distinguished for devotion and vision. In both areas the divided seceders were united (1817 and 1818), earlier than in Scotland. Other Presbyterian fragments came together into larger units, 1860 and 1868, leaving four branches of an original nine. The Dominion of Canada was formed by the union of four provinces in 1867, and three others were added by 1873. While a solid nation was being formed of a series of settled areas from Cape Breton to Vancouver Island, the churches were contributing their part to this unity and strengthening their impact upon the young nation by the progressive stages of their own unification. The four Presbyterian churches were united in 1875 to form the Presbyterian Church in Canada. Two geographically separated units in communion with the Scottish Kirk were included in this union, which thus anticipated in 1875 the parallel event of 1929 in Scotland.

At the inauguration of the Presbyterian Church in Canada, its first moderator, Dr. John Cook, a former Kirkman, was loudly applauded when he declared for 'far larger union . . . than that which we effect this day.' This expectation had already been voiced by others, and never ceased to be felt. The adoption by the Protestant Episcopal Convention in Chicago in 1886 of the four points later (1888) known as the Lambeth Quadrilateral aroused interest throughout Canadian Protestantism. Discussion toward union with the Anglicans was entered upon in 1889, and in the subsequent decade there was a good deal of exploring by joint committees of the possibility of union, especially between

Presbyterians and Methodists. The needs of the home mission in the rapidly expanding Canadian West; the value placed upon Christian fraternity, and the danger of losing it in competition; and a realization cultivated by some theological teachers, such as William Caven, Principal of Knox College, Toronto, of the full Calvinist doctrine of the Church as One, Holy, and Catholic were factors that prompted the effort toward unity. In the 'eighties, Principal George M. Grant of Queen's university warned divinity students not to become perpetuators of the disunited state of the churches.

The leading advocates of the union movement were the heads and professors of the theological and arts colleges which the churches had been careful to establish and maintain. In 1902 Principal William Patrick of Manitoba College, bearing Presbyterian greetings to the Methodist Conference, struck the note of union, and the Conference took formal action by which continuous negotiation was begun. Congregational churches were few, though by no means insignificant; they readily linked themselves with the movement. The Church of England in Canada and the Baptist churches were invited to participate in the negotiations (1906); both courteously, and for different reasons, declined. A doctrinal basis of union containing nineteen articles (another article was later added) was agreed upon in 1908 by a joint committee. Fourteen of the articles were based upon those found in a statement of the Presbyterian Church in the United States of America (1902), representing a modified Calvinism.

Then followed a long period of animated discussion and delay caused by the spirited resistance of a Presbyterian minority. Not only were the presbyteries consulted, in accordance with the Barrier Act of 1697, but two plebiscites (1911, 1915) were taken of the elders, members, and adherents. Both were favorable, and after the second the Presbyterian Assembly pledged the Church to union. The highly organized minority did everything possible to prevent the union, and carried the struggle to the Dominion and provincial legislatures. The long controversy did much harm but had its benefits in a deepened realization of the Reformed conception of the nature of the Church and of the distinction between essential and accidental elements of church polity. A young Presbyterian professor who had, so to speak, grown up in the midst of the battle wrote in 1925:

It should be recorded that in the heat of the conflict mutual courtesies and acts of goodwill have occurred which will later be remembered for good. The patience and sympathy of leaders and people in the Methodist and Congregational churches have been beyond all praise. Controversy is more noisy than progress; and while the observer today sees the evidence of strife, it is not strife but union that is the great reality of the hour. The United Church of Canada has indeed spiritually existed for many years. As she now comes formally into being, it is not to be regretted that her spirit is chastened and her fellowship deepened by the years of difficulty and delay.

Some years later Dr. W. T. Gunn, a former Congregationalist, wrote: 'To our happy surprise we found that we had been united before we met.'

The union that formed the United Church of Canada took place 10 June 1925 in a service of great impressiveness, though of necessity held in a large public hall. Louis Bourgeois' Old Hundredth pealed from the great assemblage, followed, after a prayer, by Charles Wesley's 'Oh, for a Thousand Tongues.' The first moderator of the United Church, Dr. George C. Pidgeon, a former Presbyterian, has presented in his book, *The United Church of Canada* (1950), the vivid story of how this important union was achieved.

The United Church with its General Council, conferences, presbyteries, and local official boards, including sessions, possesses a polity that is distinctly of the Reformed type. It has exhibited on the whole exemplary internal concord and communion and has grown more rapidly than the population as a whole. Property issues were arbitrated by a government commission. The Presbyterian minority continued to function under the old name and to maintain churches in the more populous parts of the country. The United Church, with membership in the world organizations of the Congregationalist, Methodist, and Presbyterian-and-Reformed communions, has a strong ecumenical consciousness. Mainly through the influence of Professor Richard Davidson of Toronto, a free liturgical development has taken place, and the Church has adopted a Book of Common Order. A new statement of faith for optional use in instruction was prepared by a committee and adopted in 1940. The

United Church affirms its respect for the Westminster Standards, and while it cannot be said to speak today the language of classical Calvinism, the Calvinist tradition remains strong within it.

— III —

In Australia and New Zealand the Scottish churches entered with the settlers in the early and middle nineteenth century. An energetic and combative pioneer, John Dunmore Lang, from 1823 labored in New South Wales, greatly promoting and then dividing Presbyterianism. Reunion of the parts was largely effected by 1864; but Presbyterianism arose and was organized separately in the other colonies. Victoria saw the equivalent of the Scottish Disruption in 1847, a United Presbyterian Church in 1850, and a Presbyterian Church of Victoria in 1859, with its General Assembly. A similar development took place in South Australia (1892) and in West Australia (1892). The Federation of Australian Churches (1885) and the formation, largely through the able leadership of John Meiklejohn, of the Presbyterian Church of Australia (1901) marked the stages of unification; the formation of the Commonwealth of Australia (1900) brought political union. Proposals for union with the Methodists and Congregationalists have been hopefully engaged in.

The New Zealand development was independent of that in Australia but in some respects similar to it. The Free Church of Scotland was strongly represented in New Zealand settlement, and its growth owed much to the service of Thomas Burns (a nephew of the poet, Robert Burns), who from 1848 built up a Presbyterian community at Dunedin. The Presbyterianism of the Southern and the Northern Island of New Zealand became united in 1901. Negotiations for a union of Presbyterians with Methodists and Congregationalists have reached an advanced stage.

Dutch settlements in South Africa began in 1652. The early settlers included some Germans; in 1688 there was a considerable influx of French Protestant refugees, who were rapidly merged with the others. The first regular minister arrived in 1665, and church organization thereafter followed the new settlements. The British occupation from 1806 gave opportunity for Scottish settlers, and after 1822 a Presbyterian Church slowly developed. The great Boer trek to the Transvaal of 1835–8 was followed by a separation in 1859 of opponents of the use of hymns and other innovations (under the influence of the Christian Reformed in the Netherlands) and the formation of the Reformed Free Church of South Africa. The four territorially separated branches of the Dutch Reformed of the Cape Colony, the Orange Free State, Transvaal, and Natal were associated in a Federal Council in 1906.

— IV —

We have alluded in passing to the early missions to the Indians undertaken from the New England colonies, especially those of John Eliot, David Brainerd, and Jonathan Edwards. Contemporary with Eliot (d. 1691) were the two Thomas Mayhews, father and son, who worked with the Indians on the island of Martha's Vineyard. The Dutch colonial settlements in America also show some effort of this sort, but it was in Southeast Asia that Dutch missionary activities were energetically carried on. The German Pietists and Moravians, with their devotion to missions independent of political governments, led the way to modern Protestant world missions.

If everywhere today men are learning to think in global terms, this is in no small degree the result of the outreach of mind brought about by the Christian Gospel, with its injunction to go into all the world to preach, teach, and baptize. Christianity, save where it has been grossly misinterpreted, has recognized no geographical or racial boundaries. At the Reformation conditions were, as Coligny's enterprises in Brazil and Florida showed, unfavorable to a Protestant world mission. With the rise of British and Dutch overseas power these conditions were greatly changed, and missionary opportunity began to fill the visions of earnest Protestants.

It is deplorable but not surprising that in the early stage of this development, a period of close Church-state relationships, Dutch authorities in colonial territories attempted to impose upon the inhabitants Christianity in its Dutch form. Thus when the Netherlands took Ceylon from the Portuguese (1656) the Singhalese were commanded to adopt the statements of faith of their Calvinist rulers. Large numbers of them were baptized by ministers who had to use interpreters in administering the rite. This unfortunate beginning was in part redeemed by an active mission, employing schools and Bible translations. The British occupation in 1796 interrupted this work and temporarily hindered the Christian mission. In Java and Malay, the Dutch were similarly active. A seminary was instituted at Leyden in 1622 to prepare missionaries for colonial fields, and in 1814 a Bible society was organized to promote the already well-established work of translating and spreading the Scriptures. But the achievements of these missions, perhaps for reasons external to them, lacked depth and permanence. Early attempts to evangelize the Hottentots in South Africa were not very effective. On the other hand the heroic labors of Robert Junius in Formosa (1631–43) left the promising beginning of an indigenous church; but this was soon extinguished through piratical conquest and massacre.

The relations of empire and commerce to Christian missions have been anomalous. At times missionaries have been hampered and opposed by the wealth-seeking settlers and rulers of the colonies; at other times the two elements have co-operated with some measure of harmony. Plainly, it would have been impossible to girdle the world with missions, as has been done since William Carey's time, without the vast secular achievement of exploration and settlement and the development of transportation involved in this. The ships that took St. Paul to Italy, St. Anskar to Sweden, and Adoniram Judson to Burma were built for commercial uses; and the voyages of Vasco da Gama, Christopher Columbus, and James Cook aroused in devout minds projects of evangelization beyond the seas. Through refugees for religion, by colonization and trade, and by missionary enterprise, Calvinism has been spread about the world. In the process it has adapted itself to new circumstances and has undergone many changes, but its essential features of polity, doctrine, and social attitude are still recognizable. Its modern expansion may in some degree be thought of as a part of the 'expansion of Europe,' the penetration of all the continents and islands by Western power and culture. At the same time it has gone into all the world in partnership with other Protestant communions, energized by the fresh religious force of the great era of missions to which the Evangelical Revival gave birth.

William Carey's association with the Calvinist Evangelicals was close. He was deeply indebted to the books of Doddridge, to the example of Brainerd, who died before Carey was born, and not less to his elder contemporaries Thomas Scott and John Newton. Scott on many occasions personally counseled him, and later attested his approval of Carey's work by generous support. Newton gave Carey his blessing before his departure to India (1793) and later wrote: 'Carey is more to me than bishop or arch-bishop: he is an apostle.' No denominational barrier prevented these Anglicans from appreciating the Baptist missionary's devotion. The Baptist Missionary Society (1792) was soon followed by others too numerous to be named here, in England, Scotland, America, Switzerland, France, Holland, and Germany.

The leadership in most of these was prevailingly Calvinist. They were an expression of the buoyant spirit of the Evangelical Movement, which, apart from Wesleyan Methodism, was informed with Calvinist piety. Henry Martyn (d. 1812), son of a Cornwall miner, pupil and friend of Charles Simeon, and a missionary of great talent and devotion in the Near East, best represents the Evangelical zeal for missions in Anglicanism. In the Scottish Church the Evangelicals contended for the promotion of missions, while the Moderates opposed it — a conflict dramatized in an Assembly debate of 1796 that was ingloriously won by the Moderates with a majority of twelve. But the enthusiasm for missions mounted in Scotland, and in 1829 the Kirk commissioned Alexander Duff to India. Duff's exceptional work, and his effective voice when on furlough, gave courage and vision to the movement in Britain and America. The American Board of Commissioners for Foreign Missions, established by the General Association of Massachusetts in 1810, took its rise out of the prayerful zeal of a group of Congregationalist students first at Williams College and later at Andover Seminary.

An examination of the famous names among pioneering missionaries of the nineteenth century will show that a very large proportion of them, under whatever denominational flag they labored, were of Calvinist extraction and piety, though in most instances they did not wear the whole doctrinal armor of Westminster or Dort. This statement would apply, for example, to William Carey (d. 1834), Robert Morrison (d. 1834), Henry Martyn (d. 1812), Alexander Duff (d. 1863), Adoniram Judson (d. 1850), David Livingstone (d. 1873), and François Coillard

(d. 1904). Livingstone was son-in-law to Robert Moffatt (d. 1883), another Scot in the service of the London Missionary Society, whose work as pioneer and translator in South Africa would shine brightly if it had not been eclipsed by the splendor of Livingstone, the greatest of missionary explorers. The achievement of Coillard, who worked for forty-six years in South East Africa under the Paris Evangelical Society, included the development of a highly successful school system and of a church in Basutoland strong enough to furnish aid in his mission to the neighboring Barotze people.

— V —

Denominationalism for the most part shrank out of sight in the foundation and support of the missionary societies, and a strong hope was engendered that they heralded a new day of Christian unity. The Scottish Congregationalist, David Bogue, at the foundation of the London Missionary Society (1795) drew thunderous applause when he exclaimed: 'Behold us here assembled . . . to attend the funeral of bigotry.' But in the next generation, when the churches themselves were so awakened to missions as to assume corporate responsibility for their maintenance, this spirit of fraternity was endangered. To forestall the waste of competition, the American Board introduced the policy of consulting with missionaries previously placed in the region where a new mission was contemplated (1838). Carey was apparently the first to propose world missionary conferences; but the first of such conferences to be held took place in New York in May 1854 as a result of a visit of Alexander Duff to Philadelphia three months earlier. The 'Century Conference,' meeting in London in 1885, adopted the principle of comity in missions and encouraged the growth of its application. The churches affected were at first for the most part Presbyterian, Congregationalist, Baptist, and Methodist. The Philippines, China, Japan, Indonesia, India, and Africa saw the development of this system. It promoted good will between communions and led to co-operation in education and other Christian activities and in some instances to the union of indigenous churches. Of these unions the most conspicuous is that which has produced the United Church of South India (below, p. 388). The comity system has unfortunately suffered some infringement in the postwar situation through the movement of displaced missionaries into areas not assigned to their churches.

Since about 1936 Christians have talked nimbly about 'The Ecumenical Movement,' but the movement was of earlier inception. We mentioned above some of the evidence of a zealous advocacy of international Christian unity by Reformed churchmen of the sixteenth and seventeenth centuries. Through half a century the apostolate of John Dury (d. 1680) in this cause remains a precious fragment of the history of quixotic frustration. Philip du Plessis Mornay, John Amos Comenius, and Richard Baxter are also among the eminent advocates of what today would be called ecumenism. In the Europe of their day, and for a century and a half later, it seemed a lost cause. Christian unity was believed in but was left to God. Or it was promoted for political ends and imposed by state authority. In pre-Revolutionary France, and in many other countries, it was assumed that the way to do this was to crush the religious minority out of existence. A different device was adopted by Frederick William III of Prussia, where Pietism and Rationalism had tended to reduce the dogmatic separation of Lutherans and Reformed. At the tercentenary of Luther's Theses (1817) the king introduced a scheme for a 'United Evangelical Church' of Prussia, and later he tried to impose a common polity and a common worship upon this comprehensive Church. The arbitrary methods adopted for introducing the proposed changes antagonized many. The result was a nominal union only, although in the Rhine Provinces and Westphalia the union became real in 1835 by synodical action of both churches. Church unity by government decree has been tried more than once since, where Protestant churches were concerned; but the Erastian principle it involves makes it uncongenial to the sons of Calvin and Knox.

The contemporary Ecumenical Movement was anticipated not only by the spirit engendered in missions but also by a series of co-operative efforts in the nineteenth century, the historic significance of which was hardly realized by their participants. The Evangelical Alliance arose in part as a result of the bicentenary celebration of the Westminster Assembly, and was organized at London in 1846. Its basis testified to Evangelical orthodoxy in such matters as 'the utter depravity of human nature' and 'justification by faith alone.' Through many later world and hemisphere meetings it cultivated a strong fraternity that penetrated the numerous churches represented. The Alliance was concerned with spiritual and not organic unity: but where the former is enjoyed, the obstacles to the latter disappear, and aspirations for the union of churches found some cautious expression in its programs. In 1864 it commemorated Calvin's death in a meeting in Geneva. One of its chief interests has been liberty of worship in countries where this was denied to minorities.

Some of the leaders of this world organization were also among the founders of the Alliance of Reformed Churches throughout the World Holding the Presbyterian System, which took shape in London in 1875 and held its first General Council in 1877. Professor William G. Blaikie in opening the first meeting of the Alliance rested the adoption of the term 'General Council' on the projects of Calvin and Beza. He also indicated that his colleague, Professor James Macgregor of New College, Edinburgh, had proposed such an organization in 1868, as had James Mc-Cosh of Princeton in 1870. The sixteenth General Council was held in Geneva in 1948. 'Western Section' (American) meetings were begun in 1888 and have usually been annual. The Alliance is one of the most active of those numerous world-wide associations of denominational families that have come into existence since the inception of the Lambeth Conferences of bishops of the Anglican communion (1867). And certainly no other family of churches has been more consistently favorable to ecumenical co-operation and unity.

— VI —

A new stage in the rise of ecumenism was reached with the World Missionary Conference at Edinburgh, 1910, sometimes thought of as originating the present Ecumenical Movement. The story of the progress of the movement through the confused later period of world history must be excluded from these pages.* It would be virtually impossible, and even if possible, hardly fruitful, so to dissect the movement as to be able to recite the

* The reader is referred to the co-operative work edited by Ruth Rouse and Stephen Charles Neill, *A History of the Ecumenical Movement, 1517–1948*. London, S.P.C.K., 1954.

contributions to it of the Calvinist branches of Protestantism; but with few exceptions these have heartily participated in all its phases and have been therein spiritually rewarded by an enriched sense of the world fellowship of the Christian faith.

Calvin's words to Cranmer that he would not hesitate to cross ten seas if he might help in uniting the severed members of the Church's body express an attitude that has been revived in the churches of the Calvinist family. Their willingness to join with those of Cranmer's communion is strikingly manifest in the formation of the Church of South India. It was among Presbyterians that the union movement in South India began, and the first objective was the consolidation of Presbyterianism itself. Proposals for the union of the various Presbyterian elements in North and South India were voiced as early as 1865. In 1901 the Dutch Reformed and United Free Church Mission churches came together in the United Church of South India. In 1904 this Church was embraced in the Presbyterian Church of India as its South India Synod. This synod was released in 1908 to form with the Congregationalist churches of a neighboring area the South India United Church. The basis of this union included a simple evangelical confession of faith in five articles and a typical Reformed polity, with General Assembly, synods, and 'councils' corresponding to what Presbyterianism usually calls 'presbyteries.'

In 1919 negotiations were begun between the South India United Church and the Anglican dioceses of adjacent provinces of South India, and in 1925 the Wesleyan Church in South India joined the discussions. The union, involving as it did episcopal and presbyterial polities and variant forms of worship, could not be brought about without protracted study of many differences and searching revaluation of traditions. Anglicanism was inwardly disturbed by sharply divergent views of the acceptability of the terms of union, and in the end a High Church minority remained aloof. The plan provided for the mutual recognition of existing ministries together with a constitutional episcopate. When thirty years have elapsed from the date of the union the question of the continued admission of ministers not episcopally ordained is to be reviewed. Five of the fifteen bishops who took office when the Church was formed had already been Anglican bishops; the rest came from others of the uniting churches. The

Church of South India was inaugurated with due solemnity in St. George's Cathedral, Madras, 27 September 1947. The event marked the most impressive step toward church unity yet taken; and the continued harmonious operation of this strong and ably led united church furnishes a challenging example to the sister communions of its contributory churches in other lands.

That churches of the Calvinist stamp should recover fellowship with others from which they have been severed would have caused the sixteenth-century fathers of Reformed Protestantism to rejoice. They would have stipulated, no doubt, that an evangelical Trinitarian faith, reverence for the Scriptures, and the means of sound discipline be secured. Certainly the Ecumenical Movement portends no revival of traditional and unmodified predestinarian Calvinism. This is not to be looked for in our century; even where it is professed, new forms of thought are in evidence. Churches and conceptions of the Church inevitably change with changing circumstances and philosophies. The important thing is not to waste great values, to cast away a precious heritage in the haste of a revolutionary age. This can happen through that tenacity which clings too narrowly to the accidents of the tradition as well as through repudiation of the substance of it. The world we live in constantly presents to the churches a seductive secularism which makes inroads among the self-protective traditionalist churches as well as among those more fraternally oriented. In union, strength may be increased to contend with this. Calvin himself taught many doctrines that he did not regard as terms of communion. He adopted what he called 'the judgment of charity,' which acknowledges 'as members of the Church all those who by confession of faith, exemplary life, and participation in the sacraments profess the same God and Christ with ourselves.' The members of the universal church were to be found, he said, dispersed in countries widely separated throughout the world (*Institutes* IV, 1, 9). On such a basis sectarian limits of fellowship and communion are excluded.

CHAPTER XXIII

CALVINISM IN A CHANGING
WORLD OF THOUGHT

— I —

THE world in which the Reformation was cradled has since known such tumults and fluctuations that we can comprehend it only by historical labor and imagination. The physical changes have removed many a Protestant shrine and overshadowed others with the accumulations of modern industry and commerce. A loyal posterity seeks to counter this obliterative process by means of memorial tablets and statuary. But such visible reminders are of the nature of museum specimens, which lend little to the recovery of the spirit of an epochal movement. Population changes instantly affect the strength of a communion in a given area, and the modern situation (from the Peace of Westphalia to the Iron Curtain) has encouraged the interpenetration of people of Calvinist and other communions. Roman Catholicism is today strong in Geneva, and there are Waldensian and Scottish Presbyterian churches in Rome. Geographical isolation cannot be expected to prevail in a world of ever-increasing facility of travel. Nor can a spiritual isolation be perpetuated. Those sects that have most tenaciously clung to an exclusive faith and practice, the Huterites and Doukhobors, have had to move from the place of their origin and to cross a continent and an ocean. We may say that New England Puritanism began in a similar flight from an environment that threatened the integrity of its testimony. It attempted to establish its own exclusive holy commonwealth, but this was not proof against the assaults of a changing culture.

Calvinism and Puritanism never said an emphatic *No* to the current forces of secular culture. In so far as Barthianism does this, it diverges from Calvinism. The typical attitude was not indiscriminatingly negative but selective. That 'the truth wherever it appears' is God-given was a principle by which Calvin defended classical learning. It was equally applicable to science and philosophy. 'You see the Calvinists. They stick where he [Calvin] left them, a misery much to be lamented,' John Robinson is alleged to have said in 1620. The complainant was among the most 'Calvinist' of his contemporaries, a stout champion of the canons of Dort, but also one who eagerly looked for 'new light yet to break forth.' Believing that God alone can know whom He saves, Robinson was also one of the most tolerant men of his age. In the minds of their framers the formulations of sixteenth- and seventeenth-century Calvinism were never of absolute authority. Confessions of faith were always secondary standards: the baseline of doctrinal argument was the Bible.

Before Biblical criticism became a serious factor for theology, Calvinism had already felt deeply the impact of new forces. Philosophy will never let religion alone. The bold anti-Aristotelian, Peter Ramus, who had been a pupil of John Sturm in Paris, made disciples of Caspar Olevianus of Heidelberg, of John Althusius (d. 1603), Reformed political philosopher, and of William Temple, friend of Philip Sidney and Provost of Trinity College, Dublin. Ramus fascinated and stimulated young Arminius, and under his influence Andrew Melville revitalized Scottish education. His system of logic was excluded from Oxford but admitted to Cambridge. It reigned in a number of the nonconformist academies and enjoyed its greatest vogue in late seventeenth-century New England. Although his system had been framed before the day in 1561 when, persuaded by Beza's plea at Poissy, he became a Huguenot, and although Beza's Geneva did not favor him, his logic proved attractive to Calvinists almost everywhere else. Since Ramus died in the St. Bartholomew massacre and was revered as a Protestant martyr, his teaching came with an attraction that made it the more acceptable. His denunciation of Aristotle had the ring of youthful intolerance and appealed to the young as a challenge to a new kind of thinking. Logic was reshaped so as to deal with evidence and was based upon the practice of argumentative rhetoric, in contempt of the 'categories' and the syllogism. It involved reference to an invented series of dichotomies, but resolved itself into the art of discussion and was nothing if not a thing of use for living. Ramus

was said to have prayed when he was dying that God would il-
lumine all good spirits with the light of logic for the deliverance
of man from error. Thus the strange new logic was for his disciples a passion, or a form of piety; it was something utterly different from the logic of the school text, with its 'Barbara Celarent
Darii Ferioque' that some of us encountered in youth. Or ought
we to call it the annihilation of logic and the substitution of a
kind of rhetoric therefor? Whatever judgment is rendered on
Ramus as a thinker, his impact upon the Western mind and on
the Reformed churches for a century and a half was stimulating
and liberating. Both Arminianism and Amyraldism (above, pp.
250, 265 ff.) owed something to this pervasive stimulus, but it
was influential also with such men as Melville, whose Calvinist
orthodoxy was not in question.

Francis Bacon showed a similar impatience with the old logic,
which he said aimed 'to provide an answer' rather than to discern
'the inner truth of things.' He challenged men to a long struggle
for knowledge, an effort 'with humility and veneration to unroll
the volume of creation.' This was to open the door to the realm
of scientific search both for truth and for man's comfort and
power. Bacon's chief interest in religion was to keep it from exercising a restrictive control of science. René Descartes completed
the break with the Aristotelian habits of mind by making knowledge rely upon intuition. He adopted the method of doubt, by
which all is surrendered that can be doubted, so that the residue
may be utilized as the basis of a reconstruction of knowledge.
There is left the thinking mind, and he can say, 'cogito, ergo sum,'
not as a syllogistic proof but as 'a direct inspection of the mind.'
Descartes' mathematical discoveries, too, were to prove weapons
to undermine the Aristotelian science.

A certain ambiguity attends the relation of Bacon's thought
to Calvinism. The weight was thrown upon the instrument of
sense in the acquisition of knowledge, yet the knowledge that
was revealed in Scripture was not assailed or questioned. Calvinism had no basic quarrel with the effort of science to 'unroll
the volume of creation.' Calvin had given his approval to the
sciences in the Institutes, and made way for the astronomers in
his treatment of Genesis. His rejection of Copernican views was
an echo of the general voice of the learning of his age. Even the
speculations of Giordano Bruno regarding infinitude did not

greatly frighten Calvinists. Bruno received kindly treatment in Beza's Geneva until he wantonly attacked one of the ministers, and even after this was restored to the city's hospitality. In England his closest friends were Philip Sidney and Fulke Greville, both favorers of Puritanism. Not until much later did Christianity have to consider the astounding disclosures of geology and biology. Comenius, who shared the alliance of his church, the Unity of Brethren, with Calvinism, adopted Bacon's philosophy as the basis of his educational theory of sense-realism. Indeed, throughout the seventeenth century, save for a few instances such as that of Galileo, science was looked upon as an innocent maidservant of religion. There was more fear of purely theological novelties than of any lurking danger in the discoveries of the sciences.

— II —

This attitude survived even the teaching of Descartes, and many a Calvinist became a Cartesian. The Augustinians Pierre Bérulle, founder of the French Congregation of the Oratory, and Guillaume Gibieuf, who placed Augustine above Aquinas and Plato above Aristotle, were personal friends of Descartes, and apparently it was they who induced him to devote himself to philosophy. His use of Augustinian and Anselmic language in his argument for the existence of God could not fail to appeal to Calvinist minds. As early as 1630 he wrote to Father Marin Mersenne, another of Bérulle's circle, 'I hold that all those to whom God has given the use of reason are bound to use it mainly in the effort to know Him and to know themselves.' This is in substance Augustine's language; but it is also in substance Calvin's first sentence in the *Institutes* of 1536.

It is not, then, surprising that Descartes, who wrote in the Netherlands, had his followers among the more liberal Dutch Calvinists. The conservative mind of Gijsbert Voet (d. 1676) of Utrecht reacted quite unfavorably, however. Voet was offended by the Cartesian Henri le Roi (Regius), his colleague at Utrecht and the pupil of Henri Renier (Reneri), a French convert from Roman Catholicism exiled to Holland, who had brilliantly espoused Cartesianism. Voet found in the Cartesian method of doubt not only skepticism but atheism, and drew a powerful rejoinder from Descartes himself. But Voet secured the rejection of Descartes' teaching by the university of Utrecht in 1642, and other condemnations of it followed in the Netherlands. Yet Descartes had bold defenders. The Reformed minister, Balthasar Bekker, wrote his *Admonition on the Cartesian Philosophy* (1658) to show that Cartesianism was not in contradiction with Reformed theology. Bekker was unfortunately to be later deposed from the ministry for his book against the witchcraft delusion, *The World Bewitched* (1691). Though the reigning orthodoxy still permitted no skepticism about witchcraft, it did not depose its members for Cartesianism. John Cocceius (d. 1669) of Leyden and his party, opposing the Voetians on other matters, countenanced or championed the philosophy of Descartes, and this became a divisive issue in the Dutch universities and the Reformed Church. Josef Bohatec's study of seventeenth-century Cartesianism indicates also its rapid — though always resisted — penetration of the Reformed schools of Germany, France, and Switzerland. Wherever it went, it drew attention away from the basic interests of the Reformation and especially weakened the hold of the dogmatic Calvinism of men such as Gomarus and Voet.

But, even before Descartes, Calvinism had its own part in the rise of mathematics. The invention of logarithms (1614) by John Napier of Merchiston ranks among the great mathematic achievements. Napier apparently owed nothing to other specialists but stands alone as a genius wholly original and significantly creative. He was a Scottish baron who had become an intense partisan of the Reformation through the preaching of Knox's colleague, John Goodman, and had expressed his zeal against Rome in a hotly controversial work on the Apocalypse. What Napier did for trigonometry, Descartes did for algebra (1637): both were valuable tools for the great development of science in the seventeenth century, which culminated in Newton's *Principia*. The era of science was dawning with brilliant promise.

Moreover, Descartes, by his doctrine of 'extension,' gave existence to the world of matter apart from mind. Although Nicholas Malebranche in his doctrine of 'occasionalism' attempted to restore contact between the two and offered an ingenious spiritualization of Cartesian principles, the more arresting doctrines of Spinoza led rather to deism and pantheism. Spinoza's God was the object of 'intellectual love' but not the hearer of prayer; and the decrees of God were identified with the laws of nature.

In England the pursuit of the laws of nature, though not exclusively indebted to any one philosophy, was extremely active. There was little thought that science imperiled religion, and some of the scientists were devout and active in the churches. The foundation of the Royal Society (1661) rested upon the work of a group of whom Robert Boyle (d. 1691) was the most eminent. He had spent two years of his education in Geneva and a collection of his works appeared there in his lifetime. He was equally zealous to correct the errors of chemistry, the field of his greatest originality, and to promote evangelical missions and the spread of the vernacular Scriptures.

Descartes followed Ramus into the nonconformist schools and served there to aid the new emphasis upon the teaching of science. Olive Griffiths in *Religion and Learning* gives some particulars of this, and quotes a dissenting minister's complaint (1812) that his brethren were 'better mathematicians and experimentists than scholars.' The fruit of this trend was gathered in the new secular interests of the eighteenth century, when science, still not recognized as religion's enemy, had already drawn many minds from theology. It was not unusual that the stated purpose of a Presbyterian academy in Pisgah, Kentucky (1797), was 'the promotion of science, morals and religion in a young country,' and that in Nova Scotia the Pictou Academy founded by Rev. Thomas McCulloch (1818) did not fail to teach mathematics and chemistry. McCulloch, indeed, assembled scientific apparatus and a collection of birds, beasts, and insects.

— III —

It was the age of the Deists and of the Scottish Moderates, when Calvinism was best represented in protest movements. The Deists, with their world of immutable law, had some affinities with the Calvinists who thought in terms of divine decrees. The English Presbyterians, now turned more than half Unitarian, had, as Miss Griffiths points out, 'many interests in common with the Deists'; but some of them attacked the Deists from the standpoint of a liberalized Calvinism armed with John Locke's doctrine of the use of reason to discern truth. Such, for example, was the work of George Benson, author of *The Reasonableness of the Christian Religion* (1743), a work that on purely rational grounds confuted the Deist views of the fraudulence of Scripture.

In Scotland the moral philosophy of Francis Hutcheson (d. 1746) (above, p. 356) shattered in many minds the Calvinist concept of depravity, and David Hume (d. 1787) called in question all intellectual support of belief. His *Essay on Miracles* (1755) proved especially alarming, and his 'impious and infidel principles' were condemned by the General Assembly. In denying the proofs alleged for miracles Hume did not explicitly deny the possibility of miracles or assail Christian doctrine as such. He probably retained much of it in his own belief. His attack was on the trustworthiness of reason, not on faith. A Scottish minister, Henry F. Henderson, writing in 1905, remarked that Hume really 'conferred benefit on both philosophy and religion.' But in this and other works he staggered the philosophers and despoiled their garden. Thomas Reid, Sir William Hamilton, and, with more distinction, Immanuel Kant toiled to repair the ravages of Hume's skepticism, but with little comfort to religion.

One effect of the deflation of philosophy was that religion perforce turned for support from speculative argument to Scripture and experience. We have seen that Calvinism as a theological system had undergone a variety of modifications. Its efforts to combat the philosophies, and to enlist them, had met with indifferent success. It had now to begin over again as a scriptural piety.

While this was happening among the Evangelicals, a brilliant theologian appeared in the person of the parish minister of Row, Argyllshire: John M'Leod Campbell (d. 1872), author of *The Nature of the Atonement* (1856) and less celebrated works. He had been under the influence, but had outgrown the thought, of the scholarly and saintly Thomas Erskine of Linlathen, a friend of Alexandre Vinet. Campbell brought to new force in Scotland the doctrine of the love of God. In the light of this, the important things in a minister's message were 'not destruction and salvation' but 'sin and holiness.' 'The contrast is not between things present and future, but between things spiritual and carnal.' He taught that according to the Scripture all men are through Christ 'redeemed from the curse of sin' — a doctrine he carefully distinguished from Arminianism, which, in his view, withholds God's love until the sinner qualifies for it by repentance. His other emphasis is on 'the assurance of faith,' a view enforced by his reading of Luther.

As early as 1831 his opinions on the atonement of Christ occasioned his trial and deposition by the General Assembly. He quoted at his trial the Confession of 1560 on 'ane assured faith in the promise of God'; but he was confronted with the cautious treatment of assurance in the Westminster Confession and was obliged to acknowledge that to him it was inadequate.

Such an admission was, to many in the Kirk, the sure mark of heresy. Campbell's attitude is in sharp contrast to that of William M'Gill of Ayr, who may be thought of as in a sense his forerunner. M'Gill, best known today for the admiration expressed for him by Robert Burns, in his *Practical Essay on the Death of Jesus Christ* (1786) had treated Christ's death as the fulfilment of His teaching by His example. This might have been ecclesiastically overlooked in the era of the Moderates, but when in defending himself he referred to the 'unscriptural phrases' of the Confession of Faith, he found himself in so much trouble that he abandoned his whole position and made an act of retraction worthy of a Soviet biologist. Campbell exhibited more conviction and courage. He demanded to be judged by the Scripture, the supreme standard of the Church of Scotland, not by its subordinate standards, and with an exalted boldness he declared in the Assembly:

> I lay it down as a principle that the Church never took to herself the character of infallibility from the time she became a reformed church, and that every member of the Church is at liberty to express freely how far he believes that the Church has been . . . advancing or retrograding . . . The Westminster Confession has not set forth the whole truth. It is absurd to cry 'treason' when criticism is passed on a document of this kind. What profit is it to think of our fathers in such a way . . . in that in which they may have erred?

The Confession, he said, ought not to be thought of as something 'to stint and stop the Church's growth in light and knowledge.'

It was on this issue that Campbell was condemned; but the dignity of the young prophet's behavior and the sincerity of his thought had won the approval of many good men, and the outcome may be said to have given to the Church a bad conscience. He was heartened by many tributes, and shortly before his death he received belated honors and wide acclaim as one of the great theologians of the era. Campbell's assertion of the divine love was a prophecy of the teaching that since his time has increasingly prevailed in Scottish Presbyterianism.

Campbell had been trained in Scottish philosophy under Sir William Hamilton, through whom he was favorably introduced to Kant. He was not uninstructed in Hegelianism, whose Scottish interpreter Edward Caird was his friend. Jonathan Edwards was among the theologians whom he cited and honored. He had affinities with Schleiermacher, but differs from him in his emphasis on thinking as well as feeling in religious knowledge. A widely read scholar, he was not the disciple of any school. He broke through philosophies, theologies, and confessions to his own construction of the Scripture revelation. He was no less a scriptural theologian than Calvin himself, and was wholly innocent of the problems of modern Biblical criticism. He is perhaps the last theologian of real originality of whom this statement can be made.

A lesser light but an able theologian, trained in Hamilton's philosophy, was James Morison, whose revolt against traditional predestinationism and broad view of the atonement of Christ caused his deposition by the United Secession Synod in 1841. He formed the Evangelical Union, known as the Morisonian Church, later united with the Scottish Independents. His *Nature of the Atonement* (1890) presented his case so effectively that the doctrine of a limited atonement virtually ceased to be advocated by Scottish theologians.

— IV —

In America during the same period the Mercersburg theology was imparting a new element to Reformed Church Calvinism. Among its founders (above, p. 368) John Williamson Nevin stands out with greatest distinction, although the name of his associate, the church historian and Biblical scholar Philip Schaff, is more widely known. Though little disturbed by Biblical criticism, Nevin (and Frederick Rauch before him) felt strongly the impact of German thought. Nevin had turned from his Scotch-

Irish heritage and Princeton training to the fresh excitements of German idealism, and imbibed the teachings of Schleiermacher, Hegel, and Schelling. His sermon *On Catholic Unity,* Schaff's inaugural address on *The Principle of Protestantism* (both of 1844, published together in 1845), and Nevin's weighty book, *The Mystical Presence, a Vindication of the Reformed or Calvinistic Doctrine of the Holy Eucharist* (1846), are typical expressions of Mercersburg's new Calvinism. While Schaff (a year before John Henry Newman's *Doctrine of Development*) regarded Protestantism as embracing a principle of development that permitted the hope of reunion with Roman Catholicism, Nevin stressed the centrality of the Person of Christ in salvation, and showed the forgotten evidence of the acknowledgment in the Reformed Confessions and in Calvin of the mystical presence in the Eucharist. He did not hesitate to charge Calvin with an inadequate exposition of his own principles, which through the new German psychology might now be better clarified.

The high sacramental doctrine of Nevin had affinities with the teaching of Edward Bouverie Pusey and the Anglican High Church party. Schaff conversed with Pusey, who knew well some of Schaff's German teachers, at Oxford in 1843 and again in 1854, and heard him deplore the Reformation. The Mercersburg men remained loyal to the Reformation, but reinterpreted it freely, and were more favorable to Luther's teaching than to Calvin's in their emphasis upon Christology and their attitude toward liturgical worship. Schaff was a true pupil of Johann August Wilhelm Neander (d. 1850), the most spiritual of historians and a follower of Schleiermacher in theology. Adolf Harnack, who after an interval became Neander's successor, greeting Schaff in 1892 compared him with Martin Bucer as one who carried abroad 'the light of German theology.' He was like Bucer, too, in his unfailingly fraternal attitude toward Christians of other communions than his own, and in his utopian optimism regarding church unity.

Charles Hodge (d. 1878), for fifty-six years a professor in Princeton, was in his day the reigning theologian of American Presbyterianism. He, too, was trained in Germany and was warmly attached to Neander and August Tholuck. Hodge recorded in his diary an incident of New Year's Eve, 1827, that indicates the nature of this fellowship. He was at Neander's house, Tholuck and others being present. The discussion was of predestination, and Neander declared that Calvin made God the author of sin.

> In coming away Neander shook me very affectionately by the hand and said to Tholuck: 'Tell our friend Hodge that though we dispute with him we belong to the same Lord and are one in heart.'

Such experiences may have helped to give the irenical character to Hodge's firm Calvinism that was marked and appreciated by Lutheran scholars. His *Constitutional History of the Presbyterian Church* (1840) and *Discussions on Church Polity* (1878) offer a liberal treatment of Calvinist polity, but his *Systematic Theology* (1873) is a reaffirmation, with studied avoidance of novelty, of Calvin's own teaching, and with emphasis upon the inerrancy of Scripture, which he defends from Darwin and the higher critics. Attractively pious and gracious in his personal life, Hodge was idolized by his students and esteemed by a wide circle. He left two sons to continue his work in Princeton. But the real later champion of Calvinism there was the learned Benjamin B. Warfield (d. 1921), whose *Calvin and Calvinism* (1931) is a republication of special studies contributed to the journal established by Hodge, *The Princeton Theological Review*.

Over against the motionless Calvinism of Hodge stands the creative liberalism of Horace Bushnell (d. 1876), Congregationalist preacher and author, of Hartford, Connecticut. Against the assumptions of revivalism gone stale with its concept of conversion that involved a helpless waiting for its manifestation, Bushnell in *Christian Nurture* (1846) affirmed the startling view that the child is 'to grow up a Christian and never know himself as being otherwise.' The argument involves a basic attack upon the individualistic presupposition of New England religion of his time, the isolation of souls that makes nothing of family, Church, state, and school but 'takes every man as if he existed alone.' Bushnell did not attempt to support his view, as he might have done, from the history of religious education in the Reformation era. He was not interested in attacking or defending the older Calvinism but was severely critical of its contemporary expression. It is of interest that while the Congregationalists were startled by his condemnation of individualistic religion, both Hodge and Nevin treated favorably this criticism and his assertion of the reality of the Church and the family. They were both critical, however, of the naturalism that seemed to emerge in his concept of nurture, the tendency to make conversion a natural development rather than a work of grace. His *Nature and the Supernatural* (1858) affords an answer to such criticisms; but the answer is novel and unorthodox. There is no denial of the supernatural: nature is not enough. 'The cross of redemption is the all-dominating idea' that explains the universe. But man, as man, is supernatural in his endowments of will and personality. 'We act supernaturally ourselves,' and we live in a world full of miracles. What is properly called nature stands under the 'grand supernatural empire' of God. In *The Vicarious Sacrifice* (1865) he took up the much discussed doctrine of atonement, presenting the 'moral' view which had its prototype in the work of Abailard on Romans. Calvin held, on the contrary, as did Anselm, that Christ 'bore the weight of the divine anger' that was incurred by man's sin. Campbell has an element of the moral-influence theory. Bushnell drew analogies from the identification in the family of the innocent with the guilty in suffering. God in Christ identifies Himself with His sinning human children, and by the revelation of love on the cross calls forth the response that is the condition of forgiveness.

— V —

The churches everywhere were disturbed by new movements and new ideas. In Scotland, as in America, a widespread revival took place in the late 1850's. It was accompanied by lay preaching and new attitudes toward worship. To the use of the Psalms and the versified paraphrases of Scripture passages of 1781 was now added the singing of hymns — first employed by the Relief Church. The organ as an aid to worship was first introduced in 1807 but was suppressed, and not until half a century later was it widely and permanently employed in Scotland. In the United States and Canada the introduction of hymnology and organ music came with hesitation and through contention into Presbyterian practice. Some now living remember well the precentor and the tuning fork and the local strife over the introduction of organs. Hymns became popular through revival meetings and the singing schools that gave an elementary training chiefly in rural communities. The Oxford Movement led to much ques-

tioning of worship practices everywhere. Various proposals for
worship were keenly debated. The principal Scottish innovator
was Robert Lee of Edinburgh University, who introduced in his
services in Greyfriars Church the strange practices of standing
to sing and kneeling to pray. Standing in prayer had been common for some generations. Lee also used a liturgy of his own
compiling. He was charged before the Assembly with forbidden
innovations (1858). Through his influence the Church Service
Society was formed (1865) for liturgical study. Lee died worn out
by controversy (1869), not having seen the full victory of his party.
But nothing could resist the tide of change which in later decades
affected hymnody, organ music, and architecture as well as freedom to use liturgical forms.

Meanwhile the gravest of theological controversies was in the
making. In the 1860's and 1870's there were scholars of a new
type, such as Andrew Bruce Davidson and John Tulloch, in Scottish theological chairs. They were alert to the rising interest on
the Continent in philosophy, science, and Biblical criticism. Darwin's *Origin of Species* (1859) had been followed by the startling
Essays and Reviews (1860), in which liberal Anglicans countenanced the new science and critical learning. A demand arose,
first voiced by elders of Paisley (1865), for relaxation of the subscription formula in the Church of Scotland. The pulpit began
to show the impact of the new criticism.

In 1870 William Robertson Smith (d. 1894) became professor
of Oriental Languages and Old Testament Exegesis in the Free
Church College of Aberdeen. He had already won distinction for
his originality in electrical experiments in Edinburgh. He wrote
for the *Encyclopedia Britannica* a series of articles that aroused
opposition. To the horror of the evangelically orthodox Free
Church, he expressed views derived from German criticism, to
which he had been introduced in periods of study at Bonn and
Göttingen. For the first time a Scottish Church met the terrific
onset of modern Bible criticism, and the reaction was intense.
The Anglican Church was already deep in controversy over the
similar studies of Bishop John William Colenso. Robertson
Smith was charged with heretical teaching and in the end was
deposed by the General Assembly from his chair (1881). It was
his views on the book of Deuteronomy that were most alarming
to his brethren, since his study of that book forced him to con-

clude that the books ascribed to Moses were of late composition. Smith defended himself from charges of heresy and sincerely professed the primary doctrines of his Church. Heresy was not proved: but his retention of the Aberdeen chair was felt to be a peril to the faith of students. He continued to make important contributions to Semitic studies, especially when (from 1883) he occupied a chair and various offices in Cambridge. Smith's published answers to his critics were in themselves contributions to scholarship, and his speeches in the church courts were convincing evidence of his sincerity and drew to him many warm sympathizers. As in the case of M'Leod Campbell, the excluded heretic drew his Church after him into the positions for which he had been condemned.

In America, somewhat later, occurred the parallel case of Charles Augustus Briggs (d. 1913), professor of Hebrew and later (1890) of Biblical Theology in Union Theological Seminary, New York. The Seminary was at that period under the aegis of the Presbyterian Church. His appointment to the theological chair was vetoed by the General Assembly of the Church, and he was brought to trial for heresy, condemned, and suspended from the ministry (1892). As a result, the Seminary's tie with the Presbyterian Church was severed. Though orthodox to the point of a vigorous defense of the Virgin Birth, Briggs stoutly insisted on the freedom of Biblical studies, and his literary labors in this field, as well as his numerous doctrinal and historical writings, mark him as a gifted and industrious scholar. In his *Whither? A Theological Question for the Times* (1889) he confuted Hodge and Warfield with respect to their doctrine of the inerrancy of Scripture, and learnedly argued that this was not taught by the Westminster divines. In 1898 he took orders in the Episcopal Church, a course consistent with his deep interest in Christian unity.

A man who did much to cushion the impact of scientific thought and even to enlist it in the service of religion was Henry Drummond (d. 1897), the much admired evangelical lecturer to students, whose 'tours for religion' took him to America, Africa, Australia, and the New Hebrides. An Edinburgh graduate well equipped in science, he was secured for evangelism by D. L. Moody in 1874, and three years later was appointed to lecture in natural science to Free Church theological students. His *Nat-*

ural Law in the Spiritual World (1883) and *The Ascent of Man* (1894) offered readable and reassuring interpretations of Darwinian evolution in the light of religious faith. Drummond had the art of suggesting religious analogies for biological terms and concepts in a most fascinating way. His personal attractiveness and unquestioned consecration made his message the more persuasive, and thousands owed to him the recovery of faith. His emphasis on altruism in nature as a factor in survival helped to light up Darwin's grim picture of the 'survival of the fittest.'

Modification of the doctrine of the Confession may be, and in fact has been, possible under the terms of subscription to it. Although in 1567 it was enacted that 'no other face of Kirk' than that based on the Confession of 1560 should be permitted in Scotland, the terms of subscription to this Confession were not very clearly stated. It was only in 1690, when the Westminster Standards had been adopted anew, that the General Assembly required 'all entrants into the ministry and all other ministers and elders' to subscribe to it: in 1694 each was required to declare it 'the confession of his faith.' So the Church of Scotland used the words, 'the confession of my faith,' in the questions for admission; for elders, however, the phrase was 'my approbation of the confession of Faith.' American Congregationalist ministers were asked to accept the Westminster Confession with the words, 'freely and fully consent thereunto for the substance thereof' (1648). The American Presbyterian formula of 1729 qualified acceptance of the Westminster documents by the phrase, 'in all essential and necessary articles.' The United Presbyterian Church used the form (1879), 'an exhibition of the sense in which you understand the Holy Scriptures,' and the United Free Church had its ordinands accept the Confession 'as expressing the sense in which you understand the Holy Scriptures.' The Presbyterian Church in Canada adopted the phrase, 'founded on and agreeable to the Word of God,' and the Presbyterian Church in the United States of America uses the words, 'as containing the system of doctrine taught in the Holy Scriptures.'

There have also been modifications through the adoption of declaratory statements. Thus the Free Church declared in 1846 that it regarded the Confession as 'not favoring intolerance or persecution,' and a statement was made by the United Presbyterian Church (1847) repudiating anything in the standards 'which teaches or may be supposed to teach . . . intolerant principles.' The latter Church adopted in 1879 a declaratory act in which the standards are spoken of as 'necessarily imperfect,' and the doctrine of decrees is 'held in harmony with the truth that God is not willing that any should perish and . . . has provided a salvation sufficient for all.' The Free Church's declaratory act of 1892 had a similar emphasis on the love of God and denied that the Confession teaches 'the foreordination of men to death irrespective of their own sin.' In 1903 the Presbyterian Church in the United States of America declared that 'the doctrine of God's eternal decree is held in harmony with the doctrine of His love to all mankind,' and that God 'has provided in Christ a salvation sufficient for all mankind.'

It was easier to make declarations regarding the sense of the Confession than to alter it outright; yet in several instances this has been done. The Scottish Church, as we saw, altered it in taking it from the Westminster Assembly in 1647. Three chapters were altered by the American General Synod in 1788, notably chapter XXIII, 'Of the Civil Magistrate.' In 1903 the Presbyterian Church in the United States of America added two notable chapters (XXXIV, XXXV), 'Of the Holy Spirit' and 'Of the Love of God and Missions.' Theologians have habitually regarded the Westminster documents as neither flawless nor sacrosanct; but there has been marked hesitation about subjecting them to fundamental alteration. They were, however, replaced by a more contemporary statement in the, partly Presbyterian, United Church of Canada, and in 1966 the United Presbyterian Church in the U.S.A. adopted an entirely new Confession clearly reflecting the new theological thought and biblical scholarship of our time, but affirming continuity with earlier Presbyterian and Reformed confessions.

— VI —

We saw that Continental Reformed thought was subjected to severe shocks in the seventeenth century. While most of the moderate conservatives came to adopt the Covenant theology of Cocceius, they turned against the 'hypothetical universalism' of Moïse Amyraut of Saumur. Thus John Henry Heidegger of Zurich, François Turretin of Geneva, and Lucas Gernler of Basel drew up the famous *Formula Consensus Helvetica* (1675) to combat the Saumur doctrine of grace and other innovations. The document is celebrated for its affirmation of the inerrancy of the vowel points of the Hebrew Scriptures — a device introduced by rabbis of the early Middle Ages. The *Formula* became authorative in some cantonal churches, but caused controversy and was abandoned in 1723. Turretin was the author of a lucid and complete textbook of systematic theology, *Institutio Theologiae Elenchticae* (1679–85), so long influential that it was republished in Edinburgh in 1847; Charles Hodge made much use of it. Turretin's son, Jean Alphonse (d. 1737), however, showed the early eighteenth-century trend to more liberal views.

That century saw a flood of deistic, rationalistic, and naturalistic literature. Theology quailed before the great names of Wolff, Reimarus, Voltaire, Diderot, Rousseau, d'Holbach, and Gibbon. Religion was best represented in Reformed lands by men such as Caspar Lavater (d. 1801) of Zurich, more poet than theologian, who had little preference among the churches but looked for the appearing of a spiritual universal Christianity. A little earlier the Westphalian, Gerhard Teerstegen (d. 1769), moved from a Reformed background to a strange ascetic mysticism; he became a counselor to inquirers from far and near and a writer of hymns. These men were in some sense forerunners of the great founder of modern theology, Friedrich Daniel Ernst Schleiermacher, who was nursed in Reformed and Moravian piety. By his persuasive *Addresses on Religion to Its Cultured Despisers* (1799) Schleiermacher laid the basis of a new and effective Christian appeal. His treatise on *The Christian Faith* (1821–2) brought new life to theology; but his view of doctrines as 'accounts of Christian religious affections' shows an approach far removed from that of Calvinism. He was the theologian of the Romantic Movement: in him Scripture yielded authority to religious emotions, and theology relied on psychology. Yet his moderating influence upon Calvinist minds has been incalculable. Some who had forgotten the emotional element in Calvin recovered it through Schleiermacher's influence; others bade John Calvin farewell. The new theology of feeling was expressed in Friedrich August Tholuck, a consecrated scholar, and John August Wilhelm Neander, whose *Church History* rescued from oblivion innumerable fine Christian names and Christian utterances. These men profoundly influenced Scottish and American students in Berlin, some of whom later gave leadership in their churches. Tholuck's Calvin studies included an edition of the Latin *Institutes*.

The rich contribution to theology and homiletics of Alexandre Vinet (d. 1847) of Lausanne was marked by attention to psychology and the emotions. His genius sprang to life under the influence of the *Réveil,* an Evangelical awakening of which Robert Haldane was the chief inspirer. Vinet was also a writer on literary history, a consummate interpreter of Pascal, and a religious poet. He possessed a critical mind and recognized the emerging problem of Scripture authority, but never yielded the essentials of faith. The Evangelical Movement, however, was ill prepared for the mounting impact of critical thought. In Geneva the *Ecole Evangélique,* founded by the church historian, Merle d'Aubigné, had among its professors in the 1840's the brilliant Edmund Scherer (d. 1887). He had been converted in England, his mother's homeland, to the most literalistic Evangelicalism. His studies, under Hegelian influence and that of the new Tübingen school of Biblical scholars, drew him unwillingly away from his colleagues and from Calvinist orthodoxy. He left his chair and lived out his life as a subdued and saddened agnostic, winning distinction in France as a literary critic and a political figure.

Strasbourg in the same period saw the expression of a new liberal and spiritual Protestantism begun by Edouard Reuss (d. 1891), Lutheran Biblical scholar and Calvin editor, and his pupil Timothée Colani (d. 1888), founder (with Scherer) of the Strasbourg *Revue de théologie et de philosophie chrétienne* (1850). August Sabatier (d. 1901) was briefly connected with the Strasbourg faculty, but the Franco-Prussian War in 1870 caused his removal to Paris, where he became dean of the Protestant faculty that was a continuation of that of Strasbourg. His best-known work, *Religions of Authority and the Religion of the Spirit* (1901, English 1904), appropriates Calvin's doctrine of 'the inward attestation of the Spirit' in the reading of Scripture, but turns away from dogmatic formulations, and with support from Schleiermacher sets forth a highly subjective piety, which Sabatier believes consistent with critical scholarship.

In America one of the most effective disturbers of the old Calvinism was Charles G. Finney (d. 1875), who after an intense religious struggle turned from law to theology (1821) and was largely self-taught. His independent revision of Calvinism went beyond what prevailed in the Presbyterian New School; but it was his tremendous power as an evangelistic preacher in New York villages, in the cities of Boston and New York, and in England that made him famous. As president of Oberlin College he gave currency to what was called the Oberlin Theology, which, moving on from the position of Edwards, stressed the freedom of the will and the duty of a watchful and constant obedience to God, in which lies sanctification. Finney passed from a Presbyterian to a Congregationalist connection: he was the founder of Broadway Tabernacle in New York City.

The same change of ecclesiastical attachment marked the lives of a number of leaders of American thought. Henry Ward Beecher (d. 1887) lived through the early phase of controversy over Darwinianism. He had been called to Plymouth Congregational Church, Brooklyn, after a pastorate in an Indianapolis Presbyterian congregation. In his eloquent preaching and writing he exhibited the process by which he reached a conviction of the truth of evolution; he also increasingly proclaimed the divine love. This doctrine, as we have indicated, occupied a central place in the teaching of Edwards. In part, no doubt as a compensation for the harsh realities of nature revealed by Darwin, it was now stressed by men who adopted Darwin's biology, and became a characteristic emphasis in the pulpit message of the generation after Beecher. It was Henry Drummond who in his popular address, *The Greatest Thing in the World* (1890), perfectly voiced this theme for the ministers of that generation.

Newman Smyth (d. 1925) during his ministry in Illinois wrote books in which he adopted evolutionary science and cautiously applied a parallel principle of Bible study. His *Orthodox Theology Today* (1881) treats in a liberal spirit the doctrines of the Westminster Confession. As a Congregationalist minister in New Haven (from 1882) he turned to biological experimentation, with results favorable to Darwin's conclusions. *Through Science to Faith* (1902) is one of the fruits of his reflections on evolution, in which he followed a course parallel to that of Henry Drummond. His *Passing Protestantism and Coming Catholicism* (1908) looks for ecclesiastical reunion on a grand scale. Smyth hails the 'mediating modernism' of Loisy and Tyrell, then being suppressed by the Vatican, as offering the answer — 'an answer for us all' — to the new problems, and as prophetic of 'the greater Christianity.'

It was not only in such minds as Smyth's that liberal optimism reached a peak. From the middle 'eighties America saw the development of what came to be called the Social Gospel; this will be briefly noticed in the next chapter. Union Theological Seminary in New York, in touch with British and German theology, was a testing ground for new elements of thought. After the Briggs trial Arthur Cushman McGiffert (d. 1933), a former pupil of Adolf von Harnack, was accused of heresy for his *History of Christianity in the Apostolic Age,* and left the Presbyterian to join the Congregational Church (1899). William Adams Brown (d. 1943), another of Harnack's students, similarly accused in 1911 for his lectures, *The Old Theology and the New,* was not found heretical. There was, however, a great deal that was positive and traditional in the 'new' theology of Dr. Brown, and his later work indicated a deepened sense of the basic evil in man and society; the Old Testament myth of the Fall 'tells in substance a true story.'

— VII —

Thus the Calvinism of Dort and Westminster was being discarded or altered almost beyond recognition. Only some of the smaller members of the Reformed family of churches remained immune to the liberal leaven. To the optimists, man seemed on his way toward the Kingdom of Heaven, which tended to take the form of a happy earthly state of economic sufficiency and orderly co-operation. It is true that the abler minds, and those experienced in the evils of the teeming cities, were not so superficially optimistic as a later generation has supposed. The Augustinian type of thought, with its deep sense of human sin and evil, also found some fresh expression. Vinet had mingled an interest in Pascal with his Calvinism; Kierkegaard, on Lutheran soil, revived, with a terrific force born of experience, the consciousness of man's helplessness in guilt. But who read Kierkegaard? Not many; but one who did was Peter Taylor Forsyth (d. 1921), an Aberdeen Congregationalist theologian in London. Forsyth had a limited following: some of us as students were introduced to his work about 1910 but were a little bored. In 1953, in Robert McAfee Brown's title, he is called *P. T. Forsyth, Prophet for Today.* Theology has caught up with him. His dozen books now attract a good many theological students for their pre-Barthian critique of liberal theology. In psychology Freud and in literature such disillusioned writers as Dostoyevsky, Nietzsche, Ibsen and Thomas Hardy mocked the optimists. The impression grew that scientific liberalism was yielding diminishing returns.

In America not only liberalism in doctrine but the entire academic modernization of theological study was attacked by the Fundamentalist movement. Organized in 1909 and greatly expanded after World War I, this movement entered on a highly financed campaign to gain decisions in the Churches affirming, among other test points of doctrine, the literal inerrancy of the Bible. Though it gained a large following among Baptists and Presbyterians, and actually obtained qualified approval of its doctrines in Presbyterian assemblies, the attempt to have ministers bound to assent to its reactionary positions was effectively resisted. Among its leaders were the celebrated layman William Jennings Bryan, defeated candidate for the moderatorship of the Presbyterian Church U.S.A. General Assembly in 1923, and John Gresham Machen, Princeton New Testament scholar who became the leader of a small secession under the name 'The Presbyterian Church of America' (1936). From this body, later called 'The Orthodox Presbyterian Church,' a further schism formed 'The Bible Presbyterian Synod' (1937). Campaigning evangelism, since 1947 ably represented by Baptist William Franklin (Billy) Graham, retains a strong deposit of Fundamentalism while largely abandoning its schismatic dogmatism. A turning point in the Fundamentalist controversy as it concerned Presbyterianism came with the *Auburn Affirmation* 'to safeguard the unity and liberty of the Church' presented with about 1300 signatures to the Assembly of 1924. This earnest and moderate appeal spoke on behalf of the many evangelical believers who were not Fundamentalists. Fundamentalism has since that period been less aggressive, and apart from some extremists has largely been replaced by a more moderate conservative and evangelical trend.

CHAPTER XXIV

CALVINISM AND PUBLIC AFFAIRS

— I —

THE political and social earthquakes of the modern era have been attended by an abundant growth of political and social theory. To this body of thought Calvinist authors have contributed a large share. Calvinists, too, as might have been predicted from the attitudes of their founding fathers, have participated energetically in political and social action. To recount these writings and activities would be to write the history of public affairs through four centuries. Here we can discuss only what seem to be the marks of Calvinism's impact on society. This is a realm of history that has called forth much research but still requires satisfyingly balanced and comprehensive treatment.

While Calvinists have, in given circumstances, adopted a variety of political attitudes, it is possible to affirm in this connection one generalization that admits of few exceptions. They have favored and fought for representative government and rejected the various forms of absolutism. It is, of course, erroneous to claim originality here for the Reformers. Concepts of representation and consent in government became familiar in the medieval provincial and diocesan organization of the Church and in the monastic and friar orders of the twelfth and thirteenth centuries. The Conciliar Movement was an attempt to effect a reorganization of the whole governing structure of the Church in a representative system. But it was in Calvinism that a uniformly representative polity appeared. While the Anabaptists exhibited a direct democracy, the Calvinist structure of government was a representative democracy, and thus capable of co-ordinating the churches over an area of indefinite extent, authority being exercised by bodies of elected delegates. The republican background

of Calvinism was probably reflected in this, but it was persistently defended in Scotland against kings who wanted absolute
rule. It has been argued that Buchanan and Knox, pupils of
John Major, did not advance beyond the notions of limited monarchy presented by that Conciliarist and historian. This may be
true in strictly political terms; but they had learned from Geneva something that gave them assurance in the defense of their
pattern of church polity and in their resistance to royal absolutism.

Oliver Cromwell was the most tolerant of dictators, yet in the
end he was truly a dictator. It is hard to find another Calvinist
in history who has played that role. One of the ablest of the later
expressions of British political Calvinism is *Lex Rex, a Dispute
for the Just Prerogative of King and People,* written in the midst
of the problems of the Westminster Assembly by the Scottish
delegate, Samuel Rutherford (1644). Rutherford utilizes the then
familiar argument of a contract relation between people and
king, and on scriptural grounds, as well as on those of natural
law, denies all absolute royal claims. He takes up the Roman
law maxim, 'the welfare of the people is the supreme law'; but
for him this welfare, or safety (*salus*), rests upon the people's
sovereignty. Power does not come directly from heaven to those
who use it: it comes from God to the people as a birthright and is
borrowed from the people, who may recall it 'when a man is
drunk on it.' Rutherford stands among the exponents of limited
monarchy and responsible government; but his later advocacy
of intolerance has reduced his credit among modern lovers of
freedom. Milton disliked Rutherford both for his admission of
a delegated kingship and for his persecuting principles. Yet
Rutherford strongly affirmed some of the principles indispensable to liberty.

Cromwell's younger contemporary, John de Witt (d. 1672),
was for nineteen years Grand Pensionary of Holland and leading
statesman of the Netherlands. The apology of William of Orange
(1581), perhaps the work of Languet (above, p. 248), affirmed in
high terms a doctrine of liberty and resistance to tyrants. But
De Witt led the party that feared tyranny from the House of
Orange itself. Though he died by mob violence, he was a staunch
advocate of a free republic. This he describes as 'a state in which
an assembly duly elected by the people, which is the fountain

of all legitimate power, has the right to make laws and the ability to enforce them.' He argued that this elective form of government promotes the wealth and welfare of the people and avoids the corruption of courts and the oppression of cities by kings. He showed favor to Algernon Sidney, whose strongly anti-monarchical *Discourses Concerning Government* appeared after his execution for treason under Charles II (1683). Sidney had favored the Independent party; but he always championed the cause of Parliament and when the Parliament was dismissed in 1653 had finally parted from Cromwell.

We have seen in early chapters other phases of the Calvinist spirit as expressed in political situations, and noted its relation to the American Revolution. In general it has asserted the basic authority of the people, and conceived of this as divinely bestowed through natural law. Its proponents do not assert that political rights are for the elect only; the approach to this in New England was not typical. The Calvinist who tries in this way to be politically exclusive is embarrassed by his own Calvinist affirmation that he does not know who the elect are. God alone knows. On this presupposition John Robinson, logically enough, advocated a wide tolerance. But it was direct, attentive reading of the New Testament that gave Roger Williams his horror of persecution and induced him to contend manfully against it throughout his ministry. His *Bloody Tenent of Persecution* (1644) and the tracts in which he defended this treatise may be considered among the great prophetic works of modern times. To his published principles he was unfailingly true in practice. Though not gentle as a controversialist, he saw to it that Rhode Island in his day exhibited a pattern of religious liberty.

— II —

The development of political doctrines in French Protestantism shows parallels to that in British Calvinism, and there was a great deal of intercourse between the two. François Hotman, a close friend of Calvin, in his *Franco-Gallia* (1573) interpreted French history in the light of a doctrine of popular sovereignty and representation, just as George Buchanan viewed the history of Scottish kingship (above, p. 304). Hotman was an admirer of the English Parliament. He sent his son to Oxford and through him was in touch with Leicester's circle. He may have felt at

Strasbourg, as Winthrop S. Hudson suggests, the influence of the Marian exile, John Ponet, author of the *Shorte Treatise of Politike Power* (1556). He shares with Ponet a more radical conception of resistance than Calvin's. It was against Mary Tudor that Ponet concocted his strong medicine of resistance, while Hotman was aroused by the Massacre of St. Bartholomew — which he narrowly escaped by hurried flight to Geneva — and Buchanan was justifying the deposition of Mary of Scots. In such crises of bloodshed and peril the doctrines of radical Calvinist political writers were forged. Many such works were written to guide the faithful and to explain to the world their attitudes in political affairs, all laden with proofs from Scripture and history.

Calvin had invoked 'the three estates in the several kingdoms' as a defense of the people against tyrannical kings, well knowing that the Estates General in France had held no significant meeting since 1484 and none at all since 1506. The meeting of 1561 failed to establish a policy toward the Protestants, nor did any of the few later meetings of the Estates before the Revolution fulfill the function assigned by Calvin to this agency of government. Yet French Protestants from Hotman down repeatedly expressed hope of redress of their grievances through action of the Estates. Pierre Jurieu, writing from exile, complains in *The Sighs of Enslaved France Aspiring toward Liberty* (1689–90) that the French king has assumed the place of the state itself and taken away the people's imprescriptible right. The Estates, he holds, are superior to the king in some matters and share authority with him in others. The monarchy was originally elective and under check from the Estates; it should return to this condition. In this and other works of this period Jurieu called for a meeting of the Estates to depose Louis XIV. Jurieu was reviving some of the arguments both of Hotman and of Languet and Mornay in their *Defense against Tyrants* (1579).

These authors were not republicans; they were not even 'democratic.' They would not have extended the suffrage to the uneducated masses. They thought of the Estates in traditional terms. The Estates General would represent a restricted electorate of three classes, clergy, nobles, and townsmen — the *populus* but not the populace. The peasant masses would have no voice in their deliberations. The church discipline authorized in new congregations the election of elders and deacons 'by the common voice of people and pastors,' and in well-established charges the consent of the people to such elections had to be secured. But there was no thought yet of so liberal a franchise in the state.

It would be erroneous, too, to suppose that the Huguenots showed constancy in their demand for a constitutional limitation of royal power. Guy Howard Dodge, in his study of Jurieu's theories, observes that during the period 1630–60 they 'sang a chorus of praise for royalism.' He holds that this was motivated by a desire to dissociate themselves from the English Puritan revolt, which had its turning point in the execution of Charles I. But Viénot notes that by 1625 the grand seigneurs and bourgeois favored full submission: 'forgotten were the theories of Hotman.' We may perhaps assume that the public declaration, made by Jean Daillé and others, that the royal authority is derived directly from God was less a conviction than a device to ward off charges of sedition and qualify for the king's good will. After the Revocation, save in the case of the Camisard insurrectionists, who were animated by Jurieu's exhortations, Daillé's position was generally adhered to by the persecuted remnant in France. The synod of the 'Desert' pastors that dared to meet in 1763 repeated Daillé's declaration of the divine right of kings.

Jean Claude's *Complaints of the Protestants* (1686), a devastating arraignment of Louis XIV's government, was circulated in England and was burned by James II before his loss of power, although Louis had advised him prudently to ignore it. The hope was raised that the writings of Jurieu and Claude would not only aid William III's claims against James but also so ally William with the Huguenot cause that he would lead an effort to have Louis deposed or compel him to return to the Edict of Nantes. William's policy disappointed this hope. The progressive loss of the toleration promised in 1598 and the cruelties inflicted on the Huguenots reduced the remnant to the pure pursuit of religious ends. They made little attempt to advance their cause publicly or even to voice their grievances. It was not Paul Rabaut (though he modestly did what he could) but Voltaire who most effectively exposed the false charges on which the Huguenot Jean Calas of Toulouse was legally murdered (1762). The Huguenots lamented their loss of toleration. But the new tide of revolutionary thought, charged with the eighteenth-century humanitarianism of Voltaire, Rousseau, and Cesare Beccaria (*On Crimes and Punishments,* 1764), awakened all France to an issue that went beyond toleration alone. When the Revolution came, Paul Rabaut's son, Rabaut St. Etienne, declared before the National Assembly (23 August 1789), speaking, as he said, on behalf of 'two million Protestants': 'It is not toleration that I claim, but liberty.' Exultantly he cited the adoption by the American Republic of 'the sacred maxim of universal religious freedom.' The French Protestants, like the English nonconformists, had abandoned sentiments of intolerance, and hopes of mere toleration no longer allured them; they were prepared to share in a common liberty. The lesson had been well learned in America; there, and in Scotland, as we have seen, it came to be reflected in official declarations of the Churches.

— III —

The political thought of Netherlands Calvinists and Arminians was concerned with wide issues. Johannes Althusius (d. 1628), a German trained in law in Basel and Geneva, became a local official at Emden and wrote *Politics Methodically Set Forth* (*Politica Methodice digesta,* 1603 with later and altered editions). Though written to defend the political course of Dutch Calvinism in the struggle with Spain, the work is a fundamental treatise on politics, which he defines as 'the science of linking human beings to each other for social life.' Dr. P. S. Gerbrandy has pointed to the remarkable intermixture of 'planned construction and natural growth, of organization and organism' in this work. According to this author, a distinguished Netherlands statesman, Althusius was no forerunner of Rousseau and presents no pattern of a 'corporative state' but 'shows himself a consistent pupil of the University of Geneva.' He was also a pupil of Peter Ramus in his abandonment of Aristotle and attention to contemporary facts. His great emphasis is upon the co-operation of all citizens under two contracts, social and governmental, in an integrated and organic society in which both the 'ephors,' or lower magistrates, and the chief ruler function as delegates of the people, while 'rulers and people acknowledge that they hold their power from God.'

Hugo Grotius (d. 1645), classicist, theologian, statesman, and political writer, unlike Althusius espoused Arminianism and

Erastianism, so that his connection with Calvinism is more negative than positive. As he was the foremost early expounder of international law (*The Rights of War and Peace*, 1625) his interests are, on the surface at least, mainly secular. Troeltsch regards him as outside the Calvinist tradition. His debt to Alberico Gentili, an Italian Protestant refugee in England, befriended by Leicester and Sidney, has been recognized. He shared with Calvin, too, a universal concern for the world and a desire for Christian reunion. The man of the eighteenth century who gave new currency to the international ideas of Grotius was Emeric de Vattel (d. 1767), the son of a Swiss pastor. Attention to *The Rights of War and Peace* has been revived in our war-torn age.

The 'Grand Design of Henry IV,' which some suppose to have been invented by his Huguenot minister, the Duc de Sully, aimed at the peace of Europe by way of the humiliation of the Hapsburgs and the Empire. Oliver Cromwell is reported also to have entertained utopian plans of a supernational organization of Protestantism. As this is described by a Huguenot in England, it resembles the project of John Amos Comenius earlier presented to the Long Parliament. Certainly Cromwell's foreign treaties take a comprehensive pattern and show an interest in promoting the security of Protestantism.

Not all Calvinist political writers have been ardent protagonists of the people's liberty. Where they have gained status and security for their own class, they have sometimes exhibited a stubborn political and social conservatism, marked, for example, by an unwillingness to extend the franchise beyond narrow limits. One of the greatest of nineteenth-century Frenchmen was François Pierre Guizot (d. 1874), brought up in Geneva by his pious Huguenot mother; he was an eminent writer on politics and history and for many years was prime minister of France. He was one of the most tolerant spirits in his era with respect to religious differences. In many works he assails the vice of absolute power and affirms that free institutions are necessary for the stability of government. He writes as a political liberal; nevertheless, since his administration was conservative, he has been charged with having failed to forestall, as he might have done by timely reforms, the revolution of 1848. He represented the supposed interests of a narrow electorate of wealth.

It would be unsafe to associate the statesmanship of Lincoln with the fact that he attended the sermons of a Scottish-born Presbyterian (one of whose elders was Lincoln's physician and intimate friend) or that his tutor, a 'hard-shell' predestinarian Baptist, was a friend of all three. (Lincoln's own religion was apparently expressed in a universalistic interpretation of the verse, 'in Christ shall all be made alive.') A great deal is still left obscure about these relationships and about the sources of Lincoln's political ideals. There is no such ambiguity, however, in the case of Woodrow Wilson (d. 1924), scion of a line of ministers, saturated with Calvinism from childhood, and sturdily loyal to his father and his family tradition. Though stern with himself and sometimes with those about him, he zealously espoused at every opportunity the cause of the unprivileged at home and of the weak and war-devastated nations abroad.

— IV —

We had occasion to notice (pp. 221 ff.) the fresh attention that has been given to the economic aspects of Calvinism in the present century. Nevertheless it is the judgment of this writer that the whole subject cries out for more adequate and comprehensive study than it has received. Ideas that have been brought to expression by late Calvinists have been read back into Calvin to the confusion of history. Thus it is stated that Calvin set loose an individualistic business activity, sanctioned by the view that worldly prosperity is evidence of the favor of God. We have referred to some evidence that this doctrine, which has become the lurking bourgeois heresy of the modern era, actually called forth from Calvin the most emphatic words of condemnation. He keeps repeating these judgments almost to weariness; but the impressive weight of this evidence was long almost completely ignored. The true attitude of Calvin to usury is not difficult to ascertain. The same cautious permission of moderate interest, under the strict rule of love and for the good of the borrower, reappears in the Reformed Church and in Puritanism. R. H. Tawney has called attention to the disagreement of Beza and his fellow ministers with the Geneva councils over the relaxation by the latter of laws in restraint of usury and speculation. It is curious that Dr. Tawney sees in the Calvinist defense of the poor only a system 'legalistic, mechanical, without imagination or compassion,' connected with the New Testament only by a 'coincidence of phraseology.' This judgment could have been reached only by ignoring a great body of evidence. The Church spoke with authority in these matters, but not without love. In its compressed style the French Protestant Book of Discipline states: 'All usury shall be strictly forbidden and repressed, and in the matter of loans people are to act according to the king's enactments and the rule of charity' (edition of 1675, XIV, 21). The Book of Discipline of the Church of Scotland (1560) pleads for the relief of 'the laborers and manurers of the ground' and expresses 'the grief of our hearts' over cruelty to poor tenants by 'some gentlemen.'

In England church opinion long remained negative on concessions to usury. Henry VIII's statute of 1545 permitting interest of 10 per cent was strongly opposed under Edward VI by Robert Crowley, an early Puritan and poor man's advocate, and by Bullinger's friends, John Hooper and Thomas Lever. In 1552 the law was repealed and interest made illegal. A. Hyma and H. M. Robertson have pointed to evidence here that confutes the views of Max Weber associating Calvinism with capitalism. High Churchmen and Calvinists shared many of the same opinions regarding interest, the Puritans being only the more vocal in condemning it. Thomas Wilson wrote strongly against the 5 per cent law of 1571; Thomas Norton, Calvin's translator, George Wither, a Heidelberg doctor, and later Thomas Adams, eminent Puritan preacher, were outstanding contenders against the legal permission of interest. Certain Continental Lutheran scholars were more liberal to business enterprise than Calvin was. In a work of 1638, however, the French Calvinist, Claude Saumaise, broke through some of Calvin's cautions and restrictions.

Certainly the bourgeois heresy of wealth as a mark of divine approval entered into later Calvinism, though always under the restraints of insistence upon charity and service. It may have broken in during the era of Puritan individualism, with the triumph of the Independents and the growth of foreign trading interests. Cromwell saw in his military victories the manifest favor of God and made of this something quite personal. In Charles II's reign this view is out in the open. When Baxter's friend Thomas Gouge (d. 1681) declares, 'what thou givest to the poor is not lost but sent to heaven before thee,' we may say that the old doctrine of merit has returned in a new form. And when, in his *Surest and Safest Way of Thriving*, he illustrates at length the point that generous giving is rewarded in this life, we recognize the serpent in the garden.

Despite a prudential element in Richard Baxter's ethics he does not reach the affirmation that prosperity is a proof of God's acceptance. 'Remember,' says Baxter, 'that riches do make it harder for a man to be saved . . . Remember that riches are not part of your felicity.' The full cup of prosperity may be presented by the devil. But Richard Steele in *The Tradesman's Calling* (1684) stated that 'Prudence and piety were ever very good friends; you may gain enough of both worlds if you will mind each in its place.' Dr. Tawney explains that for Steele 'trade itself is a kind of religion.' But Steele's talk is of the 'calling'; and we might interpret his meaning more generously by saying that he insists on the sanctification of the calling.

It is a little surprising that Dr. Tawney omits from consideration the fact that the eminent Anglican, Isaac Barrow (d. 1677), had earlier gone somewhat beyond Steele as a comforter of the wealthy. In Barrow's sermon on 'Godliness Is Profitable' (I Timothy 4:8), the promotion of piety is declared to be 'the concernment of all men who would safely and sweetly enjoy their dignity and power in wealth'; piety leads 'to preferments of all sorts, to honor dignity, wealth and prosperity.' His long discourse 'On the Duty and Reward of Bounty to the Poor' (Psalm 102:9) stresses the lesson that the generous man's horn is exalted 'here in this world' and 'in the future state': indeed, 'exercising bounty is the most advantageous method of improving and increasing an estate.' It was left for William Law to say (in 1728) that to waste property is to lose 'that which might purchase for ourselves everlasting treasures in heaven.' Of Law, however, Dr. Tawney merely remarks in passing that he 'reasserted with matchless power the idea that Christianity implies a distinctive way of life.'

The purpose in mentioning such overlooked details is to point to the unbalanced nature of the argument that traces the rise of economic individualism through Puritan and nonconformist writings alone, and to the need of a more comprehensive and balanced approach. I believe it will come to be seen that in this field much of what has been ascribed to Calvinism is not distinctively Calvinist at all, and that the prudential element in Puritan ethics was fully shared by typical Anglicans — indeed, also by Lutherans of the period. By the early eighteenth century, the era of William Law and Jonathan Edwards and the anonymous (Anglican) *New Whole Duty of Man,* the divine sanction of the acquisition as well as the charitable use of wealth had become a commonplace lodged in most Christian minds, Calvinists included. Let us take a strong passage from Edwards; the book is *Charity and Its Fruits* (1738):

> But if you place your happiness in God, in glorifying Him and in serving Him by doing good, in this way above all others you will promote your wealth and honor and pleasure here below, and obtain hereafter a crown of unfading glory and pleasures forevermore at God's right hand.

In a sermon on Deuteronomy 15:7–12, referring to the words of verse 10, 'the Lord shall bless thee in all thy works,' Edwards remarks: 'We find in Scripture many promises of temporal blessings to moral virtues.' Barrow had been rather more explicit in his view, which was 'to make the best of two worlds,' and to have treasures in both earth and heaven. But it never became for Barrow or Law, for Steele or Edwards, the service of God and mammon: it was always, by intention at least, kept on the plane of the service of God and man.

The story of the many Calvinist political administrators who had to do with political economy and tried out their theories cannot be told here. It would include an account of the almost incredible career of Barthelemy de Laffemas (d. 1611), a devout Huguenot of the Dauphiné, who from abject poverty and almost without formal education rose in the service of Henry IV to be 'controller general of commerce,' and introduced a drastic economic policy based mainly upon his own original ideas. We should probably call his system not mercantilism but national autarky. Prosperity was to be purchased by austerity and planned co-operation, the rejection of foreign luxury goods, and the encouragement of useful inventions. Neither Laffemas nor the more renowned Sully after him favored free enterprise in business.

— V —

One aspect of the Industrial Revolution was an increase of poverty and misery for many in the growing centers of population. One of the first to realize the Church's obligation and function in this situation was Thomas Chalmers, whose leadership of Scottish Evangelicalism we have noticed. His experience with the poor in Glasgow led him to give great effort to the amelioration of their conditions. The Reformation in Switzerland had attempted to put an end to economic destitution and begging. Scotland had been able to do something by parish co-operation to relieve poverty, but at times there had been much of it. The new factory economy enormously intensified the problem. Chalmers adopted the *laissez-faire* theory that Adam Smith propounded in *The Wealth of Nations* (1776), by which commerce and industry were to be freed of state regulations and wages determined by a 'dispute' between employer and worker. For Chalmers the deliverance of the poor was not to come from government restriction or action. Nevertheless his numerous and well-informed studies in political economy (volume IX of his *Works*, Edinburgh, 1856) show a great concern for the permanent abolition of dependent poverty. He placed great faith in the activity of 'parochial associations' such as he had developed during his ministry in Glasgow, and upon the socially regenerating power of religious and moral education based on the Bible. With this went his campaign for church extension in the neglected districts. His tract *The Connexion between the Extension of the Church and the Extinction of Pauperism* (1817) treats this theme with urgency, and it runs through many of his pamphlets and discourses. He believed that Christianity had power to give the moral energy that would enable the poor to rise out of their poverty with only the timely and temporary help of parish agencies.

The fact that the retreat and ultimate extirpation of crippling poverty was envisioned and sought meant something for later responses to the same problems. After the emergence of (Anglican) Christian Socialism, which offered a Christian answer to Marx's Manifesto of 1848, and the appearance of numerous British Christian social discussions, the 'Social Gospel' appeared in America. It was called forth by the increasing labor problems and conflicts during the industrial expansion after the Civil War. The theology of Albrecht Ritschl (d. 1899), with its value judgments, countering the emotionalism of Schleiermacher, and with its emphasis on the Kingdom of God, was a factor in this movement, whose leaders owed a debt also to British writers such as F. D. Maurice and W. R. Fremantle, and to Bushnell.

The first prominent exponent of this movement was Washington Gladden (d. 1918), a liberal Congregationalist minister and prolific writer on the Bible, theology, and social ethics. 'If liberalism is mainly criticism and denial . . . then we are not liberals,' he wrote in 1899, in a book suggestively entitled *How Much Is Left of the Old Doctrines?* Conditions in his own Columbus, Ohio, parish led him to take up the cause of labor. The theologian of the movement was Walter Rauschenbusch (d. 1918), of the Rochester (Baptist) Seminary, whose *Theology for the Social Gospel* (1917) crowned his numerous writings. Dean Shailer Mathews of the University of Chicago Divinity School contributed in many books to the progress and interpretation of the movement. His liberal faith was accompanied by the historian's critical appreciation of the theologies of history, especially of Calvin. Presbyterian and Reformed Churches have joined with others in the Federal Council (later National Council) of Churches in the Social Creed of the Churches (1912) and the 1932 revision of this. The Social Creed subordinates the acquisition of wealth to the principle of social well-being, calls for equal rights for all, and the maintenance of free speech, free assembly, and a free press. It also takes a stand for the repudiation of war, the reduction of armaments, and the building of a co-operative world order. In practice the repudiation of war has meant generally for Calvinists not an absolute refusal to participate in a war believed to be in justice unavoidable, but a real effort to establish 'a just and durable peace.' During World War II, John Foster Dulles, a prominent Presbyterian layman, later Secretary of State, led the American churches in discussions that helped to form opinion on the organization of peace.

In its forthright attack upon social evils and demand for reform, the Social Gospel partook of the spirit of Calvinism. But its leaders shared the prevalent liberal hopes of amelioration and operated with a minimum attention to theology and with no consistent doctrine of the Church. Late in its development, rather than at the outset, Rauschenbusch and Mathews tried to supply this defect, but its theology remained unstable and fragmentary. 'In our time,' wrote Charles Clayton Morrison in *The Unfinished Reformation* (1953), 'there is emerging in theological circles a more profoundly Christian undergirding of the social gospel.' The Social Gospel movement was developed under attack from different quarters; but it has left an enduring influence, leavening Christian life and thought.

The Industrial Revolution, which called forth chiefly the new social and economic interests of the churches, began a generation or two before the abolition of slavery in the British colonies and almost a century before the emancipation of the slaves in America. In this country Christian leaders debated the slavery issue with intensity for nearly three decades before 1865. On both sides the debaters found their arsenal in Holy Scripture. Presbyterian protagonists of slavery, such as George Junkin in Ohio and James H. Thornwell in South Carolina, cited passages in abundance from both Testaments. On the other side Albert Barnes and Theodore Dwight Weld sought to show that the servitude tolerated in the Bible was not comparable to Negro slavery. The declaration of the Free Church of Scotland (1845) that Christians should labor for the abolition of slavery, and the similar attitude of Scottish secessionists, may have had some influence in America. When the Civil War came (1861), however, most of the churches upheld the cause espoused by the states in which they were located. The Reformed were not so much involved as the Presbyterians, and generally opposed slavery. It is probably true that Lincoln was more troubled than his Southern opponents by the hesitancy or opposition of church people, including those of Calvinist tradition. On the other hand, Calvinists were prominent in the small minority of anti-slavery men who remained in the South.

After the war, the principle of white supremacy was asserted by the former advocates of Negro slavery. This has prevailed in the Southern states, though with decreasing rigidity in the present century. Church leadership has been very prominent in the civil rights movement and in this the churches of Calvinist origin have been among the most concerned. But in South Africa, where the whites are outnumbered by non-whites about four to one, the units of the Dutch Reformed Church have generally lent support to the government policy of *apartheid*, or separation of the races, by which negroes are deprived of many human rights. This policy has been repudiated, however, by a minority of the Reformed and by churches of British origin. No attempt can be made in this book to relate world Calvinism to the numerous current issues involving racial, cultural and economic tensions throughout the world.

— VI —

The record, then, is rather more ambiguous in economic, social, and racial matters than in political matters. Most Calvinists have always associated with their faith in the sovereignty of God a feeling for the cause of human liberty and public justice and a strong preference for representative and responsible government. While many of them have advanced beyond Calvin in tolerance, many have remained far behind him in consecration to the aid of their fellowmen and the betterment of society. Some have exhibited an austere social detachment from the grosser life of the masses or have become victims of what Calvin (On Psalm 30:6) calls that 'carnal confidence' that 'creeps upon the saints' in prosperity, rendering them complacent toward their own faults and insensitive to the wrongs endured by others. But some Calvinists of recent generations are truly described in the words of the Reformer (On Job 36:6–14):

> To prove ourselves to be God's children let us beware that we lend our helping hand to such as are wrongfully persecuted, and that according to the ability that God giveth us we do succor such as are trodden under foot.

CHAPTER XXV

THE SPIRIT OF CALVINISM
IN THE WORLD TODAY

— I —

IN THE foregoing chapters an attempt has been made to portray and interpret a great branch of Protestantism that has made an incalculable impact on the life of mankind. Is it still possible to speak of Calvinism in the present tense? Yes; but this answer must be qualified in the light of some particulars.

Calvinism, like the Church in the thought of St. Paul, may be considered in terms of body and spirit. The body consists of the visible ecclesiastical elements, the structures and mechanisms by which churches function, and the written laws and official rules of procedure to which they refer for direction. These outward manifestations of Calvinism as they exist today show strong evidence of continuity with the past. They are perhaps more complicated than they were in the sixteenth century, but there is nothing esoteric or subtle about them. They can be observed and described by any competent reporter. This body of Calvinism has its local congregational or parish units, with their busy sessions and boards. It has also its graded territorial representative agencies of government, called by such names as classes, presbyteries, synods, assemblies, councils, each with its scope of authority defined in relation to those above and below it in rank. Among churches of the Presbyterian and Reformed family the system varies in detail, but it is everywhere recognizably the same in essentials. It exhibits a pyramided structure of representative and responsible governing bodies, to which laymen and ministers are elected and in which they co-operate on formally equal terms. The system was thus described by Alexander Henderson in his *Government and Order of the Church of Scotland* (1641):

Here there is superioritie without tyrannie . . . Here there
is a paritie without confusion and disorder. For the pastors
are in order before the elders, and the elders before the
deacons. The Church is subordinate to the Presbyterie,
the Presbyterie to the Synod and the Synod to the Nationall
Assembly.

Through the centuries Calvinism has exhibited this outward
form and has struggled to maintain it, often asserting it as a
matter of loyalty to the Scriptures. Even today in some Calvinist circles the traditional principles of the Reformed polity
are defended on strictly scriptural grounds. But thoughtful students of history acknowledge that the older Calvinists often expressly tolerated a constitutional episcopacy and saw in their
existing differences from episcopal churches no barrier to intercommunion or to reunion. It is significant that this view has
been acted upon in the formation of the Church of South India.
It cannot be said, however, that the strictly synodical and presbyterial Calvinism is declining in vigor throughout the world.
Instead, apart from China, where it was in process of development before World War II, the system seems to be expanding
and taking on increased strength and unity. It lacks, indeed, the
rigor of the old-fashioned discipline, which was marked by a
paternal supervision of the people's daily lives. Legal controls
have been for the most part abandoned, and to some extent the
mores are being changed; but it can hardly be argued that present-day morality among members of the Calvinist churches suf-
fers by comparison with that of a century or more ago.

'The body without the spirit is dead.' Even in an active body
there may be a spiritual feebleness. The passing of Calvinism
as a type of religious life might conceivably take place before
its outward weakening would become apparent. Its opponents
have often celebrated its decline and fall, and at times its supporters have voiced grave apprehension for its future. Benjamin
B. Warfield, that uncompromising Calvinist, showed such disquiet even when he wrote in 1909, 'There are very likely more
Calvinists in the world today than ever before,' since he found
extremely few of them whom he could regard as true to the type,
and most of these in Holland. In 1913 Professor James Stalker
of Aberdeen, at a meeting of the Alliance of Reformed Churches,
deplored the decay of the Calvinist spirit in Scotland and Ge-

neva. What, he asked, would Calvin say if he could see Geneva
now, or Knox if he could revisit the Scottish cities? Before the
twentieth-century scourge of war, the spirit of Calvinism seemed
to these representatives of it to have become almost extinct. There
are many in the churches of Calvinist tradition who have neglected the deep things of Calvinism or claimed Calvin's sanction
for economic or racial privilege in ways that he would have repudiated with scorn.

— II —

When Europe was plunged into war in 1914 it became dev-
astatingly clear that the prevailing liberalism had not taken
the measure of man's wickedness and the stubborn strength of
evil. P. T. Forsyth, who had earlier affirmed the authority of the
Bible and recalled to the vocabulary of theology the disused word
'grace,' published an arresting book, *The Justification of God:
Lectures for Wartime on a Christian Theodicy* (1917). Forsyth
lacks the peremptory tone of Karl Barth: his pages are strewn
with interrogation points; but the questions penetrate to the
joints and marrow. When he deplores 'an anthropocentric religion which has displaced the theocentric' and declares that 'in
the seeming failure of a God of order we are cast upon a God
of crisis,' we are in the new theological atmosphere of the war
era. About the same time, in a Swiss parish, while he could in
imagination hear (as he has said) the sound of guns to the northward, Karl Barth wrote a declaration of theological war. It was
his *Römerbrief,* and it appeared in 1919, while statesmen were
shaping an all too fragile political peace.

Barth's warfare was against the presuppositions of the old
complacent liberalism and every element of natural theology.
Many were soon recruited to his banner. Some of these — notably Emil Brunner — could not go all the way with Barth in the
negation of philosophy and secular culture. Barth's own thought
has developed far since 1919, to the inconvenience of admirers
and critics alike. The hot debates have involved divergent interpretations of the Reformation and particularly of Calvin.
Meanwhile a new historical industry in this field was manifest,
and the literature of research on Calvin and Reformed origins
mounted. Much of this literature dealt with economic, political,
and cultural aspects of the Calvinist teaching. The world crisis

of World War II heightened the vogue of Barthianism and allied views. What Barthianism may ultimately mean for Calvinism is not easy to guess. But this fact at least is inescapable: It is helping to bring Calvin's half-forgotten teachings to close attention in theological education and in the ecumenical exchange of thought.

The Theology of Crisis, with its ever-fresh manifestations in many lands and churches, is a topic far too extensive (and perhaps too familiar) to be discussed here. It is inevitably concerned with the Reformation, finding in its leaders allies and, in a limited sense, authorities. While exception may be taken to its lack of appreciation of Calvin's affirmations in the realms of culture and politics, it has undoubtedly brought a fresh realization of many aspects of his teaching. Barth has shown, indeed, a secondary interest in the scholastic Calvinism of the seventeenth century. He has referred to 'the sheer beauty of its trains of thought.' But he manifestly owes little to any of Calvin's interpreters; and the typical modern judgments rendered upon Calvin, from Schleiermacher to Ernst Troeltsch and Karl Holl, he vigorously repudiates. The fact that he treats both Luther and Calvin with unfailing deference has the effect of leading friend and foe into their company.

Once in Calvin's company, even though led thither by Barth, one may readily discover in his thought some things that Barth would like to exclude from theology. Calvin was willing, with all his teaching on depravity, to concede to the human far more than Barth does, and to take very seriously the cultural heritage of Western man. It is therefore conceivable that the outcome will be more like the Calvinism of Calvin than the widely variant Calvinism of Barth. It will not, of course, to judge by the fate of all isms, be exactly either. Barth's sincere refusal to absolutize his own theology is sometimes overlooked. He is emphatic; but he recognizes that finality is not for the theologian. Nor is he now embarrassed, as formerly, by the callow dogmatism of his converts. Many who are grateful to Barth for stimulation are quite strong enough to criticize his more extreme judgments and the perilous paradoxes of his dialectic.

The harrowing experiences of World War I, and its exposure of moral bankruptcy in the West, led to a widespread new spiritual quest. There arose a craving to recover the Calvinist awareness of God and the moral tonic of the Calvinist ethic. The new interest expressed itself in an unprecedented body of historical labor on the Reformed branch of the Reformation, and particularly on the thought of Calvin. Calvin's doctrines became a field of research and an arena of animated debate, but also the object of religiously motivated inquiry. While this revived Calvin interest was greatly stimulated by Barthianism, some elements of it were independent of the new Swiss theology.

The work of Abraham Kuyper (d. 1920) (above, p. 369) bore fruit in Holland, Germany, France, and America. In his two volumes on *Common Grace* (1902) he sought to show that Calvin's teaching could be harmoniously and usefully related with science and applied to the common life of moderns. Kuyper himself became an able conservative politician and prime minister of the Netherlands. He was highly influential in the Christian Reformed (*Gereformeerd*) Church. In 1924 the Christian Reformed in America strongly affirmed against dissentients the doctrine of common grace and its accord with Calvin's theology. D. Berkhof of Grand Rapids, in the 1941 edition of his *Systematic Theology,* reflecting the views of Kuyper and his follower H. Bavinck, amicably disagreed with Barth on this doctrine. Cornelius van Til has presented (1949) a cautious reinterpretation of the doctrine finding 'a certain good before God in the life of the historically undeveloped believer.' Although these writers tend to view Calvin as an infallible oracle, they give to his teaching a distinct emphasis that has possibilities for his wider influence. In a number of historical writings Albert Hyma of the University of Michigan has included favorable interpretations of social aspects of Calvinism.

In French Calvinism Auguste Lecerf (d. 1943) of the Free Faculty of Theology in Paris has held a notable place. Lecerf began as a convert of the older evangelical type. Born in London of unbelieving French refugee parents, he was religiously awakened at the age of twelve in an evangelical Sunday school there, and later in France, after studying Romans and Calvin's *Institutes,* he became an earnest Protestant. At seventeen he was baptized. He studied under Auguste Sabatier but turned away from that master's vague spirituality to write a thesis on *Determinism and Responsibility in Calvin's System* (1895). Lecerf, too, was indebted to the Dutch school of new Calvinists and was only slightly stimulated by the Barthians. It was he who organized the Calvinist Society of France (1927). His philosophical *Introduction to the Reformed Faith* and his posthumously collected *Etudes calvinistes* (1949) contain vivid, if somewhat hastily written, materials in advocacy and historical interpretation of Calvinism. These studies cover essential topics in theology and include an illuminating essay on 'Calvinism and Capitalism' (in which he assails Weber, Troeltsch, and especially their popularizers) and others in which he relates Calvinism to philosophy and science. The impression that Calvinism is a remedy for the twentieth century is conveyed in these vigorous essays.

In his *God-Centered Religion* (1942) Dr. Paul T. Fuhrmann places in a clear light aspects of the new Calvin-ward trend between the two world wars. He begins the book with a fifteen-page account of 'the return of French and Swiss Protestants to the principles of the Reformation.' Here we see men turning to the Reformers in eager quest for guidance during the crisis of the Hitler era, which had exposed the utter inadequacy of the worldly liberalism of earlier decades. Fuhrmann says that he was one of those who in the fashion of the time had turned up their noses at the mention of Calvin's name when he decided to make 'the titanic effort to read a few pages of Calvin himself.'

That day the writer discovered a new world, and became suddenly aware that the current notion of Calvin was purely imaginary. He realized that many modern theologians have, though unconsciously, used Calvin as a scarecrow in order to have us throw ourselves in their arms, and to keep us there in slavish admiration of their own teachings . . . A multitude of Swiss and French Protestants understood anew that greatness and sublimity, and turned to read all those publications that had kept the memory of Calvin alive through the years (*God-Centered Religion,* Grand Rapids, 1942, p. 17).

Fuhrmann points to the two strands, 'classical' and Barthian, in the movement, but also discerns a significant group (Jean de Saussure, Jaques Courvoisier, Max Dominicé) that goes to school to Calvin rather than to Barth, yet without taking over the entire body of Calvin's thought. Interpreting their position, he remarks:

Calvin's true legacy is, indeed, not a system but a method, the method of striving to see everything — man, Christ, faith, the world, the Bible, religion, life . . . — not from man's point of view but from the viewpoint of God (op. cit. p. 23).

A revival of Calvinism, modified in various ways, is also apparent in the Anglo-Saxon world. It is apparently not much affected by Christian Reformed books in English but has arisen through a discriminating reconsideration of Calvin's thought by writers such as Thomas M. Lindsay, Herbert Darling Foster, A. Mitchell Hunter, and later Quirinus Breen, Georgia Harkness, R. N. Carew Hunt, James Mackinnon, and Arthur Dakin. More recently the Barth and Brunner discussions have deeply affected without controlling such Calvin scholars as Thomas F. Torrance, Edward A. Dowey, Jr., and T. H. L. Parker. The theology of John Whale is essentially an independent restatement of Calvinism. Characteristic of Scottish theologians, as represented, for example, by John Baillie, is a respect for Calvin and historic Calvinism that was rarely discoverable in their late predecessors. Among the periodicals in English the *Evangelical Review* (Edinburgh) and the *Calvin Forum* (Grand Rapids) present what is regarded as undeviating Calvinism; *Theology Today* (Princeton), the *Scottish Theological Review* (Edinburgh), and the *Reformed Theological Review* (Melbourne) are scholarly organs primarily of Calvinist thought.

— III —

We ought, however, to speak guardedly of the revival of Calvinism. The Calvinism that is being revived is nowhere a replica of that of Calvin's time or of any other generation. That our little systems have their day has been a commonplace for a century and has become an ever more obvious fact. Because of the fertility of the modern mind and the ceaseless interchange of ideas, the survival or revival of any system of theology cannot be looked for. Karl Barth's impressive effort to create a new theology on Reformed soil exhibits from decade to decade so much variation that potential disciples are perplexed or alienated. He himself has called it merely 'the theology of correction.' Where can one find reproduced the authentic Barthianism of Barth — or the Hegelianism of Hegel, or the Lutheranism of

Luther? It is important to know the Calvinism of Calvin; but the mind of today can profess it in unaltered form only at too great expense and with considerable, if unacknowledged, deviations. To reconstruct original Calvinism in detail we should have to restore the society and thought patterns of the sixteenth century.

Indeed, a recovery of the spirit of Calvinism does not require a restoration of the entire system. Any such reappropriation is bound to be selective with respect to specific doctrines and practices. We have seen some of the influences and conditions under which the new Calvin movement began. It is proceeding along two lines. First, by historical scholarship Calvinism is being rescued from its defamers and from its too zealous partisans. And second, its permanently valuable elements (as they are judged) are being restored and recovered for the enrichment of modern Christianity. This process may be compared with the somewhat earlier exploration and recovery of Thomism, though the latter has been more ecclesiastical in motivation. There are many who cannot make St. Thomas Aquinas the arbiter of all theological issues, yet they obtain a wholesome stimulation from his thought and hold him in sincere respect. This is assuredly happening in the process of the renewed acquaintance of contemporary religion with the Calvinist tradition. The revival is not a complete conversion to Calvinism but is marked by a willingness to learn from it and to appropriate its usable elements. There are zealous Calvinists who do not like to think of this eclectic procedure, yet they themselves are forced in some degree to practice it. Who can approve today, for example, Calvin's defense of the condemnation of Servetus? It is foolish to say that the spirit of Calvinism demands a revival of its early intolerance. Nor can its spirit any longer be reasonably held to be tied to the doctrine of reprobation, or to any specific treatment of the divine decrees, or to any assumption of the inerrancy of Scripture. Its true spirit is found in faithful response to the Scripture revelation of a sovereign and redeeming God. While much else may be abandoned, the renewal of this vital principle truly means the revival of the Calvinist spirit; and it may well prove the most creative force in twentieth-century Christianity.

There are some who deplore the return to an interest in Calvin's thought. For one thing, it imports discomfort among those who would like to attain a blissful state of intellectual neutrality and detachment. It is also supposed to bear a threat of discipline to the wayward and, some would say, danger of moral tyranny. The view has been expressed that 'Calvinism' is a basic cause of the personality disorders now prevalent in America, especially those that involve an exaggerated sense of guilt. It may be that the word is used in this context in a loose way to include excessive parental control wherever it is found. Certainly this can still be found in America; but the instances best known to this writer happen to occur in homes that are distinctly non-Calvinist. It would be interesting to have comparative statistics on these matters; I have been unable to find any, and generalizations based on hearsay may be ultimately based on prejudice. Statistics of a sort are available with regard to imprisonment for crimes; whether reliable or not, they give a report favorable to the groups under Calvinist influence. But I do not think that it has been alleged that our prisons are filled with Presbyterians.

There exists today no distinctively Calvinist society corresponding to a political unit. The characteristics of life in such a society have been admiringly depicted by James Anthony Froude in his lecture on 'The Influence of the Reformation on the Scottish Character' (1865). Rarely, says Froude, has any people 'thought more about right and wrong' than the Calvinist Scots. He marks in them thrifty industry, a sound hatred of waste and extravagance, and an emphasis upon the 'worldly virtues,' especially honesty. He discusses the charge that Scottish life has been gloomy and austere and points to the fact that the Scots are noted for 'kindly, genial humor which half loves what it laughs at.' He adds:

> I should rather say that the Scots had been an unusually happy people. Intelligent industry, the honest doing of daily work, with a sense that it must be done well, under penalties; the necessities of life moderately provided for; and a sensible content with the situation in life in which men are born — this through the week, and at the end of it the 'Cotter's Saturday Night' — the homely family gathered reverently and peacefully together and irradiated by a sacred presence. Happiness!

This is Froude's description of the Scots not of his time but chiefly of the age before the social ravages of the early Industrial Revolution. It is no doubt an idealization, but it is not so much a falsification as are the opinions that reverse the judgment. It

is often charged or assumed that Calvinism produces an op
pressively austere, dour, or dreary type of personality. Although
the charge is sometimes uttered in the censorious spirit it condemns, it is not to be dismissed without consideration. What
substance is there in the view that Calvinists are gloomy folk?
Is it anything more than a reflection of the fact that they do not
much frequent the amusement factories created to serve up a
little merriment to those who have no means of producing their
own supply? It is a generalization on one of those imponderable
matters on which judgment cannot well be evaluated. The theme
has been widely treated in fiction: Nathaniel Hawthorne, Ian
Maclaren, and George Macdonald are among the more familiar
writers who treat the problems of somber personality in a Calvinist setting, mingling high respect with critical judgment. Macdonald, who can speak of the 'nightmare memory of a Scottish
Sabbath,' views the harsher aspects of parish life as 'degeneracy'
caused by stressing views that the leader (Calvin), 'urged by the
necessity of the time, spoke loudest, never heeding what he loved
most.' Calvin, too, distinctly rebuked those who would make
Sunday a 'nightmare' on the ground of Old Testament injunc-
tions — a 'Jewish rigor' in which Christians have no part.

It may be that too many Calvinists show a depressing gravity
of behavior. But most of us know innumerable religious folk
best classed as Calvinists who are always the life of the company
and possess a high capacity for social fun and cheerful wit. C. S.
Lewis has felt strongly the influence of George Macdonald, who
shed his boyhood Calvinism; but Lewis describes Macdonald's
father, a Scottish Congregationalist minister, as 'hard, tender
and humorous all at once, in the old fashion of Scotch Christianity.'

An unctuous and pretentious Calvinism was caricatured by
Robert Burns in 'Holy Willie.' No religion, however, is responsible for its hypocritical imitators; and in real life Holy Willie
Fisher was disciplined by the Kirk. The poet William Cowper,
John Newton's close friend, is alleged to have been a case of
mental derangement induced by Calvinist theology; but this
view has been effectively refuted. The verdict of an astute historian of literature, Hoxie Neale Fairchild, is that Newton 'did
not scare Cowper into madness with threats of hell fire,' and
that another theology would have made no difference to his diseased mind. Readers of Sir Walter Scott's description of the Rev-

erend Habakkuk Mucklewrath in *Old Mortality* (if they do not
have Thomas McCrie's devastating exposure of this characterization) may turn to Scott's *Tales of a Grandfather* to observe the
novelist's warm laudation of the old-time ministers. They were
'endeared to their people' by the purity of their lives and their
willingness to suffer poverty, hardship, and danger, and they
yielded effective service in correcting the ancient revengeful fury
of the Scots.

Anyone familiar with psychology and humane letters knows
that many things besides religion enter into temperament. We
tend in these matters to measure too superficially the evidence
of the health or sickness of a soul. A sense of security in God may
be accompanied by a disturbing compassion for men: there is
always a Jerusalem to weep over. Happiness is little related to
the decibels of laughter. The true Calvinist finds his blessedness
in a faith that glorifies God and enjoys Him. He who is weak in
faith will miss this welling gladness. And there is something that
makes the Calvinist less demonstrative than some other believers.
It is sad that he should conceal his joy in God and forget Calvin's
reminder that 'We are nowhere forbidden to laugh.'

— IV —

The Christianity of the twentieth century assuredly feels anew
the strength of the spirit of Calvinism. Not only is this true in
the denominations in which what we have called the body of
Calvinism may be discerned. It is a spirit suffused through many
churches, encouraging the rise of a type of piety familiar in the
old Calvinism and once distinctive of it. This is a piety not much
identified with peculiar words and rites of worship. It is char-
acterized by a combination of God-consciousness with an urgent
sense of mission. The triune God, Sovereign Creator, Redeemer,
and Comforter, is an ever-present reality through both prosperity
and disaster. Guilt is real, but it is submerged under grace. The
Calvinist may not know how it happens; he may be a very simple-
minded theologian; but he is conscious that God commands his
will and deed as well as his thought and prayer. This is what
makes him a reformer and a dangerous character to encounter
on moral and political issues. He is a man with a mission to bring
to realization the will of God in human society.

He knows, too, that the human heart, including his own, is
deceitful and desperately wicked. This makes him a little dis-

trustful of the sincerity of idealistic utterances and professions, and likely to deliberate long on the choice of a cause to espouse. Yet when he knows what is God's will, and how it is to be translated into action of the hour, he will espouse it with courage, energy, and tenacity. God has not given him the spirit of fear. In many instances he appears to be charged with that apostolic *parrēsia*, or outspoken boldness, which men saw with wonder in the early apostles. The members of the Jerusalem council anxiously said to one another, 'What shall we do with these men?' Calvinists, too, have often been troublers of Israel, assailants of the evils countenanced by the majority. We might almost say that this has been their trade and that when we find them acquiescent in a bad society they have given up working.

Those who have been taught to think of Calvinism as important chiefly for some (usually misunderstood) connection with capitalism and middle-class society will have difficulty in discovering its real significance. The spirit of Calvinism has been most treasured among the less prosperous of its adherents. In Calvin's sermons, the Gospel is preached unto the poor; if economic historians have not found this it is because they have looked in another direction. Burns knew the 'cotter,' who led his children in prayer and in reverent reading of the family Bible that had been his father's pride. Wordsworth found typical in Scotland:

> *A virtuous household, though exceeding poor!*
> *Pure livers were they all, austere and grave,*
> *And fearing God: the very children taught*
> *Stern self-respect, a reverence for God's Word,*
> *And an habitual piety . . .*

Dr. Kuyper's conversion to Calvinism came through the testimony of his poor parishioners and the protests against his very un-Calvinistic sermons expressed by a humble woman, who became his monitor and led him to the sources that such as she had prized while the privileged folk became religiously indifferent. Many of the prosperous nominal members of churches of Calvinist tradition would be offended if they were confronted by Calvin's demands upon men of wealth. Capitalists who are in reality ethically Calvinist are those whose chief concern is not to gain wealth but to apply it to beneficent uses. Blindly to accumulate wealth is no more a mark of Calvinism than waste is; it regards both equally as reprehensible disobedience to God and rejection of Christian social duty. We are entering on a phase in the revaluation of Calvinism in which perhaps the ultimate religious ideal of the Geneva Reformation may be allowed to express itself.

We must not forget that this religious ideal is intimately associated with a sense of the reality of 'the Church, One, Catholic, and Holy.' Living Calvinism has always reached beyond its existing ecclesiastical status, seeking union and intercommunion. As we have seen, the Calvinist element in Protestantism has taken a prominent part in the twentieth-century ecumenical advance. It is well adapted to activity in a situation in which (as is the case today) the denominational fragmentation of the Christian Church is especially indefensible. In the next half-century (if a pun may be permitted) many church units may yield to church unity. The Calvinist churches are likely to participate in extensive reconstructions, carrying with them into wider communions what is felt to be essential to their tradition, and leaving behind the inferior and archaic elements to which in separate existence they have adhered. The spirit of Calvinism can no longer be solely associated with, or exclusively claimed by, the churches of Reformed origin. No longer spoken of with contempt, or apology, it goes forth into the commerce and exchange of ecumenical Christianity, there to survive or perish.

But we humans will, perhaps, still be for the most part fickle, as we have been. If we should presently move into an era of world prosperity and human comfort, suffering the spiritual debility that usually attends worldly ease, the Calvinist scriptural faith, awareness of a present God, and austere devotion to His will may again seem forbidding and become rare, until reckless secularism brings on a new crisis. But if life is hard for us and we encounter new dramatic manifestations of Antichrist in the forms of tyranny and war, the sturdy faith of Calvinism will be sought out again, and its spirit will be reborn in the hour of trial.

The alternatives are, of course, not exhausted in this prognosis. Calvinism has a message, if it could be heard in our time, not only for the distressed but also for the prosperous. It reminds every man who will hearken to reflect that always, in good or evil circumstances, he has to do with God — *ut sibi in tota vita negotium cum Deo esse reputet* (*Institutes* III, VII, 2).

POSTSCRIPT

mainly bibliographical,
to the paperback edition

SINCE this book first appeared in 1954, the province of history within which it is set has been a remarkably active field of scholarly research. So copious is the production that a reasonably comprehensive list of new titles would be absurdly disproportionate to the book itself. The book-list of the former edition has here been revised with the omission of about fifty of the original titles and the inclusion of about one hundred items of later date. For Parts I and II at least, the majority of the weightier books and studies are of non-English origin. Although some of the most informative of these have been appearing in English translation, there remain many that are not likely to be soon translated. Of these a number have been selected for their special worth. Noteworthy editions of source materials in the original and in translation have also been cited. It is hoped that the following brief comments on the new literature in the field will prove of interest to the reader. One generalization may be permitted at the outset, and it is a most agreeable one: historical labor on all phases of Reformed Protestantism has been increasingly tinged by the ecumenical spirit of our time and delivered from the blight of denominational prejudice.

PART I

Zwingli and the German-Swiss Reformation have received attention from an increasing number of scholars. Father J. V. Pollet, in a work of 1963, indicates that in the previous ten years over two hundred and fifty studies of Zwingli appeared. The *Corpus Reformatorum* edition of Zwingli approaches completion (in 16 volumes), as does also the *Zwingli-Hauptschriften* edited for more ready use by Fritz Blanke and others. Oskar Farner has completed in 4 volumes his detailed and authoritative biography of the Reformer; but this does not discourage others from presenting fresh interpretations of his life and teaching. Jaques Courvoisier has treated Zwingli as a Reformed theologian, and Jean Rilliet, in a book written from the sources but in a semi-popular style, presents an intimate personal portrait of the man and places him with Luther and Calvin as 'third man of the Reformation.' Fritz Blanke, in two of his reprinted essays on the Reformation, has examined the evidence on Zwingli's (not immodest) judgment of himself and of Calvin's (critically favorable) judgment of Zwingli. Father Pollet lays emphasis on Zwingli's points of agreement with Luther and on their unacknowledged common debt to the scholastics.

PART II

Edward A. Dowey's carefully descriptive bibliographical articles in *Church History*, that are on our list, will guide the reader through the progress of research on Calvin from 1948 to 1960. Wilhelm Niesel has compiled a numbered list of nearly 1600 titles of twentieth-century Calvin items to 1959. These include a number that are themselves bibliographical, chiefly within his numbers 131 to 184. During the present decade the stream of production has risen in volume. Scholars today go to Calvin with a greater variety of interests than formerly, and their studies exhibit more adequately the range of his thought and the qualities of his mind. Thus students are being gradually introduced to a new Calvin who is not only biblical scholar, theologian, preacher, and guide of souls, but also humanist, ecumenical churchman, and political and social thinker. The field of Calvin studies has been enlivened by the contribution of numerous competent Roman Catholic historians, clerical and lay, ranging from the laborious tabulation of Augustine-Calvin parallels by Luchasius Smits to Alexandre Ganoczy's discussion of 'collegiality' in Calvin and in Vatican II. Calvin's teaching on the Christian life, in its religious basis and secular manifestations, has been closely examined by Ronald S. Wallace. The Weber thesis on Calvinism and Capitalism has been more than ever subjected to devastating criticism, *e. g.*, by Kurt Samuelson and Herbert Leuthy; while André Biéler has given us a major work on Calvin's economic and social thought that would have opened Weber's eyes.

A. M. Hugo has brought to fresh notice Calvin's early humanism in his study of the Seneca Commentary and is now co-operating with Ford Lewis Battles in a much more extended treatment of this work, to contain ample essays, translation, and notes. A foretaste of this volume can be seen in an essay by Battles in the book edited by G. E. Duffield and noted below. Jean Boisset's scholarly volume, also listed, features the

Platonic element in Calvin's thought. Q. Breen has examined Calvin's style in relation to the history of rhetoric. E. G. Léonard, looking broadly at his impact on history, has dubbed him 'the founder of a civilization.'

The 400th anniversary of Calvin's death was widely observed in Europe and America, calling forth some published work of quality. In this connection may be mentioned Richard Stauffer's discourses contained in his book on the 'humanity' of Calvin, which clarifies, with evidence, 'certain misunderstood aspects of his personality,' and the same Paris scholar's attempt to penetrate the Reformer's reticence by a study of his use of the first person singular in sermons. The latter study appears in a volume emanating from a symposium held in Strasbourg, in which many of the best-known Calvin scholars participated. These annotated discourses constitute a stimulating and highly informative miscellany. One of the contributors to the Strasbourg *Colloque*, Jean Daniel Benoît, has two valuable studies also in G. E. Duffield's *Collection*, one of which, 'Calvin the Letter-Writer,' again brings us close to Calvin's personality. Something is being learned of his personal relationships also from Beza's *Correspondance*, now published to a date near that of Calvin's death.

It is of interest that, between 1955 and 1964, two annotated editions of the French *Institution* of 1560 appeared, Cadier's modernized version and Benoît's minutely edited reproduction, and that there were also new and improved translations of the 1559 Latin into German by Weber and into English with ample indexes by Battles, and Introduction and Notes by the present writer. Within the same period a (second) complete translation was made into Japanese by Nobuo Watanabe under the auspices of the Japan Calvin Translation Society, which has already issued a number of the commentaries, tracts, and sermons. Extensive excerpts from the *Institutes* have appeared in Chinese, in a project begun by Nanking Theological Seminary and guided by Francis Jones, the translator being Ching Yu Hsu. The expansion of Calvin's reading public may be suggested by the appearance of a Gaelic version of his *Catechism* and by five printings between 1956 and 1963 of the *Instruction in Faith* in Japanese.

Notable among the new source publications is the series *Supplementa Calviniana* which offers a new mass of textual material consisting of hitherto unpublished sermons. These substantial, well-edited volumes are being produced by an international corps of devoted scholars led by Erwin Mühlhaupt, under the sponsorship of the World Presbyterian Alliance. Many of these sermons are obtained only after laborious search, and the project is not yet half completed.

PARTS III AND IV

Within the range of Parts III and IV of our book, historians have been relatively less busy, but there have been many challenging studies. Among general works of distinction, the palm should be awarded to the late Emile G. Léonard's three-volume history of Protestantism, Volume III of which was completed from Léonard's notes by Jean Boisset. Volume II will be found extremely valuable for the seventeenth century, and the whole work has many points of contact with the present volume. It is weighted with references and bibliographical lists. For the period after 1650, James Hastings Nichols offers safe guidance on the general history and its Calvinist strain. A very different approach, theological and Calvinist, is offered in the work of John S. Whale in our list. An excellent compressed study of the Reformation by the Roman Catholic historian Jean Delumeau gives due attention to Calvin and the Reformed Churches. Robert W. Henderson's revised Harvard dissertation sheds much light on the history of the doctoral ministry, and the theme has been pursued by W. F. Dankbaar in the *Colloque Calvin* referred to above. Elwin Allen Smith has shown the interaction of the Presbyterian ministerial mind with the changing culture through two centuries of American history. George L. Hunt has edited a series of informative lectures on political ideas and personalities in the world of Calvinism, from Calvin to Woodrow Wilson.

Among works of national and area extent, Scotland and the United States are well represented, and Puritanism has continued to attract the interest of historians. The Scottish Episcopalian Gordon Donaldson views Knox and Melville in sharp contrast; under the latter, the Reformed Church took its distinctly Presbyterian shape. Stuart Louden, from a position within the Church of Scotland, interprets its ethos with emphasis on its unfailing sense of participation in the Church Catholic. The spice of biography lends savor to history in the volume edited by Ronald S. W. Wright, with its 23 sketches of leading figures in the Kirk since Knox. On a wider canvas, Geddes MacGregor studies the doctrine of the Church in the Reformed tradition. The late George David Henderson of Aberdeen left us, among numerous valuable writings, a compressed but authoritative book on Presbyterianism; and John H. S. Burleigh of Edinburgh is the author of a reliable history of the Scottish Church.

For the history of Calvinism in America, Jacob Hoogstra has edited a 'survey' volume, in part arranged by regions of the country, concerned chiefly with the more conservative churches. Lefferts A. Loetscher has clearly traced and explained the 'broadening' of thought and outlook in the United Presbyterian Church since 1869, and this among other themes can be examined in the source documents on Presbyterianism edited by Maurice W. Armstrong, Loetscher, and Charles A. Anderson. Issues in Presbyterian history, as these were met in the area of New York State, are also vividly reviewed by Robert H. and James H. Nichols. T. Watson Street's short history of Southern Presbyterians, stressing the later decades, has been followed by the first of Ernest Trice Thompson's two volumes presenting in some detail the colorful story of Southern Presbyterianism to 1861, when the Presbyterian Church of the Confederacy was formed. The prolific Presbyterian writer, Clifford M. Drury, has assembled more than fifty manuscripts from as many authors, some of them internationally known scholars, sketching the history of Reformed and Presbyterian Churches in all the world, and containing a considerable body of otherwise unavailable data. The sketches, many of them translations, have not been finally edited for publication. The film copy records 914 pages of typed text.

The other titles in the revised Book List must be left to speak for themselves. They are not necessarily of less value than those I have mentioned, but they may not be so close to the story told in this book.

BOOK LIST

PART I

HULDREICH ZWINGLI AND THE REFORMATION
IN GERMAN SWITZERLAND

Blanke, Fritz, *Aus der Welt der Reformation: fünf Aufsätze*, Zurich, 1960.

Bouvier, André, *Henri Bullinger, Réformateur et conseiller oecuménique* . . . , Neuchâtel, 1940.

Courvoisier, Jaques, *Zwingli*, Geneva, 1947; *Zwingli, A Reformed Theologian*, Richmond, Va., 1963.

Davies, Rupert Eric, *The Problem of Authority in the Contiental Reformers*, London, 1946.

Farner, Oskar, *Huldrych Zwingli*, 4 vols., Zurich, 1943-60; *Zwingli, the Reformer: His Life and Work*, tr. D. G. Sear, New York, 1952.

Fast, Heinold Heinrich, *Bullinger und die Taüfer*, Neustadt, 1959.

Garside, Charles, 'The Literary Evidence for Zwingli's Musicianship,' *Archiv für Reformationsgeschichte*, Jahrg. 48, 1957, 56-75.

Good, James Isaac, *History of the Swiss Reformed Church* . . . , Philadelphia, 1913.

Hauser, Henri, *La Naissance du protestantisme*, Paris, 1940.

Hyma, Albert, 'Hoen's Letter on the Eucharist and Its Influence upon Carlstadt, Bucer and Zwingli,' *Princeton Theological Review*, XXIV, 1927, 124-31.

Jackson, Samuel Macaulay, *Huldreich Zwingli, The Reformer of German Switzerland* . . . , with a historical survey of Switzerland before the Reformation by John Martin Vincent and a chapter on Zwingli's theology by Frank Hugh Foster, New York, 1901.

Köhler, Walther, *Das Marburger Religionsgespräch, 1529*, Leipzig, 1929; *Ulrich Zwingli und die Reformation in der Schweiz*, Tübingen, 1919.

Ley, Roger, *Kirchenzucht bei Zwingli*, Zurich, 1948.

Oechsli, Wilhelm, *History of Switzerland, 1499-1914*, tr. Eden and Cedar Paul, New York, 1922.

Pollet, J. V., O.P., *Huldreich Zwingli et la réforme en Suisse*, Paris, 1963.

Richardson, Cyril Charles, *Zwingli and Cranmer on the Eucharist*, Evanston, 1949.

Rilliet, Jean, *Zwingle, le troisième homme de la réforme*, Paris, 1959; tr. Harold Knight, *Zwingli, Third Man of the Reformation*, Philadelphia, 1964.

Thompson, Bard, 'Zwingli Study since 1918,' *Church History*, XIX, 1950, 116-28.

Zwingli, Huldreich, *Huldreich Zwinglis sämmtliche Werke*, ed. Emil Egli *et al.*, Berlin and Zurich, 1905—; *Aus Zwinglis Predigten*, ed. O. Farner, 2 vols., Zurich, 1957; *The Latin Works and the Correspondence of Huldreich Zwingli, together with Selections from His German Works*, ed. Samuel Macaulay Jackson, 3 vols., New York, 1912, Philadelphia, 1922, 1929; *Selected Works of Zwingli*, ed. S. M. Jackson, New York, 1901; *Zwingli and Bullinger*, selected translations with introductions and notes by George W. Bromiley (Library of Christian Classics, Vol. XXIV), Philadelphia, 1953; *Huldreich Zwingli: Auswahl seiner Schreiben*, ed. Edwin Künzli, Zurich, 1962.

PART II

JOHN CALVIN AND THE REFORMATION IN GENEVA

Bainton, Roland H., *Hunted Heretic: The Life and Death of Michael Servetus*, Boston, 1953.

Beza (De Bèze), Théodore, *Correspondance de Théodore de Bèze*, recueillie par Hippolyte Aubert, publié par Fernand Aubert et Henri Malan, Geneva, 1960— [Vol. IV, 1965, to 1563].

Benoît, Jean-Daniel, *Calvin, directeur d'âmes*, Strasbourg, 1947; *Jean Calvin: la vie, l'homme, la pensée*, Carrières sous Poissy, 1948.

Bieler, André, *La Pensée économique et sociale de Calvin*, Geneva, 1959; *The Social Humanism of Calvin*, tr. Paul T. Fuhrmann, foreword by Visser 't Hooft, Richmond, Va., 1964.

Bohatec, Josef, *Budé und Calvin: Studien zur Gedankenwelt des französchischen Früh-humanismus*, Graz, 1950.

Boisset, Jean, *Sagesse et sainteté dans la pensée de Calvin: Essai sur l'humanisme du réformateur français*, Paris, 1959.

Bratt, John H., *The Rise and Development of Calvinism*, Grand Rapids, 1959.

Breen, Quirinus, *John Calvin, A Study in French Humanism*, Grand Rapids, 1932; 'John Calvin and the Rhetorical Tradition,' *Church History*, XXVI, 1957, 5-21.

Cadier, Jean, *L'Homme que Dieu a dompté*, Geneva, 1958; tr. O. R. Johnson, *The Man God Mastered: A Brief Biography of John Calvin*, London, 1960.

Calvin, Jean, *Ioannis Calvini opera quae supersunt omnia*, ed. G. Baum, E. Cunitz, E. Reuss and continuators, 59 vols., Brunswick and Berlin, 1863—1900 (*Corpus Reformatorum* series); *Ioannis Calvini opera selecta*, ed. P. Barth and G. Niesel, 5 vols., Munich, 1926—36; *Supplementa Calviniana*, ed. Erwin Muhlhaupt with 11 associates, Neukirchen, 1961—; (vol. I, *Sermons on II Samuel*, ed. Hans Rückert; vol. II, on Isaiah 13—29, ed. George Barrois; and vol. V, on Micah, ed. Jean-Daniel Benoît, have appeared.) ; *Unterricht in der Christlichen Religion: Institutio Christianae religionis, nach der letzten Aufgabe übersetzt und bearbeitet von Otto Weber*, Neukirchen, 1955; *Institution de la religion chrétienne, edition nouvelle publié par la Société Calviniste de France*, ed. Jean Cadier, 4 vols., Geneva, 1955–58; *Institution de la religion Chrestienne*, ed. Jean-Daniel Benoît, 5 vols., (vol. V is apparatus), Paris, 1957–63; *Institutes of the Christian Religion*, ed. John T. McNeill; tr. Ford Lewis Battles, 2 vols. (Library of Christian Classics, vols. XX, XXI), Philadelphia, 1960; *Calvin: Commentaries*, newly tr. and ed. by Joseph Haroutunian, in collaboration with Louise Pettibone Smith (Library of Christian Classics, vol. XXIII), Philadelphia, 1958; *Calvin: Theological Treatises*, tr. with introduction and notes by J. K. S. Reid (Library of Christian Classics, vol. XXII), Philadelphia, 1954; *A Compend of the Institutes of the Christian Religion*, ed. Hugh Thompson Kerr, Philadelphia, 1939; 2nd ed., 1962; *A Calvin Treasury: Selections from the Institutes of the Christian Religion*, ed., William F. Keesecker, New York, 1961; *John Calvin on God and Political Duty*, ed. John T. McNeill (Library of Liberal Arts, vol. 23), New York, 1950; 2nd ed., 1956; *John Calvin on the Christian Faith: Selections from the Institutes, Commentaries and Tracts*, ed. John T. McNeill (Library of Liberal Arts, vol. 93), New York, 1957; *Thine is My Heart: Devotional Readings from John Calvin*, ed. John H. Kromminga, Grand Rapids, 1958; *Concerning the Eternal Predestination of God*, tr. with introduction by J. K. S. Reid, London, 1961; 'Against Luxury and License in Geneva: A Forgotten Fragment of Calvin,' tr. F. L. Battles, *Interpretation XV*, 1965, 182–202; *Calvin tel qu'il fut; textes choisis* par le Chanoine (Léon) Cristiani, préface par H. Daniel-Rops, Paris, 1965; Calvin, *Textes choisis* par Charles Gagnebin, préface de Karl Barth, Paris, 1948; *The Deity of Christ and Other Sermons*, tr. Leroy Nixon, Grand Rapids, 1950; *Sermons from Job*, tr. Leroy Nixon, introductory essay by Harold Dekker, Grand Rapids, 1952; *Commentaries*, 45 vols. (reprint of Edinburgh edition), Grand Rapids, 1948; *Calvin's Commentaries*, ed. David W. and Thomas F. Torrance (new translations by T. H. L. Parker *et al.*), Edinburgh and Grand Rapids, 1959–; *Instruction in Faith (1537)*, tr. with an historical foreword and notes by Paul T. Fuhrmann, Philadelphia, 1959; *Letters of John Calvin*, compiled from the original manuscripts and edited with historical notes by Jules Bonnet, 4 vols., Philadelphia, 1858; *Tracts and Treatises on the Reformation of the Church*, tr. H. Beveridge, notes and introduction by T. F. Torrance, 3 vols., Grand Rapids, 1959.

Clavier, Henri, *Etudes sur le Calvinisme*, Paris, 1936.

Courvoisier, Jaques, *La Notion d'église chez Buccr dans son developpement historique*, Paris, 1933.

Dakin, Arthur, *Calvinism*, London, 1941.

Dankbaar, W. F., *Calvijn, zijn Weg en zijn Werk*, Nijkerk, 1958.

Delumeau, Jean, *Naissance et affirmation de la réforme*, Paris, 1965.

Doumergue, Emile, *Jean Calvin, les hommes et les choses de son temps*, 7 vols., Lausanne, 1899–1927.

Dowey, Edward A., jr., *The Knowledge of God in Calvin's Theology*, New York, 1952; 'Studies in Calvin and Calvinism since 1948,' *Church History*, XXIV, 1955, 360—67; 'Studies in Calvin since 1955,' *Church History*, XXIX, 1960, 196—204.

Duffield, G. E., ed., *Courtenay Studies in Reformation Theology I: John Calvin*, London, Sutton Courtenay Press; Grand Rapids: Eerdmans, 1966.

Freschi, Renato, *Giovanni Calvino*, 2 vols., Milan, 1934.

Geisendorf, Paul F., *L'Université de Genève 1559—1959*, Geneva, 1959.

Gloede, Günter, *Theologia naturalis bei Calvin*, Stuttgart, 1935.

Gutersohn, Ulrich, *Calvin als Mensch, Mann der Kirche und Politiker*, St. Gallen, 1945.

Grimm, Harold J., *The Reformation Era*, New York, 1954.

Hall, Basil, *John Calvin, Humanist and Theologian*, London, 1956.

Harbison, E. Harris, *Christianity and History* (essays 11 and 12), Princeton, 1964.

Harkness, Georgia Elma, *John Calvin; the Man and His Ethics*, New York, 1931, 1958.

Herminjard, Aimé Louis, *Correspondance des réformateurs dans les pays de langue française*, 9 vols., Geneva, 1878—97.

Hogstra, Jacob T., *John Calvin—Contemporary Prophet*, Grand Rapids, 1959.

Hugo, André Malan, *Calvijn en Seneca: Een inleidende Studie van Calvijns Commentaar op Seneca* De Clementia, Groningen, 1957.

Hunt, R. N. Carew, *Calvin*, London, 1933; 'Calvin's Theory of the State,' *Church Quarterly Review*, VIII, 1929, 56—71.

Hunter, A. Mitchell, *The Teaching of Calvin*, 2nd ed., Glasgow, 1950.

Imbart de la Tour, P., *Les Origines de la réforme*, Vol. IV, *Calvin et l'institution chrétienne*, Paris, 1935.

Jansen, J. F., *Calvin's Doctrine of the Work of Christ*, London, 1956.

Lecerf, A., *Etudes Calvinistes*, Neuchâtel and Paris, 1949.

Lefranc, A., *Calvin et l'éloquence française*, Paris, 1935.

Linder, Robert Dean, *The Political Ideas of Pierre Viret*, Geneva, 1964.

Mackinnon, James, *Calvin and the Reformation*, London, 1936.

McNeill, John T., 'The Democratic Element in Calvin's Thought,' *Church History*, XVIII, 1949, 153—71; 'Calvin as an Ecumenical Churchman,' *Church History*, XXXII, 1963, 379—91; 'Natural Law in the Teaching of the Reformers,' *Journal of Religion*, XXVI, 1946, 168—82; 'The Church in Sixteenth-Century Reformed Theology,' *Journal of Religion*, XXII, 1942, 251—69; 'The Significance of the Word of God for Calvin,' *Church History*, XXVIII, 1959, 140—45; 'Thirty Years of Calvin Study,' *Church History*, XVII, 1948, 207—240; *Unitive Protestantism: The Ecumenical Spirit and Its Persistent Expression*, Richmond, Va., and London, 1964.

Moltmann, Jürgen, ed., *Calvin-Studien 1959*, Neukirchen, 1960.

Monter, E. William, *Studies in Genevan Government, 1536—1605*, Geneva, 1964.

Mueller, William A., *Church and State in Luther and Calvin*, Nashville, 1954.

Niesel, Wilhelm, *Calvin-Bibliographie 1901—1959*, Munich, 1961; *Die Theologie Calvins*, 2nd ed., Munich, 1957; tr. (from 1938 edition) Harold Knight, *The Theology of Calvin*, London, 1956; *Calvins Lehre vom Abendmahl*, Munich, 1930.

Nijenhuis, W., *Calvinus Oecumenicus: Clavijn en de Eenheid der Kerk in het Licht van zijn Briefwisseling*, 's Gravenhage, 1958.

Pannier, Jacques, 'Calvin à Strasbourg,' *Revue d'histoire et de philosophie religieuses*, IV, 420-48; 504-33.

Parker, T. H. L., *The Doctrine of the Knowledge of God: A Study in the Theology of John Calvin*, Edinburgh, 1952; *The Oracles of God; an Introduction to the Preaching of John Calvin*, London, 1947; *Portrait of Calvin*, London, 1954; Philadelphia, 1955.

Pauck, Wilhelm, 'Calvin and Butzer,' *Journal of Religion*, IX, 1929, 237-56; *The Heritage of the Reformation*, Glencoe, Ill., 1950.

Petry, Ray C., 'Calvin's Conception of the *Communio Sanctorum*,' *Church History*, V, 1936, 227-38.

Pfister, Oskar Robert, *Calvins Eingreifen in die Hexer- und Hexenprozesse von Peney, 1545*, Zurich, 1947.

Quistorp, Heinrich, *Calvin's Doctrine of the Last Things*, tr. Harold Knight, London, 1955.

Registres de la Compagnie des Pasteurs de Genève au Temps de Calvin, ed. R. M. Kingdon and J. F. Bergier with the collaboration of A. Dufour, Geneva, vol. I, 1964; vol. II, 1962; ed. and tr. P. E. Hughes, *The Registers of the Pastors of Geneva in the Time of Calvin*, Grand Rapids, 1966.

Reyburn, Hugh Young, *John Calvin, His Life, Letters and Work*, London, 1914.

Rilliet, Jean Horace, *Calvin, 1509-1564*, Paris, 1963.

Schmidt, Albert Marie, *John Calvin and the Calvinistic Tradition*, tr. Roland Wallace, New York, 1960.

Smits, Luchasius, *Saint Augustine dans l'oeuvre de Jean Calvin*, 2 vols., Assen, 1957-8.

Stauffer, Richard, *L'Humanité de Calvin*, Neuchâtel and Paris, 1964.

Street, T. Watson, *John Calvin on Adiaphora: An Exposition* (Union Theological Seminary typed dissertation), New York, 1954.

Strohl, H., *La Pensée de la réforme*, Paris, 1951.

Stuermann, Walter Earl, *A Critical Study of John Calvin's Concept of Faith*, Tulsa, 1952.

Torrance, Thomas F., *Calvin's Doctrine of Man*, London, 1949.

Van Halsema, Thea B., *This was John Calvin*, Grand Rapids, 1959.

Veerman, A., *De Stijl van Calvijn in die Institutio Christianae Religionis*, Utrecht, 1943.

Walker, Williston, *John Calvin, the Organizer of Reformed Protestantism, 1509-64*, New York, 1906.

Wallace, Ronald S., *Calvin's Doctrine of the Christian Life*, Edinburgh, 1959.

Warfield, Benjamin B., *Calvin and Calvinism*, New York, 1931.

Wencelius, Léon, *L'Esthétique de Calvin*, Paris, 1937.

Wendel, François, *Calvin: Sources et évolution de sa pensée religieuse*, Paris, 1950; tr. Philip Mairet, *Calvin: the Origins and Development of his Religious Thought*, London, and New York, 1963; François Wendel *et al.*, *Regards contemporains sur Jean Calvin: Actes du colloque Calvin*, Strasbourg, 1964, Paris, 1965.

Whitney, Harold J., *Profile of John Calvin in the Institutes*, Brisbane, 1957.

Wilbur, E. Morse, *The Two Treatises of Servetus on the Trinity*, Cambridge, Mass., 1932.

Witte, J. L., S.J., 'Die Christologie Calvins' in *Das Konzil von Chalkedon*, ed. A. Grillmayer, vol. III, Würzburg, 1954, 487-529.

Zweig, Stefan, *The Right to Heresy: Castellio against Calvin*, tr. Eden and Cedar Paul, New York, 1936.

PART III

THE SPREAD OF REFORMED PROTESTANTISM
IN EUROPE AND EARLY AMERICA

Armstrong, Maurice Whitman, Lefferts A. Loetscher and C. A. Anderson, eds., *The Presbyterian Enterprise: Sources of American Presbyterian History*, Philadelphia, 1956.

Bainton, Roland H., *Studies on the Reformation*, Boston, 1962.

Bangs, Carl, 'Arminius and the Reformation', *Church History*, XXX, 1961, 155-70.

Bates, Miner Searle, *Religious Liberty: An Inquiry*, New York, 1945.

Beardslee, John W., III, ed., *Reformed Dogmatics: J. Wollebius; G. Voetius; F. Turretin*, (selections) New York, 1965.

Burleigh, John H. S., *The Church History of Scotland*, London and New York, 1961.

Bucsay, Mihaly, *Geschichte des Protestantismus in Ungarn*, Stuttgart, 1959.

Byington, Ezra Hoyt, *The Puritan in England and New England*, London, 1896.

Chambon, Joseph, *Der französische Protestantismus, sein Weg bis zur französischen Revolution*, 5th ed., Zurich, 1943.

Citron, Bernard, *New Birth: A Study of the Evangelical Doctrine of Conversion . . .*, Edinburgh, 1951.

Classen, Peter Claus, *The Palatinate in European History, 1559-1660*, Oxford, 1963.

Claude, Jean, *La Défense de la réformation*, 2 vols., The Hague, 1682.

Cremeans, Charles Davis, *The Reception of Calvinistic Thought in England*, Urbana, 1949.

Crouch, Joseph, *Puritanism and Art: An Inquiry into a Popular Fallacy*, London, 1910.

Daniel, Robert, *Textes et documents relatifs à l'histoire des églises réformées en France*, Geneva, 1962.

Davies, A. M., *The Presbyterian Heritage*, Richmond, Va., 1965.

Davies, Horton, *The Worship of the English Puritans*, London, 1948.

Dodge, Guy Howard, *The Political Theory of the Huguenots of the Dispersion, with Special Reference to . . . Pierre Jurieu*, New York, 1947.

Donaldson, Gordon, *The Scottish Reformation*, Cambridge and New York, 1960.

Drummond, Andrew Landale, *German Protestantism since Luther*, London, 1951.

Flynn, John Stephen, *The Influence of Puritanism in the Political and Religious Thought of the English*, London, 1920.

Foster, Herbert Darling, *Collected Papers of Herbert Darling Foster*, New York, 1929.

Gaer, Joseph, and Ben Siegel, *The Puritan Heritage: America's Roots in the Bible*, Philadelphia, 1964.

Gaustad, Edwin Scott, *The Great Awakening in New England*, New York, 1957.

Gerbrandy, Pieter Sjverds, *National and International Stability: Althusius, Grotius, Van Vollenhoven*, Cambridge, Mass., 1944.

Gerrish, Brian A., 'The Lord's Supper in the Reformed Confessions,' *Theology Today*, XXIII, 1966, 224-43.

Gierke, Otto von, *The Development of Political Theory*, tr. Bernard Freyd, New York, 1939.

Green, Robert Waldo, *Calvinism and Capitalism: The Weber Thesis and the Critics*, Boston, 1959.

Haller, William, ed., *Tracts on Liberty in the Puritan Revolution, 1638-1647*, 3 vols., New York, 1965.

Hastie, William, *The Theology of the Reformed Church in its Fundamental Principles*, Edinburgh, 1904.

Haroutunian, Joseph, *Piety versus Moralism: The Passing of the New England Theology*, New York, 1932.

Henderson, G. D., *The Burning Bush: Essays in Scottish Church History*, Edinburgh, 1957; *Presbyterianism*, Aberdeen, 1954.

Henderson, Robert W., *The Teaching Office in the Reformed Tradition: A History of the Doctoral Ministry*, Philadelphia, 1962.

Heppe, Heinrich, *Reformed Dogmatics, Illustrated from the Sources*, rev. and ed. Ernst Bizer, foreword by Karl Barth, tr. G. T. Thomson, London, 1950.

Hillerbrand, Hans J., *The Reformation: A Narrative History Related by Contemporary Observers*, New York and London, 1964.

Howse, Ernest Marshall, *Saints in Politics: The Clapham Sect and the Growth of Freedom*, Toronto, 1952.

Hunt, George Laird, ed., *Calvinism and the Political Order: Essays Prepared for the Woodrow Wilson Lectureship of the National Presbyterian Center, Washington, D.C.*, Philadelphia, 1965.

Kromminga, John H., *In the Mirror: An Appraisal of the Christian Reformed Church*, Hamilton, Ontario, 1957.

Johnson, F. Ernest, ed., *Foundations of Democracy*, New York, 1947; ed., *Wellsprings of the American Spirit*, New York, 1948.

Jordan, Wilbur Kitchener, *The Development of Religious Toleration in England*, 4 vols., Cambridge, Mass., and London, 1936-40.

Kingdon, Robert W., *Geneva and the Coming of the Wars of Religion in France, 1533-63*, Geneva, 1956.

Knappen, Marshall M., *Tudor Puritanism*, Chicago, 1939.

Knox, S. J., *Walter Travers, Paragon of Elizabethan Puritanism*, London, 1962.

Kuyper, Abraham, *Calvinism*, 2nd ed., Grand Rapids, 1931.

Lechler, Gotthard Victor, *Geschichte der Presbyterial- und Synodalverfassung seit der Reformation*, Leiden, 1854.

Léonard, Emile G., *Histoire générale du protestantisme*, 3 vols., vol. III ed. Jean Boisset, Paris, 1962-5; vol. I, *The Reformation*, tr. Joyce M. H. Reid, London, 1965.

Leube, Hans, *Canlvinismus und Luthertum im Zeitalter der Orthodoxie*, Leipzig, 1928.

Leuthy, Herbert, 'Once again, Calvin and Capitalism,' *Encounter*, XXII, 1964, 26-38.

Levy, Babette May, *Preaching in the First Half-century of New England History*, Hartford, 1945.

Lorimer, Peter, *John Knox and the Church of England*, London, 1875.

Louden, Stuart, *The True Face of the Kirk*, London, 1963.

MacGregor, Geddes, *Corpus Christi: The Nature of the Church according to the Reformed Tradition*, Philadelphia, 1959; *The Thundering Scot, A Portrait of John Knox*, Philadelphia, 1957.

MacGregor, Janet Girdwood, *The Scottish Presbyterian Polity . . . Its Origins in the Sixteenth Century*, London, 1926.

Maxwell, W. D., *John Knox's Genevan Service Book*, Edinburgh, 1931; *A History of Worship in the Church of Scotland*, London, 1955, 1965.

McCrie, C. G., *The Confessions of the Church of Scotland*, Edinburgh, 1907.

McEwen, James S., *The Faith of John Knox*, London and Richmond, Va., 1961.

McNeill, John T., *The Presbyterian Church in Canada, 1875-1925*, Toronto, 1925; 'Foundations of Presbyterian Ecumenicity,' *Journal of Presbyterian History*, XLIV, 1966, 1-23; *Unitive Protestantism: The Ecumenical Spirit and Its Persistent Expression*, Richmond, Va., and London, 1964.

Miller, Perry, *The New England Mind: The Seventeenth Century*, New York, 1937; *The New England Mind: From Colony to Province*, Cambridge, Mass., 1953; Miller, Perry and Thomas H. Johnson, eds., *The Puritans*, 2 vols., New York, 1963, 1964.

Moffatt, James, *The Presbyterian Churches*, London, 1928.

Mours, S., *Le Protestantisme en France au XVIe siècle*, Paris, 1959.

Moltmann, Jürgen, *Christoph Pezel und der Calvinismus in Bremen*.

Moore, Will Graburn, *La Réforme allemande et la littérature française*, . . . Strasbourg, 1930.

Patry, Raoul, *Philippe du Plessis-Mornay, un Huguenot homme d'état, 1549-1623*, Paris, 1933.

Pearson, A. F. Scott, *Thomas Cartwright and Elizabethan Puritanism, 1535-1603*, Cambridge, 1925.

Percy, Lord Eustace, *John Knox*, new edition with a foreword by the Duke of Hamilton, London and Richmond, 1965.

Perry, Ralph Barton, *Puritanism and Democracy*, New York, 1944.

Pauck, Wilhelm, *The Heritage of the Reformation*, revised and enlarged edition, Glencoe, 1961.

Ramsay, Mary Paton, *Calvin and Art, Considered in Relation to Scotland*, Edinburgh, 1938.

Reid, H. M. B., *The Divinity Principals of the University of Glasgow, 1545-1654*, Glasgow, 1917.

Reid, J. K. S., *The Authority of Scripture: A Study of Reformation and Post-Reformation Understanding of the Bible*, London and New York, 1957.

Reid, J. M., *Kirk and Nation: The Story of the Presbyterian Church of Scotland*, London, 1960.

Renwick, A. M., *The Story of the Scottish Reformation*, London, 1960.

Revesz, Imre, *History of the Hungarian Reformed Church*, tr. George A. F. Knight, New York, 1956.

Samuelson, Kurt, *Religion and Economic Action: The Protestant Ethic, the Rise of Capitalism, and the Abuses of Scholarship*, New York, 1961.

Schneider, Herbert Wallace, *The Puritan Mind*, New York, 1930.

Scholes, Percy Alfred, *The Puritans and Music in England and New England*, London, 1954, 1962.

Slosser, Gaius J., ed., *They Seek a Country: The American Presbyterians: Some Aspects*, New York, 1955.

Simpson, Alan, *Puritanism in Old and New England*, Chicago, 1955.

Smith, H. Shelton, Robert T. Handy and Lefferts A. Loetscher, *American Christianity*, 2 vols., New York, 1960, 1963.

Starkey, Marion L., *The Congregational Way: The Role of the Pilgrims and Their Heirs in the Shaping of America*, Garland City, New York, 1966.

Stauffer, Richard, *Un Précurseur français de l'oecuménisme, Moise Amyraut*, preface de Paul Conord, Paris, 1962.

Street, T. Watson, *The Story of the Southern Presbyterians*, Richmond, Va., 1960.

Sweet, William Warren, *Religion in Colonial America*, New York, 1949; vol. I, *Religion on the American Frontier*, vol. II, *The Presbyterians, 1783-1840*, New York, 1936; vol. III, *The Congregationalists*, Chicago, 1939.

Tawney, R. H., *Religion and the Rise of Capitalism*, London, 1926.

Thompson, Bard, ed., *Liturgies of the Western Church*, Cleveland, 1961; Bard Thompson, *et al.*, *Essays on the Heidelberg Catechism*, Philadelphia, 1963.

Torrance, Thomas F., *The School of Faith: The Catechisms of the Reformed Church*, London and New York, 1959.

Trinterud, Leonard J., *The Forming of an American Tradition: A Re-examination of Colonial Presbyterianism*, Philadelphia, 1949.

Viénot, John, *Histoire de la réforme française des origines à l'Edit de Nantes*, Paris, 1926; *Histoire de la réforme français de l'Edit de Nantes à sa revocation*, Paris, 1934.

Whale, John S., *The Protestant Tradition*, Cambridge University Press, 1954.

Walker, Williston, *Creeds and Platforms of Congregationalism*, introduction by Douglas Horton, Boston, 1960.

Wright, Louis B., *Religion and Empire: The Alliance between Piety and Commerce in English Expansion, 1558-1625*, Chapel Hill, 1943.

Wright, Ronald Selby, *Fathers of the Kirk: Some Leaders of the Church in Scotland from the Reformation to the Reunion*, London, 1960.

PART IV

CALVINISM AND MODERN ISSUES

Beaver, R. Pierce, *Ecumenical Beginnings in Protestant World Mission*, New York, 1962.

Cailliet, Emile, *The Christian Approach to Culture*, New York, 1953.

Cavert, Samuel McCrea and Henry Pitney Van Dusen, eds., *The Church through Half a Century: Essays in Honor of William Adams Brown*, New York, 1936.

Drury, Clifford M., *Four Hundred Years of World Presbyterianism* (typescript and film) San Anselmo, 1961.

Dunn, David, *et al.*, *History of the Evangelical Reformed Church*, Philadelphia, 1961.

Elliot-Binns, L. E., *The Early Evangelicals: A Religious and Social Study*, London, 1953.

Fleming, J. R., *A History of the Church of Scotland 1843-1874*, Edinburgh, 1927; *A History of the Church of Scotland 1875-1929*, Edinburgh, 1933.

Foster, Frank Hugh, *The Modern Movement in American Theology*, New York, 1939.

Fuhrmann, Paul T., *Extraordinary Christianity: The Life and Thought of Alexander Vinet*, Philadelphia, 1964; *God-Centered Religion*, Grand Rapids, 1942.

Furniss, Norman F., *The Fundamentalist Controversy 1918-1931*, New Haven, 1954.

Gombos, Gyula, *The Lean Years: A Study of Hungarian Calvinism in Crisis*, New York, 1960.

Hodge, Charles, *Constitutional History of the Presbyterian Church in the United States of America*, Philadelphia, 1851; *Discussions on Church Polity*, New York, 1878.

Horton, Douglas, *Reformation and Renewal: Exploring the United Church of Christ*, Philadelphia, 1966.

Houghton, Lewis Seymour, *Handbook of French and Belgian Protestantism*, New York, 1919.

Howse, Ernest Marshall, *Saints in Politics: the Clapham Sect and the Growth of Freedom*, Toronto, 1952.

Hudson, Winthrop S., *American Protestantism*, Chicago, 1961.

Lingle, Walter Lee, *Presbyterians, Their History and Beliefs*, rev. by T. Watson Street, Richmond, Va., 1958.

Loetscher, Lefferts A., *The Broadening Church: A Study of Theological Issues in the Presbyterian Church since 1869*, Philadelphia, 1954; art. 'Presbyterians,' *Twentieth Century Encyclopedia of Religious Knowledge*, Grand Rapids, 1955.

Maury, Léon, *Le Réveil religieux dans l'église réformée à Genève et en France, 1810-30*, 2 vols., Paris, 1892.

McDermott, R. P., *Irish Protestantism Today and Tomorrow*, Dublin, 1945.

McGiffert, Arthur Cushman, *The Rise of Modern Religious Ideas*, New York, 1915.

MacLeod, John, *Scottish Theology in Relation to Church History Since the Reformation*, Edinburgh, 1943.

Mead, Sidney E., *The Lively Experiment*, New York, 1963.

Nash, Arnold Samuel, ed., *Protestant Thought in the Twentieth Century*, New York, 1951.

Nichols, James Hastings, *Democracy and the Churches*, Philadelphia, 1951.

Nichols, Robert Hastings and James Hastings Nichols, *Presbyterianism in New York State*, Philadelphia, 1963.

Orr, James Edwin, *The Light of Nations: Evangelical Renewal and Advance in the Nineteenth Century*, Exeter, 1966.

Schneider, Herbert Wallace, *Religion in Twentieth Century America*, Cambridge, Mass., 1952.

Smith, Elwin A., *The Presbyterian Ministry in American Culture; A Study in Changing Concepts, 1700-1800*, Philadelphia, 1962.

Smith, Timothy L., *Revivalism and Reform*, Nashville, 1957.

Steele, David N., *The Five Points of Calvinism Defined, Defended and Documented*, Preface by Roger Nicole, Philadelphia, 1963.

Stokes, Anson Phelps, *Church and State in the United States of America*, 3 vols., New York, 1950.

Tillich, Paul, *The Protestant Era*, Chicago, 1951.

Van der Velde, *The Presbyterian Churches and the Federal Union, 1861-1869*, Cambridge, Mass., 1962.

Vanderlaan, Eldren C., *Protestant Modernism in Holland*, London and New York, 1924.

Van Til, Cornelius, *The Case for Calvinism*, Philadelphia, 1964.

Whitney, Harold J., *The Teaching of Calvin for Today*, New York, 1961.

Williams, Daniel Day, *The Andover Liberals*, New York, 1941.

Zenos, Andrew Constantinides, *Presbyterianism in America, Past, Present and Prospective*, New York, 1937.

INDEX

Absolution, 150, 303

Absolutism, royal, 305f., 321, 323, 329, 337

Academies, science in, 395; Dissenting, 330, 395

Adlischweiler, Anna (wife of Bullinger), 68f.

Adrian VI, Pope, 38

Agende (Basel), 81

A Lasco, John, 191, 259, 309; in England, 258, 282, 315; in Poland, 282f.; his Emden catechism, 282; *Forma ac ratio*, 282

Alciati, Andrea, 103

Alexander VI, Pope, 12, 129

Alliance of Reformed Churches, 387, 427

Alstedt, John Henry, 276, 285

Althusius, John, 416

Ambrose, St., 50, 68

America, Calvinism in, 331–50, 377f., 408

American Board of Commissioners for Foreign Missions, 384f.

American Revolution, 347f., 413

Amyraut, Moïse, and Amyraldism, 250, 265, 349, 392, 405

Anabaptists, 39, 41ff., 55, 68, 71f., 75, 119f., 141, 146, 156, 163, 411

Anhalt, 277f.

Anti-Trinitarians, 72, 119, 155, 182f., 207, 274, 356

Apartheid, 424

Appenzel, 7, 58, 60, 62, 79

Aquinas, St. Thomas, 134, 393, 433

Aristotle, 105, 391, 396, 416

Arminianism, 265ff., 392, 410; five points of, 264; in England, 314, 321, 337; in Scotland, 356, 396; tolerated, 368

Arminius, Jacob, 263, 266, 391

Athanasian Creed, 141f.

Auburn Affirmation, 410

Auburn Declaration, 367

Augsburg Confession, 197, 272f., 282, 286. *See also* Confessio augustana variata

Augusta, John, 283

Augustine, St., 30, 255, 393

Australia, churches in, 381

Bacon, Sir Francis, 101, 392

Baden, diet of, 60; disputation of, 61–4

Baillie, John, 432

Bale, John, 178, 312

Ball, John, 19

Bancroft, Richard, 319ff., 323

Bannerman, James, 372f.

Baptism, 86, 88, 218; of infants, 43, 88, 164

Baptismal font, 142

Baptists, in England, 328; in Massachusetts, 341; in Scotland, 360; Missionary Society, 384

Barnes, Albert, 367

Barrier Act, 355

Barrow, Isaac, 420f.

Barth, Karl, 428f., 432

Barth, Peter, 202

Barthians, 229